Al-Qa'ida Ten Years After 9/11 and Beyond

Yonah Alexander
Michael S. Swetnam

 POTOMAC INSTITUTE PRESS

Cover Design: Evan Lundh
Usama bin Laden image courtesy, FBI, Department of Justice
http://www.fbi.gov/wanted/topten/usama-bin-laden/
Ayman al-Zawahiri image courtesy, National Counterterrorism Center,
Counterterrorism Calendar 2011
http://www.nctc.gov/site/profiles/al_zawahiri.html
World Trade Center Attack image: Robert Fisch/CC BY-SA 2.0

ISBN: 978-0-9678594-7-7 Hardback
ISBN: 978-0-9678594-6-0 Paperback

Published, 2012 by the Potomac Institute Press
Potomac Institute for Policy Studies

Potomac Institute for Policy Studies
901 N. Stuart St, Suite 200
Arlington, VA, 22203
www.potomacinstitute.org
Telephone: 703.525.0770; Fax: 703.525.0299
Email: webmaster@potomacinstitute.org

Al-Qa'ida
Ten Years After 9/11
and Beyond

*This book is dedicated to the victims of
al-Qa'ida's terrorist network and in honor
of those who serve in combating terrorism
nationally, regionally, and globally.*

Table of Contents

CHAPTER 3

Selected List of Acronyms

AAIA	Aden-Abyan Islamic Army
AD	*Anno Domini*
AK-47	Avtomat Kalashnikova, Russian made assault rifle made in the year 1947
AQAP	al-Qa'ida in the Arabian Peninsula
AQI	al-Qa'ida in Iraq
AQIM	al-Qa'ida in the Islamic Maghreb
ARC	Advice and Reform Council
BBC	British Broadcasting Corporation
CEO	Chief Executive Officer
CIA	Central Intelligence Agency
CNN	Cable News Network
CRS	Congressional Research Service
CSIS	Center for Strategic and International Studies
D	Democrat
DEA	Drug Enforcement Administration
DHS	Department of Homeland Security
EIJ	Egyptian Islamic Jihad
FARC	Revolutionary Armed Forces of Columbia
FATA	Federally Administered Tribal Areas
FBI	Federal Bureau of Investigation
FIU	Financial Intelligence Unit (Peru)
GIA	Armed Islamic Group
GSPC	Group for Preaching and Combat
GWOT	Global War on Terror
IAA	Islamic Army of Aden
ICU	Islamic Courts Union
IED	Improvised Explosive Device
ISI	Islamic State of Iraq
ISI-P	Inter Services Intelligence (Pakistan)

IU	Islamic Union
KDP	Kurdistan Democratic Party
LeT	Lashkar-e-Taiba
LIFG	Libyan Islamic Fighting Group
MAK	Maktab al-Khadamat
NATO	North Atlantic Treaty Organization
Navy SEALs	United States Navy's Sea, Air, and Land Team
NCTC	National Counterterrorism Center
NEFA Foundation	Nine Eleven Finding Answers Foundation
NGO	Non-Governmental Organization
NSC	National Security Council
NYPD	New York City Police Department
OAE	Operation Active Endeavor
PETN	Pentaerythritol tetranitrate, an explosive
PUK	Patriotic Union of Kurdistan
RAND Corporation	Research and Development Corporation
TTP	Tehrik-e-Taliban
UAE	United Arab Emirates
UK	United Kingdom
UN	United Nations
US	United States
USIP	United States Institute of Peace
USS	United States Ship
VBIED	Vehicle Borne Improvised Explosive Device
WMD	Weapon of Mass Destruction

Preface

Some 2,000 years ago, Cornelius Tacitus, the keen Roman historian, famously observed that, "even the bravest are frightened by sudden terrors."[1] It is not surprising, therefore, that the "free and brave" people of America were traumatized by extraordinary personal and national insecurity when 19 suicide terrorists mounted simultaneous and massive attacks on September 11th, 2001.

The perpetrators, members of the radical Islamist international network al-Qa'ida ("the base"), hijacked four United States (US) commercial airlines and crashed them into the Twin Towers of the World Trade Center in New York City, New York and the Pentagon in Arlington, Virginia, and a third unintended target, a field in Shanksville, Pennsylvania. This dazzling assault that killed approximately 3,000 Americans, including nationals from over 90 different countries, represented the deadliest non-state terrorist operation in world history.[2]

The catastrophe of 9/11, like the "day of infamy" some sixty years earlier, has dramatically defined America's vulnerability to external attacks by both sub-state and state actors. But unlike the December 7, 1941 attack on Pearl Harbor by Japan, the one unprecedented strike by al-Qa'ida has resulted in more devastating human, political, social, economic, and strategic costs to the US than World War II.[3]

Indeed, the "long war" against "militant Islam" as declared by President George W. Bush on September 20, 2001 is still intact a decade later.[4] Subsequently, on October 6, 2001, America, leading an international coalition of allied countries, launched a massive military operation against al-Qa'ida's sanctuary and its Taliban protectors in Afghanistan. This effort, labeled "Operation Enduring Freedom," was intended to keep the homeland safe.[5] Similarly, US President, Barack Obama, has regarded the battle in Afghanistan (also adversely affected by al-Qa'ida members and Taliban insurgents from "no-man's land" in Pakistan) as a "war of necessity."[6]

As of November 2011, about 95,000 American troops remain in Afghanistan, and the Administration has called for a gradual withdrawal from that region in the time frame of 2012-2013. In the interim, direct and indirect negotiations are being conducted by Afghanistan, Pakistan, and the US with the Taliban insurgents to end terrorism and other forms of violence.[7]

Moreover, another long and costly war was undertaken by the Bush presidency in March 2003 against Iraq. The rationale for this new military action was based on the assessment that the Baghdad regime led by Saddam Hussein had links with al-Qa'ida and was engaged in a campaign to develop weapons of mass destruction (WMD). Although the US and its coalition partners defeated Iraq's military, and executed Saddam after his capture and trial, the US has continued to endure mounting terrorist and insurgent attacks with high costs in human lives, economic damage, and dire political consequences.[8] Thus, for nearly nine years, over 4,000 American soldiers have been killed (out of more than a million troops who served), and the cost to the US has been roughly $800 billion to conduct the war.[9] President Obama declared on October 21, 2011, that the American military engagement in Iraq will end on December 31, 2011, when the last US soldiers will exit the country.[10] This full withdrawal strategy has already raised concerns regarding Iraq's security capabilities to confront continuing threats of sectarian violence and Iran's growing influence in the region.[11]

Definitional Focus: Terrorism and Insurgency[12]

In connection with Afghanistan and Iraq and the general strategies against al-Qa'ida military operations, it is prudent to provide some clarity to the existing confusion over the meaning of what constitutes "terrorism" and "insurgency." The United Nations (UN), for instance, has thus far failed to establish an international consensus on those "acts, methods and practices of terrorism as criminal and unjustifiable wherever and by whomever committed."[13] Even after 9/11, the world body adopted a "zero-tolerance" approach strategy (e.g., a terrorist attack against one country is deemed an assault on humanity in general) without agreeing on a universally accepted definition.

Similarly, the North Atlantic Treaty Organization (NATO), the regional security multilateral organization that is currently developing into a global security provider (most recently operating in Libya), has after 9/11 launched "Operation Active Endeavor" (OAE) in supporting the Afghanistan mission without a formal definitional unanimity on "terrorism."[14]

Thus, the absence of a conceptual agreement by members of the international community as to who are the "terrorists" in contradiction to "freedom" or "resistance" fighters is clearly one of the contributing factors that encourages violence in the name of higher theological and ideological "principles."[15]

It is not surprising, therefore, that the US, like other countries, has developed its own unique definitional approaches relevant to the al-Qa'ida challenge. Basically, the following details constitute the American perceptions and policies:[16]

1. the term *international terrorism* means terrorism involving citizens of the territory of more than one country;
2. the term *terrorism* means the premeditated, politically motivated violence perpetrated against noncombatant targets by subnational groups or clandestine agents;
3. the term *terrorist group* means any group practicing, or which has significant subgroups that practice, international terrorism;
4. the terms *territory* and *territory of the country* mean the land, waters, and airspace of the country; and
5. the terms *terrorist sanctuary* and *sanctuary* mean an area in the territory of the country
    A. that is used by a terrorist or terrorist organization
        i. to carry out terrorist activities, including training, fundraising, financing, and recruitment; or
        ii. as a transit point; and
    B. the government which expressly consents to, or with knowledge, allows, tolerates, or disregards such use of territory.

What is particularly noteworthy about this definition is the American meaning of *noncombatant targets*.[17] While indiscriminate attacks on civilians appear to always be regarded as illegal in war and peacetime, the US also includes in *noncombatant targets* military personnel who are at the time of a terrorist incident unarmed and/or not on duty. Additionally, attacks on military bases, installations, and residences are considered illegal, such as the bombing of the Marine Headquarters in Beirut in 1983 perpetrated by Hezbollah (the Shiite terrorist group based in Lebanon and supported by Iran).[18]

Clearly, al-Qa'ida's operations, as early as the 1990s, have also been classified by the US as violations of the laws of armed conflict. It is suffice to mention the November 13, 1995, car bombing at the Saudi National Guard training center in Riyadh, killing five Americans; the June 25, 1996, attack at Khobar Towers (a US Air Force housing complex in Dhahran) with a toll of 19 soldiers dead and injuring hundreds more; and the October 12, 2000, bombing of the *USS Cole* in Aden harbor in Yemen, killing 17 and wounding 39 American servicemen.[19]

Other clarifications of the meaning of the terms *international terrorism* and *domestic terrorism* are also detailed in American jurisprudence. Thus, the USA PATRIOT Act, US Code 18 Section 233a (18 U.S.C. Section 233a) states the following:[20]

1. the term *international terrorism* means activities that—
    A. involve violent acts or acts dangerous to human life that are a violation of the criminal laws of the US or of any State, or that would be a criminal violation if committed within the jurisdiction of the US or of any State;
    B. appear to be intended—
        i. to intimidate or coerce a civilian population;
        ii. to influence the policy of a government by intimidation or coercion; or
        iii. to affect the conduct of a government by mass destruction, assassination, or kidnapping; and
    C. occur primarily outside the territorial jurisdiction of the US, or transcend national boundaries in terms of the means by which they are accomplished, the persons they appear intended to intimidate or coerce, or the locale in which their perpetrators operate or seek asylum;
2. the term *domestic terrorism* means activities that—
    A. involve acts dangerous to human life that are a violation of the criminal laws of the US or of any State;
    B. appear to be intended—
        i. to intimidate or coerce a civilian population;
        ii. to influence the policy of a government by intimidation or coercion; or
        iii. to affect the conduct of a government by mass destruction, assassination, or kidnapping; and
    C. occur primarily within the territorial jurisdiction of the US.

The foregoing definitional sources of American law do not, however, clarify the conclusion that nonetheless exists concerning the US: policies and activities vis-à-vis terrorism. For instance, during the Bush administration (2001-2009), the official concept *Global War on Terror* (GWOT) was utilized to characterize the juridical and political nature of asymmetric warfare challenge.[21] Once President Barack Obama assumed power, the conceptual approach has apparently been shifted from previous *warlike* disposition to a new terminology labeling *terrorism* as *human-caused disaster* and GWOT as *overseas contingency operations.*[22]

Another term, no less confusing than *terrorism* relates to the concept of *insurgency.*[23] In general, this form of warfare has traditionally been considered as a condition of armed revolt against a recognized sovereign entity that does not reach the proportions of organizing a revolutionary government or being recognized as a military belligerent. Its targets are usually military forces or installations, and it follows the international rules of armed conflict. Insurgent activity seeks a basis of popular support for the goals the revolutionaries espouse. If successful, insurgents eventually conduct guerrilla military operations and organize a revolutionary regime.

Insurgency, then, is merely the first phase of a legitimate revolution in which physical violence is used for specific political and military gains rather than for private benefits. Despite this favorable status, whenever insurgents employ terrorist tactics, they are not entitled to a legal exemption for the crime they have committed.

Yet despite these general elements of such a level of conflict, each nation, according to its own perceptions of the challenge presented, has developed conceptual, doctrinal, and operational dispositions and actions.

The US Department of Defense provides three specific relevant definitions and strategies:[24]

- *Insurgency*: An organized movement aimed at the overthrow of a constituted government through use of subversion and armed conflict. (Joint Publication 3-05, Special Operations)
- *Insurgent*: Member of a political party who rebels against established leadership. See also antiterrorism; counterinsurgency; insurgency. (Joint Publication 3-07.2, Joint Tactics, Techniques, and Procedures for Antiterrorism)
- *Counterinsurgency*: Those military, paramilitary, political, economic, psychological, and civil actions taken by a government to defeat insurgency. (Joint Publication 3-05, Special Operations)

Moreover, the US Department of the Army's field manual on "Counterinsurgency" offers further details on the insurgency doctrine highlighting the longevity of this form of "small war," and "irregular warfare."[25] One often-cited document on the subject is "Tactics in

Counterinsurgency," dated March, 2009.[26] This manual asserts, for example, that establishing civil control in Afghanistan requires plans "to serve the population and areas that remain loyal; reclaim the populations and areas that support the insurgency; and eliminate the insurgency, politically, militarily, and philosophically." Additional "lines of effort" include "support host nation forces, support governance, restore essential services, support economic and infrastructure development and conduct information engagement."[27]

This twin "hard" and "soft" power approach was also applied in the Iraq war. The objective in both strategic theaters then was to ultimately establish stable, self-reliant, and dependable geopolitical regional zones serving the security interests of the US.[28]

The "Just War" and "Jihad" Concepts: Some Perspectives [29]

Aside from the foregoing difficulties in developing a universal consensus over the meaning, implications, and strategic resources to "terrorism" and "insurgency," the international community, particularly since 9/11, has faced the complex theological challenge presented by al-Qa'ida's global "jihad," thus justifying unlimited use of force against the "enemies of God." This "sacred" mindset has brought the world's attention once again to an understandable concern regarding the frightening strategic dangers of the "clash of civilizations" as demonstrated by the "just war," "jihad" concepts and their relevancy to the "battle of ideas" between the culture of life and the culture of death. In the context of our study it is, therefore, useful to better understand the legacy of these doctrines, their historical lessons, and application to current and future al-Qa'ida threats.

More specifically, the rudimentary beginnings of the "just war" doctrine may be attributed to the Romans. It was an outgrowth of the association of religions with international relations. The performance of such religious rites was delegated to the *collegium fetaialium*, and the priests or fetiales were entrusted with the task of deciding if a foreign country had failed to perform its duties toward the Roman State. If a foreign country subject to Roman rule refused to perform the specified religious rites, and no settlement was reached within an allocated period for negotiation and deliberation, a "just cause of war" was said to exist, and the matter was placed before the Senate.[30]

During subsequent eras, Saint Augustine justified Christian participation in war on such grounds as injury to the country, or unjustified occupation of territory. While punishment out of all proportion to the original act would be considered unjust, the redress of grievances was justifiable, the ultimate purpose of war being the achievement of peace.[31] It was Thomas Aquinas who laid down three criteria for the justified initiation of war: First, it must be authorized by the prince; second, there must be a just cause for it, such as un-redressed grievances; and third, the belligerents must attempt to achieve a just peace. This theory was both used to curb feuds within a state and applied to conflicts between independent states.[32]

In the Middle Ages, Spanish jurists such as Francisco Vitoria (*circa* 1480-1546) held that not only is self-defense justifiable, but also defense of one's friends or allies where requested. In addition, he held that subject peoples may rebel against an unjust prince and request another nation to intervene on their behalf. An innovation, later discredited, held that the prince whose cause is just may act as judge in a conflict even where he has been one of the belligerents.[33]

Another Spanish legal scholar, Francisco Suarez (1548-1617), emphasized this "judicial" theory, holding that the opposing prince becomes subject to the dominant prince. While he advocated for arbitration, he found it sufficient for the prince to consult several wise men and then decide.[34]

To be sure, the "Dutch" school was most influential. Hugo Grotius (1583-1645), the famed writer on international law and the "just war" doctrine, held that the declaration of hostilities allowed either of the belligerents to harm the enemy. This right did not extend to prisoners, and he believed that good faith must be kept with the enemy in all instances. He also maintained that neutral nations should not support an unjust cause, and the army fighting for a just cause should have the right of marching through a neutral country and take command of bases within it if necessary. Grotius extended the doctrine of the "just war" to include such matters as hostages and defeated countries.[35]

The 18th century's legal scholars also elaborated on the meaning of the doctrine. For instance, Christian Wolf (1679-1754) justified war for unjustified injury, but held that a war could be considered just on both sides and that neutrals could not be required to aid the belligerent whose cause was "just." Also, Emmerich de Vattell (1714-1767) held that the theory of a "just war" was moral, and did not affect the legality of the war.[36]

By the beginning of the 19th century, the concept of a "just war" underwent a period of disuse. The theory that a war could be considered legal or illegal was discarded. It was replaced by the concept of supreme sovereignty. To judge the legality of a war would necessitate the deliberation and judgment of sovereignty by a third party, and this would be considered an impairment, as states were considered equal. This did not mean that violence was sanctioned, but rather that the doctrine of "just war" no longer met the needs of the political actualities of Europe in the 19th century. Methods were adopted in an attempt to restrict the worst consequences of conflict, such as political alignments and the formulation of rules of warfare to reduce widespread destruction.[37]

The 20th century brought a revitalization and reformulation of the "just war" doctrine developed in earlier periods. It condemned certain wars and condoned others. It returned to the theory that wars of aggression were illegal, while self-defense was justifiable. This theory was implemented in the Versailles Peace Treaty of 1919.[38]

The Treaty also demonstrated the concept that war may be used to right a wrong or punish an aggressor, by requiring Germany to forfeit territories such as the Saar coal fields and its colonies in South Africa, as well as to pay monetary reparations. Germany was required to accept a "war guilt" clause, stating that it "accepted the responsibility" for damage caused by the war "… imposed upon them [the Allies] by the aggression of Germany and her allies." Aggression was explicitly condemned.[39]

The opinion of the Allies is clearly illustrated by George Clemenceau in the Letter to the President of the German Delegation covering the Reply of the Allied and Associated Powers: "In the view of the Allied and Associated Powers the war which began on 1 August, 1914, was the greatest crime against humanity… that any nation… has ever consciously committed… not less than several million dead lie buried in Europe… Because Germany saw fit to gratify her lust for tyranny by resort to war… the Allied and Associated Powers believe that they will be false to those who have given their all to the freedom of the world if they consent to treat this war on any other basis than as a crime against humanity and right."[40]

This general philosophy is reflected in the Covenant of the League of Nations, which envisioned an organization to provide for arbitration in matters of dispute, with enforcing sanctions to punish violators. The implication of the concept of a "just war" was reflected in the fact that while the Covenant provided for substitutes to conflict, it relied upon "self-help" in the event that these substitutes failed.[41]

The Pact of Paris (or the Kellogg-Briand Pact) of 1928 supposedly outlawed all forms of conflict in settling international disputes. Article I reads: "The…Contracting Parties…condemn recourse to war for the solution of international controversies, and renounce it as an instrument of national policy in their relations without another." Article II strengthens that purport, by extending the definition of conflict, thus: "The settlement or solution of all disputes or conflicts of whatever nature or of whatever origin they may be, which may arise among them, shall never be sought except by pacific means."[42]

But certain wars were still considered to be just. Negotiations for the ratification of the Pact illustrated that the right to self-defense was not denied. In the words of US Secretary of State Frank B. Kellogg: "Every nation is free at all times to defend its territory from attack or invasion, and it alone is competent to decide whether circumstances require recourse to war in self-defense." A signatory of the Pact of Paris could engage in a "just war" and yet remain within its terms.[43]

The "just war" doctrine was invoked before the Second World War to justify American aid to the Allies, and after it to justify the punishment of those allegedly responsible for starting it. In 1945, the concept of "just war" had been embodied in the Charter of the UN.[44] Although the Charter provides for arbitration and adjudication, the right of self-defense has been maintained. Article 51 says: "Nothing in the present Charter shall impair the inherent right of individual or collective self-defense if an armed attack occurs against a member of the UN, until the Security Council has taken the measures necessary to maintain international peace and security."[45] The UN thus recognized "just" wars begun in self-defense against armed aggression.

These are, however, divergent opinions as to what constitutes "self-defense." Does a state have the right to anticipate an attack? To use force to thwart it? Would a state be justified in using force as a means of self-defense against indirect aggression? The General Assembly has, to a degree, set a precedent by recognizing the Nuremberg Judgment: "Preventative action in a foreign country is justified only in case of an instant and overwhelming necessity of self-defense, leaving no choice of means, and no moment of deliberation."[46] The action of the Netherlands in World War II was also recognized: "Faced by the imminent threat of invasion on her Far Eastern Territories which the conspirators had long planned and were now about to execute, the Netherlands in self-defense declared war against Japan."[47] On the whole, the UN has been reluctant to recognize cases that may expand the definition of self-defense.

It is against the foregoing background of mostly "Western" perspectives and experiences of the "Just War" concept that the "Jihad" doctrine must be understood. According to numerous Islamic scholars, it is apparent that Muslims have consistently used theologically based criteria for distinguishing between "just" and "unjust" violence. For instance, violence was justified to defend an Islamic society from "religious impurity" threats or from a foreign invading army. "Jihad" therefore represented a sanctified form of resistance force directed against disobedience to the command of Allah. "Jihad's" comprehensive meaning thus represents a struggle for personal and public faithfulness rather than an inevitable call for war. In fact, Muslim communities are duty-bound to explore every peaceful means available for conflict resolution before they resort to violence. And then when hostilities are undertaken, the Muslims are obligated to utilize measured and proportional responses to the threat. Their fighters are obligated during battles not to kill civilians, including women and children, and to treat prisoners of war humanely.[48]

Regardless of record, for militant Islam as graphically illustrated by al-Qa'ida's declared intentions and actions, the concept of "jihad" has projected a new ominous level of brutalization against humanity. Its ideological foundation has been nourished by radical Islamic concepts, doctrines, and interpretations. For example, the Middle Age school of Salafiyya (the venerable forefathers) in advocating that Islam had been corrupted by idolatry and therefore must be purified has influenced al-Qa'ida's thinking.[49] A more profound impact on al-Qa'ida's theological radicalization was made by Islamic scholars in the 20th century who argued that Islam was in real danger of being destroyed by Western influences. The teachings, for instance, of Maulana Maudoodi and Rashid Rida who developed the theory that modern Western culture represented the pre-Islamic period (jahiliyya) coupled with the assertions of Sayyid Qutb that the US is Islam's most challenging spiritual adversary have particularly impacted al-Qa'ida's extremist attitudes and violent actions against America and its friends and allies.[50]

Al-Qaida's Foreign Affinity Terrorism

Al-Qaida's challenge to the US did not begin with 9/11. The first wake-up call took place on February 3, 1993, when a car bomb detonated in the parking garage of the World Trade Center in New York City, killing six civilians and injuring 1,042 others, and causing widespread damage. This shocking attack, marking the largest international terrorist attack in America, was perpetrated by foreign terrorists from the Middle East (e.g., Egypt, Iraq, Jordan, and the Palestinian Authority) operating as the "long-arm" of al-Qa'ida in the homeland.

It was not, however, until July 6, 2003, with the creation of the Department of Homeland Security (DHS), consisting of some 180,000 employees in 22 agencies, that an extraordinary framework to provide intergovernmental cooperation on national, state, and local levels focused on threats to America from al-Qa'ida and other like-minded foreign groups. What became of particular concern to the DHS and related governmental bodies was the alarming expansion of the foreign-affinity terrorism challenge. That is, the concern to homeland security, as well as to American interests abroad, stemmed not only from foreign members of al-Qa'ida and their affiliated groups around the world, but more increasingly from American citizens and permanent residents who belong to a specific national "Diaspora" with loyalties to radical, ethnic, racial, religious, and political movements.[51]

Detailing the nature and extent of this emerging trend, US Government officials in a public briefing to the Senate on February 16, 2011, explained that these American foreign-affinity operatives, "...have occupied a variety of roles with extremist groups overseas, such as foot soldiers and front line combatants, operational planners, propagandists, attack operatives for homeland plots, and even senior leaders, with some American extremists combining multiple roles. American extremists will likely remain a small part of the jihad but play a disproportionately large role in the threat to US interests because of their understanding of the US homeland, connections to compatriots back in the US, and relatively easy access to the homeland and potentially to US facilities overseas."[52]

The success of foreign terrorist organizations in recruiting and radicalizing American and other Western citizens increased most noticeably between 2009-2010. The ease of creating and spreading extremist messages on Internet platforms and other media has made an easy target of American citizens susceptible to al-Qa'ida's rhetoric. Notably, from September 2001 to May 2009, there were arrests for 21 terrorist plots in the US, including two attacks; this figure increased between May 2009 and November 2010 to 22 terrorist plots, including two attacks.[53] These shocking numbers demonstrate that al-Qa'ida's efforts to inspire radical Islam and violence in American citizens have proved effective. However, initiatives implemented by the Intelligence Community, such as law enforcement and intelligence fusion centers and FBI sting operations, have successfully thwarted terrorist efforts overall and prevented large-scale attacks against the homeland.[54]

The following list of American foreign-affinity terrorists (selected from open-source information collected from public reports, court proceedings, and news outlets) details some recorded plots, attacks, arrests, and trials since 9/11:[55]

- John Walker Lindh: Imprisoned to 20 years for serving with the Taliban in Afghanistan
- Jose Padilla: The "dirty bomb" plotter sentenced to 17 years in prison
- Najibullah Zazi: An Afghan-American who planned to target the New York City Subway system, awaiting sentencing
- Michael Finton: Plotted to use a weapon of mass destruction against a federal building in Springfield, Illinois, sentenced to 28 years in prison
- Christopher "Kenyatta" Paul: Planned terrorist attacks in the US and Europe and is serving a 20-year sentence
- Mohammad Abdi Yusuf: A naturalized American from Somalia provided financial support to al-Shabaab and is awaiting trial
- Nadal Malik Hassan: An Army psychiatrist who killed twelve military personnel and one civilian in Fort Hood, Texas, and is awaiting trial
- Sharif Mobley: A New Jersey member of al-Qa'ida in the Arabian Peninsula (AQAP) is awaiting trial in Yemen
- Paul Gene Rockwood: A self-radicalized convert to Islam who created a jihadist hit-list and is serving eight years in Alaska
- Farooque Ahmed: A Pakistani-born American sentenced to 23 years in prison for a plot to bomb Washington, DC Metro
- Mohamed Osman Mohamud: A naturalized American from Somalia planned a Vehicle Borne Improvised Explosive Device (VBIED) attack in Portland and is awaiting sentencing
- Rezwan Ferdaus: Indicted for an alleged plot to fly model airplanes, filled with C-4 plastic explosives into the Pentagon and US Capitol

To be sure, over the past decade many other al-Qa'ida plots were identified by media reporting, according to specific locations and types of attacks. Some of the more familiar cases include "Lackawanna Six"; "Columbus Shopping Mall Bombing"; the "Financial Building Bombing in New York City, Washington, DC, and Newark, New Jersey"; the "Liquid Bombing of 10 Planes from the UK to the US"; the "Northwest Airlines Flight 253 Underwear Bomber"; and the "Times Square Car Bombing Attempt."[56]

The most spectacular recent tactical success was the targeted killing in Yemen of two American-born al-Qaida senior propagandists, namely cleric Anwar al-Awlaki (member of AQAP) and Samir Khan, the editor of al-Qa'ida's English journal *Inspire*.[57]

Additionally, the US has been successfully engaged in numerous missions abroad directed against non-American senior terrorist leaders. For instance, Khalid Sheikh Mohammed, the mastermind of 9/11 and al-Qa'ida's chief of operations, was arrested in cooperation with Pakistan.[58] The major modus operandi strategy adopted by the US was based on the calculated elimination of key leaders of al-Qa'ida and its affiliates in precise drone strikes in Afghanistan, Iraq, Pakistan, and Yemen. Suffice to mention the assassination of the following senior operatives: Muhammad Atef; Abu Musab al-Zarqawi; Abu Laith al-Libi; Sayeed al-Masri; Abu Hafs al-Najdi; Ilyas Kashmiri; and Atiyah Abd al-Rahman.[59]

While the foregoing tactical successes degraded al-Qa'ida's operational capabilities, at least temporarily, the ultimate strategic accomplishment of the US counterterrorism objectives was the killing of Usama bin Laden. On May 1, 2011, President Obama reported to the American people, and, indeed, to the entire international community, that a US military operation, conducted by Navy SEAL commandos in the town of Abbottabad in Pakistan shot the "Prince" who personified the most dangerous terrorist challenge in contemporary times.[60]

Although justice was finally done, the battle against al-Qa'ida, under the new leadership of Ayman al-Zawahiri, is still intact simply because bin Laden's legacy is a permanent fixture in radical Islam.[61] The latest demonstration of this disposition is the message communicated in the October 2011 issue of *Talae Khurasan* ("The Vanguard of Khurasan"), a journal published by al-Qa'ida's central leadership, asserts that bin Laden's movement "...had paved the way for the Arab Spring by kindling the spirit of defiance and willing for self-sacrifice in the hearts of the Muslims."[62] Similarly, in the Fall 2011 issue of the English *Inspire* publication, its editor Samir Khan (who was killed in Yemen) warned that this "...battle will continue until they find themselves powerless under our domination."[63]

Finally, our study contains an "Acknowledgements" section on the methodological approach as well as on the contributions of individuals and institutions to our work. An "Introduction" by Charles Allen, the foremost authority in the US on terrorism and al-Qa'ida follows. The analytical and descriptive narrative is then presented in eight chapters, each of which is focusing on a specific aspect of al-Qa'ida. Thus, chapter one examines the

"Ideological and Theological Perspectives and Goals." A review of the "Key Leadership" such as bin Laden, al-Zawahiri, and other senior associated figures is presented in chapter two. "Selected Modus Operandi," particularly those dealing with recruitment, funding, and links with organized crime, are discussed in chapter three. "Propaganda and Psychological Warfare" aspects, including the media and the Internet, are covered in chapter four. Al-Qaida's "Key Networks" in Iraq, the Arabian Peninsula, and the Islamic Maghreb are reviewed in chapter five. Profiles of selected affiliated groups such as al-Shabaab, Lashkar-e-Taiba (LeT), and the Taliban are analyzed in chapter six. Case studies and brief descriptions of selected individuals and groups with alleged connections to al-Qa'ida in the US are presented in chapter seven. And chapter eight, "Operation Neptune and Beyond" surveys the hunt for bin Laden, the May commando raid, and offers some perspectives on the post-bin Laden era. The "Appendixes" contains both al-Qa'ida's selected electronic communications during the past decade as well as selected official US statements and documents representing executive perspectives and policies. A selected bibliography and an Index are also included.

It is hoped that this work will serve to clarify and verify the proliferation of literature currently available on al-Qa'ida's past, present, and future.

Notes and Bibliographic References

Note to the reader: Due to the different English translations of Arabic terms, in some instances, different spellings are used in literature and in the media (e.g., al-Qa'ida vs. al Qaeda). We have tried to provide consistency of the English translations, wherever possible, in the work.

1. Cornelius Tacitus was a Roman historian who analyzed the reigns of several Roman Emperors in his works *Annals* and *Histories*. Tactius is considered one of the Roman eras greatest historians, famous for his prose and insight in philosophy and politics. Tacitus, Cornelius "*Annals*," (109) *http://classics.mit.edu/Tacitus/annals.html*

2. The literature on al-Qa'ida before 9/11 was rather limited. See, for example, Yonah Alexander and Michael S. Swetnam, *Usama bin Laden's al-Qa'ida: Preface of a Terrorist Network*, (Ardsley, NY: Transnational Publishers, Inc., 2001). The best account of 9/11 is Kean, Thomas, and Lee Hamilton. 9-11 Commission, "9/11 Commission Report." Last modified July 22, 2004. *http://www.911commission.gov/ report/911Report.pdf*. In the post September 11 period a proliferation of

studies were published. One of the latest major books is Peter Bergen, *The Longest War: America and Al-Qaeda Since 911*, (New York, NY: The Free Press, 2011).

3. For a media report on Pearl Harbor, selected at random, see Kluckhohn, Frank. "Japan Wars on U.S. and Britain; Makes Sudden Attack On Hawaii; Heavy Fighting At Sea Reported." 1941. *http://www.nytimes. com/learning/general/onthisday/big/1207.html*.

4. See, Bush, George. "War on Terror". Joint Session of Congress. US Congress. Washington, DC September 20, 2001.

5. See, Richard Stewart, *US Army in Afghanistan: Operation Enduring Freedom*, (Washington, DC: Defense Department, Army, Center of Military History, 2004).

6. See, Williamson, Elizabeth and Peter Spiegel. *Wall Street Journal*, "Obama says Afghan War 'of Necessity." Last modified August 17, 2009. *http://online.wsj.com/article/SB125054391631638123. html*. This "War of Necessity" has already cost the US according to Defense Department reports, 1,727 Service members killed. A latest source for this statistic is *The New York Times*, "U.S. Military Deaths in Afghanistan." Last modified August 17, 2011. *http://www.nytimes. com/2011/08/18/us/18list.html*.

7. For some of the extensive media sources on developments related to Afghanistan as of November, 2011 See, Borger, Julian. *The Guardian*, "Afghan government ready to resume negotiations with Taliban." Last modified Novemeber 23, 2011. *http://www.guardian.co.uk/world/2011/ nov/23/afghan-government-negotiations-taliban?newsfeed=true*. The complicated relationships between Afghanistan, Pakistan, the US, NATO, and other actors are covered by some of the latest press reports such as, Nordland, Rod. *The New York Times*, "Taliban Attack US-Afghan Meeting in Border District." Last modified November 10, 2011. *http:// www.nytimes.com/2011/11/11/world/asia/taliban-attack-united-states- army-and-afghan-meeting-in-chamkani-district.html*; and, Anthony, Augustine, and Qasim Nauman. Reuters, "NATO attack could hurt war on Terror." Last modified December 1, 2011. *http://www.reuters.com/ article/2011/12/01/us-pakistan-nato-idUSTRE7B00OU20111201*.

8. *The New York Times*, "Iraq News- Breaking World Iraq News." Last modified November 11, 2011. *http://topics.nytimes.com/top/news/ international/countriesandterritories/iraq/index.html*.

9. See, Belasco, Amy. Congressional Research Service, "The Cost of Iraq, Afghanistan and Other Global War on Terror Operations Since 9/11." Last modified March 29, 2011. *http://www.fas.org/sgp/crs/*

natsec/RL33110.pdf. The latest report on US casualties was cited by Global Security, "U.S. Casualties in Iraq." Last modified December 1, 2011. *http://www.globalsecurity.org/military/ops/iraq_casualties.htm*.

10. *Ibid*. 8.

11. Martinez, Michael. CNN, "U.S. pullout in Iraq raises concerns about Iran." Last modified October, 2, 2011. *http://articles.cnn.com/2011-10-21/middleeast/world_meast_iraq-iran-influence_1_iran-and-iraq-iran-iraq-war-iraqi-militias?_s=PM:MIDDLEEAST*. For a recent report on Iraq's outlook see: Cigar, Norman. *Al-Qaida, The Tribes, and the Government: Lessons and Prospects for Iraq's Unstable Triangle*, Quantico, VA: Marine Corps University Press, 2011.

12. Governmental and non-governmental experts and observers (including the media) speak with a bewildering variety of voices on the subject of "terrorism" and "insurgency." This section represents an updated overview of the definitions of the terms. For earlier perspectives see, for example, a report prepared by Ray S. Cline and Yonah Alexander for the Department of the Army and Published by the Subcommittee on Security and Terrorism (for the use of the Committee on the Judiciary, US Senate (Washington, DC: U.S. Government Printing Office, June 1985)). For other sources definitions and general related literature see, for instance, Alexander, Yonah. *Terrorism: An International Resource File*, (Ann Arbor, MI: UMI, 1991) and Schmidt, Alex P., and Albert J. Jongman. *Political Terrorism*, (Piscataway, NJ: Transaction Publishers, 2005).

13. UN General Assembly, 84th plenary meeting. "Resolution 49/60 [Measures to eliminate international terrorism]". 9 December 1994. (A/RES/49/60)

14. See, for example, discussion by Colak, Levent. "The Importance of Partnership and Cooperation in Light of Experiences Gained in Afghanistan." *Partnership for Peace and Review*. I. no. 1 (2010): 31-44. For a broader analysis of NATO's new strategic concept see NATO, "NATO 2020: Assured Security; Dynamic Engagement." Last modified May 17, 2010. *http://www.nato.int/cps/en/natolive/official_texts_63654.htm*.

15. See, for instance, Alexander, Yonah and Eli Tavin. *Terrorists or Freedom Fighters?*, (Fairfax, VA: Hero Books, 1986).

16. U.S. Code Title 22, Ch.38, Para. 2656f(d)

17. *Ibid*. 16.

18. BBC, "1983: Beirut blasts kill US and French troops." Last modified October 23, 1983. *http://news.bbc.co.uk/onthisday/hi/dates/stories/*

october/23/newsid_2489000/2489117.stm. It should be noted that Hezbollah has also operated abroad such as mounting attacks in Buenos Aires, destroying the Israeli Embassy in 1992 and the office building of Argentinian Jewry in 1994. See, for instance Alexander, Yonah. *Middle East Terrorism: Selected Group Profiles*, (Washington, DC: Jinsa, 1994).

19. The international press and other publications have covered extensively al-Qa'ida's operations. See for example Global Security, *"USS Cole* bombing." *http://www.globalsecurity.org/security/profiles/uss_cole_bombing.htm*.

20. US Congress. 2006. *USA PATRIOT improvement and reauthorization act of 2005*. 109th Cong., 2d sess., P.L. 109-177. *http://w2.eff.org/patriot/20020925_patriot_act.php*.

21. MSNBC, "'America Will Not Retreat,' Bush Vows." July 11, 2005. *http://www.msnbc.msn.com/id/8541812/ns/us_news-security/t/america-will-not-retreat-bush-vows/#.TtfKYrJFuso*.

22. Wilson, Scott and Al Kamen. *The Washington Post*, "'Global War on Terror' is Given New Name." March 25, 2009. *http://www.washingtonpost.com/wp-dyn/content/article/2009/03/24/AR2009032402818.html*.

23. For one of the most illuminating studies see Walter Laqueur, *Guerrilla Warfare: A Historical and Critical Study*, (Ardsley, NY: Transaction Publishers, 1997).

24. US Army, "Counterinsurgency." Last modified December, 2006. Accessed November 28, 2011. *http://www.fas.org/irp/doddir/army/fm3-24.pdf*.

25. *Ibid*. 24.

26. US Army, "Tactics in Counterinsurgency." Last modified March, 2009. *http://www.fas.org/irp/doddir/army/fmi3-24-2.pdf*.

27. *Ibid*. 26.

28. Wipfli, Ralph, and Steven Metz. US Army War College and the Brookings Institution, "Coin of the Realm: U.S. Counterinsurgency Strategy." Last modified January 10, 2008. *http://www.strategicstudiesinstitute.army.mil/pdffiles/pub846.pdf*.

29. Initial research on this segment began over 40 years ago during field work in the Middle East, Asia, Europe and the US. The academic effort focused on the question: is it ever justifiable to engage in hostilities and war? If so, under what circumstances may groups or countries mount sporadic or all-out acts of violence within the framework of law and morality. This academic effort has benefitted from the extensive studies available such as Wright, Quincy. *A Study of War*, (Chicago, IL:

University of Chicago Press, 1942). Additionally, the literature on the religionization of politics produced by Western and Eastern scholars was most useful. The contributions of Bernard Lewis including, *The Crisis of Islam: Holy War and Unholy Terror*, (New York, NY: Random House, 2004) and *Faith and Power: Religion and Politics in the Middle East*, (Oxford, UK: Oxford University Press, 2010) are cases in point.

30. Draper, Gerald. *Reflections on Law and Armed Conflicts*, (The Hague, Netherlands: Kluwer Law International, 1998).

31. Lang, Peter. *Augustinian Just War Theory and the Wars in Afghanistan and Iraq*, (New York, NY: Peter Lang Publishing Inc., 2011).

32. Aquinas, Thomas. *Summa Theologica*, (London, UK: Benziger Brothers, 1911).

33. Scott, James. *The Spanish Origin of International Law: Francisco De Vitoria and His Law of Nations.*, (Clark, NJ: The Lawbook Exchange, Ltd., 2008).

34. Ralston, Jackson. *International Arbitration from Athens to Locarno.* (Palo Alto, California: Stanford University Press, 1929).

35. Grotius, Hugo. *On The Law of War and Peace*. 1625. *www.munseys. com/diskone/djbp.pdf.*

36. Schiffman, Lawrence, and Joel Wolowelsky. *War and Peace in the Jewish Tradition*, (Jersey City, New Jersey: KTAV Publishing House, 2007).

37. US Military, "History of the Law of War." *http://www.au.af.mil/au/ awc/awcgate/law/low-workbook.pdf.*

38. Yale Law School, "Avalon Project- The Versailles Treaty." Last modified 2008. *http://avalon.law.yale.edu/subject_menus/versailles_menu.asp.*

39. *Ibid.* 38.

40. Clemenceau, George. Archives, "Reply of the Allied and Associated Powers to the observations of the German delegation on the conditions of peace...." Accessed November 29, 2011. *http://www.archive.org/ stream/replyofalliedass00allirich/replyofalliedass00allirich_djvu.txt.*

41. Walters, F. P. *A History of the League of Nations*, (Oxford, UK: Oxford University Press, 1952). See also, O'Brien, William V., and Anthony C. Arend. *Military Medical Ethics*. Vol. 1. 2009. *http://www. bordeninstitute.army.mil/published_volumes/ethicsvol1/ethics-ch-08. pdf.* chap. 8, "Just War Doctrine and the International Law of War."

42. Hoover, Herbert. Miller Center: University of Virginia, "Remarks Upon Proclaiming the Treaty for Renunciation of War." *http://millercenter. org/president/speeches/detail/3813.*

43. "Treaty for the Renunciation of War", Department of State Publications No. 268 (1933), p.57.

44. Goodrich, Leland, and Edvard Hambro. *Charter of the United Nations: Commentary and Documents*. (Boston: World Peace Foundation, 1946).

45. United Nations, "Charter of the United Nations." *http://www.un.org/en/documents/charter/chapter7.shtml*.

46. John O'Brien, *International Law*, (London, UK: Cavendish Publishing Ltd., 2001). Also, see, for example, Hans Kelsen, *Law of the United Nations*, (New York, NY: Frederick A. Praeger, 1964) and Roselyn Higgins, *Development of International Law Through the Political Organs of the United Nations*, (Oxford, UK: Oxford University Press, 1963).

47. Gabrielle McDonald, and Olivia Swaak-Goldman, *Substantive and Procedural Aspects of International Criminal Law*, (The Hague: Kluwer Law International, 2000), 806.

48. A vast collection of literature exists on the Jihad concept, history, current practice, and future implications. See, for instance, Brachman, J. *Global Jihadism Theory and Practice*. (New York, NY: Rutledge, 2009); Keppel, G. *The Trail of Political Islam*. (Boston, MA: Harvard University Press, 2002); Maghadam, Assaf. *The Globalization of Martyrdom:Al Qaeda, Salafi Jihad, and the Diffusion of Suicide Attacks*. (Baltimore, MD: John Hopkins University Press, 2011).

49. Bernard Lewis, *What Went Wrong? The Clash Between Islam and Modernity in the Middle East*, (Oxford, UK: Oxford University Press, 2002).

50. Irwin, Robert. *The Guardian*, "Is this the man who inspired Bin Laden?." Last modified October 31, 2001. *http://www.guardian.co.uk/world/2001/nov/01/afghanistan.terrorism3*. See also, Brynjar Lia, *Architect of Global Jihad: The Life of Al Qaeda Strategist Abu Mus'ab Al-Suri*, (London, UK: C. Hurst & Co. , 2009).

51. Alexander, Yonah. *Terrorists In Our Midst: Combating Foreign-Affinity Terrorism in America*, (Santa Barbara, California: Praeger Security International, 2010).

52. Clapper, James. Director of National Intelligence, "Statement for the Record on the Worldwide Threat Assessment of the U.S. Intelligence Community for the House Permanent Select Committee on Intelligence." Last modified February 10, 2011. *http://www.dni.gov/testimonies/20110210_testimony_clapper.pdf*.

53. Bjelopera, Jerome P., and Mark A. Randol. Congressional Research Service, "American Jihadist Terrorism: Combating a Complex Threat." 2010. *http://www.fas.org/sgp/crs/terror/R41416.pdf.*

54. Federal Bureau of Investigation Press Release. US Attorney's Office, District of Massachusetts, "Massachusetts man charged with plotting attack on Pentagon and U.S. Capitol and attempting to provide material support to a foreign terrorist organization." September 28, 2011. *http://www.fbi.gov/boston/press-releases/2011/massachusetts-man-charged-with-plotting-attack-on-pentagon-and-u.s.-capitol-and-attempting-to-provide-material-support-to-a-foreign-terrorist-organization.*

55. New American Foundation, "Homegrown Terrorism Cases 2001-2011: The Homegrown Threat." *http://homegrown.newamerica.net/.*

56. Davey, Monica. *The New York Times*, "Would-Be Detroit Plane Bomber Pleads Guilty, Ending Trial." Last modified October 12, 2011. *http://www.nytimes.com/2011/10/13/us/umar-farouk-abdulmutallab-pleads-guilty-in-plane-bomb-attempt.html.*

57. Griffin, Jennifer, and Justin Fishel. Fox News, "Two U.S.-Born Terrorists Killed." Last modified September 30, 2011. *http://www.foxnews.com/politics/2011/09/30/us-born-terror-boss-anwar-al-awlaki-killed/.*

58. Ressa, Maria, Mike Boettcher, Ash-Har Quraishi, Kelli Arna, and Suzanne Malveaux. CNN, "Top al Qaeda operative caught in Pakistan." Last modified March 1, 2003. *http://articles.cnn.com/2003-03-01/world/pakistan.arrests_1_qaeda-ahmed-abdul-qadoos-pakistan-officials/3?_s=PM:asiapcf.*

59. Global Security, "Full Directory." *http://www.globalsecurity.org/security/profiles/terrorism_directory_home.htm.*

60. MSNBC, "US Forces kill Osama bin Laden in Pakistan." Last modified May 2, 2011. *http://www.msnbc.msn.com/id/42852700/ns/world_news-death_of_bin_laden/t/us-forces-kill-osama-bin-laden-pakistan/*

61. CNN, "Al-Zawahiri appointed al Qaeda's new leader, jihadist websites say." Last modified June 16, 2011. *http://articles.cnn.com/2011-06-16/world/al.qaeda.new.leader_1_al-zawahiri-al-qaeda-statement-counterterrorism-official?_s=PM:WORLD.*

62. MEMRI, "Al-Qaeda leader 'Attiyat Allah Affirms Organization's Role in Arab Spring." Last modified October 5, 2011. *http://www.memrijttm.org/content/en/report.htm?report=5697&m=JT.*

63. SITE Monitoring Service, "Site Intelligence Group." *http://news.siteintelgroup.com/.*

Acknowledgements

It is a truism that research is the beginning of scholarship rather than the end of a process of learning. Indeed, any scholarly effort in both the social and exact sciences necessarily requires fierce verification in the quest of understanding complex issues and challenges.

Thus, striving to accomplish with completeness and finality the challenge of an academic examination of the intricate and secretive components of the most notorious global terrorist network in the history of humanity was traditionally perceived as "mission impossible." A major reason for failing to completely expose al-Qa'ida's multifaceted mystique, such as its precise intentions and capabilities, are the inevitable built-in constraints imposed by the limitations of open-source research methodologies.

Despite the effect of these intellectual and practical difficulties casting some doubts on a scientific inquiry, contemporary academic work in this general area did not begin with a vacuum of knowledge. In fact, a historical accumulation of extensive data in the broad interdisciplinary field of terrorism, from antiquity through the middle ages and modern times, was already available to a new generation of contemporary students and scholars. Benefiting from this extraordinary knowledge-base, incorporating the experiences of humanity's recorded memory, we were able to undertake a preliminary study of al-Qa'ida as early as 1988, when Usama bin Ladin first established its "Base" in Afghanistan and Pakistan for the purpose of continuing his "Jihad" regionally and globally.

Initially, we were able to draw from published and unpublished material on radical Islam and terrorism at several educational institutions, such as the International Center of Terrorism Studies (at the State University of New York) and the Terrorism Studies Program (at The George Washington University). Both universities administered research activities for the Inter-University Center for Terrorism Studies (IUCTS: a consortium of universities and think tanks in dozens of countries). Useful information was also made available by other academic bodies, including Georgetown University's Center for Strategic and International Studies (CSIS) and University Microfilms Incorporated (a Bell and Howell Information Company) based at Ann Arbor, Michigan. These institutions deserve our gratitude for their cooperation and initial support.

Some ten years later, after the devastating bombings of the US embassies in Nairobi, Kenya, and Dar es-Salaam, Tanzania, killing 234 civilians including 12 Americans, and injuring more than 5,000 others, the International Center for Terrorism Studies (ICTS), newly formed by the Potomac Institute for Policy Studies in Arlington, Virginia, undertook a major research project culminating in the release of *Usama bin Ladin's al-Qa'ida: Profile of a Terrorist Network* (Ardsley, New York: February 2001), some six months before 9/11.

In the aftermath of the September 11 attacks, this work immediately served as a reference source for academics, policy makers, the media, and other interested individuals and institutions around the world. In fact, that volume underwent several printings and was instantly translated into over a dozen languages, including Dutch, Korean, Polish, and Turkish. Currently, that product is still "in print," published by Brill in the Netherlands.

After consultations with academic and professional colleagues in the US and abroad, the co-authors of the pre-9/11 book decided to continue to conduct extensive research on al-Qa'ida's expanding challenges to US security interests as well as to the entire international community. Their new study, *al-Qa'ida: Ten Years Later and Beyond*, has been released by the Potomac Institute Press to mark the anniversary of those fearful times with the hope of creating a safer America and a more secure world.

The methodology designed for this newly published volume has consisted of two major levels of activities. First, daily research on the post-9/11 al-Qa'ida was conducted at both the ICTS and the Inter-University Center for Legal Studies (IUCLS) based at the International Law Institute (ILI) in Washington, DC. Special appreciation is therefore due to these institutions for their continuous support over the past decade. The co-authors are particularly grateful to the leadership of the Potomac Institute for Policy Studies, including General Alfred Gray, USMC (Ret.), Chairman, Board of Regents; Thomas O'Leary, Executive Vice President, Strategy, Planning and Programs; Gail Clifford, Vice President for Financial Management and Chief Financial Officer; and BGen. David Reist, USMC (Ret.), Vice President, Strategy and Planning. Acknowledgement is also due to Professor James Giordano, Vice President for Academic Programs, and Executive Director, Potomac Institute Press, as well as Sherry Loveless, Managing and Production Editor at the Press, for their dedication in producing the volume under a tight time publishing schedule.

Moreover, our colleagues at the ILI, Professor Edgar H. Brenner, co-director, IUCLS; Professor Don Wallace, Jr., Chairman, ILI; and Bill Mays, copyeditor of the manuscript, also deserve our highest praise for their constructive professional comments on the work. Professor Herbert Levine, our academic advisor, has also reviewed several drafts over the years, and we appreciate his dedication.

As indicated previously, our ten-year study is partially based on daily updates of extensive open-source material collected at the IUCTS (both at the Potomac Institute for Policy Studies and the ILI). This effort has been undertaken by numerous interns (undergraduate, graduate, and law students) as well as other young researchers from dozens of universities and think tanks throughout the world. Those individuals who were involved in this research project came from institutions such as: Amsterdam University; Ankara University; University of California, Berkeley; Brown University; Cairo University; University of Copenhagen; Dartmouth College; Haifa University; Harvard University; Hebrew University; Istanbul University; Johns Hopkins University; London School of Economics; University of Maryland; Massachusetts Institute of Technology; McGill University; Moscow State University; National University of Singapore; New York University; University of Notre Dame; Oxford University; Princeton University; Stanford University; University of Stockholm; Tel Aviv University; University of Virginia; Uppsala University; and Yale University.

We would like to thank all of the interns and researchers for their devotion and hard work and to mention specifically those individuals who assisted preparing the manuscript for publication in the Summer and Fall 2011: Jacob Butz (Indiana University School of Law); Courtney Byrne (University of San Diego School of Law); Philip Canton (University of Arizona); Erin Grimes (University of San Diego); Felix Huesken (University of Glasgow); Alex Knight (Middlebury College); Kevin McCrory (College of William and Mary); William Pentis (Arizona State University); Angela Rasmusson (University of Arizona School of Law); Sarah Scott (University of Alberta); Jesse Sedler (Emory University); Benjamin Snyder (Pennsylvania State University); David Spunzo (New England School of Law); Matthew Vogel (The George Washington University School of Law); Willmetta Warholyk (Seton Hall University); and Michelle Wiggett (Western New England University).

Moreover, special thanks are due for the extraordinary coordinating efforts of Patrick Cheetham (Research Coordinator, University of California,

Los Angeles); John Cooke (Research Assistant, Georgetown University); Evan Lundh (Research Assistant, University of California, Los Angeles); Amy Glazier (Research Assistant, Tufts University); and Jesse Sedler (Research Assistant, Emory University).

Another significant aspect of our study focused on organizing and participating in numerous courses, seminars, and conferences aiming at identifying al-Qa'ida's current and future threats on the conventional and unconventional levels and developing counterterrorism strategies to meet these challenges. For example, NATO's Center of Excellence-Defence Against Terrorism conducted a course (with the academic support of the IUCTS) in Ankara on "Weapons of Mass Destruction" (November 9-13, 2009) with participation of civilian and military representatives from many countries. More recently, a co-sponsored conference between IUCTS and the European Parliament in Brussels was held on July 12, 2011, on "al-Qa'ida and the South Asia Experience: Regional and Global Responses."

Similarly, ICTS and the IUCLS organized other events both at the Potomac Institute for Policy Studies and the ILI. Thus, on September 15, 2010, a seminar was held on "al-Qa'ida: Quo Vadis? (Nine Years After 9/11)" with contributions from Charles Allen, Philip Mudd, Paul Pillar, and Stephen Simon. The second event held on June 28, 2011, focused on "Cutting Through the Fog of Law: Was Killing bin Laden an Illegal 'Extrajudicial Execution,' a 'War Crime,' or a Lawful Act During Armed Conflict" with Bob Turner, Marion (Spike) Bowman, Jeffrey Addicott, and W. Hays Parks as panelists. Our co-sponsors at home and abroad as well as the numerous speakers who contributed to our research efforts deserve our deepest gratitude.

Finally, thanks are due to Jim Wolfe, Director of Security, US Senate, for arranging to formally review the manuscript.

Introduction— Charles E. Allen

This fall, as of September 11th, it will have been ten years since we had a successful inbound al-Qa'ida attack directly against the US. I think this is pretty remarkable, given the fact that we have engaged in two multi-year wars in Afghanistan and in Iraq and we have had a global, intelligence-led offensive against al-Qa'ida in all dark corners of the world, not just Iraq and Afghanistan. And given the complexity of the attacks that occurred back on September 11th, 2001, the Intelligence Community forecast there would likely be future attacks of equal if not greater intensity than what occurred ten years ago.

Part of the reason for this pessimistic forecast was the Intelligence Community's lack of understanding of the full capabilities of al-Qa'ida and its ability to conduct intercontinental attacks against the US. I was never that pessimistic— never quite believed that— but I did believe there were going to be additional attacks: small, violent attacks here in this country. And we now know there would have been successful attacks repeatedly had the US not gone on the offensive at home and abroad to disrupt a series of plots that would have resulted in serious loss of American life as well as damage to our critical infrastructure and to our national psyche. I only have to cite the aviation plot of August 2006 to illustrate a disrupted attack because of excellent British intelligence.

The same thing could be said of the attacks that occurred back on the 26th and 27th of October last year, when we had AQAP attempting to bring down airliners using pentaerythritol tetranitrate (PETN), a low-pressure vapor-type explosive that was disguised in Hewlett Packard laser desktop printer components. Again, excellent intelligence, this time from the Saudis, prevented that event from occurring. And I have learned through my long career in intelligence that there will be "abrupt discontinuities," as we used to call them (today they are called "black swans"), where profound events emerge with the power to change history. We may be seeing that today in Tunisia and in Egypt.

We live in a world with deep political, economic, ethnic, religious, and geographic fault lines; some of these are certain to cause conflict. They cannot be avoided. The events that are occurring in Lebanon illustrate this clearly. We will be very fortunate to resolve issues there without real conflict.

We also have a great "youth bulge" around the world. Part of this is reflected in what has occurred in Tunisia, where an enormous percentage of the national population under 25 is unemployed or underemployed. Combined with the fault lines of the Middle East centered in the Arab-Israeli dispute, I think I can see a "witch's brew" developing over the next decade, which will test the West, and will test this country in particular. For this reason, I think we have to look at terrorism in a much broader context. We also have to look at the global threat from al-Qa'ida as standing apart from predecessor terrorist organizations. The diffusion of technology and science means that some of the world's most dangerous capabilities can be placed in the hands of a few violent extremists. The recipes are on the Internet for anyone to study. Al-Qa'ida in the Arabian Peninsula just issued a new explosives manual, in English, that contains some highly accurate information on how to make bombs.

Global communications and mass media provide a mechanism that can be used to fuel terrorism internationally. Communications today provide terrorists and terrorist groups with the ability to coalesce across national boundaries and sustain a common ideology and a narrative. They permit groups to recruit new members, train them, and coordinate attacks virtually.

Let's look back at what happened in 2010. Little has changed when it comes to the objectives of al-Qa'ida. Al-Qa'ida's goal is to attack the US, inflict mass casualties, damage US critical infrastructure, and cause permanent psychological damage to the US. Al-Qa'ida takes a long term view; Usama bin Laden has written about this. He does not believe that the US or the West has the resiliency to remain steadfast, to take heavy losses, and to resist over the long term. Al-Qa'ida leaders have taken pleasure in viewing the US as a society that recoils when there is a threat, or that invokes the "blame game" when there are unsuccessful attempts to attack this country.

The US and global allies in 2010 continued their relentless attack to disrupt, dismantle, defeat, and destroy al-Qa'ida's leadership in the Federally Administered Tribal Areas (FATA). According to the press, in 2010 we launched 115 so-called drone strikes against al-Qa'ida leaders, operatives, propagandists, and trainers in the FATA. The strikes reportedly killed a number of al-Qa'ida leaders. Al-Qa'ida acknowledges that Shaikh Sa'id, the number three man within al-Qa'ida, and its general manager, died last May. So al-Qa'ida "central" is not entirely cohesive. The National Counterterrorism Center (NCTC) says there are only about 300 al-Qa'ida members active in the FATA, and it estimates that maybe fewer than a hundred are active inside Afghanistan.[1] And contrary to popular thought, and to what I read in the press, al-Qa'ida leaders are not easily replaced. It takes a long time to replace good leaders.

Al-Qa'ida's diminished strength in the FATA, however, is offset by the fact that we have the Tehrik-e-Taliban (TTP), which is a tribally based Pakistani group led by Hakimullah Mehsud. The TTP has deep links into al-Qa'ida central, and is involved in supporting cross-border operations into Afghanistan. It has vowed to take vengeance on the US, which it blames for the August 2009 death of Baitullah Mehsud. Faisal Shahzad, the Times Square bomber, allegedly was trained by the TTP for about six weeks before he made his unsuccessful attempt last May. The TTP is challenged, however, in extending its threat transcontinentally to the US. It is primarily a tribally based Pashtun movement.

The other regional tribal supporter of al-Qa'ida is the Haqqani network led by Siraj Haqqani, son of the famed mujahideen fighter Jalaluddin Haqqani, who once was Minister of Tribal Affairs in the Taliban Government. The Haqqani network, *inter alia*, provides manpower to al-Qa'ida for cross-border operations into Afghanistan. The al-Qa'ida network allegedly, according to the press, may groom extremists for suicide operations. There is also LeT, which is a Kashmiri-based group focused primarily on conducting attacks in India. But none of these affiliated groups is the type that has the intent and the objective of attacking the US.

Al-Qa'ida affiliated networks continued to decline in 2010. Jemaah Islamiyah, which was decimated back in 2007, 2008, and 2009, remains dormant. The Abu Sayyaf group, in the Philippines, has had its leaders killed or captured. This was more of a thuggish group than a purveyor of Islamic extremism. But I do have concerns about North Africa and East Africa. Let's look at al-Qaida in the Islamic Maghreb (AQIM). It functions as an umbrella organization for a disparate collection of Sunni Muslim terrorist elements determined to attack what they see as "apostate regimes" in Algeria, Tunisia, Libya, Mauritania, and Morocco. The bulk of AQIM forces are located in southern Algeria, northern Mali, and Mauritania. They have raided archaeological sites and tourist areas in Mali and Mauritania. They specialize in kidnapping and extracting significant ransom in order to fuel their operations. They have kidnapped a significant number of Westerners, including a number of Frenchmen whom they still hold. We have not seen them attack Western Europe, but they may become emboldened as the result of the disturbances that have occurred in Tunisia. I think we have to watch AQIM very closely, and we are all indebted to Professor Alexander for studying this issue in depth.

We know that AQAP merged with al-Qaida in Saudi Arabia in January 2009. It is very much an insurgent group, determined in its efforts to attack the US and the West. It thrives in the ungoverned areas of Yemen. It conducted numerous attacks in 2010 inside Yemen, particularly in the southern governance. Its most prominent extremists are well known; for example, Anwar al-Awlaki, a US citizen who provided "spiritual sanction" for those who may wish to commit suicide in the name of al-Qa'ida. Awlaki supported AQAP's propaganda efforts against the West. He continued to speak from hiding until he was killed by a drone strike in 2011. On November 9, 2010, he issued a new video. If you read the transcript, it can be summed in two words: kill Americans.

We have already noted AQIM's efforts to bring down airliners using PETN in laser jet toner cartridges, but it has also done something else that is quite interesting. Last year, it published the first edition of *Inspire*, which is a web-based journal of propaganda directed at inciting violent acts, especially by young Muslims living in the US, the UK, and other Western states. This is an electronic, web-based magazine, with the potential to induce young and alienated Muslims to commit acts of violence in the US and Canada.

Let us consider al-Shabaab, in East Africa. Professor Alexander has noted that it is directly linked to al-Qa'ida central, operating from Somalia. And of course it continues to wage a fairly successful insurgency against Somalia's Transitional National Government, which is backed by the UN and the US. Several dozen young Americans of Somali descent have traveled to Somalia to fight for al-Shabaab. At least a couple have martyred themselves there— committed suicide operations in that fight. Our concern is not about an inbound threat directly from al-Shabaab central, but about those who've gone to Somalia, trained there, fought there in military operations— and returned— still radicalized and capable of committing terrorist acts. And al-Shabaab remains a fertile ground for recruiting extremists not only in the US but also in Western Europe.

One development that has occurred in the last year is a greater prominence of radicalization, especially among Muslim youth in the West— in Europe as well as in North America. According to a RAND corporation study that was published in 2010, there were only 46 publicly reported cases of radicalization and recruitment to jihadist terrorism in the US between September 11, 2001, and the end of 2009. Only 125 people were identified as part of these 46 cases. Thirteen of those cases, however, occurred in 2009, which is a very sharp uptick. And in 2010, the number of cases has increased further. On November 26, Mohamed Osman Mohamud, in Portland, Oregon, tried to detonate a car bomb at a Christmas tree lighting. Antonio Martinez, also known as Muhammad Hussain, was going to attack an armed forces recruiting center in Maryland with a bomb. These individuals were self-inspired and self-motivated. They were not directed from al-Qa'ida central in the FATA or from AQAP in Yemen. These persons were all US citizens or held legal immigration status. The central theme of each plot involved placing explosives in areas that would murder innocent Americans.

Western Europe is also a primary focus of al-Qa'ida plotting. There have been arrests across a number of countries in Europe, including Spain. There are reports involving radicalized individuals, some of whom were allegedly preparing to stage a Mumbai-type attack, as occurred during November, 2008. This threat was so severe that the Department of State issued an "advisory alert" warning Americans of possible attacks on Europe's public transport system or tourist attractions. British authorities arrested, in December 2010, nine men on terrorism charges. The individuals found encouragement and bomb-making instructions in AQAP's Internet journal, *Inspire*. *Inspire* is well worth reading. The electronic journal is published in simple, easily understood English. It is not heavy on ideology, like many of the old tomes that used to come out of as-Sahab, the propaganda arm of al-Qa'ida central. It is much cleverer in its message.

We must keep our perspective on radicalization here in this country. The Pew Research Center, in a study published in May 2007, has pointed out that American Muslims are overwhelmingly American in outlook, values, and attitudes. They believe hard work pays off in society. They have high income levels, and good educations. Most American Muslims, by a two to one margin, do not see any conflict between being a devout Muslim and living in a modern society. So our concerns are only over a tiny minority of Muslims, a number of whom are converts to Islam, who remain strongly linked with Islamic countries in which extremist groups are flourishing.

Many new immigrants have arrived in the US during the last fifteen to twenty years as refugees and asylum seekers. Some of these immigrants have become strongly attracted to anti-Western, especially anti-US, forces in their countries of origin. Political, religious, and social tensions that exist in a particular community in the US may mirror tensions in these other countries. These tensions may be reflected in the belief held by many Muslims in other countries that the US is "at war with Islam."

This affinity with violent groups abroad is reflected again in the case of Somalia. Somali immigrants coming to this country have found assimilation to be difficult; many have felt alienated. Many retained their clan/sub-clan affinities in Somalia. With civil war raging in Somalia, they felt attracted to radical imams here in this country. Some of the first generation of these fighters have returned and others will. And we should be just as concerned about the second generation. These are not naturalized Americans like the first generation of Somali-Americans; they were born as Americans—young men who are in their teens and who are still influenced by the first generation of Somalis and radical Imams.

To date, the self-radicalized cells detected in the US and Canada have lacked the level of sophistication, experience, and access to resources of terrorist cells overseas. Their efforts have been in the nascent stages, and many have been amateurish. But it is not the success that is important, it is the intent. Eventually, they will get it right.

Given what I have outlined, I believe we have every reason to be concerned about terrorism in 2011 and beyond. We know how quickly al-Qa'ida metastasized after 9/11. Al-Qa'ida central may be slowly dying, but its tentacles around the world live on. These tentacles will remain alive for years to come. I cannot overstate the power of the Internet for fueling the growth of radicalization in this country, as well as in Western Europe. Many of the extremists recruited in the US began their journey on the Internet, where they readily found resonance and reinforcement for their own discontented views. So the outlook for al-Qa'ida and its objective of inflicting major damage to the US and Western countries has not changed, and the threat is very much with us and will remain so in 2011 and beyond.

Bibliographic Reference

1. Sanger, David E. and Mark Mazzetti. *The New York Times*, "New Estimate of Strength of Al Qaeda is Offered." June 30, 2010. *http://www.nytimes.com/2010/07/01/world/asia/01qaeda.html*.

CHAPTER 1

Ideological and Theological Perspectives and Goals

Unlike conventional terrorist organizations, al-Qa'ida does not aim to achieve a political goal within the existing national or international levels of governance. Instead, al-Qa'ida wishes to establish a new world order based on Islamic principles and law.

In a 1997 interview, Usama bin Laden asserted this idea, stating, "It is a great pride and a big hope that the revelation unto Muhammad, 'Peace be upon him,' will be resorted to for ruling. When we used to follow Muhammad's revelation we were in great happiness and in great dignity, to God belongs credit and praise."[1]

This overarching goal and fundamental ideology of al-Qa'ida can be attributed to three factors: (1) the Islamic fundamentalist movement of Salafism, (2) the radical teachings of Sayyid Qutb and Abdullah Azzam, and (3) a number of circumstances surrounding the Soviet invasion of Afghanistan.

Salafism

The term Salafism, as it is commonly used today, refers to a Sunni Islamic movement that emphasizes the sole religious authority of the Quran and the hadith (the Prophet's practices).[2,3] Salafis (translated as "disciples of the forbears") seek to emulate the salaf, the earliest practitioners of Islam. [4,5] Salafis deny the merit of Islamic scholars who offer broad interpretations of the Quran and denounce Shi'as as rafidi, or rejectionists of Islam's first three caliphs. Furthermore, Salafis are often wary of other religions, including Judaism and Christianity (dhimmi, or "people of the book"), which share a common origin with Islam.[6] The origins of Salafism are often associated with Ibn Taymiyya, a 14th century Islamic scholar.[7] Wahhabism, another fundamentalist Islamic movement, is seen largely as a subsidiary of Salafism that is practiced mainly in Saudi Arabia.[8]

There exists a broad spectrum within Salafism regarding political engagement. While some followers advocate nonviolent political activism,

1

others argue against overt political participation.[9] On the other end of the spectrum lie Salafi jihadists, who advocate the use of violence to achieve political goals.

Sayyid Qutb

Sayyid Qutb's teachings emphasize the necessity of Islam in the modern world. Born in Egypt in 1906, Qutb received both a traditional Islamic education as well as a Western university education. An influential member of the Muslim Brotherhood, Qutb spoke of the encroachment of jahiliyyah, or ignorance and unbelief, which he felt was in conflict with Islam.[10] In his seminal work, *Milestones*, Qutb explains the necessity of Islam's spread:

> *Islam is the way of life ordained by God for all mankind, and this way establishes the Lordship of God alone—that is, the sovereignty of God—and orders practical life in all its daily details. Jihad in Islam is simply a name for striving to make this system of life dominant in the world.*
>
> ...
>
> *It is in the very nature of Islam to take initiative for freeing the human beings throughout the earth from servitude to anyone other than God; and so it cannot be restricted within any geographic or racial limits.*[11]

The spread of Islam through jihad was Qutb's solution for combating the evils associated with jahiliyyah. Jailed and eventually hanged for his radical beliefs, Qutb died a martyr, adding further authority to his teachings. Usama bin Laden's second in command, Ayman al-Zawahiri, was greatly influenced by Qutb's teachings, stating, "Sayyid Qutb's call for loyalty to God's oneness and to acknowledge God's sole authority and sovereignty was the spark that ignited the Islamic revolution against the enemies of Islam at home and abroad."[12]

Abdullah Azzam

Abdullah Azzam stressed the importance of fard al-'ayn, or the obligation of Muslims to defend Islamic lands from foreign and secular invasion.[13] Born in 1941, Azzam's Palestinian roots became the driving force behind his call for defensive jihad, which he promoted while teaching at the King Abdulaziz University in Saudi Arabia and the Islamic University in Pakistan. It was at the King Abdulaziz University that Usama bin Laden and Azzam first crossed paths. Originally concentrating on Israel, Azzam shifted his focus to Afghanistan, establishing the Maktab Khadamat al-Mujahideen (MAK) (Office of Services for the Mujahideen) with bin Laden to aid the jihadists opposed to the Soviet invasion.[14] Through their collaboration they produced the idea of al-Qa'ida al-Sulbah, or the "solid base" of Muslim vanguards, set to pave the way for an Islamic society.[15] Through jihad, these vanguards would liberate Muslim territories held by nonbelievers and secular regimes.[16] After Azzam's assassination in 1989, bin Laden adopted the name "al-Qa'ida" for his newly established organization, embracing the legacy of Azzam's teachings.[17]

In a statement entitled "al-Qa'ida's Creed and Path," the organization showed its support for Azzam's idea of fard al-'ayn, declaring, "We believe that the ruler who does not rule in accordance with God's revelation, as well as his supporters, who substitute the shari'a [with some other law], are infidel apostates. Armed and violent rebellion against them is an individual duty on every Muslim."[18]

The Soviet Invasion of Afghanistan

The Soviet invasion of Afghanistan in 1979 acted as a catalyst for the rapid spread of radicalism amongst Muslims. First, Soviet aggression seemed to confirm the growing belief that Islam was facing a cultural attack (al-ghazw ath-thaqaf) from the non-Muslim world.[19] Second, the international scope of the resistance in Afghanistan, which included Muslims from all over the world, allowed for the proliferation of radical ideas amongst jihadists. Finally, the perception of jihadi success in repelling the Soviet invasion shaped Usama bin Laden's views regarding the viability of jihad in shaping global affairs. In a 1997 interview, Usama bin Laden argued that, "If Russia can be destroyed, the US can also be beheaded."[20]

Al-Qa'ida's Ideology and Goals

Al-Qa'ida is guided by a fundamentalist Islamic ideology that adheres to the belief that Islam is the only legitimate authority on earth, spanning all aspects of life, especially governance.

3

From this ideology flows a number of goals. First, al-Qa'ida seeks to rid Islam of alien influences. These influences include Western ideals such as secularism and revisionism, as well as competing sects of Islam, primarily that of the Shi'a. Second, al-Qa'ida seeks to liberate Muslim territories "occupied" by foreign forces. This includes areas in the Arabian Peninsula, especially Saudi Arabia, as well as areas in Palestine, North Africa, and the Asian Subcontinent where US, NATO, and Israeli troops are stationed. This goal also calls for the overthrow of secular governments in Muslim nations, such as Egypt. Third, al-Qa'ida seeks to establish a global Islamic caliphate so that all of humanity has the opportunity to accept Islam.[21] A caliphate is an Islamic political system ruled by a caliph who unites the Muslim community (umma) and rules according to Islamic law (sharia). Historically, the caliphate was a vast and sophisticated empire responsible for many innovations in mathematics and science. At its height, the caliphate stretched from Spain, across portions of North and West Africa and into the Middle East, as well as India.[22] While the global caliphate is often discussed in the media, the first two goals constitute al-Qa'ida's chief objectives.[23]

Al-Qa'ida's Ideology Today: Signs of Change?

In the final recorded message before his death, Usama bin Laden praised the revolutions sweeping across the Arab world. He asserted his belief that such revolutions would spread, putting an end to the regimes of Western-backed "tyrants."[24] While bin Laden professed support for the overthrow of governments with ties to the West, he seemed to be ignoring the pro-democratic spirit of the uprisings. The system of governance proposed by al-Qa'ida is theocratic and undemocratic in nature. Does Usama bin Laden's final message indicate a shift in al-Qa'ida's ideology? With the Muslim world overwhelmingly calling for democracy, was this message bin Laden's final attempt to make al-Qa'ida's ideology once again relevant? The answer remains uncertain.

Notes and Bibliographic References

1.   CNN, "Interview with Usama bin Laden." March 1997. *http://www.cnn.com/video/#/video/world/2011/05/02/video.vault.bin.laden.jihad.cnn.*

2.   Blanchard, Christopher M. CRS Report for Congress, "The Islamic Traditions of Wahhabism and Salafiyya." January 17, 2007.

3. Salafism can also refer to a reformation movement in the late 19th and early 20th centuries, which sought to adapt Islam in the face of Western modernization and expansion. This movement is often associated with Jamal al-Din al-Afghani and Muhammad 'Abduh. For more information on this movement, see Meijer, Roel. *Global Salafism: Islam's New Religious Movement*, (New York, NY: Columbia University Press, 2009), 45-47.

4. "Salafists in Gaza: The Real Thing." *The Economist*. May 15, 2010. *http://www.economist.com/node/16117240*.

5. Moghadam, Assaf. *The Globalization of Martyrdom: Al Qaeda, Salafi Jihad, and the Diffusion of Suicide Attacks*, (Baltimore, MD: The John Hopkins University Press, 2008), 95.

6. *Ibid*. 2, 3; and Moghadam, Assaf. *The Globalization of Martyrdom: Al Qaeda, Salafi Jihad, and the Diffusion of Suicide Attacks*, (Baltimore, MD: The John Hopkins University Press, 2008), p. 95.

7. Meijer, Roel. *Global Salafism: Islam's New Religious Movement*, (New York, NY: Columbia University Press, 2009), 38.

8. *Ibid*. 2.

9. *Ibid*. 7, 48-49.

10. Kepel, Gilles. *The War for Muslim Minds: Islam and the West*, (Cambridge, MA: Belknap, 2006),136.

11. Qutb, Sayyid. *Milestones*. *http://web.youngmuslims.ca/online_library/ books/milestones/hold/index_2.htm*.

12. Musallam, Adnan A. *From Secularism to Jihad: Sayyid Qutb and the Foundations of Radical Islam*, (Westport, CT: Greenwood Publishing Group, Inc., 2005), 167.

13. Shavit, Uriya. "Al-Qaeda's Saudi Origins." *Middle East Quarterly*. 13. no. 4 (Fall 2006): 5.

14. Maliach, Asaf. "Abdullah Azzam, al-Qaeda, and Hamas: Concepts of Jihad and Istishhad," Military and Strategic Affairs 2:2 (October 2010): 80.

15. *Ibid*. 14, 80.

16. *Ibid*. 14, 82.

17. *Ibid*. 14, 83.

18. *Ibid*. 7, 53.

19. *Ibid*. 13, 3.

20. Foreign Broadcast Information Service (FBIS), "Pakistan Interviews Usama Bin Ladin". Interview with Hamid Mir. March 18, 1997. Available electronically from *http://hdl.handle.net/10066/4735*.

21. For more on these goals see Blanchard, Christopher M. CRS Report for Congress, "Al Qaeda: Statements and Evolving Ideology." July 9, 2007.

22. Livesey, Bruce. Public Broadcasting Service (PBS), "The Salafiist Movement." *http://www.pbs.org/wgbh/pages/frontline/shows/front/special/sala.html*.

23. Pankhurst, Reza, "The Caliphate, and the Changing Strategy of the Public Statements of Al-Qaeda's Leaders." *Political Theology*. 11. no. 4 (October 2010): 532.

24. Aboudi, Sami. Reuters, "Al Qaeda Releases Posthumous bin Laden Audio Recording." May 19, 2011. *http://www.reuters.com/article/2011/05/19/us-binladen-audio-idUSTRE74I0DJ20110519*.

CHAPTER 2

Key Leadership

*Usama bin Laden**

Usama bin Laden was born in 1957 in Saudi Arabia as the 17th son of 51 children of Muhammad bin Laden. His father was of Yemeni descent from the village of al-Ribat; his mother was a Saudi. Muhammad bin Laden left al-Ribat in 1931 and founded the construction company the Bin Laden Group with his brothers. The company became heavily involved in Saudi government contracts building everything from the holy mosques in Mecca and Medina to highways and palaces. The bin Laden family business proved to be incredibly lucrative and the family amassed a fortune estimated at billions of dollars.

From an early age, Usama bin Laden was raised as a strict Islamist. Due to his close relationship with Mecca's mosques and the Saudi royal family, his father welcomed many pilgrims during the Hajj season. Even after his father died, visitors continued to pour into the home of the then thirteen-year-old Usama bin Laden.

Usama bin Laden is believed to have received a civil engineering or public management degree around 1980 from King Abdulaziz University in Jeddah, Saudi Arabia, though some contend that he fell short of obtaining a diploma. During his education he had two very distinguished teachers: Abdullah Azzam, who later collaborated with him in Afghanistan; and Mohammed Qutb, the famous Islamic philosopher. While bin Laden was attending university one of the most formative experiences of his adolescence occurred: the Soviet invasion of Afghanistan.

During the early stages of the mujahideen resistance, bin Laden traveled to Afghanistan and Pakistan to meet with scholars and leaders who had been guests at his family's house. He began lobbying for the mujahideen and successfully raised large amounts of money for their cause.

After university, bin Laden left Saudi Arabia for Afghanistan to join the mujahideen. He not only brought fresh recruits but also large amounts of cash and badly needed construction machinery. In 1984, he built a "guesthouse" in Peshawar, Pakistan, which would be the first station for new recruits for the mujahideen. The Maktab al-Khadamat (MAK) was established by Abdullah Azzam at bin Laden's guesthouse and was active in supporting the resistance. MAK was successful in funneling money into the war zone; building tunnels and hospitals; generating media and publications; and drawing support for the mujahideen around the world, especially in Afghanistan, but also in places like Yemen. The MAK was known to have a recruiting office in Brooklyn, New York, at the Alkifah Refugee Center.

Around 1986, bin Laden decided to chart a separate course from MAK. He built his own camps and trained his own fighters. Within two years he had six camps such as al-Masadah- The Lion's Den. He ran several successful assaults, with help from ex-military advisers from Egypt and Syria who brought much-needed experience, and participated in several battles, including the battle of Jalalabad.

Around 1988, bin Laden realized that it was necessary to keep documentation of the people who traveled through his guesthouse, camps, and Afghanistan. He wanted to be able to track his friends and fellow mujahideen fighters as well as to be able to give answers to families with missing loved ones and friends who were out of touch. This network became known as "al-Qa'ida" (or the base). Following the Soviet withdrawal from Afghanistan in 1989 he went back to Saudi Arabia, while al-Qa'ida remained headquartered in Peshawar, Pakistan.

The Afghan war, however, did not end with the Soviet retreat. The rebels' hostilities continued initially against the Moscow-backed government and then between opposing factions (the Taliban and the Northern Alliance). On November 24, 1989, MAK suffered a major blow when a car bomb killed Azzam and his two sons in Peshawar.

During the same period in Saudi Arabia, bin Laden gave several public speeches relating to the Afghan victory, the failures of the Saudi government, and the impending Iraqi invasion. The Saudi government became concerned with his activities and placed a travel ban on him.

In August 1990, American troops arrived in Saudi Arabia at the invitation of the Saudi government to protect the Kingdom from a potential Iraqi attack. Bin Laden was furious that the Saudi government had sought and received a Western government's help and that non-Muslim forces were based in the same country as the Muslim holy sites of Mecca and Medina. Consequently, bin Laden met with several religious leaders to begin rounding up recruits. The Saudi government then attempted to stop his activities, and by 1991 bin Laden had been expelled from Saudi Arabia.

Bin Laden used his connections to leave the country for Pakistan and later travel back into Afghanistan. There, he tried to work out a settlement between the warring factions battling for power while gathering support for a new jihad. In late 1991, after his efforts at mediation in the Afghan civil war had failed and several attempts were made on his life, bin Laden left for the Sudan.

Bin Laden was attracted to the Sudan for several reasons. The strict Islamist ideology of the new regime under the National Islamic Front appealed to him, and the regime sought his help. There were also several business opportunities for construction projects, including major highways, ports, and airports. Bin Laden set up several new companies in Sudan which would use these projects to provide income and support al-Qa'ida's activities while serving as a front to transport weapons and men. He also found employment and homes for several hundred "Arab-Afghans," who could not or would not return home after the jihad in Afghanistan.

While in Sudan, bin Laden set up al-Qa'ida's headquarters in the Riyadh section of Khartoum. It is reported that bin Laden funded and had remote, if not direct, involvement in several terrorist operations that took place in the early-to-mid 1990s in Yemen, Saudi Arabia, Somalia, Egypt, as well as the 1993 World Trade Center bombing in New York. Bin Laden and other members of al-Qa'ida worked to put aside their differences with other Shi'a terrorist organizations and trying to unify them under al-Qa'ida against their perceived common enemies. Bin Laden and al-Qa'ida held several talks with elements within the Iranian government and the terrorist organization Hezbollah; it is believed that bin Laden sent members of his group to Hezbollah camps in Lebanon to receive training.

While bin Laden was living in Sudan, Saudi intelligence conducted several assassination attempts against bin Laden. The Saudi government froze his assets in the early 90s and publicly withdrew his Saudi citizenship in 1994. Usama was also denounced by members of his family. Following his public denunciation, bin Laden formed the Advice and Reform Council (ARC) as the political arm of al-Qa'ida. Through the ARC, bin Laden and his associates published several statements condemning the Saudi and Western governments. By 1996, Sudan was under extreme international pressure to deport bin Laden and his followers. The Sudanese government, seeking relief from an embargo against its country, asked bin Laden to leave whereupon he relocated to Afghanistan.

Upon his return to Afghanistan, bin Laden began to issue several public statements and fatwas calling for all Muslims "to kill Americans and their allies, civilian and military, [as] an individual duty." The first notable fatwa issued by bin Laden, "Message from Usama bin Laden to his Muslim Brothers in the Whole World and Especially in the Arabian Peninsula: Declaration of Jihad Against the Americans Occupying the Land of the Two Holy Mosques; Expel the Heretics from the Arabian Peninsula," came in 1996. During this time he increased his media exposure, giving his first interview to CNN, in 1997, as well as declaring additional fatwas.[1]

Bin Laden set up several training camps for his new jihad against the US. From these camps, bin Laden financed and helped plan several terrorist operations, such as the Khobar Towers bombing in 1996 in Saudi Arabia, the 1998 bombings of the American embassies in East Africa, and the 2000 attack on the *USS Cole* in Yemen. While the US retaliated for the 1998 embassy bombings with cruise missile strikes on al-Qa'ida training camps in Afghanistan and thwarted several other plots linked to bin Laden, such as the 2000 millennium plot, bin Laden's vast network of resources and his devoted following enabled him to continue his jihad. The umbrella framework of the International Islamic Front for Jihad against Jews and Crusaders which bin Laden and associates set up in Afghanistan in February 1998 served as a "clearing house" and coordinating body for many groups worldwide.[2] From Afghanistan, al-Qa'ida was able to launch its most spectacular attack: the September 11, 2001, attacks on the World Trade Center and the Pentagon.

Early in the 2001 invasion of Afghanistan, US forces were believed to have been close to locating bin Laden in the mountain region of Tora Bora. However, he managed to elude the US and remained at large for the next decade despite the $25 million bounty offered for his capture. It remains unclear how much influence bin Laden had on the planning of operations or how much contact al-Qa'ida central had with its affiliates during his time in hiding. Bin Laden remained active in the public sphere, releasing occasional audio and video messages aimed at followers worldwide and remaining the international face of al-Qa'ida.

Though he was believed to be hiding somewhere in the Afghanistan-Pakistan border region, bin Laden had been living in a compound in Abbottabad, Pakistan, near the Pakistani capital of Islamabad since 2005. US officials first became alerted to the possibility of bin Laden's presence in the area in the summer of 2010. Several months of intelligence work confirmed bin Laden's location in the compound. Early in the morning on Monday, May 2, 2011, Pakistani time, a US Navy SEAL team raided the compound, killing bin Laden.

Ayman al-Zawahiri

Ayman al-Zawahiri has long been considered to be the second highest ranking member of al-Qai'da, outranked only by Usama bin Laden. Since the killing of Usama bin Laden by US Navy Seals, al-Zawahiri now tops the Federal Bureau of Investigation's (FBI) "Most Wanted Terrorists" listing. On June 16, 2011, al-Zawahiri was named the successor to Usama bin Laden on numerous jihadist websites, and is now considered the leader of the world's most notorious terrorist organization.[3]

Al-Zawahiri was born in Egypt on June 19, 1951. He was trained as a physician and founded Egyptian Islamic Jihad (EIJ). This organization has opposed the secular Egyptian government and sought its overthrow through violent means. Al-Zawahiri fought in the Afghan-Soviet war, where he became a close confidant of bin Laden. In 1998 the EIJ effectively merged with al-Qai'da to posture against the Egyptian government and ultimately the US.[4] Three days before his sixtieth birthday, Ayman al-Zawahiri was named successor to Usama bin Laden. The alleged al-Qa'ida "general command" stated that "Hereby the General Command of the Qaeda al-Jihad—and after the end of the consultations—we declare that Sheikh Dr. Abu Muhammad Ayman al-Zawahiri (may God bless him) will take over the responsibility of command of the group."[5] Ayman al-Zawahiri has many aliases including: Abu Muhammad, Abu Fatima, Muhammad Ibrahim, Abu Abdallah, Abu al-Mu'iz, The Doctor, The Teacher, Nur, Ustaz, Abu Mohammed, Abu Mohammed Nur al-Deen, Abdel Muaz, and Dr. Ayman al Zawahiri. He speaks Arabic and French.

Currently, there is a $25 million reward for information leading to the apprehension or conviction of al-Zawahiri, the same amount previously offered for Usama bin Laden. Most notably, al-Zawahiri is wanted for his operational role in the August 7, 1998, bombings of two US embassies in Dar es-Salaam, Tanzania; and Nairobi, Kenya.[6] In the span of 9 minutes, suicide bombers launched simultaneous attacks on both sites. There were over 5,100 injuries with estimates of victims' deaths ranging from 224 persons (FBI) to 302 persons (State Department).[7] Though the attacks were on US facilities, only 12 US citizens were killed, with the majority of casualties being Kenyans. Al-Qa'ida and Ayman Al-Zawahiri were identified as being major players in planning the bombings through the interrogation of Mohammed Sadeek Odeh, a Nairobi cell-operative detained in Pakistan following the attacks.[8]

Major Audio and Visual Publications since the inauguration of Barack Obama:

2011

> *June 8th, 2011*: In a statement posted on jihadist websites, al-Zawahiri spoke for the first time since the death of Usama bin Laden. In the 28 minute video, al-Zawahiri dedicated much of the time to a eulogy to bin Laden, stating that "… the sheikh has departed, may God have mercy on him, to his God as a martyr and we must continue on his path of jihad to expel the invaders from the land of Muslims and to purify it from injustice." Al-Zawahiri continues to denounce Americans for burying bin Laden at sea, and has given his support to the wave of Arab unrest occurring throughout the Middle East. He has specifically called for sharia to be implemented in Egypt.[9]

Many analysts believed bin Laden's control over al-Qa'ida eroded in recent years while in hiding and which increased al-Qa'ida's decentralization. Some said bin Laden had become little more than an inspirational figure, as well as an occasional propagandist for the anti-American terror movement, and that the planning and operational controls belonged to al-Zawahiri.[10] However, a senior US intelligence official said that "[the] compound in Abbottabad was an active command-and-control center for al-Qaeda's leader. He was active in operational planning and in driving tactical decisions within al-Qaeda."[11]

Furthermore, intelligence analysts note that, despite speaking for 28 minutes in his eulogy, al-Zawahiri not only neglected to present himself as al-Qa'ida's new leader, but even called for new leaders to step up in the jihadist movement.

> *April 14th, 2011*: In a one-hour and nine-minute video, Ayman al-Zawahiri incited Muslims to rise up against both NATO and Muammar Gaddafi's forces. Al-Zawahiri also reiterated al-Qa'ida's backing for the ousted Tunisian and Egyptian presidents, accusing the Egyptian government of "separation from Islam" and "subservience to the West."

Al-Zawahiri accused the US of installing sympathetic new regimes in Tunisia and Egypt, demanding that Muslims rise up against the "whippers" and "invaders."[12]

2010

July 20th, 2010: In this video, al-Zawahiri slammed Arab leaders as "Zionists" who were helping Israel's siege of the Gaza Strip. He also mocked US President Barack Obama for saying that the Taliban will not regain power in Afghanistan, hailing, at the same time, the "victory" of the Islamist militant group against coalition forces.

Al-Zawahiri went on to criticize Egyptian President Hosni Mubarak for planning to curb cross-border smuggling, which, at the time, was the only lifeline for the Hamas-run enclave amid Israel's blockade. Al-Zawahiri also criticized Jordan's King Abdullah II for providing "intelligence service to… [the] US and [Israel's] Mossad."[13]

2009

December 14th, 2009: In a 26-minute audio recording, al-Zawahiri renewed calls to establish an Islamic state in Israel and urged followers to "seek jihad against Jews." Al-Zawahiri criticized US allies in the Middle East, calling Egyptian President Hosni Mubarak, Jordanian King Abdullah II, and Saudi Arabian King Abdullah Abdulaziz "brothers of satan."

In this audio recording, al-Zawahiri called for attacks against Americans who imprisoned Ramzi Yousef, the mastermind of the 1993 World Trade Tower attack, and Khalid Sheikh Mohammed, the mastermind of the September 11, 2001, attack.

2008

November 19th, 2008: In an 11-minute audio web posting, al-Zawahiri warned then President-elect Barack Obama that "a heavy legacy of failure and crimes awaits" him. Al-Zawahiri criticized Obama's foreign policy positions on Afghanistan and Israel and ridiculed his worldview. Al-Zawahiri said Obama, former and current Secretaries of State Colin Powell and Condoleezza Rice, and "your likes" fit Malcolm X's description of "house slaves."

Al-Zawahiri attributed President-elect Obama's stance on withdrawing troops from Iraq to the demands of Usama bin Laden, who had called for the withdrawal of troops prior to the web posting.[14]

Selected Associate Key Leaders

Abdullah Ahmed Abduallah

Abdullah was born in or around 1963 and is estimated to be at a height of 5'8". He has a medium build with dark hair, dark eyes, and an olive complexion. He has a scar on the right side of his lower lip.[15]

Abdullah is an Egyptian national and one of five individuals indicted by a US federal grand jury on December 20, 2000 for the 1998 African embassy bombings. Abdullah Ahmed Abdullah faces the death penalty for training al-Qa'ida operatives. He reportedly played an active role in both embassy bombings as well as in the murders of US servicemen in Mogadishu. During the Afghan war, he trained soldiers in the use of explosives at the Jihad Wal camp in Khost. It is believed he sat on al-Qa'ida's consultation council as well as the religious/fatwa committee.

After leaving Nairobi, Kenya, in 1998, Abdullah Ahmed Abduallah is believed to have fled to Pakistan. His current whereabouts are unknown.[16]

Saif al-Adel

Al-Adel was born on April 11, 1960 or 1963, has dark hair, dark eyes, and an olive complexion with no known scars or marks.[17]

Al-Adel, an Egyptian national, was indicted by a federal grand jury on December 20, 2000. He became al-Qa'ida's number three military commander following the death of Muhammed Atef in 2001 and the capture of Khalid Sheikh Mohammed in 2003.[18] Although reports indicated that he did not have an active role in the actual bombing of the embassies, it is reported that al-Adel sat on al-Qa'ida's consultation council as well as its military committee. It is also believed he played an active role in Somalia, where eighteen US servicemen were murdered by al-Qa'ida-affiliated men. Al-Adel is also attributed with being one of the masterminds of the assassination of Egyptian President Anwar al-Sadat. Upon the death of Usama bin Laden, al-Adel took over as interim chief for al-Qa'ida. Since he was released from Iran in March of 2011, his whereabouts have been unknown.

Muhammed Atef*

Atef was 6'4" to 6'6" in height with a thin build, dark hair, dark eyes, and olive complexion with no known scars or marks. Atef was an Egyptian national, the co-founder of al-Qa'ida, and the military chief under bin Laden. While at large, he was indicted for his connection to the East African embassy bombings. Atef's daughter is married to Usama bin Laden's son. It was believed that in the event of bin Laden's capture or death, Atef would have become al-Qa'ida's leader. However, Atef was killed in Afghanistan in November 2001.

Abu Ubaidah al-Banshiri*

Al-Banshiri was a co-founder of al-Qa'ida and was a member of the Majlis al-Shura and the "emir" (or head) of the military committee from 1991-1996. According to testimony by his brother-in-law, Ashif Mohamed Juma, al-Banshiri drowned in a ferry accident on Lake Victoria in May 1996. The name "Banshiri" derives from the Banshir Valley, where he supposedly went when he first arrived in Afghanistan to fight the Soviets. It is believed he was a police officer in Egypt before he went to fight in Afghanistan.

Abu Yahya al-Libi

Abu Yahya al-Libi, born in 1963 in Libya, is currently one of the top leaders in al-Qa'ida, and is serving on the Sharia Committee. The US State Department has identified al-Libi as a key motivator in the global jihad movement.[19] Although not much is known about his origin, al-Libi is thought to have been a member of the Libyan Islamic Fighting Group (LIFG) that attempted to remove Libyan ruler Muammar Gaddafi from power in the 1990s. A former member of the LIFG said that al-Libi spent five years in Mauritania as a religious student and is considered a theological scholar.[20] Al-Libi was arrested in 2002, but later escaped from a high-security prison in Bagram, Afghanistan, with three other terror suspects in 2005.[21] Since his escape, al-Libi has risen through the ranks of al-Qa'ida and has become one of its top strategists. He has also appeared in numerous websites promoting global jihad.[22] Most recently, he appeared in a video in March 2011, directed at the people of Libya and calling on them to fight against Gaddafi.[23]

Anas al-Liby

Al-Liby is believed to have been born on either March 30, 1964 or May 14, 1964, in Tripoli, Libya. His height is estimated at 5'10" to 6'2" with a medium build, and he has dark hair with dark eyes and an olive complexion. Al-Liby has a scar on the left side of his face.

Al-Liby is a Libyan national who allegedly sat on al-Qa'ida's consultation council. He was indicted in the US on December 20, 2000, for his role in the East African embassy bombings. He allegedly took photographs of the embassies that were later used by bin Laden to pinpoint where the explosives should be positioned. While not officially recognized, a Human Rights Watch Report claims that al-Liby may have been held in a secret Central Intelligence Agency (CIA) detention facility.[24] However, there is reason to believe that al-Liby may still be at large due to the fact that he still appears on the FBI's Most Wanted Terrorist list.[25]

Khalid Sheikh Mohammed†

Khalid Sheikh Mohammed acted as al-Qa'ida's chief of operations and is the self-described mastermind of the September 11th terrorist attacks. He was born in Kuwait on April 24, 1965.[26] Mohammed holds citizenship in Kuwait, Pakistan, and Bosnia.[27] He was captured in Pakistan in 2003 and has remained in US custody since then. In 2006, Mohammed was moved to Guantanamo Bay.[28] He is believed to be responsible for the following attacks, attempted attacks, or plots: the September 11, 2001, terrorist attacks; the 1993 attack on the World Trade Center; the bombing of nightclubs on Bali in 2002; the bombing of a Kenyan hotel in 2002; the attempted shoe bombing by Richard Reid; a plot to blow up the Panama Canal; plots to hit other towers and nuclear plants across the US; and plots to assassinate Pope John Paul II and President Bill Clinton. He has also admitted that it was he who beheaded reporter Daniel Pearl in 2002.[29] Mohammed is currently awaiting trial at Guantanamo Bay, following Congress' decision to impose restrictions against moving him back to the US.[30]

16

Abu Hafs al-Najdi*

Al-Najdi was a senior al-Qa'ida member and the number two overall targeted insurgent in Afghanistan.[31] Al-Najdi, a native of Saudi Arabia, served as al-Qa'ida's operations chief for the Kunar province. As chief of operations, his role entailed establishing training sites and camps in the province, directing recruitment, organizing al-Qa'ida's finances, weapons, equipment, and planning attacks against Coalition forces.[32] On April 13, 2011, following a four-year manhunt, al-Najdi was killed in an airstrike while meeting with other al-Qa'ida members in the Kunar province. He is reported to have directed the suicide attack that killed Malik Zarin the morning of his death.[33]

Omar Mahmoud Othman Omar†

Omar, of Palestinian origin and a Jordanian national, obtained political asylum in Britain after being convicted twice in absentia by a Jordanian court for his connections to terrorist activities. Jordanian officials have asked for his extradition due to his previous involvement in planned attacks and to his involvement in al-Qa'ida. He was arrested by British authorities in early February 2001, but was released without charge. He has known ties with the Armed Islamic Group (GIA) and is a known fundraiser for the Chechen rebels. Omar has been identified by Jamal al-Fadhl, in his testimony in the US District Court for the Southern District of New York on February 6, 2001, as a member of al-Qa'ida's Fatwa Committee under the name "Abu Qatada." Omar was later arrested again in England; and on February 18th, 2009, he was deported to Jordan where he had outstanding convictions for two bombings.[34]

Qari Zia Rahman

Qari Zia Rahman is believed to be a Taliban and al-Qa'ida commander. He is said to have had close ties with both Usama bin Laden and Faqir Mohammed, a Taliban leader. Rahman's areas of operation include: the Kunar and Nuristan provinces of Afghanistan and the Bajaur and Mohmand tribal agencies in Pakistan. Rahman is credited with establishing suicide camps in Kunar intended to train female suicide bombers.[35] Rahman has become a prominent target for raids and airstrikes. In the spring of 2010, the

Pakistani government reported that they had killed Rahman, but this claim was later disproven by Rahman himself, who spoke to the media, mocking Pakistan for its mistake.[36] He most recently condemned Predator airstrikes occurring in Pakistan, stating that both al-Qa'ida and the Taliban will seek vengeance against US troops in Afghanistan.[37]

Mamdouh Mahmud Salim†

An Iraqi, Salim was born in 1958 and established links between al-Qa'ida and groups in Iraq and Lebanon. He was arrested in Germany on September 16, 1998. It is believed that Salim cofounded al-Qa'ida and managed some camps and guesthouses in Afghanistan and Pakistan, as well as extensive financial dealings within al-Qa'ida and bin Laden's front companies. On November 20, 2000, Salim stabbed a prison guard in the eye, stabbed another in the body, and sprayed irritants on others during a failed escape attempt. Salim was re-sentenced and now faces 32 years to life imprisonment.[38]

Adnan G. El Shukrijumah

Shukrijumah is 5'3" to 5'6" in height and is estimated to weigh 132 pounds with an average build. He has black hair, black eyes, and a dark, mediterranean complexion with no known scars or marks. Shukrijuman occasionally wears a beard, has a pronounced nose, and is asthmatic.[39]

Born on August 4, 1975 in Saudi Arabia, Shukrijumah moved to the US in the 1980s with his family, and was a resident of the US for 15 years.[40] It is believed that he joined an al-Qa'ida training camp in the late 1990s while visiting Afghanistan, and quickly rose through al-Qa'ida's ranks due to his knowledge of the US. Shukrijumah is now believed to have replaced Khalid Sheikh Mohammed as chief of the terror network's global operations, making Shukrijumah the highest-ranking al-Qa'ida member who has held residency status in the US.[41] Shukrijumah is believed to be responsible for numerous terrorist plots, such as the 2004 plot against financial targets in New York and New Jersey, the plot targeting JFK airport in 2007, and the terror plot targeting the New York and London subways in 2009.[42] In 2010, a federal grand jury sitting in the Eastern District of New York indicted him for his alleged role in planning terrorist attacks against the UK and the US. Shukrijumah currently remains at large.[43]

Notes and Bibliographic References

* Individual is deceased

† Individual is detained

1. CNN, "Timeline: Osama bin Laden, Over the Years." May 2, 2011. *http://articles.cnn.com/2011-05-02/world/bin.laden.timeline_1_bin-laden-group-usama-bin-king-abdul-aziz-university?_s=PM:WORLD.*

2. *Ibid.* 1.

3. Bajoria, Jayshree, and Lee Hudson. Council on Foreign Relations, "Profile: Ayman al-Zawahiri." July 14, 2011. *http://www.cfr.org/terrorist-leaders/profile-ayman-al-zawahiri/p9750.*

4. Federal Bureau of Investigation, "FBI–Ayman al-Zaqahiri." *http://www.fbi.gov/wanted/wanted_terrorists/ayman-al-zawahiri/view.*

5. CNN, "Al-Zawahiri Appointed al Qaeda's New Leader, Jihadist Websites Say." June 16, 2011. *http://articles.cnn.com/2011-06-16/world/al.qaeda.new.leader_1_al-zawahiri-al-qaeda-statement-counterterrorism-official?_s=PM:WORLD.*

6. *Ibid.* 5.

7. Global Security, "East African Embassy Bombings." January 11, 2006. *http://www.globalsecurity.org/security/profiles/east_african_embassy_bombings.htm.*

8. PBS, "The Trail Of Evidence- Notes On The Interrogation Of One Suspect." *http://www.pbs.org/wgbh/pages/frontline/shows/binladen/bombings/interrogation.html.*

9. CBS, "Al-Zawahri: Bin Laden will still terrify U.S." June 8, 2011. *http://www.cbsnews.com/stories/2011/06/08/501364/main20070009.shtml.*

10. Hoskinson, Charles. *Politico,* "Osama Bin Laden Was Still in Control, U.S. Says." May 9, 2011. *http://www.politico.com/news/stories/0511/54508.html.*

11. *Ibid.* 10.

12. AFP, "AFP: Al-Qaeda Number Two Broaches Libya in New Video." April 14, 2011. *http://www.google.com/hostednews/afp/article/ALeqM5j3C_aFhG1EZatQWSyGxGj81UnXzQ?docId=CNG.9baeed4b77985cc23322a6a1edf5ef6e.851.*

13. Khalil, Ali. AFP, "AFP: Zawahiri Slams Arab Leaders as 'Zionists' in New Tape." July 19, 2010. *http://www.google.com/hostednews/afp/article/ALeqM5gX2M8bJ7vEIzB_h2NvZXWo17o2bg.*

14. CNN, "Al Qaeda Leader Mocks Obama in Web posting." November 19, 2008. *http://edition.cnn.com/2008/US/11/19/obama.alqaeda/index.html*.

15. Federal Bureau of Investigation, "FBI–Abdulah Ahmed Abdullah." *http://www.fbi.gov/wanted/wanted_terrorists/abdullah-ahmed-abdullah*.

16. Windrem, Robert. MSNBC, "At large: Al-Qaida leaders, associates." *http://www.msnbc.msn.com/id/4686491/ns/world_news-hunt_for_al-Qa'ida*.

17. Federal Bureau of Investigation, "FBI–Said al-Adel." *http://www.fbi.gov/wanted/wanted_terrorists/saif-al-adel*.

18. *Ibid.* 16.

19. US Department of Justice, "Rewards for Justice-Abuyahya-English." *http://www.rewardsforjustice.net/index.cfm?page=abuyahya*.

20. Whitlock, Craig, and Munir Ladaa. *The Washington Post*, "Al-Qaeda's New Leadership: Abu Yahya al-Libi." *http://www.washingtonpost.com/wp-srv/world/specials/terror/yahya.html*.

21. Wiseman, Paul. *USA Today*, "4 Terror Suspects Escape from U.S. Base in Afghanistan." July 11, 2005. *http://www.usatoday.com/news/world/2005-07-11-afghanistan-escapees_x.htm?csp=N009*.

22. Moss, Michael. *The New York Times*, "Rising Leader for Next Phase of Al Qaeda's War." April 8, 2008. *http://www.nytimes.com/2008/04/04/world/asia/04qaeda.html?ref=abuyahyaallibi*.

23. Moreau, Ron. *The Atlantic*, "Al Qaeda vs Qaddafi." March 16, 2011. *http://www.theatlantic.com/daily-dish/archive/2011/03/al-qaeda-vs-qaddafi/174370/*.

24. Human Rights Watch, "US: Close CIA Prisons Still in Operation." April 26, 2007. *http://www.hrw.org/en/news/2007/04/26/us-close-cia-prisons-still-operation*.

25. Federal Bureau of Investigation, "FBI–ANAS AL-LIBY." *http://www.fbi.gov/wanted/wanted_terrorists/anas-al-liby*.

26. *The New York Times*, "Khalid Shaikh Mohammed–KSM." April 4, 2011. *http://topics.nytimes.com/top/reference/timestopics/people/m/khalid_shaikh_mohammed/index.html*.

27. "Global Security, "Khalid Sheikh Mohammed." *http://www.globalsecurity.org/security/profiles/khalid_shaikh_mohammed.htm*.

28. Ressa, Maria, Mike Boettcher, Ash-Har Quraishi, Kelli Arena, John King, Suzanne Malveaux, and Phil Hirshkorn. CNN, "Khalid Shaikh Mohammed: Life of Terror." September 23, 2003. *http://edition.cnn.com/2003/WORLD/asiapcf/south/03/02/mohammed.biog/*.

29. BBC, "Profile: Khalid Sheikh Mohammed–al-Qaeda 'Kingpin.'" April 4, 2011. *http://www.bbc.co.uk/news/world-12964158.*

30. *The Huffington Post,* "Khalid Sheikh Mohammed Met With Jose Padilla, Ex-Chicago Gang Leader, In 2002: Wikileaks." June 26, 2011. *http://www.huffingtonpost.com/2011/04/26/khalid-sheikh-mohammed-me_n_853729.html.*

31. CNN, "A Top Insurgent in Afghanistan Killed, Coalition Confirms." April 26, 2011. *http://edition.cnn.com/2011/WORLD/asiapcf/04/26/afghanistan.insurgent.killed/.*

32. Roggio, Bill. *The Long War Journal*, "Saudi al Qaeda leader Killed in Kunar Airstrike." April 26, 2011. *http://www.longwarjournal.org/archives/2011/04/saudi_al_qaeda_leade.php.*

33. *Ibid.* 32.; and Taylor, Rob. Reuters, "Senior Qaeda Leader in Afghanistan Killed: NATO." April 2, 2011. *http://www.reuters.com/article/2011/04/26/us-afghanistan-insurgent-idUSTRE73P1EE20110426.*

34. *The New York Times*, "Omar Mahmoud Mohammed Othman." February 18, 2009. *http://topics.nytimes.com/topics/reference/timestopics/people/o/omar_mahmoud_mohammed_othman/index.html.*

35. Roggio, Bill. *The Long War Journal*, "Al Qaeda, Taliban Create Female Suicide Cells in Pakistan and Afghanistan." December 31, 2010. *http://www.longwarjournal.org/archives/2010/12/al_qaeda_taliban_create_female_suicides_cell_in_pakistan_and_afghanistan.php.*

36. Roggio, Bill. *The Long War Journal*, "Taliban Commander Qari Zia Rahman Denies Reports of His Death." April 14, 2010. *http://www.longwarjournal.org/archives/2010/04/taliban_commander_qa_1.php.*

37. Roggio, Bill. *The Long War Journal*, "Afghan al Qaeda/Taliban Commander Threatens to Avenge Pakistan Drone Strike." March 22, 2011. *http://www.longwarjournal.org/archives/2011/03/afghan_al_qaedatalib.php.*

38. Weiser, Benjamin. *The New York Times*, "Suspected Al Qaeda Leader to be Resentenced in Stabbing of Guard." December 2, 2008. *http://www.nytimes.com/2008/12/03/nyregion/03sentence.html?_r=1.*

39. Federal Bureau of Investigation, "FBI–Adnan G. Shukrijumah." *http://www.fbi.gov/wanted/wanted_terrorists/adnan-g.-el-shukrijumah.*

40. Alfano, Sean, and Corky Siemaszko. *NY Daily News*, "Adnan Shukrijumah, Believed To Be The New Head of Global Operations for Al Qaeda, FBI says." August 6, 2010. *http://articles.nydailynews.com/2010-08-06/news/27071963_1_terror-plots-attacks-najibullah-zazi.*

41. *Ibid*. 40.
42. Temple-Raston, Dina. NPR, "Al-Qaida Mastermind Rose Using American Hustle." October 11, 2010. *http://www.npr.org/templates/ story/story.php?storyId=130434651.*
43. *Ibid*. 39.

CHAPTER 3

Selected Modus Operandi

Recruitment

Recruitment is an absolute necessity for al-Qa'ida's operational ability. Despite this, no specific recruitment division of al-Qa'ida or standardized recruitment method remains.[1] Al-Qa'ida's recruitment tactics have often been hard to define due to the largely personalized and constantly evolving application process; however, by examining three distinct eras of al-Qa'ida's development, common trends in recruitment can be identified.

Recruitment Before 9/11

Al-Qa'ida was founded as the mujahideen fought to expel the Soviets from Afghanistan. The war itself acted as Usama bin Laden's original recruitment tool, attracting many young men to Afghanistan who were eager to fight Soviet aggression against a Muslim state. During the war, Usama bin Laden established the MAK to recruit, fund, and deploy combatants. As the war came to a close, bin Laden founded al-Qa'ida, utilizing the contacts and networks he had generated during the war. This group of battle-hardened jihadists left over from the Afghan war became the original members of al-Qa'ida.[2]

Recruitment After 9/11

Following 9/11 and the subsequent US invasion of Afghanistan, al-Qa'ida's operational structure was drastically altered. Prior to 9/11 al-Qa'ida was similar to a corporation, with bin Laden acting as the CEO; orders were issued from the top and officials received a salary.[3] Under this structure, bin Laden was able to oversee recruitment by observing and instructing new members in his training camps. After 9/11, many of al-Qa'ida's senior staff were captured, killed, or forced into hiding, rendering the "corporate" structure of al-Qa'ida a thing of the past.

With scattered leadership and few physical bases left, a new paradigm of recruitment arose. The senior leadership no longer handed down orders, but acted as an inspiration for those who associated themselves with the organization. For instance, during the Iraq War, Usama bin Laden was not mobilizing jihadists as he had done during the Soviet invasion of Afghanistan, but merely called on Muslims to combat American forces.[4] This era of recruitment was defined by an expansion of less formal outlets for radicalization and recruitment. In his testimony to Congress, Brian Michael Jenkins of the RAND Corporation explained these terms:

> *Radicalization comprises internalizing a set of beliefs, a militant mindset that embraces violent jihad as the paramount test of one's conviction ... Recruitment is turning others or transforming oneself into a weapon of jihad.*[5]

Radicalization and recruitment have shifted into the digital world. One estimate puts the number of militant jihadist websites at 4,000.[6] These sites offer a wide range of content, from bomb making to weapons handling. Potential recruits now have the ability to research radical teachings, study terror tactics, and connect with likeminded individuals in front of a computer screen rather than in a training camp.[7] As-Sahab, al-Qa'ida's media division, has effectively utilized the Internet, issuing a number of videos aimed at potential recruits.[8]

While the Internet has become a key recruitment tool for al-Qa'ida, a number of recruitment methods still play a role in reaching out to potential members. A study on terrorism issued by the New York City Police Department (NYPD) reported that: "Though the locations can be mosques, more likely incubators include cafés, cab driver hangouts, flophouses, prisons, student associations, non-governmental organizations (NGO)s, hookah (water pipe) bars, butcher shops and book stores."[9] While these locations have the potential to harbor radical thinkers, they do not necessarily promote militancy or have links to al-Qa'ida. However, such environments may provide a meeting ground for individuals sympathetic to terrorist actions.

Madrassas are also included in the list of radicalization and recruitment nodes. For instance, the 9/11 Commission Report stated:

Millions of families, especially those with little money, send their children to religious schools, or madrassas. Many of these schools are the only opportunity available for an education, but some have been used as incubators for violent extremism.[10]

Such claims have led to fears that the future generation of al-Qa'ida may be even more radicalized than the previously residing order. Many have pointed out that madrassas, like other potential nodes, are not necessarily militant in nature and are often the only educational option for students of impoverished families.[11]

Finally, US foreign policy was one of the largest contributors to al-Qa'ida's recruitment during this period. American military engagements in Afghanistan and Iraq gave a new generation of young Muslims the opportunity to fight perceived Western encroachment in Muslim lands. Hearkening back to the idealized jihadist success during the Soviet invasion of Afghanistan, al-Qa'ida has called for a new mujahideen to resist foreign occupation.[12] Furthermore, it was common for recruitment during this time to be linked to regional movements, such as those in the Philippines, Indonesia, Pakistan, and Chechnya.[13]

Recruitment Today: Recent Trends

The death of Usama bin Laden marked a huge blow for the future of al-Qa'ida's recruitment. As prominent journalist and terrorism expert Peter Bergen explained in a recent interview:

When you join al-Qa'ida, you swear an oath of allegiance to bin Laden, not to al-Qa'ida or al-Qa'idaism. Similarly, when groups join al-Qa'ida in Iraq, they swear a personal fealty to bin Laden. He's the grand fromage of al-Qa'ida and the jihadi movement. No one can replace him.[14]

Usama bin Laden's death also came at a time of a general operational decline for al-Qa'ida. Increased drone strikes, primarily in Pakistan, have put pressure on al-Qa'ida's leadership and have led to the deaths of a number of top officials. It has become increasingly difficult for al-Qa'ida to replace veteran leadership with young, inexperienced recruits.[15] There is further evidence that al-Qa'ida is also losing funding, as exemplified in the June 2009 audio message in which al-Qa'ida's leadership in Afghanistan reported a shortage of food, weapons, and other supplies.[16] Additionally, testimonies from captured Western recruits suggest disillusionment with the organization that promised glorified jihad, but delivered a strenuous lifestyle with few observable results.[17]

Attempts have been made by al-Qa'ida central to shift some of its recruitment to affiliated groups in areas such as the Middle East and North Africa, but the organizations in these regions are less organized and struggle to maintain popular support.[18] Furthermore, support for al-Qa'ida in Iraq has foundered, as Sunni tribes have rejected al-Qa'ida's tactics.[19]

Realizing their limitations in operational capabilities, al-Qa'ida has adopted a new method of recruitment. In a recent video released by al-Qa'ida, English-speaking, US-born Adam Gadahn urged Americans to buy automatic weapons at local gun shows for the purpose of mounting attacks in the US.[20] Such calls can also be found in al-Qa'ida's English language online magazine *Inspire*, which debuted in June 2010. As of September 2011, seven issues had been released, each featuring essays, photographs, and instructions on how to wage jihad. For example, the January 2011 issue has a section entitled "Destroying Buildings," outlining how to create a bomb with the intention of causing structural damage to small buildings.[21] It is important to note that *Inspire* is a publication of AQAP, not al-Qa'ida central, highlighting the recent dissemination of power to affiliated groups. With approximately 100 English-language websites aimed at radicalization and recruitment, al-Qa'ida appears to be targeting marginalized Muslims living in the West.[22]

Who Joins al-Qa'ida?

There is no cohesive "profile" for al-Qa'ida members. Recruitment is not isolated to one geographical region, and there are al-Qa'ida cells and associates in approximately 70 countries.[23] Furthermore, the motivation for seeking membership remains largely varied and reflects individual experiences.

A report on terrorism issued by the NYPD concluded that fifteen to thirty-five year-old males are the demographic most at-risk for resorting to terrorist tactics. These individuals tend to be action-oriented and are at an age when self-identification becomes important.[24] A group with a strong ideological message, like al-Qa'ida, can provide direction and meaning to these often alienated and lonely individuals.[25] A special report by the US Institute of Peace (USIP) identified four motivations for potential recruits: "… revenge seekers looking for an outlet for their frustration, status seekers looking for recognition, identity seekers looking for a group they can belong to, and thrill seekers looking for adventure."[26]

While some consider poverty a contributing factor to recruitment, of the 2,032 foreign fighters interviewed in the USIP Report, economic motivations were the least common reason for joining.[27] The NYPD report on terrorism found that recruits were usually "not economically destitute."

When discussing al-Qa'ida's recruitment, it is necessary to keep in mind that a low yield of recruits still has the potential to produce large-scale attacks. As Peter Bergen has said, "Even backed into a corner like a snake, these groups continue to have, and will continue to have, some capacity."[28]

Funding

Prior to the events of 9/11, al-Qa'ida was able to raise and access its funds easily. Most of al-Qa'ida's funding was garnered from simple fundraising sources, including donations from wealthy individuals, mosques and sympathetic imams, Islamic charities, soft state sponsorship, and Usama bin Laden's personal network of wealthy friends and family. There is little indication that Usama bin Laden used his personal fortune to finance al-Qa'ida activities, and speculation has arisen about the size and scope of his wealth.[29] As al-Qa'ida's command structure evolved from a centralized system to a franchised organization over the past decade, so too did its means of raising revenue. Each al-Qa'ida franchise typically garners funds on the local level, resorting to crime, kidnapping, racketeering, smuggling, and black market deals, though some of the money raised today comes from the traditional donation network and corrupt charities.

Charities

Charities were the primary financial instrument al-Qa'ida used to generate funds prior to 9/11, and are still a significant source of funds for the organization today. One of the reasons why charities are a lucrative source of revenue is the Muslim notion of zakat. Zakat is one of the five pillars of Islam, which provides that it is every Muslim's duty to donate a percentage of their earnings to help the less fortunate. The idea of charity in Islam is far more pervasive than it is in Western culture. Some nations, such as Saudi Arabia, have tenets of zakat incorporated into their constitution.[30] Thus al-Qa'ida was able to siphon state-sanctioned donations to Islamic causes. Some charities were run under corrupt pretenses; in many cases, al-Qa'ida was able to take advantage of lax oversight and the charities' own ineffective financial controls to obtain money. It is unclear the extent to which some of these charities knew about the final destination of their funds.

The size and scope of funding operations have been reduced following international pressure, criminal investigations, and the arrests and deaths of core members of the al-Qa'ida financial system. For instance, the al-Haramain Islamic Foundation was exposed as an al-Qa'ida financier following the arrest of Omar al-Farouq on June 5, 2002, in Indonesia. Farouq confessed to his interrogators that "money was laundered through the foundation by donors from the Middle East."[31] Initially, the US took traditional steps in prosecuting al-Haramain by submitting members' names to the UN sanctions committee. This eventually proved ineffective, and the US moved to designate the entire al-Haramain Islamic Foundation as an al-Qa'ida financier.[32]

It was not until the terrorist attacks in Riyadh in May 2003, that Saudi officials began to focus on inhibiting terrorist finances. The attack in Riyadh provoked the Saudi government into action and in some cases curbed public support of al-Qa'ida, as many Saudis believed the war had come to their homeland.[33] Saudi law enforcement began to crack down on both individuals and charities; an al-Qa'ida facilitator and "Swift Sword," the alias for AQAP's representative in Saudi Arabia, were captured or killed in the aftermath of the Riyadh attack.[34] Even today, al-Qa'ida relies on donations from wealthy individuals and supporters to provide al-Qa'ida with enough revenue to continue its operations.

Individuals

In many cases al-Qa'ida was able to obtain funds directly through a network of personal contacts and individual donors. Usama bin Laden was well connected with the Saudi elite, as he was raised and taught in the upper echelon of Saudi society. This network, along with other wealthy individuals radicalized and inspired by al-Qa'ida, provided significant funding for the organization. There were several cases in which individuals were responsible for directly financing terrorism; one individual, Abd al Hamid al Mujil, dubbed "the million dollar man" by fellow jihadists, personally raised thousands of dollars to distribute to al-Qa'ida:

He was executive director of the eastern province branch of the International Islamic Relief Organization, a charitable group. He provided donor funds directly to al Qaeda, says the US government, and was particularly focused on helping al Qaeda affiliates in the Philippines.[35]

Al Mujil has since been placed on a UN sanctions list, had his finances frozen and been put under a travel ban. Another case in 2007 involved two South African family members: Farhad Ahmed Dockrat and Junaid Ismail Dockrat. They were arrested for funding al-Qa'ida: "one by providing funds to Al Akhtar Trust, a globally-recognized al-Qa'ida fundraiser, and another by facilitating travel for individuals to train in al-Qa'ida camps."[36] The pair has been accused of raising $120,000 for Hamza Rabia, who was at that time an operations chief in al-Qa'ida.[37] Though prosecuting individuals connected to al-Qa'ida has been somewhat successful, the issue of the personal financing of terrorism is still a relevant problem which must continually be addressed.

Passive State Sponsorship Support

There is little evidence to support the claim that al-Qa'ida received direct financial aid from a state sponsor, although this does not indicate that al-Qa'ida did not indirectly benefit from states such as Syria or Iran. Matthew Levitt and Michael Jacobson, researchers for the Washington Institute for Near East Policy, define the aid given from Syria and Iran as "Passive State Sponsorship," wherein a state will not directly support the organization, but rather provide a climate in which al-Qa'ida could thrive and grow without interference from outside forces. Levitt and Jacobson found:

At times, the greatest contribution a state can make to a terrorist's cause is by not acting. A border not policed, a blind eye turned to fund-raising, or even the toleration of recruitment all help terrorists build their organizations, conduct operations and survive.[38]

One of the main passive state sponsors is Iran, which has allowed senior al-Qa'ida leadership to stay in their country with impunity under what they call "house arrest." Iran has been accused not only of housing al-Qa'ida leadership, but also acting as a conduit for militants and funds to al-Qa'ida in Afghanistan.[39] Specifically, "Iran's Islamic Revolutionary

Guards Corps–Qods Force has established the Ansar Corps to facilitate, arm, and train al-Qa'ida and Taliban fighters in Afghanistan.'[40] Syria has also been accused of providing fertile ground for al-Qa'ida to grow and develop. Al-Qa'ida in Iraq (AQI) has benefitted enormously from Syria's tolerance of the organization. AQI was able to use Syria as a hub to direct financial support as well as European and other recruits into Iraq.[41] Syria, Iran, and other passive state sponsors allowed al-Qa'ida the means to transport money and personnel to their areas of operation, providing the organization with a means of conducting terrorism around the world. The slaying of Usama bin Laden in Pakistan does lead to questions concerning members of the Pakistani government providing passive state sponsorship to al-Qa'ida.

Criminal Activity

Since 9/11, al-Qa'ida has increasingly sought new sources of income as the US and other nations' financial international law enforcement bodies have stymied their traditional forms of fundraising. Al-Qa'ida has used several illicit methods to raise funds to compensate for budgetary shortfalls. Typically, these criminal activities are delegated to al-Qa'ida's franchises in the Islamic Maghreb, the Arabian Peninsula and Iraq; though before al-Qa'ida became a franchised organization it was reported to be using crime as a means to finance some of its operations. In an interview, Ahmed Ressam, an al-Qa'ida operative who attempted to blow up Los Angeles International Airport, discussed how he was able to fund himself while undercover in Canada before the bombing attempt. He admitted that burglary and fraud were his main sources of income while he was living in Canada.[42] Since 9/11, al-Qa'ida and its franchises have increased their profitable criminal activities, resorting to the international drug trade, smuggling, kidnapping for ransom, and theft.[43] These methods will be described later when discussing the franchises individually.

How al-Qa'ida Transports Its Money

Al-Qa'ida relied on a variety of methods to transport its funds to areas of operation. The main methods were: couriers, the use of the traditional hawala system, and financial institutions.

The Courier System

The courier system, which has been a well-known method of moving illicit funds, consists of using recruits within the al-Qa'ida organization to move large cash amounts from one operation to another. Typically, these couriers are new recruits who maintain a low profile and usually do not know the exact purpose of the funds. In some cases, a single courier is used, though the use of multiple couriers traveling different routes has also been reported. The 9/11 attacks had some of their resources transported by courier. Khalid Sheikh Mohammed, the mastermind of the 9/11 attacks, was believed to have been a courier, transporting roughly $120,000 to Abdul Aziz Ali, the perpetrator of the attack.[44] Couriers are still successfully used by al-Qa'ida, as they are very difficult to track. Couriers often rely on sympathetic states, such as Iran, to passively support them, allowing safe transit through their country. The regime in Tehran has gone so far as to create special task forces with the responsibility to assist al-Qa'ida in this regard.[45] Couriers are a widely employed intermediary for al-Qa'ida; though this process is slow and sometimes dangerous, it allows the organization to distribute its finances with no international oversight and little paper trail.

Hawala System

One of the financial tools most frequently used by al-Qa'ida has been the hawala system, an ancient and informal network used to transport money within the Muslim world.[46] It was especially attractive to al-Qa'ida after its relocation to Afghanistan as Afghanistan's banking system was limited in size, scope, and reliability.[47] The hawala system was first created during the time of the Silk Road, when Arab traders needed a method to transfer funds without being robbed.[48] The transaction begins when a customer seeks the assistance of a hawaladar, a broker in the hawala system. The client would request to send a sum of money to a specific location, and the hawaladar would contact his counterpart in the area where the funds were to be sent. The client would give the broker a sum of money including a small commission, usually five percent, the name and location of the recipient, as well as a password. The hawaladar would then contact the recipient's broker and negotiate the transfer of funds. The hawala system is based on mutual trust fostered over years of financial interaction. A direct money transfer would usually not take place; if there were large imbalances between brokers, then the debts would be addressed by sending money or jewelry to settle the discrepancy.[49]

The system is not based on any legal foundation and it does not keep any permanent records, providing al-Qa'ida with a nearly untraceable means of sending and receiving money.[50] In some cases, particularly when hawaladars know that their clients are breaking the law, no notes or records are kept at all.[51] On September 15, 2010, Mohamad Younis, a hawaladar from New York, was indicted on charges of illegally transferring money in support of terrorism. Mr. Younis was engaged in transferring money, via the hawala system, from Pakistan to Faisal Shahzad. Faisal Shahzad was responsible for the attempted car bombing in Times Square, in May of 2010.[52] Hawala transactions are still widely used by al-Qa'ida despite crackdowns from the US and the international community.

Financial Institutions

Al-Qa'ida did not rely solely on archaic forms of financial transactions. There is evidence that operatives working for the organization were able to access funds from modern financial institutions, especially before 9/11. The use of the international banking system was generally not directly linked to al-Qa'ida. Often proxies would utilize bank transfers to move money indirectly to areas of operation, with the money being sent either by hawala or courier to distribute funds for al-Qa'ida's operations.[53] A typical case of proxies using the banking system would consist of hawaladars using wire transfers to settle debts involved in money transfers, or corrupt charities using their own bank accounts to transfer funds to couriers who would then distribute the funds to al-Qa'ida.

In some cases, al-Qa'ida operatives would directly use the banking system to carry out attacks. The most notorious example of this was the 9/11 attacks. The main financial facilitator of 9/11 was Ali Abdul Aziz Ali, a computer wholesaler who worked in a free trade zone in Dubai, United Arab Emirates (UAE). Ali used wire transfers between UAE banks and banks in New York and Florida six times between April 16, 2000 and September 17, 2000, providing the hijackers with $120,000.[54] Typically, transfers would amount to between $5,000 and $10,000, although Ali sent roughly $70,000 to the 9/11 hijackers, knowing that transferring amounts of that size was common in his line of work and would not merit further scrutiny by authorities.[55] While financial institutions are not the main means to transfer illicit funds for al-Qa'ida, they are routinely accessed by al-Qa'ida affiliates.

How al-Qa'ida Spent Its Money

There is no evidence to suggest that funds raised by al-Qa'ida were taken to a central location such as a "war chest" or treasury. Money that was acquired would be transferred to local operations, mainly in Afghanistan and used for operational expenses. Most of the finances were spent on maintenance for training facilities, salaries for jihadists, and a small amount to aid other terror groups. Al-Qa'ida's command system was highly organized and based on a committee structure. These committees were responsible for handling the logistics of the organization, including finance. Besides bin Laden, the next chief financial leader in al-Qa'ida was Mustafa al-Yazid, also known as Sheik Sa'id. Sa'id, an Egyptian, was a trained accountant who joined al-Qa'ida after fighting alongside bin Laden in Afghanistan during the Soviet occupation. Sa'id is believed to have been miserly with the group's finances, even withholding funds for operational expenses. Sa'id was killed in a predator drone attack on May 28, 2008.[56] This was a huge blow to the al-Qa'ida network, as he was one of the chief operational commanders who was actively involved in day-to-day operations of the organization.

Before 9/11, some of the money raised was donated to the Taliban in exchange for a base of operations and safe haven, as well as for assisting the Taliban in acquiring arms, goods, vehicles and, in some cases, for social projects. It is estimated that al-Qa'ida paid the Taliban between $10 and $20 million annually in exchange for a safe base of operations and resistance against foreign pressure to evict them from Afghanistan.[57] The CIA estimated that it cost al-Qa'ida roughly $30 million annually to sustain itself before 9/11. Al-Qa'ida funded a number of terrorist operations, including the 1998 US embassy bombings in East Africa (which cost approximately $10,000), the 9/11 attacks (approximately $400,000–$500,000), the October 18, 2002, and Bali bombings (approximately $20,000).[58] Since the September 11th attacks al-Qa'ida has had a huge reduction in its budget. This is a result not only of international police and intelligence prosecution, but also due to structural changes in the organization itself.

Selected al-Qa'ida Franchises' Funding

Since AQI was founded in 2004, it has utilized a variety of means to fund its operations and compensate their members including kidnapping for ransom, extortion, theft, hijacking, and black market sales.

A 2010 report by the National Defense Research Institute of RAND provides a comprehensive analytical compilation of AQI's financial ledgers between 2005 and 2006 in Anbar, Iraq's largest geographical region.[59] Between June 2005 and May 2006, AQI's administration in the Anbar province raised a reported $4.5 million, averaging a monthly sum of $373,000.[60] Stolen goods accounted for approximately half of AQI's total revenue during this period. The total amount of AQI's profits during this period was enough to allow it both to obtain self-sufficiency internally, and to send excess AQI revenues outside of the Anbar province.

Since 2006, AQI's funds have dwindled, correlating with the organization's reduction of power within Iraq and resulting in its increasing inclination to turn to crime to reconstitute itself.[61] AQI's criminal activity centers on kidnapping, extortion, and robberies. Both US and Iraqi officials note that AQI militants resort to these measures to compensate for a significant decrease in cash received from external donors and organizations, which were responsible for financing AQI-affiliated attacks in the past.[62] Decreases in funding from sources outside of Iraq indicate a more general weakening of the al-Qa'ida organization; however, it has led to a vast upshot in deadly criminal activity by AQI militants within Iraq. In February 2008, AQI militants abducted Archbishop Paulos Faraj Rahho, a prominent Christian from Mosul, for the second time after his first kidnapping yielded a $200,000 ransom.[63] Gunfire assailed Rahho's vehicle after he led a Stations of the Cross procession at the Cathedral of the Holy Spirit; his driver and two other companions were killed during his abduction.[64] AQI kidnappers demanded a reported $3 million for his release; however, Church officials had been instructed by Rahho not to offer any ransom in exchange for his release, as the funds would be used for more crimes and killings.[65] A month later when no ransom money had been received, Rahho's body was recovered in a shallow grave.

Threats and intimidation as forms of extortion are commonly used tactics to obtain critical funding by AQI members. When an army unit came across a half-burned passenger bus in September 2008, its owner claimed he had received telephone calls from AQI members, assuring that he would "suffer the consequences" unless he paid the group a sum of $20,000.[66]

Banks and shops are prime robbery targets for AQI insurgents because they can provide quick access to cash. AQI was blamed for a string of robberies and attacks with cash-incentives throughout 2010. In May 2010, masked men equipped with assault rifles and rocket-propelled grenades shot up a crowded jewelry market in the capital city of Baghdad, leaving 15 civilians dead and allowing the perpetrators to flee with a substantial quantity of gold.[67] The following month, insurgents wearing Iraqi military uniforms targeted Iraq's central bank, culminating in a three-hour standoff with security forces after bombs were detonated nearby, killing 26 people.[68] In August, individuals dressed in Iraqi army uniforms attacked a convoy of Iraqi vehicles in Haditha that was en route to compensate oil workers, resulting in five deaths and a looted $400,000.[69] Rarely are the AQI culprits responsible for such robberies caught or prosecuted.

In July 2011, AQI made an online appeal for new fundraising ideas in an effort to fund its organization and "feed the widows and the orphans" of the mujahideen.[70] Reports indicate that their major sources of funding, crime and foreign donations, have dried up and that the group no longer has the ability to effectively function. Those who responded contributed a variety of suggestions, from the extortion of money from foreign companies, or the forcing of wealthy Iraqis to pay zakat to the organization, to the imposition of fines upon Shi'as, whom they regard as infidels.[71] This online appeal has been seen as a desperate attempt to recover from the financial losses that have stricken AQI over the past 10 years of counterterrorism operations.

Although these criminal activities accumulate tens of millions of dollars, the single most profitable endeavor for AQI insurgents derives from oil rackets. Known as "illegal oil bunkering," militants pierce holes in oil pipelines, tap the oil into trucks, and sell it on the black market. Net profits from this activity are a reported $2 million a month, with additional payments coming from the owners of hijacked trucks transporting kerosene and gasoline, "protection payments" from reputable businesses, and quasi-legitimate fuel-trucking companies and gas stations established by AQI members. AQI militants frequently target the Kirkuk-Yumurtalik pipeline, which serves as a key line linking Iraq's northern oilfields around Kirkuk to the Turkish port of Ceyhan. Insurgents specifically target this location as a way to exploit the political vacuum created by a failure of Shi'a, Sunni, and Kurdish factions to agree on a coalition government.[72]

AQIM has proven itself to be a resourceful fundraiser, having shifted its financial base from international donations to local criminal acts. The predecessor of AQIM, the Group for Preaching and Combat (GSPC), could trace much of its support to international terror networks in Europe, especially in the UK.[73] However, as the group matured and sought more global exposure after the July 2005 bombings in London, traditional sources of revenue fell victim to prosecution by law enforcement. The GSPC officially transformed itself into AQIM in April of 2007, when GSPC's leader Abdelmalik Drukdal swore allegiance to Usama bin Laden.[74] From the outset of 2007 until 2011,

AQIM has increasingly relied on kidnapping for ransom as its primary means of finance. It is estimated that up to 90% of AQIM's funding comes from kidnapping, each captive person can generate up to $7 million from foreign governments.[75] The first recorded case of jihadist militants capturing and ransoming foreign nationals in the Maghreb region occurred in February 2003 led by Ammari Saifi. Saifi was able to hijack a bus carrying 32 European tourists in the Algerian Sahara.[76] According to Algerian sources, there were nine recorded cases of AQIM capturing and ransoming civilians between 2008 and 2010 in Algeria.[77] It is estimated that since 2003, at least $70 million has been paid in ransoms, largely by Spain and France.[78]

Other sources of revenue are largely based on smuggling contraband into Europe, mainly counterfeit cigarettes, money, and other goods. There have been reports that AQIM has been involved in smuggling narcotics, mainly cocaine, from South America.[79] In 2009, three suspected al-Qa'ida members were indicted in New York for attempting to smuggle narcotics to finance terrorism. The Drug Enforcement Administration (DEA) arrested Oumar Issa, Harouna Toure and Idress Abelrahman after their group was infiltrated by a paid informer posing as a Lebanese militant. The group offered to transport cocaine from Colombia through West Africa to markets in Europe for $4,200 per kilo.[80] The size and scope of al-Qa'ida's connection to the Revolutionary Armed Forces of Columbia (FARC) has been called into question, and there is speculation as to the extent to which drug smuggling has contributed to AQIM's finances.

AQAP still relies on al-Qa'ida's original sources of income, donations. Most evidence suggests that wealthy donors and corrupt charities make up the financial backbone of this al-Qa'ida franchise.[81] Much of AQAP's material and personnel derive from Saudi Arabia. Efforts by the US as well as Saudi Security forces have hindered the flow of this aid. In April 2009, the US Embassy in Saudi Arabia reported that the Kingdom was "on target" with its counterterrorism plan.[82] The Embassy report noted counterterrorism progress:

The Saudi government's implementation of cash courier regulations, ban on the transfer of charitable funds outside the Kingdom without government approval, and arrest and prosecution of individuals providing ideological or financial support to terrorism.[83]

The crackdown on financial support from Saudi Arabia was demonstrated on March 14, 2010, when Ibrahim Saleh Mejahid al-Khalifa, the chief financial officer of AQAP, was killed.[84] AQAP addressed its financial woes in an edition of *Inspire*. In *Inspire's* fourth issue, senior al-Qa'ida recruiter Anwar al-Awlaki encourages jihadists residing in the West "to assist the financing of jihadist activities through any means possible, including theft, embezzlement, and seizure of property."[85] He specifically names the American government and American citizens as principal targets for these attacks.[86] The US government is still concerned with the support given to AQAP by Saudi donors.

Links With Organized Crime

Al-Qa'ida has been able to maintain power because of its complex networks and large following. Since 9/11, the effort to combat terrorism has increased ten-fold. As a result of this more aggressive attitude towards terrorism, al-Qa'ida has been forced to redesign how it operates and obtain funding.[87]

Al-Qa'ida's dealings with organized crime groups are brief and forged for specific purposes such as trafficking drugs or obtaining false documents.[88] Some of the organizations it has been linked to include the FARC, Colombian and Mexican drug cartels, and the Camorra Mafia of Naples. Al-Qa'ida's limited association with FARC and the drug cartels has allowed the organization to profit from the world of drug trafficking, while the Camorra Mafia has provided them with forged documents and a network of safe houses throughout Europe. These safe houses have made it easy for al-Qa'ida operatives to move about cities such as London and Madrid.[89] By 2000 al-Qa'ida's involvement in trafficking cocaine throughout West Africa had allowed it to amass well over $400 million annually.[90]

The strengthening ties between al-Qa'ida and organized crime appear to be isolated to the al-Qa'ida franchises, such as AQIM and the Islamic State of Iraq (ISI). Top leaders remain removed from relations with organized crime syndicates as ties with criminal activities which violate Islamic law could threaten their credibility in the eyes of their followers.[91] They also continue to reject alliances with drug traffickers because they fear becoming more visible and vulnerable to being captured.[92]

While there are members of al-Qa'ida using organized criminal activities to finance their attacks, fundamentally al-Qa'ida remains a terrorist organization. The finances obtained from these alliances are only a means to continue operations driven by al-Qa'ida's fundamentalist ideology.

The Price of Globalization

Organized crime groups and al-Qa'ida have been able to connect with one another as a result of globalization, free trade, technological innovations, and an integrated global economy. In 2007 the Deputy Director of the Globalization Project at the Institute for National Strategic Studies at the National Defense University in Washington, DC stated, "Criminal organizations and terrorist groups are flourishing as a result of the conditions for heightened worldwide interdependence, increased global commerce and rapid communication and transportation."[93] Increasing globalization has caused this issue to remain in the spotlight. During a terrorism symposium in March of 2011 the Executive Director of the UN Office on Drugs and Crime (UNODC) said:

> *Today, the criminal market spans the planet, and in many instances criminal profits support terrorist groups. Globalization has turned out to be a double-edged sword. Open borders, open markets, and increased ease of travel and communication have benefited both terrorists and criminals.*[94]

Alone, each of these groups has a significant power base, however, new avenues as a result of globalization (e-mail, Facebook, YouTube, etc.) have allowed them to work in conjunction with one another, making their networks more complex and intertwined. Globalization has also been prompted by advances taking place in the financial and technological industries. These advances have allowed organized crime syndicates and terrorist organizations to expand into activities such as cybercrime and credit card fraud.[95] For example, an al-Qa'ida operative in conjunction with a Moroccan waiter was able to devise a simple credit card scam in a process known as "skimming." All that was needed to steal credit card information was a $200 skimmer and a laptop.[96]

Each of the criminal activities in which al-Qa'ida has partaken has provided it with the financial means to continue carrying out attacks. These methods include kidnapping, counterfeiting, extortion, and drug trafficking.

Kidnapping

Kidnapping operations have become very prevalent throughout the Sahel, the Horn of Africa, Yemen, East Asia, and Afghanistan. In Afghanistan alone there were 38 reported cases of kidnapping in 2008. While this number decreased in 2009, kidnapping cases remain a threat. Groups that have gained recognition in many of these cases include AQIM, al-Shabaab, and AQAP.[97] As previously noted, AQIM's growth and operations rely heavily on ransom payments; it surpasses both al-Shabaab and AQAP in the kidnapping business.[98]

When a country learns that its citizens have been kidnapped by al-Qa'ida, it has two options. It can refuse to negotiate with terrorists: in January 2011, France attempted a rescue operation resulting in the deaths of two French nationals.[99] In March of 2011, France refused to pay the 90 million euro ransom demanded by al-Qa'ida for the release of four French nationals who had been taken in September 2010. Foreign Minister Alain Juppe was quoted saying, "We do not negotiate on these terms."[100]

French nationals were kidnapped in response to France's banning of the veil in public places and the involvement of French troops in Afghanistan. In December 2010, Usama bin Laden was quoted saying, "It is very simple—as you kill, you will be killed, as you take hostages, you will be taken hostages, and as you compromise our security, we will compromise your security."[101] In bin Laden's eyes, attacks on the Western world were justified because of its suppression of Muslim culture, which had a detrimental effect on the culture's purity; "The kidnapping of your experts in Niger…is in retaliation for the tyranny you practice against our Muslim nation."[102] Overall, al-Qa'ida's global jihad can be broken down into three parts: weakening Western influences; shifting the balance of power; and establishing a caliphate.[103] France's suppression of the Muslim culture has prompted al-Qa'ida to continue the tactic of kidnapping.

The other option is to pay a ransom and/or negotiate with terrorists. This gives the terrorist organization the position of power, because when a country complies with ransom demands, the organization has more resources to continue operations and kidnappings.[104] On February 22, 2008, two Austrian citizens were kidnapped by AQIM. The demands made for their safe return included 5 million euros and the immediate release of al-Qa'ida affiliates being held in both Algeria and Tunisia. In response to these demands, the Austrian Chancellor Alfred Gusenbauser declared the kidnapping was, "… an act of violence against Austria."[105] After the deadline was pushed back and demands were negotiated, the two hostages were released in October 2008 in exchange for 4 million euros and the release of jihadists from Mauritania.[106]

Counterfeiting

Al-Qa'ida is suspected of counterfeiting since the time of the first World Trade Center bombing.[107] This form of criminal activity is enticing to terrorist organizations because it serves two important purposes. First, money gained from counterfeiting can be used to fund future operations. In December 2009, a connection between Somali pirates and al-Qa'ida was discovered when customs agents in Somalia seized over $1 million in counterfeit US bills. The currency was going to be smuggled into Hargeisa and used for financing several terrorist operations.[108] Additionally, counterfeiting can destabilize a country's economy by decreasing the public's confidence in the currency's value, both within the country and among the international community.[109]

Al-Qa'ida has not only been known to counterfeit money. In December 2010, an international counterfeiting operation of passports and immigration stamps was uncovered by Spanish and Thai authorities. While investigators did not have confirmation of the passports being directly linked to a terrorist operation, authorities believed al-Qa'ida was using this ring to successfully move members throughout the world.[110] Whether counterfeiting money or other items of value, al-Qa'ida is able to undermine the functions of society. Counterfeiting money can upset a country's commerce and trade, while counterfeiting other items, such as important legal documents, can allow members of al-Qa'ida to move undetected through the very security precautions countries rely on to prevent terrorists from entering into their country.

Extortion

Al-Qa'ida also finances its operations by extorting large sums of money from businesses and individuals. Two areas especially affected are the city of Mosul in Iraq and the town of Baghlia in Algeria.

In Mosul, the ISI uses mafia-style tactics to coerce residents who range from members of the government to vegetable vendors.[111] Operatives infiltrate construction businesses and monopolize construction projects throughout the city. City projects are then run by firms controlled by al-Qa'ida.

In response, Iraqi Prime Minister Nouri al-Maliki started a military campaign in May 2008 to curb the ISI's stronghold on the city. Al-Qa'ida responded by adopting more covert tactics to force individuals to pay money, including kidnapping and assassination.[112] This tactic reduces reliance on funding from external sources. Colonel Charles Sexton of the US Army stated, "They (ISI) are mutating into a completely criminal, monetarily driven organization with very, very loose ideological drive and purpose."[113] Either way, payments to members of al-Qa'ida has become a necessary way of life for the cities' wealthy. Political analyst Majdi al-Abdali explained, "There is a growing tendency among members of society to accept the culture of paying money in order to avoid [violent] acts and killing and in order to maintain certain positions or jobs."[114] Abu Mohammad, a store owner, was shot to death when he refused to pay the ISI.[115] This level of extortion appears to have allowed al-Qa'ida to gain a firm stronghold over communities because refusal to comply results in severe punishment.

In the town of Baghlia, AQIM has been extorting money from local farmers each summer, demanding 10% of the value gained from all crops harvested. This protection money, as two farmers called it, amounts to roughly between $1,330 and $18,620. Ahmed Alouane, a security analyst, elaborated that those who do not comply face consequences, "You have no choice but to pay. Otherwise you, or a member of your family, is kidnapped."[116] One farmer feared being killed when he began refusing to pay and said, "If we pay, we become accomplices to terrorists. If we don't pay, we may end up killed."[117]

Links to Smuggling

Al-Qa'ida has allied with Dawood Ibrahim, whose D-Company is made up of over 5,000 members and is known to operate out of Pakistan, India, and the UAE.[118] Through its alliance with Dawood, al-Qa'ida has been able to gain access to smuggling routes through India, South Asia, Africa, Europe, and the Middle East.[119]

Drug Trafficking

In the area of drug trafficking, al-Qa'ida has formed alliances with FARC and several Latin American drug cartels. In 2009, AQIM was linked to FARC after members were arrested for moving cocaine through the region of West Africa.[120] With the help of al-Qa'ida, FARC is able to access

European drug markets by utilizing trade routes in Africa.[121] In return for this access, money gained from FARC's drug trade has been used to fund terrorist operations; this was highlighted in a report done in 2010 by the Center for a New American Security.[122] Aside from cooperation in the drug trade, reports from 2003 found that al-Qa'ida may also be working with Mexican cartels to gain entry into the US.[123]

Alliances between drug trafficking rings and al-Qa'ida are also occurring in the Middle East. The terrorist organization has teamed up with Haji Juma Khan, one of the main orchestrators of the heroin trade in Afghanistan.[124] With the help of Khan, al-Qa'ida has been able to set up a heroin network throughout the Middle East, Asia, and Europe. When consulting with US and NATO officials, former US drug czar Gen. Barry McCaffrey reported funding upwards of $800 million for operations carried out by both al-Qa'ida and the Taliban.[125] Links between drug trafficking and money laundering have also surfaced. In 2009 the Peruvian Financial Intelligence Unit (FIU) estimated that around $3 billion linked to the drug trade had been laundered through Peru.[126] While al-Qa'ida may be profiting from the drug trade, a small but significant setback occurred in December 2009 when charges were brought against three members of al-Qa'ida's North African branch who were moving cocaine through West and North Africa.[127]

Conclusion

Whether al-Qa'ida is directly linked with organized crime syndicates or turning to criminal tactics on its own, it is quickly adapting to changes forced on them by globalization and increased security measures. As a result of al-Qa'ida's evolution, it is important for countries and organizations committed to eradicating terrorism to remain cognizant of what the future could bring. With increasing reliance on the virtual world, al-Qa'ida has become decentralized. This franchised method for carrying out terrorism has led to the organization's networks becoming self-sustaining, even when key leaders are captured.[128] This evolution has made it increasingly difficult for countries committed to combating terrorism to dismantle the entire al-Qa'ida organization.

Notes and Bibliographic References

1. Jenkins, Brian Michael. RAND Corporation Testimony, presented before the House Homeland Security Committee, Subcommittee on Intelligence, Information Sharing, and Terrorism Risk Assessment, "Building an Army of Believers: Jihadist Radicalization and Recruitment." April 5, 2007. *http://www.rand.org/pubs/testimonies/2007/RAND_CT278-1.pdf*.

2. Borum, Randy, and Michael Gelles. *Behavioral Sciences and Law*, "Al-Qaeda's Operational Evolution: Behavioral and Organizational Perspective." 2005. *http://goo.gl/XGk4n*.

3. Rollins, John. Congressional Research Service, "Al-Qaeda and its Affiliates: Historical Perspective, Global Presence, and Implications for U.S. Policy." February 5, 2010, *http://www.fas.org/sgp/crs/terror/R41070.pdf*; and The 9/11 Commission, "The 9/11 Commission Report." 67. *http://www.911commission.gov/report/911Report.pdf*.

4. *Ibid*. 3.

5. *Ibid*. 1.

6. Seib, Philip. *Military Review*, "The Al-Qaeda Media Machine." May-June 2008. *http://www.au.af.mil/au/awc/awcgate/milreview/seib.pdf*.

7. National Intelligence Council, "The Terrorist Threat to the US Homeland." July 2007.

8. *Ibid*. 6.

9. Bhatt, Arvin, and Mitchell D. Silber. The New York City Police Department, "Radicalization in the West: The Homegrown Threat." 2007. *http://www.nypdshield.org/public/SiteFiles/documents/NYPD_Report-Radicalization_in_the_West.pdf*.

10. The 9/11 Commission, "The 9/11 Commission Report." 365. *http://www.911commission.gov/report/911Report.pdf*.

11. Bergen, Peter and Swati Pandey. *The New York Times*, "The Madrassa Myth." June 14, 2005. *http://www.nytimes.com/2005/06/14/opinion/14bergen.html*.

12. *Ibid*. 2.

13. *Ibid*. 1.

14. MacDonald, Nancy. *Maclean's*, "The Beginning of the End?" 124:18. May 16, 2011. *http://www2.macleans.ca/2011/05/11/the-beginning-of-the-end/*.

15. *Ibid*. 3.

16. *Ibid*. 3.

17. Black, Ian, and Jason Burke. *The Guardian*, "Al-Qaida: Tales from Bin Laden's Volunteers." September 10, 2009. *http://www.guardian.co.uk/ world/2009/sep/10/al-qaida-terrorism-bin-laden?intcmp=239.*

18. *Ibid.* 3.

19. *The New York Times*, "Al Qaeda Urges Attacks in West." June 3, 2011. *http://www.nytimes.com/2011/06/04/world/04qaeda.html.*

20. *Inspire*, Winter 2010.

21. *Ibid.* 6.

22. *Ibid.* 3.

23. *Ibid.* 9.

24. Khatchadourian, Raffi. *The New Yorker*, "Azzam the American." 82:46. January 1, 2007. 62.

25. Venhaus, Colonel John M. US Institute of Peace Special Report, "Why Youth Join al-Qa'ida." May 2010. 2. *http://www.usip.org/files/ resources/SR236Venhaus.pdf*

26. *Ibid.* 25.

27. *Ibid.* 14.

28. Greenburg, Douglas, John Roth, and Serena Wille. National Commission on Terrorist Attacks Upon the US, "Monograph on Terrorist Financing." *http://www.911commission.gov/staff_statements/911_ TerrFin_Monograph.pdf.*

29. *Ibid.* 28.

30. Salim, Arskal. *Challenging the Secular State: The Islamization of Law in Modern Indonesia*, (Hawai'i: University of Hawai'i Press, 2008).

31. Brisard, Jean-Charles. The United Nations, "Terrorism Financing: Roots and Trends of Saudi Terrorism Financing." December 19, 2002. *http://www.investigativeproject.org/documents/testimony/22.pdf.*

32. Levitt, Matthew and Michael Jacobsen. The Washington Institute for Near East Policy, "The Money Trail: Finding, Following, and Freezing Terrorist Finances." November 2008. *http://www.washingtoninstitute. org/pubPDFs/PolicyFocus89.pdf.*

33. Ember, Steve. Voice of America, "Riyadh Bombing Attacks." May 16, 2003. *http://www.voanews.com/learningenglish/home/a-23-a-2003-05- 16-2-1-83116637.html.*

34. *Ibid.* 28.

35. Vardi, Nathan. "Is al Qaeda Bankrupt?" *Forbes Magazine*, March 15, 2010. *http://www.forbes.com/global/2010/0315/issues-terrorism- osama-david-cohen-is-al-qaeda-bankrupt.html.*

36. U.S. Department of Treasury, "Treasury Targets Al Qaida Facilitators in South Africa." January 26, 2007. *http://www.treasury.gov/press-center/press-releases/Pages/hp230.aspx.*

37. *Ibid.* 32.

38. Byman, Daniel. Brookings Institution, "Passive Sponsors of Terrorism." Winter 2005. *http://www.brookings.edu/~/media/Files/rc/articles/2005/winter_middleeast_byman/20051216_survival.pdf.*

39. *Ibid.* 32.

40. Roggio, Bill. *The Long War Journal*, "Germany-based Moroccan al Qaeda Foreign Fighter Facilitator Captured in Southeastern Afghanistan." May 24, 2011. *http://www.longwarjournal.org/archives/2011/05/germany-based_morocc.php#ixzz1O9YzSLmR.*

41. *Ibid.* 32.

42. PBS, "A Terrorist's Testimony." 2001. *http://www.pbs.org/wgbh/pages/frontline/shows/trail/inside/testimony.html.*

43. *Ibid.* 32.

44. *Ibid.* 28.

45. Smith, Michale S. II. Kronos, "Al-Qa;ida-Qods Force Nexus." April 29, 2011. *http://thomaspmbarnett.squarespace.com/storage/Kronos_AQ.QF.Nexus.globlogization.pdf.*

46. Anderson, Kevin. BBC, "Hawala System Under Scrutiny." November 8, 2001. *http://news.bbc.co.uk/2/hi/business/1643995.stm.*

47. *Ibid.* 28.

48. *Ibid.* 46.

49. *Ibid.* 46.

50. *Ibid.* 28.

51. US Department of the Treasury, "A Report to the Congress in Accordance with Section 359 of the Uniting and Strengthening America by Providing Appropriate Tools Required to Intercept and Obstruct Terrorist Act of 2001." November 2002. *http://www.fincen.gov/news_room/rp/files/hawalarptfinal11222002.pdf.*

52. Dienst, Jonathan. NBC New York, "LI man Charged in Connection with Times Square Bomb Plot Case." September 15, 2010. *http://www.nbcnewyork.com/news/local/LI-Man-Charged-In-Connection-With-Times-Square-Bomb-Plot-Case-102964694.html.*

53. *Ibid.* 28.

54. *The New York Times*, "Ali Abdul Aziz Ali." November 13, 2009. *http://topics.nytimes.com/topics/reference/timestopics/people/a/ali_abdul_aziz_ali/index.html.*

55. *Ibid*. 28.
56. Windrem, Robert. MSNBC, "Islamic Site: Al-Qaida's Third in Command Reported Killed." June 1, 2010. *http://www.msnbc.msn.com/id/37440747*.
57. *Ibid*. 28.
58. *Ibid*. 28.
59. Bahney, Benjamin, Howard J. Shatz, Carroll Ganier, Renny McPherson, and Barbara Sude. *An Economic Analysis of the Financial Records of Al-Qa'ida in Iraq*, (Santa Monica, CA: RAND, 2010). *http://www.rand.org/content/dam/rand/pubs/monographs/2010/RAND_MG1026.pdf*.
60. Marron, Donald. *The Christian Science Monitor,* "The Economics of Al-Qaeda in Iraq." December 29, 2010. *http://www.csmonitor.com/Business/Donald-Marron/2010/1229/The-economics-of-Al-Qaeda-in-Iraq*.
61. Arraf, Jane. *The Christian Science Monitor,* "General Odierno: Al Qaeda in Iraq Faces Serious Financial Crunch." July 2, 2010. *http://www.csmonitor.com/World/Middle-East/2010/0702/General-Odierno-Al-Qaeda-in-Iraq-faces-serious-financial-crunch*
62. Michaels, Jim. *USA Today,* "Al-Qaeda in Iraq Relying More on Bank Heists." September 7, 2010. *http://www.usatoday.com/news/world/iraq/2010-09-07-iraqrobberies07_ST_N.htm?loc=interstitialskip*
63. Carlstrom, Gregg. Al Jazeera English, "A Snapshot of Al-Qaeda in Iraq." October 24 2010. *http://www.aljazeera.com/secretiraqfiles/2010/10/20101022164635810456.html*; and O'Mahony, Anthony. *The Guardian*. "Obituary: Archbishop Paulos Faraj Rahho." April 1, 2008. *http://www.guardian.co.uk/world/2008/apr/01/catholicism.religion*
64. O'Mahony, Anthony. *The Guardian*. "Obituary: Archbishop Paulos Faraj Rahho." April 1, 2008. *http://www.guardian.co.uk/world/2008/apr/01/catholicism.religion*.
65. Carlstrom, Gregg. Al Jazeera English, "A Snapshot of Al-Qaeda in Iraq." 24 Oct. 2010. *http://www.aljazeera.com/secretiraqfiles/2010/10/20101022164635810456.html*
66. *Ibid*. 63.
67. Ahmed, Hamid. *The Washington Times*, "15 Killed in Iraq Gold Robbery." May 25, 2010. *http://www.washingtontimes.com/news/2010/may/25/15-killed-iraq-jewelry-robbery/*.
68. CBC News, "Insurgents Attack Iraq's Central Bank." June 13, 2010. *http://www.cbc.ca/news/world/story/2010/06/13/iraq-centralbank-attack.html*.
69. *Ibid*. 63.

70. The Telegraph, "Al-Qaeda in Iraq Looks for Fundraising Ideas." July 26, 2011. *http://www.telegraph.co.uk/news/worldnews/al-qaeda/8664536/Al-Qaeda-in-Iraq-looks-for-fundraising-ideas.html*.

71. *Ibid.* 70.

72. Reuters, "Iraq on Alert for Al Qaeda Oil Pipeline Attacks." August 23, 2010. *http://www.reuters.com/article/2010/08/23/us-iraq-oil-security-idUSTRE67M3AX20100823*.

73. Filiu, Jean-Pierre. Carnegie Endowment for International Peace, "Al-Qaeda in the Islamic Maghreb: Algerian Challenge or Global Threat?" October 2009. *http://carnegieendowment.org/files/al-qaeda_islamic_maghreb.pdf*.

74. *Ibid.* 72.

75. Walt, Vivienne. TIME, "Terrorist Hostage Situations: Rescue or Ransom?" October 12, 2010. *http://www.time.com/time/world/article/0,8599,2024420,00.html*.

76. Hansen, Andrew. Council on Foreign Relations, "Al-Qaeda in the Islamic Maghreb." July 21, 2009. *http://www.cfr.org/north-africa/al-qaeda-islamic-maghreb-aqim/p12717#p8*.

77. Permanent Mission of Algeria to the United Nations, "Contributions of Algeria to the Panel on the Ransoms Payment Issues as a Source of Financing Terrorism: The Intervention of M. Kamel Rezag Bara, Advisor to his Excellency the President of the Republic-Algeria." September 7, 2010. *http://jcb.blogs.com/Kamel%20Rezag%20Bara%20Key%20Notes%20Remarks.pdf*.

78. *Ibid.* 72.

79. Nagraj, Neil. *New York Daily News*, "Colombian FARC Rebels, al-Qaeda Joining Forces to Smuggle Cocaine into Europes, says DEA." January 5, 2010. *http://articles.nydailynews.com/2010-01-05/news/17943446_1_al-qaeda-smuggle-colombian-farc-rebels*.

80. Gendar, Alison. *New York Daily News*, "Al Qaeda Cocaine Ring: 3 Terror Suspects Charged in New York City on African Drug Case." December 18, 2009. *http://www.nydailynews.com/news/world/2009/12/18/2009-12-18_3_alqaida_suspects_charged_in_african_drug_case.html*.

81. Government Accountability Office, "Combating Terrorism: U.S. Agencies Report Progress Countering Terrorism and its Financing in Saudi Arabia, but Continued Focus on Counter Terrorism Financing Efforts Needed." September 2009. *http://www.gao.gov/new.items/d09883.pdf*.

82. *Ibid*. 81.
83. *Ibid*. 81.
84. Xinhua Net, "Al-Qaida Says its Fund Raiser Killed by Yemeni Forces." March 14, 2010. *http://news.xinhuanet.com/english2010/world/2010-03/14/c_13209643.htm*.
85. MEMRI. "Fourth Issue of the English-Language AQAP Magazine *'Inspire'* — A General Review." January 19, 2011. *http://www.memri.org/report/en/print4927.htm*.
86. *Ibid*. 85.
87. Wannenburg, Gail. Essex, "Links Between Organised Crime and al-Qaeda." Spring 2003. *http://www.essex.ac.uk/ecpr/standinggroups/crime/members_files/wannennberg.pdf*.
88. Rollins, John and Liana Sun Wyler. Congressional Research Service, "International Terrorist and Transnational Crime: Security Threats, U.S. Policy, and Considerations for Congress." March 18, 2010. *http://assets.opencrs.com/rpts/R41004_20100318.pdf*.
89. Chepesiuk, Ron. Global Politician, "Dangerous Alliance: Terrorism and Organized Crime." September 2007. *http://www.globalpolitician.com/23435-crime*.
90. Homeland Security Newswire. "A new threat: organized crime, terrorist links." March 2011. *http://www.homelandsecuritynewswire.com/new-threat-organized-crime-terrorists-links*.
91. *Ibid*. 88.
92. Blanchard, Christopher. CRS Report for Congress, "Afghanistan: Narcotics and U.S. Policy." May 2005. *http://fpc.state.gov/documents/organization/48610.pdf*.
93. *Ibid*. 89.
94. Fedotov, Yury. Global Security, "Growing links between crime and terrorism the focus of UN forum." March 2011. *http://www.globalsecurity.org/security/library/news/2011/03/sec-110316-unnews01.htm*.
95. *Ibid*. 88.
96. *Ibid*. 85.
97. Benjamin, Daniel. *The New York Times*, "Stop Funding Terrorists." February 2011. *http://www.nytimes.com/2011/02/18/opinion/18iht-ed benjamin18.html?_r=1*.
98. *Ibid*. 97.
99. Emirates 24/7 News, "Abducted young Frenchmen killed in Niger Desert." January 2011. *http://www.emirates247.com/news/world/abducted-young-frenchmen-killed-in-niger-desert-2011-01-09-1.339694*.

100. Reuters, "France: won't negotiate on Qaeda hostage terms." March 2011. *http://af.reuters.com/article/maliNews/idAFLDE72K1SS201103 21?pageNumber=1&virtualBrandChannel=0.*

101. Emirates 24/7 News, "Bin Laden warns France over veil ban, Afghan war." October 2010. *http://www.emirates247.com/news/world/bin-laden-warns-france-over-veil-ban-afghan-war-2010-10-27-1.309821.*

102. *Ibid.* 101.

103. Witty, David M. National Defense University, "Attacking al Qaeda's Operational Centers of Gravity." 2008. *http://www.humansecuritygateway. com/documents/NDU_AttackingAlQaedasOperationalCentersGravity.pdf.*

104. *Ibid.* 97.

105. Realite EU, "Al Qaeda in the Maghreb." March 2008. *http://www. realite-eu.org/site/apps/nlnet/content3.aspx?c=9dJBLLNkGiF&b=23 15291&ct=4066687.*

106. Shay, Shaul. International Institute for Counter-terrorism, "Al Qaeda in the Maghreb and the terror abductions." June 2010. *http://www.ict. org.il/Articles/tabid/66/Articlsid/828/currentpage/1/Default.aspx.*

107. Interpol Report, Union Des Fabricants, "Counterfeiting and Organized Crime Report." 2004. *http://www.interpol.int/Public/FinancialCrime/ IntellectualProperty/Publications/UDF.pdf.*

108. Kouri, Jim. Somalilandpress, "Somali Piracy and Counterfeiting Funding Al Qaeda." December 2009. *http://somalilandpress.com/ somali-piracy-and-counterfeiting-funding-al-qaeda-9862.*

109. *Ibid.* 87.

110. Kimery, Anthony L. *Homeland Security Today*, "Global: Al Qaeda-Linked Counterfeit Passport Ring Busted." December 2010. *http:// www.hstoday.us/channels/global/single-article-page/al-qaeda-linked-counterfeit-passport-ring-busted/629870f91f302446c5eca91f09d6e71 2.html.*

111. Salama, Ahmad. Niqash: Briefings from Inside and Across Iraq, "Kidnapping and Construction: Al-Qaeda Turns to Big Business, Mafia-Style." *http://www.niqash.org/content.php?contentTypeID=75 &id=2815&lang=0.*

112. *Ibid.* 111.

113. Rao, Prashant. AFP, "Al-Qaeda in Iraq turns to extortion." September 2010. *http://www.google.com/hostednews/afp/article/ ALeqM5iC3TN9ixQcpFK6oRrhwpO-LwRxEw.*

114. *Ibid.* 111.

115. Asharq Al-Awsat, "Iraq: Al-Qaeda Extorting Businesses in Mosul." September 2010. *http://www.asharq-e.com/news. asp?section=1&id=22250.*

116. Reuters, "Algeria killings case light on Al Qaeda extortion racket." August 2010. *http://www.dawn.com/2010/08/31/algeria-killings-cast-light-on-al-qaeda-extortion-racket.html.*

117. *Ibid.* 116.

118. Roggio, Bill. *The Long War Journal*, "al Qaeda, and the ISI." January 2010. *http://www.longwarjournal.org/threat-matrix/archives/2010/01/dawood_ibrahim_al_qaeda_and_th.php.*

119. Raman, B. South Asia Analysis Group, "The Global Terrorist." October 2003. *http://www.southasiaanalysis.org/papers9/paper818.html.*

120. Bove-LaMonica, Daniella. "Al-Qaeda and Drug Trafficking, a Dangerous Partnership." June 2011. *http://www.policymic.com/articles/504/al-qaeda-and-drug-trafficking-a-dangerous-partnership.*

121. Columbia Reports, "FARC and al Qaeda in 'Unholy' Drug Alliance." January 2010. *http://colombiareports.com/colombia-news/news/7529-farc-and-al-qaeda-in-unholy-drug-alliance.html.*

122. *Ibid.* 90.

123. *Ibid.* 89.

124. Mcgirk, Tim. "Terrorism's Harvest." *TIME Magazine*, August 2004. *http://www.time.com/time/magazine/article/0,9171,674806,00.html.*

125. Abbot, Sebastian. *The Huffington Post*, "Al-Qaeda's Drug Trade Keeps Them Afloat during the Economic Crisis." October 2008. *http://www.huffingtonpost.com/2008/10/16/al-qaedas-drug-trade-keep_n_135352.html.*

126. *Hindustan Times*, "Al Qaeda Routing Money to India via Europe." June 2011. *http://www.hindustantimes.com/India-news/NewDelhi/Al-Qaeda-routing-money-to-India-via-Europe-report/Article1-670044.aspx.*

127. BBC News, "US arrests three Africans in 'al-Qaeda cocaine sting.'" December 2009. *http://news.bbc.co.uk/2/hi/8422010.stm.*

128. *Ibid.* 85.

CHAPTER 4

Propaganda and Psychological Warfare

"We are in a battle, and more than half of this battle is taking place in the battlefield of the media . . . [We] are in a media battle for the hearts and minds of our umma."[1]

This statement by Ayman al-Zawahiri captures the current era of fighting taking place internationally in the media. Al-Qa'ida relies on the media to spread its jihadist propaganda and to recruit new members.[2] Increasingly, al-Qa'ida has utilized new avenues to spread its message, including the Internet (jihadist websites, YouTube, social networking sites, etc.) and magazines.[3] By taking advantage of different modes of communication, al-Qa'ida has been able to spread its message to a broad audience. Al-Qa'ida's message resonates with some sympathizers who will heed the call to violence and others who will echo the word of violent jihad throughout the virtual community.[4]

A New Mode of Warfare

The definition of psychological warfare in the *Encyclopedia Britannica* encompasses three important characteristics: to use propaganda against an enemy; to demoralize the enemy by breaking down its will to fight and resist; and to simultaneously strengthen the will of allies and those in favor of the cause.[5]

In many ways, al-Qa'ida has changed its approach to warfare. Rather than focusing on conventional methods, it strives to inflict both immediate harm and long-lasting fear in its victims and the wider global audience.[6] Terrorist attacks can scar a nation's populace long after the actual incident has occurred. Through the instillment of fear, al-Qa'ida is able to disrupt a nation's normal way of life. An attack can cause people to change their daily routines and to constantly fear for their safety, thereby undermining important pillars of a society such as business, culture, and trust.[7] This psychological targeting of an enemy's audience is achieved through a continuous threat of violence and can be used to encourage changes in behavior among the enemy.[8]

In psychological warfare, terrorists manipulate their enemy's populace to further their objectives. By undermining and continuously disrupting a society's ability to function, terrorist organizations are attempting to push public opinion to surrender to the demands made by the terrorist organization. Overall, the society targeted by terrorism becomes another one of the organization's tools for advancing its beliefs and agenda.[9]

Suicide terrorism is an especially effective means of psychological warfare because it serves a dual purpose. First, by releasing videos of the attack, al-Qa'ida can state the reason for the attack and threaten additional attacks if change does not take place.[10] Second, this form of terrorism acts as a recruiting tool for new members. In the time leading up to the attack the suicide bomber pledges his allegiance to the fight in a video recording. This serves as a form of inspiration for others who want to join the cause. In what is called propaganda by deed, "A terrorist operation itself is an act of personal example and is an ideal in which others should feel compelled to emulate."[11] Large-scale attacks, often characterized by brutality, are meant to demonstrate the cause's intensity, power, and legitimacy. Such attacks magnify the capabilities of the organization in the public's eye and act as a recruitment tool.[12]

Propaganda Aspects

Al-Qa'ida has been able to use both literary and technological avenues to spread its message throughout the international community.[13] Each new outlet provides the opportunity to reach new audiences, who may either join the cause or spread the jihadist message on their own. For example, Abu Omar of Jordan does not partake in the violence of jihad, but instead demonstrates his allegiance to al-Qa'ida by spreading its message through e-mails, discussion boards, and chat rooms.[14] Omar and many others are taking it upon themselves to spread the word of jihad, thus decentralizing al-Qa'ida's control over the content posted on the web. By gaining support from those not directly linked with the organization, al-Qa'ida has in many ways become a social movement.[15] Just like many social networks, membership is not fixed, but is constantly expanding.[16]

The Media

When al-Qa'ida's message is not appearing on major TV networks or being spoken about in news sources such as Al Jazeera, BBC, and *The*

Washington Post, the organization utilizes its own media resources to spread the word. As-Sahab, al-Qa'ida's largest production company, has produced a number of videos since 2005, including a "Top 20" video of IED attacks on US military forces and the beheading of businessman Nicholas Berg in 2004.[17] These videos and others like them are designed not only to inspire already committed members, but to reach out to potential recruits: "Once inspired by the videos, the prospective jihadist might move on to a Web posting such as 'How To Join Al-Qaeda.'"[18] Al-Qa'ida is also utilizing children's television shows to start radicalization early. For example, in a show titled *Pioneers of Tomorrow,* a character resembling Mickey Mouse was depicted as becoming a martyr.[19] Then, in 2008, al-Qa'ida released a video depicting young boys holding grenades, AK-47s, and pistols while wearing suicide vests. This video was targeted at young children, whom al-Qa'ida believes to be the next generation of mujahideen.[20]

In its most recent endeavor, AQAP has alluded to an upcoming cartoon movie for children titled *Al-Qaeda in the Arabian Peninsula.* This movie will teach children the history of al-Qa'ida and encourage them to carry out acts of terrorism. Will McCants, a scholar of militant Islamism and former State Department adviser, was quoted as saying, "[I]f it's legit and anywhere near like the purported screen shots and promotional banner, it would indicate that AQAP is becoming even more sophisticated in its efforts to reach out to youth."[21]

The Internet

Al-Qa'ida's message has become readily available on the Internet. With over 5,600 websites already in operation and roughly 900 more emerging on a yearly basis, al-Qa'ida's Internet presence has created a virtual community where citizens can advance the group's ideology without the risk of officially joining the organization.[22] Not only is the Internet being used to spread the message of jihad, the virtual world is being utilized to plan attacks, replacing traditional meeting sites, such as training camps or mosques.[23]

Al-Qa'ida relies on semi-official sites to spread its message. Those who run these websites may be direct affiliates of al-Qa'ida, other supporters, or those who are like-minded jihadists.[24] Two prominent websites used to distribute jihadist information among the virtual community are Azzam Publications and Al-Maqdese. Azzam Publications has been running since 1994 and has gained recognition as a supporter of jihad, receiving roughly five million hits a day throughout the world.[25] While this site can be viewed in different languages, many others are only in Arabic, but are still hosted globally.[26]

Articles on these websites are aimed at condemning America and the Western world. One author on the Al-Maqdese site stated, "Muslims and I know that you are from among the most impure, unbeliever and abject peoples in the world. ... You are the commander of the religious and moral weakening."[27] While many of these websites are regularly taken down, they usually reappear within days. As Evan Kohlmann of the NEFA Foundation and the Combating Terrorism Center reported, "If you shut down one of their websites today, they have a complete copy elsewhere and can put it up on a new server and have it up tomorrow."[28]

The social networking site Facebook is also facing the problem of removing jihadist groups, only to have them show up again the next day. Facebook administrators say that once a page is deleted, users of the account start a new page using a different email address. Once the page is reposted, they expand their network by tagging selected friends in posts. From there, the new page can be spread over Facebook.[29] Al-Qa'ida maintains a strong following on Facebook because pages like Jihad Al-Ummah act as a liaison between members of Facebook and jihadist websites such as Shumukh Al-Islam.[30] According to Kohlmann, al-Qa'ida's presence on Facebook shows "the hidden dark side of online social-networking—as a virtual factory for the production of terrorists."[31]

Al-Qa'ida has also taken complete advantage of YouTube, which has emerged as the leading website for the spread of jihadist information.[32] In January 2007, the ISI established a channel on YouTube. The goal of the channel was to use video clips and speeches by members of the ISI to draw in people interested in joining al-Qa'ida.[33] While YouTube administrators have been removing videos dealing with illegal activities and hate speech, they say any videos dealing with only religion will not be taken down. YouTube and its owner, Google, are struggling to balance security with free expression, and questionable material "that is brought to our attention is reviewed carefully."[34] The dangers of YouTube videos became obvious after an incident in the UK in May 2010 when Roshonara Choudhry stabbed MP Stephen Timms; she had been radicalized by watching video clips posted on the site. In response to this, the British Security Minister, Baroness Neville-Jones, contacted President Obama and stated, "Websites that incite cold-blooded murder would categorically not be allowed in the UK." She also demanded the removal of video postings inciting hate, which Google acknowledged when it began taking down clips of Anwar al-Awlaki.[35]

Al-Qa'ida's message is also spread via discussion boards and chat rooms. The Christmas Day bomber Umar Farouk Abdulmutallab began his discussion of radicalization on the Islamic Forum. When he first posted a thread, "I Think I Feel Lonely, Religious dilemmas," he spoke of the devotion he had for his religion, the contempt he had for those who disregarded Islamic law, and the confusion he was feeling in regard to liberalism and extremism. [36] As he began to form relationships with other members on the site, he hinted at jihadist fantasies, and instead of questioning his motives, readers urged him on. One response stated, "You could be the next Salah AdDeen..."[37] Saladin was a Muslim leader during the Third Crusade and conquered Damascus, Mosul, and the Syrian city of Aleppo between the years 1174 and 1186 AD.[38]

Farouk is only one of many who became involved with extremist conversations while on the Internet. Many youths who are curious, lonely, or looking to vent their frustrations will turn to the Internet. While they may begin looking at jihadist propaganda only casually, long-term exposure provides the opportunity for radicalization. This radicalization can be facilitated by recruiters who communicate with potential members via online forums.[39]

Magazines

Al-Qa'ida has also begun using magazines to spread their message throughout the international community. Some of the more popular ones include *Nida'ul Islam* (The Call of Islam), the *Voice of Jihad*, *Al-Battar Training Camp*, and *Inspire*. The scope of each magazine differs, but the main themes throughout them include messages from the now-deceased bin Laden, justifications for jihad, and weapons making/tactics training.[40]

Inspire magazine, written in English, is a new tool for recruiting jihadists in the West. This publication is heavily influenced by al-Awlaki's religious teachings; it contains testimonies from those already committed to the fight and instructions on how to commit violent acts. The influence this magazine has throughout America was brought to light when an article from the first *Inspire* issue, "How to Build a Bomb in the Kitchen of Your Mom," was found among the belongings of the Fort Hood bomb plot suspect Jason Abdo.[41] When Abdo was questioned, he specifically mentioned al-Awlaki, providing further evidence of Awlaki's ability to attract "lone wolf" jihadists to the cause, even within America's borders.[42] The magazine regularly criticizes America for targeting al-Awlaki, and has stated, "Not a single shred of evidence has been produced to incriminate Imam Anwar al-Awlaki; so why has the US government put him on their hit list?"[43] The March 2011 issue of the magazine answered questions asked in the previous edition regarding the steps necessary for becoming a jihadist. The writers of *Inspire* suggested partaking in a lone wolf attack in the West, stating, "Killing 10 soldiers in America…is much more effective than killing 100 apostates in the Yemeni military."[44] *Inspire's* content aims to create and enable terrorists on American soil.

An issue of *Inspire* released in July 2011 featured a spread on the death of bin Laden; it eulogized him for bravely confronting SEAL Team 6. This cover story, titled "Sadness, Contentment, & Aspiration," was written by the late American AQAP blogger Samir Khan.[45] In his article, Khan speaks of bin Laden's strength during his final minutes of life, saying, "His determination did not weaken in front of them, nor was he sapped of strength. Rather, he stood and confronted them face to face like a firm mountain, and continued to engage them in a fierce battle."[46] Other highlights in this issue include instructions on how to fire an AK-47, how to create explosives from peroxide, and a section answering questions readers had posed to Anwar al-Awlaki via email.[47]

Conclusion

Al-Qa'ida's use of propaganda has been characterized by its continuity and adaptation to modern technology. Al-Qa'ida's message has reached many communities to promote the recruitment of new members. Often the organization preys on those who feel lonely and helpless.[48] Al-Qa'ida has shifted from a cause rallying against the West to a social movement because it is a complex network of interconnected people and ideas, there is no easy way to dismantle the propaganda giant the organization has become.

Notes and Bibliographic References

1. Dictionary.com, "Ayman al-Zawahiri, July 2005 Definition of Umma— The Islamic Community." *http://dictionary.reference.com/browse/umma*.
2. Seib, Philip, J.D. *Military Review*, "The Al-Qaeda Media Machine.".
3. Anti-Defamation League, "Jihad Online: Islamic Terrorists and the Internet." 2002. *http://www.adl.org/internet/jihad_online.pdf*.
4. Fattah, Hassan. *The New York Times*, "Al Qaeda Increasingly Reliant

on Media." September 30, 2006. *http://www.nytimes.com/2006/09/30/world/30jordan.html?pagewanted=1.*

5. Encyclopedia Britannica, "Psychological Warfare." *http://www.britannica.com/EBchecked/topic/481682/psychological-warfare.*

6. Hanser, Robert D. "Psychological Warfare and Terrorism." *https://kucampus.kaplan.edu/documentstore/docs09/pdf/picj/vol2/issue1/Psychological_Warfare_and_Terrorism.pdf.*

7. EJournal USA, Countering the Terrorist Mentality. Foreign Policy Agenda: U.S. State Department/Bureau of International Information Programs. May 2007 *http://www.au.af.mil/au/awc/awcgate/state/counter_terr_mentality_may07.pdf.*

8. *Ibid.* 6.

9. Ganor, Boaz Dr. International Institute for Counter-Terrorism, "Terror as a Strategy of Psychological Warfare." July 15, 2002. *http://212.150.54.123/articles/articledet.cfm?articleid=443.*

10. Ferber, Sari and Yoram Schweitzer. "Al-Qaeda and the Internationalization of Suicide Terrorism." November 2005. *http://studies.agentura.ru/english/library/memo78.pdf.*

11. *Ibid.* 10.

12. Rabasa, Angel, Peter Chalk, Kim Cragin, Sara Daly, Heather Gregg, Theodore Karasik, Kevin O'Brien and William Rosenau. RAND Corporation, "Beyond al-Qaeda Part 1 The Global Jihadist Movement." 2006. *http://www.social-sciences-and-humanities.com/PDF/beyond_al-qaeda.pdf.*

13. *Ibid.* 12.

14. *Ibid.* 4.

15. University of Washington, Henry M. Jackson School of International Studies, "Countering Al-Qaeda's Ideology: Re-Assessing U.S. Policy Ten Years After 9/11." 2011. *https://digital.lib.washington.edu/dspace/bitstream/handle/1773/16495/Task%20Force%20O%202011.pdf?sequence=1.*

16. Telvick, Marlena. PBS Frontline, "Al Qaeda Today: The New Face of the Global Jihad." January 2005. *http://www.pbs.org/wgbh/pages/frontline/shows/front/etc/today.html.*

17. *Ibid.* 2.

18. *Ibid.* 2.

19. *Ibid.* 2.

20. CNN International, "U.S: Al Qaeda Video Shows Armed Boys in Training." February 6, 2008. *http://articles.cnn.com/2008-02-06/ world/iraq.main_1_boys-in-black-hoods-al-qaeda-roadside-bomb?_ s=PM:WORLD*.

21. Maclean, William. *The Huffington Post*, "Al Qaeda Children's Cartoon Might Be Group's Newest Propaganda Tool." July 21, 2011. *http://www. huffingtonpost.com/2011/07/20/al-qaeda-children-cartoon_n_905085. html*.

22. *Ibid*. 15.

23. *Ibid*. 16.

24. *Ibid*. 3.

25. North, Andrew. BBC News, "Pro-Jihad Website Draws Readers." February 15, 2002. *http://news.bbc.co.uk/2/hi/uk_news/1823045.stm*.

26. *Ibid*. 3.

27. *Ibid*. 3.

28. Thompson, Mark. *TIME Magazine*, "Should the U.S. Destroy Jihadist Webs?" December 23, 2009. *http://www.time.com/time/nation/ article/0,8599,1949373,00.html*.

29. Green. R. Right Side News, "Jihad Al-Ummah: Facebook's Main Jihadi Hub." December 23, 2010. *http://www.rightsidenews. com/2010122312416/world/terrorism/jihad-al-ummah-facebooks- main-jihadi-hub.html*.

30. *Ibid*. 29.

31. *Ibid*. 15.

32. Stalinsky, Steven. The Middle East Media Research Institute, "Part V: YouTube-The Internet's Primary and Rapidly Expanding Jihadi Base." December 10, 2010. *http://www.memri.org/report/ en/0/0/0/0/0/0/50/4854.htm*.

33. Bakier, Abdul. The Jamestown Foundation, "Al-Qaeda's Islamic State of Iraq Turns to YouTube." January 23, 2008. *http://www.jamestown. org/single/?no_cache=1&tx_ttnews%5Btt_news%5D=4671*.

34. *Ibid*. 32.

35. Gardham, Duncan, Gordon Rayner, and John Bingham. *The Telegraph*, "YouTube Begins Removing al-Qaeda Videos." November 8, 2010. *http://www.telegraph.co.uk/news/politics/8107264/YouTube-begins- removing-al-Qaeda-videos.html*.

36. Rucker, Philip, Julie Tate. *The Washington Post*, "In Online Posts Apparently by Detroit Suspect, Religious Ideals Collide." December 29, 2009. *http://www.washingtonpost.com/wp-dyn/content/article/2009/12/28/AR2009122802492.html.*

37. Gawaher, "Islamic Forum: Post by Umar Farouk Abdulmutallab." *http://www.gawaher.com/index.php?showtopic=7544.*

38. MiddleAges.org, "Saladin." *http://www.middle-ages.org.uk/saladin.htm.*

39. *Ibid*. 15.

40. *Ibid*. 12.

41. Thomas, Pierre, Marth Raddatz, Rhonda Schwartz, and Jason Ryan. ABC News, "Fort Hood Bomb Plot Suspect: 'Inspired by al Qaeda?" July 29, 2011. *http://abcnews.go.com/Blotter/fort-hood-suspect-nabbed-al-qaeda-inspire-magazine/story?id=14187568.*

42. *Ibid*. 41.

43. Joscelyn, Thomas. *The Long War Journal*, "Analysis: Anwar Awlaki's message to Inspire readers." October 21, 2010. *http://www.longwarjournal.org/archives/2010/10/analysis_anwar_awlak.php.*

44. *Ibid*. 32.

45. Anti-Defamation League, "AQAP Releases Sixth Issue of Inspire Magazine." July 19, 2011. *http://www.adl.org/main_Terrorism/inspire_aqap_6.htm.*

46. Ferran, Lee. ABC News, "New Al Qaeda Magazine: Bin Laden Confronted SEALs in Fierce Battle." July 19, 2011. *http://abcnews.go.com/Blotter/al-qaeda-inspire-magazine-pushes-personal-jihad-bomb/story?id=14105572*

47. *Ibid*. 46.

48. *Ibid*. 12.

CHAPTER 5

Al-Qa'ida's Key Networks

Al-Qa'ida in Iraq

AQI is a Sunni jihadist group that traces its origins to Ansar al-Islam, a group based in northern Iraq and formed in September 2001.[1] Ansar al-Islam was listed by the UN as a serious terror risk and a terrorist organization on February 24, 2003.[2] Ansar al-Islam's goals were initially fueled by local issues, but al-Qa'ida's search for a post-Saddam presence in Iraq changed its focus.

In 2001, Ahmad Fadeel al-Nazal al-Khalayleh, also known as Abu Musab al-Zarqawi, fled Afghanistan to northern Iraq, where he established himself as the leader of Ansar al-Islam, meaning "Partisans of Islam."[3] While most of Zarqawi's past is unknown, it is confirmed that he had a long-time friendship with Usama bin Laden starting in 1989.[4] After meeting bin Laden, Zarqawi did not immediately devote himself to jihad. He worked as a reporter and later began to promote the idea of an Islamic regime in Jordan.[5] Zarqawi was arrested in Jordan in 1996 and served a five-year sentence for conspiring to overthrow the government. Upon release, he fled from his native Jordan to Afghanistan in 1999, where he lived for two years before fleeing again, this time to Iraq. He stayed out of the public spotlight until 2003, when Ansar al-Islam joined forces with al-Qa'ida forming AQI.

Al-Qa'ida reached out to Ansar al-Islam, which already had a large following with the Kurdish community in northern Iraq, and asked them to support al-Qa'ida and focus their attention on al-Qa'ida's larger goal of forming a caliphate. While Ansar al-Islam was primarily focused on local issues and its domestic enemies, it became clear the US was now becoming an obstacle to its goals. Al-Qa'ida, and more specifically Usama bin Laden, began vocally endorsing Ansar al-Islam. It is alleged that as many as thirty al-Qa'ida members migrated into Ansar's camps immediately after AQI's formation, giving al-Qa'ida a significant presence in Iraq.[6] According to the UN, bin Laden provided Ansar al-Islam with between $300,000 and $600,000 in return for its support for al-Qa'ida.[7] This was the formal beginning of AQI; al-Qa'ida had found its following and a leader, a combination that would lead to countless missions in the years to come.

Zarqawi's relationship with bin Laden played a large role in the alliance of the two organizations. This connection was publicized by promoting Zarqawi to a deputy position in al-Qa'ida in 2004.[8] While the ties between Saddam Hussein, Ansar al-Islam and al-Qa'ida have been a fiercely debated topic, what is undisputed is that al-Qa'ida became a disruptive force in Iraq in 2003 with the formation of AQI.[9]

After the fall of Saddam Hussein, Iraq was in a state of chaos. While foreign troops tried to maintain peace, al-Qa'ida took advantage of the instability and quickly gained followers and power. It recruited from the large population of dissatisfied youth who had lost faith in their government under the control of Saddam Hussein and who felt they would be oppressed by the next regime.[10] AQI preached the goal of "establishing a caliphate—a single, transnational Islamic state."[11] Usama bin Laden and Zarqawi shared the same vision for al-Qa'ida, to spread their jihad into "Greater Syria."[12] As long as apostate regimes ruled in this territory, they vowed to continue attacks until their caliphate was established. The instability of the Iraqi national government and the economy made many Iraqis susceptible to AQI's message.[13] AQI provided an opportunity for security, protection, and income that the national government and local economies could not provide, which attracted many young men to AQI's movement.[14]

Zarqawi's influence on AQI was enormous. He carried out several successful bombings in Jordan prior to joining forces with al-Qa'ida, experience he used after the US-led invasion of Iraq.[15] He demonstrated that he was able to carry out large-scale attacks and inspired confidence in his followers that he was capable of conducting similar missions in Iraq.[16] He provided AQI with a direct link to bin Laden and support for their missions. AQI wasted no time planning and carrying out attacks once it established its presence in Iraq. In August 2003, AQI bombed the Jordanian embassy, a Shi'a mosque, and the UN headquarters in Baghdad. The attacks on the UN base killed the UN envoy to Iraq, prompting the UN to withdraw from the country, a strategic victory for al-Qa'ida's efforts to gain power.[17]

In August 2005, AQI attempted a rocket attack on a US Navy ship in the port of Aqaba, Jordan. It struck again in November 2005, bombing three hotels in Amman, Jordan and leaving 67 people dead and over 150 injured. This attack helped AQI gain enough support to form the Mujahideen Shura Council in January 2006.[18] The Mujahideen Shura Council was a coalition of five smaller jihadist groups from countries within their "Greater Syria" region who joined together in order to help achieve their goals and aid AQI by expanding its power and influence.[19]

In February 2006, the largely Sunni Arab AQI bombed the al-Askari Mosque, one of the holiest shrines in Shi'a Islam.[20] While there were no deaths, the attack furthered the divide between Sunnis and Shi'as in Iraq and enflamed sectarian tensions. Under Zarqawi's leadership, AQI deployed small-scale attacks aimed at prodding the country into a civil war.[21] One of Iraq's two vice presidents compared this attack to "9/11 in the US."[22] Shi'as responded immediately, killing hundreds of Sunnis in the days following the attack. The attack on al-Askari Mosque can be traced as the root cause for 168 attacks on mosques that occurred in the week following the February 22nd attack.[23] Zarqawi's campaign of attacks made him a major target for the US and its allies.

The US quickly labeled Zarqawi as a legitimate and enormous threat to national security and peacekeeping efforts in Iraq and the greater Middle East. It placed a $25 million bounty on information that could lead to his capture, the same amount that was offered for Usama bin Laden.[24] While little was known about Zarqawi prior to 2004, his whereabouts were closely monitored following his public support for al-Qa'ida.

Close attention from the Intelligence Community led to an airstrike on June 7, 2006 that targeted a safe house roughly 55 miles north of Baghdad where Zarqawi had been seeking refuge.[25] He was killed, which was a key strategic and symbolic victory for the US' efforts in Iraq. The implications of Zarqawi's death were not immediate as it struck quickly and effectively in November 2006 in Sadr City. There it set off a series of car bombs and mortar attacks that killed hundreds.[26] AQI continued this trend less than a year later, in August of 2007, by setting off more car bombs in the Yazidi villages of northern Iraq, which killed more than 700 civilians.[27] Though AQI considered the attacks a success, the large number of civilian casualties began to create a divide between the organization and the citizens of Iraq.

The attacks that followed Zarqawi's death caused a shift in how Iraqi civilians viewed AQI. Prior to 2007, when Zarqawi was focused on international issues and small-scale attacks, Sunni civilians generally either ignored or supported AQI. When the larger scale attacks began, such as the attacking of the Yazidi villages, AQI became extremely unpopular.[28] This change of heart by the civilian population has significantly decreased AQI's domestic power, as individuals who are willing to work with either Iraqi or US intelligence services now often infiltrate their system and then divulge crucial information.[29]

While AQI was crumbling from within, it continued to be on the offensive and to target those who opposed its beliefs. In 2009 AQI harassed hotels housing Western journalists in Iraq as well as other high-profile visitors to the country. It also attacked the Ministries of Finance and Foreign Affairs in 2009, the Baghdad Provincial Council, and the Ministry of Justice.[30] By September 2009, the US Defense Department reported that AQI had suffered "significant leadership losses and a diminished presence in most population centers."[31] In 2010 AQI continued to lose members, power, and influence; however, it persisted with its attacks. Following the national elections that took place in March 2010, AQI increased attacks on civilians. It bombed five civilian apartment buildings and publicly killed civilians "execution-style" to demonstrate its power.[32] Yet in 2010, the Defense Department concluded that from March 2010 to May 2010, the allies had killed or captured 34 of the top 42 AQI leaders.[33] While al-Qa'ida is far from eradicated in Iraq, it has certainly lost a significant amount of power due to the constant reshaping of its leadership in recent years.

After the death of Zarqawi, AQI struggled to find the leadership it needed to keep the organization strong and centralized. Iraq is one of many countries to have al-Qa'ida essentially "franchised" there, as the group has a loose affiliation with the headquarters and leaders of the movement. This, and the numerous foreign members, makes AQI a unique challenge to counterterrorism officials. It is estimated that between 200 to over 3,000 of the 10,000-member organization are foreign-born.[34] More than 60% of the foreign fighters are from Saudi Arabia, having crossed the border into Iraq from Syria.[35]

Al-Qa'ida in the Arabian Peninsula

AQAP, as it is currently constituted, officially traces its origins to the 2009 merger of Saudi and Yemeni al-Qa'ida affiliates, although the group has roots in several strains of jihadist activity that trace their activity as far back as the end of the Soviet war in Afghanistan.[36] Shortly after the Soviet withdrawal from Afghanistan many Yemeni veterans of the Afghan war began to return to Yemen.[37] The government of Yemen allowed al-Qa'ida to operate largely undeterred during the 1990s as part of its attempt to maintain stability while fighting challenges to its authority in the south.[38] With this détente in place, al-Qa'ida was able to plan future operations, including the attack on the *USS Cole* in Aden in 2000.[39]

After the 9/11 attacks, al-Qa'ida faced constraints in Yemen as the government of Ali Abdullah Saleh cooperated in counterterrorism efforts with the US military. These programs to capture senior al-Qa'ida members, as well as drone strikes aimed at decapitating al-Qa'ida leadership, helped significantly diminish the presence and capacity of al-Qa'ida affiliated groups in Yemen by 2003, when al-Qa'ida began to base operations in and focus attacks on Saudi Arabia.[40] Al-Qa'ida would remain largely dormant in Yemen until its reemergence in 2006.[41]

In addition to its Yemen operations, al-Qa'ida also had an active branch operating in Saudi Arabia for much of the early-to-mid-2000s, focusing its efforts mostly on Western targets in Saudi Arabia, as well as the Saudi security services.[42] Much like its Yemeni counterpart, in the immediate aftermath of 9/11, the Saudi al-Qa'ida affiliate faced a coordinated counter-terror effort from the Saudi Interior Ministry which diminished its capabilities inside the Kingdom. Prior to the merger of the Saudi and Yemeni branches, remnants of the Saudi affiliate had already fled across the border to Yemen, further bolstering al-Qa'ida's presence there.[43] Eventually, several Saudis would serve key roles in the newly constituted AQAP leadership.

In 2006, 23 alleged members of al-Qa'ida escaped from a high security Yemeni prison. Among those to escape was the current head of AQAP, Nasir al-Wuhayshi, a veteran of combat in Afghanistan and a personal associate of Usama bin Laden.[44] In addition to Wuhayshi, many of the escaped prisoners would go on to serve in core leadership roles in al-Qa'ida's Yemen branch, and later in AQAP. Rounding out the top leadership was Said al-Shihri, a Saudi who had previously been both in US custody at Guantanamo Bay and in Saudi Arabia's jihadist rehabilitation program.[45]

Since the 2009 merger, AQAP has become one of the most active of al-Qa'ida branches, perpetrating and attempting some of the highest-profile terrorist attacks in recent years. It is also one of the largest al-Qa'ida affiliates, with estimates placing active members in the hundreds, large enough to rival al-Qa'ida's central organization in Afghanistan and Pakistan.[46] The first high profile attack by the group after the 2009 merger was a failed suicide attack against Prince Mohammed bin Nayef, the Saudi counter-terror chief whose efforts were effective in driving al-Qa'ida out of Saudi Arabia and into Yemen.[47] This unsuccessful attempt has been followed up with several threats against the Saudi royal family. Since then, AQAP has followed a consistent pattern of targeting the Yemeni government, foreign nationals, and Western interests in Yemen. These attacks have included several suicide attacks and the killing of foreign tourists, as well as two attacks against the American embassy in Sana'a, the second of which killed 17 people.[48]

Although AQAP has frequently worked in its primary area of operations in the Arabian Peninsula to target Yemeni and Saudi interests (the "near enemy" in al-Qa'ida's ideological lexicon), it is also unique among current al-Qa'ida affiliates in having the reach and capacity to carry out attacks against "the far enemy," i.e., Western governments and interests. AQAP has been aggressive in its attempts to carry out terrorist attacks internationally, although with limited success so far.[49] AQAP has recently made several attempts against aviation targets including sending bombs in printer cartridges via air cargo and Umar Farouk Abdulmutallab's attempted suicide bombing.[50]

In addition to being active in planning and executing terrorist attacks, AQAP has its own substantial propaganda operation designed to appeal to a broad audience of both potential recruits in Yemen and sympathetic readers abroad. AQAP appeals to these disparate audiences with messages aimed at addressing unique grievances, and it has several publications in both Arabic and English that carry its message to audiences in Yemen and abroad.[51] One of those publications, *Sada al-Malahim*, is published in Arabic and is geared to a Yemeni and Saudi audience, with the goal of recruiting potential members from these areas and gaining the sympathy and support of the broader population.[52] While furthering the central tenets of al-Qa'ida's ideology, AQAP also uses its publications to address local concerns and tie them to the broader al-Qa'ida narrative. AQAP's message campaigns against corruption, economic inequality, and widespread poverty in Yemen. It also criticizes the Shi'a Houthi rebellion in the north of Yemen.[53]

In addition to the Arabic periodical *Sada al-Malahim*, AQAP is unique among al-Qa'ida affiliates in its attempts to appeal to an international audience with its English-language publication, Inspire, discussed in chapter four. Prior to being killed in a drone strike on September 30, 2011, Anwar al-Awlaki focused his publication on a Western and English-speaking youthful audience sympathetic to al-Qa'ida, living outside of al-Qa'ida's traditional strongholds and bases of operations.[54] Awlaki also published many of his sermons in written, audio, and video form on the Internet which influenced attacks such as the Ft. Hood shooting and attempted flight explosion on Christmas Day 2009.[55]

Al-Qa'ida in the Islamic Maghreb

AQIM officially assumed its name and pledged allegiance to al-Qa'ida central in 2007, although it has roots in Algeria that date back to the outbreak of civil war in 1992. During the civil war the Algerian military fought against

Islamist groups to prevent them from gaining power after their success in national elections in 1992. These Salafist groups and their offshoots would eventually morph into the current threat to the Maghreb (Algeria, Tunisia, Morocco, and Libya) and the Sahel (Mauritania, Mali, Niger, Nigeria, Burkina Faso, and Senegal).

One of the main groups in the Algerian civil war was the GIA. During the conflict, a disagreement over the GIA's targeting of civilians caused a GIA official, Hassan Hattab, to break away from the GIA and form another organization, the Salafist Group for Preaching and Combat (GSPC).[56] The GSPC was designated a terrorist organization by the State Department in 2002. In 2003, under the leadership of Abdelmalik Drukdel the GSPC entered into an alliance with al-Qa'ida, later pledging full allegiance in 2006 and adopting the AQIM moniker in 2007.[57] AQIM maintains a strong presence in Algeria, a reflection of these Algerian roots, and most of the membership and senior leaders are Algerian.[58] Despite adopting the al-Qa'ida name, the AQIM franchise maintains few operational ties to al-Qa'ida central.[59]

In the early part of the 2000s, the GSPC lacked sufficient resources as a result of the destructive decade-long civil war between the Islamists and the Algerian government.[60] Droukdel reached out to Zarqawi by sending him a secret letter discussing cooperation between the two groups. Among some of the specific terms, Droukdel sought Zarqawi's help in releasing a GSPC leader. In return, AQIM would play a significant role in Zarqawi's operations in Iraq.[61] The partnership with AQI, and the desire of al-Qa'ida's leadership to expand into the Maghreb, set into motion the GSPC's evolution into AQIM.[62] Droukdel ultimately hoped that an association with al-Qa'ida would allow the GSPC to expand beyond its previous focus on Algeria and become a broader North African terrorist organization, incorporating other Islamist groups from nearby Tunisia and Libya.[63]

AQIM facilitated the travel of fighters from North Africa to Iraq to aid the insurgency, building Droukdel's and AQIM's international profile. Many of these fighters passed through GSPC training camps in Algeria prior to their arrival in Iraq. AQIM sent so many jihadists to Iraq that the US Central Command estimated at one point that up to 25% of the members of the insurgency came from North Africa.[64]

After the GSPC rebranded itself as AQIM in 2007, it utilized suicide tactics which had been uncommon during Algeria's civil war, but were a hallmark of AQI.[65] The suicide bombings were largely aimed at international and foreign targets, although several attacks were also directed against the Algerian government. AQIM's first attack was a series of three suicide bombs detonated at various government installations in the Algerian capital.[66] This was followed several months later by an attack on a UN compound in Algiers.[67] AQIM continued its suicide bombing campaign into 2008, but its earlier attacks remain its most deadly.

After its initial burst of violence, popular backlash and a crackdown by the Algerian government limited the ability of AQIM to carry out suicide attacks. Increased efforts by Algerian security services drove the group out of the capital. AQIM struggled with decreased support from abroad, criticism from the Algerian public about suicide attacks, and pressure from the Algerian security services which forced the organization to leave the capital and operate instead in Algeria's desert regions. AQIM migrated to the Tanezrouft Range in the south and across the border to Mali.[68] It is currently estimated that the Algerian government has captured or killed up to 1,300 members of AQIM since the group's formation, with fewer than 1,000 members still remaining. In recent years, the number of suicide attacks committed by the group has sharply dropped.[69]

As discussed in chapter three, kidnapping foreign nationals, especially American, French, and Spanish workers in the Maghreb and Sahel regions, is AQIM's main source of revenue; ransom payments by companies and governments can reach millions of dollars.[70] This money is used to fund AQIM operations and purchase weapons and equipment. Occasionally, AQIM will make additional demands, such as the release of AQIM fighters. In the case of the hostages currently held by AQIM in Niger, the organization has demanded the withdrawal of French forces from Afghanistan.[71] The results of these kidnappings have been mixed; several times governments have given in to demands, while on other occasions refusal has resulted in the execution of hostages. AQIM's criminal enterprises also operate relatively undisturbed in the Sahel. It is active in trafficking drugs, weapons, and people across the region.

Notes and Bibliographic References

1.	Bruno, Greg, and Julia Jeffrey. Council on Foreign Relations, "Profile: Al-Qaeda in Iraq (a.k.a. al-Qaeda in Mesopotamia)." April 26, 2010. *http://www.cfr.org/iraq/profile-al-qaeda-iraq-k-al-qaeda-mesopotamia/ p14811.*

2.	United Nations Security Council, "The Al-Qaida Sanctions Committee." November 19, 2010. *http://www.un.org/sc/committees/1267/NSQE09803E. shtml.*

3. Teslik, Lee. Council on Foreign Relations, "Profile: Abu Musab al-Zarqawi." June 8, 2006. *http://www.cfr.org/iraq/profile-abu-musab-al-zarqawi/p9866.*

4. *Ibid.* 3.

5. *Ibid.* 1.

6. *Ibid.* 1.

7. *Ibid.* 2.

8. *Ibid.* 3.

9. Katzman, Kenneth. Congressional Research Service, "Al Qaeda in Iraq: Assessment and Outside Links." August 15, 2008. *http://www.fas.org/sgp/crs/terror/RL32217.pdf.*

10. *Ibid.* 1.

11. *Ibid.* 1.

12. *Ibid.* 1.

13. *Ibid.* 1.

14. Al-Jabouri, Najim and Jensen Sterling. National Defense University, "The Iraqi and AQI Roles in the Sunni Awakening." *http://www.ndu.edu/press/lib/images/prism2-1/Prism_3-18_Al-Jabouri_Jensen.pdf.*

15. *Ibid.* 1.

16. *Ibid.* 1.

17. *Ibid.* 1.

18. *Ibid.* 1.

19. *Ibid.* 1.

20. *Ibid.* 1.

21. Knickmeyer, Ellen and K.I. Ibarahim. *The Washington Post,* "Bombing Shatters Mosque in Iraq." February 23, 2006. *http://www.washingtonpost.com/wp-dyn/content/article/2006/02/22/AR2006022200454.html.*

22. *Ibid.* 21.

23. Worth, Robert. *The New York Times,* "Muslim Clerics Call for an End to Iraqi Rioting." February 25, 2006. *http://www.nytimes.com/2006/02/25/international/middleeast/25iraq.html.*

24. *Ibid.* 3.

25. *Ibid.* 3.

26. *Ibid.* 1.

27. *Ibid.* 1.

28. U.S. Department of Defense, Report to Congress, "Measuring Stability and Security in Iraq." September 2009. *http://www.defense.gov/pubs/pdfs/9010_Report_to_Congress_Nov_09.pdf.*

29. *Ibid.* 28.
30. *Ibid.* 1.
31. *Ibid.* 28.
32. *Ibid.* 28.
33. *Ibid.* 28.
34. *Ibid.* 1.
35. *Ibid.* 1.
36. BBC, "Profile: Al-Qaeda in the Arabian Peninsula." June 14, 2011. *http://www.bbc.co.uk/news/world-middle-east-11483095.*
37. Healy, Sally and Ginny Hill. Chatham House, "Yemen and Somalia: Terrorism, Shadow Networks and the Limitations of State Building." October 2010. *http://www.chathamhouse.org/publications/papers/view/177395.*
38. *Ibid.* 37.
39. *Ibid.* 36.
40. Harris, Alistair. Carnegie Endowment for International Peace, "Exploiting Grievances Al-Qaeda in the Arabian Peninsula." May 2010. *http://carnegieendowment.org/files/exploiting_grievances.pdf.*
41. O'Neill, Brian. Carnegie Endowment for International Peace, "Rebellions and the Existential Crisis in Yemen." September 9, 2009. *http://www.carnegieendowment.org/arb/?fa=show&article=23807&zoom_highlight=AQAP.*
42. *Ibid.* 36.
43. *Ibid.* 37.
44. *Ibid.* 37.
45. Al Jazeera, "Al-Qaeda in the Arabian Peninsula." December 29, 2009. *http://english.aljazeera.net/news/middleeast/2009/12/2009122935812371810.html.*
46. Boucek, Christopher. Carnegie Endowment for International Peace, "The Evolving Terrorist Threat in Yemen." September 2010. *http://www.carnegieendowment.org/files/Christopher_Boucek_CTC_Sentinel.pdf.*
47. *Ibid.* 36.
48. *Ibid.* 40.
49. Whitlock, Craig. *The Washington Post*, "Al-Qaeda's Yemen affiliate widens search for recruits and targets." November 30, 2010. *http://www.washingtonpost.com/wp-dyn/content/article/2010/11/29/AR2010112905459.html?nav=emailpage.*

50. Randall, David and Andrew Johnson. *The Independent*, "Yemen, the new crucible of global terrorism." October 31, 2010. *http://www. independent.co.uk/news/world/middle-east/yemen-the-new-crucible-of-global-terrorism-2121364.html*.

51. *Ibid*. 40.

52. *Ibid*. 40.

53. *Ibid*. 40.

54. Ghosh, Bobby. *TIME Magazine*, "Was Fort Hood Shooter Inspired by Radical Imam?" November 9, 2009. *http://www.time.com/time/nation/ article/0,8599,1936973,00.html*.

55. *Ibid*. 54.; and *Ibid*. 36.; and Mazzetti, Mark, Eric Schmitt, and Robert Worth. *The New York Times*, "American-Born Qaeda Leader Is Killed by U.S. Missile in Yemen." September 30, 2011. *http://www.nytimes. com/2011/10/01/world/middleeast/anwar-al-awlaki-is-killed-in-yemen.html?_r=1&pagewanted=all*.

56. Office of the Coordinator for Counterterrorism, "Country Reports on Terrorism 2009." August, 2010. *http://www.dtic.mil/cgi-bin/GetTRDo c?AD=ADA525847&Location=U2&doc=GetTRDoc.pdf*.

57. Rollins, John. Congressional Research Service, "Al Qaeda and Affiliates: Historical Perspective, Global Presence, and Implications for U.S. Policy." January 25, 2011. *http://www.fas.org/sgp/crs/terror/ R41070.pdf*.

58. Filiu, Jean-Pierre. Carnegie Endowment, "Al-Qaeda in the Islamic Maghreb: Algerian Challenge or Global Threat?" October 2009. *http:// www.carnegieendowment.org/files/al-qaeda_islamic_maghreb.pdf*.

59. *Ibid*. 56.

60. Mehkennet, Souad, Michael Moss, Eric Schmitt, and Elaine Sciolino. *The New York Times*, "A Threat Renewed- Ragtag Insurgency Gains a Lifeline from Al Qaeda." July 1, 2008. *http://www.nytimes. com/2008/07/01/world/africa/01algeria.html?_r=1&scp=1&sq=ragt ag&st=cse&oref=slogin*.

61. *Ibid*. 60.

62. Hansen, Andrew and Lauren Vriens. Council on Foreign Relations, "Al-Qaeda in the Islamic Maghreb (AQIM)." July 21, 2009. *http:// www.cfr.org/north-africa/al-qaeda-islamic-maghreb-aqim/p12717*.

63. *Ibid*. 62.

64. *Ibid*. 58.

65. *Ibid*. 56.

66. *Ibid*. 58.

67. *Ibid*. 58.
68. *Ibid*. 58.
69. The National Counterterrorism Center, "Al-Qa'ida in the Lands of the Islamic Maghreb (AQIM)." *http://www.nctc.gov/site/groups/aqim.html*.
70. Thurston, Alex. *The Christian Science Monitor*, "AQIM, Kidnapping, and Murder: A Brief History." January 19, 2011. *http://www.csmonitor.com/World/Africa/Africa-Monitor/2011/0119/AQIM-kidnapping-and-murder-a-brief-history/(page)/2*.
71. *Ibid*. 70.

CHAPTER 6

Selected Affiliated Groups

Al-Shabaab

Al-Shabaab is an Islamic insurgent group attempting to establish an Islamic state in Somalia. Al-Shabaab has ideological and organizational roots in the Islamic Union (IU) and the Islamic Courts Union (ICU), two powerful Somali Islamist groups. Both parent organizations worked toward the goal of implementing sharia law in Somalia and had strong ties to al-Qa'ida.[1] Al-Shabaab originated in 2004 as a militant division of the ICU, a network of tribes that controlled much of Somalia before the Ethiopian invasion in 2006.[2] After the ICU lost power to the Ethiopian forces, al-Shabaab emerged as the leader of the movement resisting Ethiopian control of the country.[3] Al-Shabaab has since grown into a powerful actor in Somalia and has gained control of much of the southern part of the country.[4]

Al-Shabaab follows a rigid form of Islam. The group rejects any governance not based on Islamic law and believes Islamic governance will solve Somalia's problems.[5] In accordance with this philosophy, al-Shabaab's primary goal is to overthrow the Transitional Federal Government, Somalia's recognized government, and establish an Islamic state in Somalia.[6] Its chosen method for achieving these objectives is "jihad against the apostates [and] regimes aiding the Crusaders' proxy war against Muslims."[7] Al-Shabaab's leaders have increasingly cast this jihadist vision as part of a larger global strategy, even claiming the establishment of a worldwide Islamic caliphate as one of the group's goals. The group's leaders see pursuit of jihad beyond Somalia's borders as a religious imperative.[8]

Al-Shabaab's official leader is Sheikh Mohamed Mukhtar Abdirahman, but the group is actually steered by a central group of leaders, including Issa Osman Issa, Ali Mahmud Ragi, Abdifatah Aweys Abu Hamza, and Mukhtar Robow.[9,10] There are three geographical divisions within the organization: the Bay and Bokool regions, southern and central Somalia and Mogadishu, and Putland and Somaliland. Each of these units has its own distinct leader, which may compromise the unity and cohesion of the organization, particularly in terms of ideology. The regional divisions operate independently of each other, and each leader must attempt to reconcile the group's broader ideology with his region's unique needs and challenges. While the extent of existing schisms within the group is unclear, the organization's structure of separate geographical factions creates an opportunity for it to be undermined by opponents. [11]

Estimates of the group's size vary between 3,000 to 7,000 fighters.[12] Al-Shabaab has engaged in forced recruitment, so it is not clear how many of these members are truly loyal to the group's ideology.[13] Membership is comprised of local Somalis, many from the Hawiye clan, as well as foreign recruits.[14] For example, al-Shabaab has been recruiting American Muslims to their cause. During the July 2011 House Committee meeting on Homeland Security, it was found that "al-Shabab has successfully recruited and radicalized more than 40 Muslim Americans and 20 Canadians who have joined the terror group inside Somalia."[15] One American in particular, Shirwa Ahmed, became the first American suicide bomber in 2008 when he carried out an attack in the northern part of Somalia.[16]

Recently, al-Qa'ida has increased its activity in Yemen; jihadists leaving Iraq often head towards Yemen. Yemen is a relative safe location for al-Qa'ida fighters' operations, although the security dynamic there is likely to change as terrorist attacks continue and pressure mounts on the government to crack down on terrorism. Somalia's history as a critical al-Qa'ida bridgehead into East Africa and its proximity to Yemen make it a plausible recipient for an influx of jihadists. Its lack of a strong central authority, porous borders, and the presence of al Qa'ida-affiliated groups make it a logical destination for al-Qa'ida fighters, particularly if Yemen increases its internal security and begins to carry out counterterrorism operations displacing the fighters.[17]

Al-Shabaab receives significant amounts of funding from the Somali diaspora.[18] Dispersed Somalis funnel money to their homeland through the hawala system.[19] This money is often intended as support for family members rather than solely as a donation to al-Shabaab.[20] The group also gains funds through a variety of criminal activities and port revenues.[21]

Al-Shabaab's methodology is characterized by the use of traditional guerrilla tactics, such as suicide bombings, roadside bombs, shootings, and assassinations.[22] Somalia's depleted condition through decades of violence has produced a citizenry of fighters familiar with asymmetrical warfare, weapons, and tactics, and thus is uniquely suited to participation in terrorist activity. While its most frequently used tactic is to bomb targets associated with al-Shabaab's opponents, the group also uses indirect ways of asserting control, such as blocking humanitarian assistance by hijacking aid or preventing its passage into certain areas of the country.[23]

Al-Shabaab's attacks have resulted in over 200 deaths and even more injuries since the beginning of 2008.[24] Although the withdrawal of Ethiopian forces from Somalia in January of 2009 eliminated one of al-Shabaab's primary opponents, the group has continued to launch attacks against a variety of other targets, including civil society actors, African Union Mission forces, and other international peacekeepers.[25] One of the group's most significant attacks in recent years occurred during the World Cup in July 2010. Al-Shabaab bombed two venues in Kampala, Uganda, where people were gathered to watch the World Cup, killing 74 and injuring 85. This attack was alarming not only because of the significant loss of life, but also because it was the first time al-Shabaab had staged an attack outside Somalia.[26]

Al-Shabaab has gradually adopted tactics focused on social and political means of advancing its agenda in addition to its violent methods.[27] Since 2008, the group has also used political strategies to recruit new members and gain power and control in Somalia. Al-Shabaab conducts town visits in which clerics affiliated with the organization speak before public gatherings and meet with the town's leaders to convince them of the purity of their intentions. Like many insurgent groups in the Middle East and Africa, al-Shabaab ingratiates itself with a town's residents by providing them with necessary services and becoming part of their daily lives, taking the place of government. In this process, al-Shabaab often establishes sharia courts to provide speedy trials for local criminals, assists in the settlement of town disputes, and gives food and money to the town's impoverished citizens.[28]

During al-Shabaab's ascent to power in Somalia in late 2006, the organization's leaders began reaching out to al-Qa'ida before publicly claiming an affiliation with al-Qa'ida in 2007.[29] The two groups' public support of each other is an indication of the strength and extent of their ties. Sheik Mukhtar Robow, spokesman for al-Shabaab, stated his wish to join with al-Qa'ida as one organization and obey bin Laden's orders in August of 2008.[30] In February 2010, the group declared that it was aligning with al-Qa'ida "to confront the international crusaders and their aggression against the Muslim people."[31] Al-Qa'ida has responded in kind, with several senior officials declaring their sympathy and support for al-Shabaab's cause and encouraging Muslims around the world to join the mujahideen in Somalia in their fight to establish an Islamic state.[32] Most significantly, Usama bin Laden released a video in which he explicitly endorsed al-Shabaab.[33]

The strongest link between al-Shabaab and al-Qa'ida is an overlapping ideology grounded in a strict Salafi interpretation of Islam.[34] Both al-Shabaab and al-Qa'ida advocate the establishment of Islamic governance and the removal of Western interests from their respective regions.[35] They also view jihad as the principal mechanism for achieving their goals and use guerrilla tactics. Al-Shabaab's national goals in Somalia increasingly fit into the framework of al-Qa'ida's global agenda as al-Shabaab expands its focus.[36]

Evidence has shown that some of al-Shabaab's fighters trained and fought with al-Qa'ida in Afghanistan, which likely reinforced ideological and methodological similarities between the two groups.[37] In addition to limited joint training and some contact between leaders of the two groups, there also appear to be some direct financial and membership linkages. [38] Overall, the ideological similarities between al-Shabaab and al-Qa'ida are fairly strong, while their organizational ties are inconclusive. The groups' shared goals have bonded them despite the lack of concrete commonalities in terms of leadership and membership.[39]

US counterterrorism officials have found text messages on portable flash drives at the compound where bin Laden was killed which offer evidence that bin Laden sought to strengthen operational ties between al-Qa'ida and al-Shabaab. According to this intelligence, al-Qa'ida's powerful branch in Yemen has provided weapons, fighters, and training with explosives over the last year. According to a Somali militant who was captured en route from Yemen to Somalia and interrogated aboard a US warship, the heads of al-Qa'ida in Yemen acted at times as bin Laden's middle-men to the Somali fighters.[40]

Lashkar-e-Taiba

Lashkar-e-Taiba (LeT) is a Pakistani militant group attempting to challenge India's control over the region of Kashmir and establish Islamic rule in India.[41] LeT was established in 1990 as the military wing of Markaz al-Dawa-wal-Irshad, a group focused on waging jihad and preaching Islam.[42] Over time, LeT has become an independent organization but it has retained these original goals, which it pursues through bombings and other violent attacks. In addition to its illegal activities, LeT has a charitable branch called Jamaat-ud-Dawa that provides services such as medical clinics and schools.[43] Providing these services has strengthened LeT and popularized it among the populations of Pakistan and Kashmir.[44] LeT has recently broadened the scope of its jihadist goals, leading to increased concerns about the dangers of the organization and the strength of its affiliation with al-Qa'ida.

Due to parallel philosophies, similar methodology, and instances of overlapping leadership and membership, LeT is often considered an affiliate of al-Qa'ida. Links between the two organizations, particularly the involvement of cohorts of bin Laden in the founding of LeT, are a central element of the relationship.[45] LeT and al-Qa'ida also share very similar ideologies: LeT's jihadist goals stem from a form of Wahhabi Islam similar to the theology espoused by al-Qa'ida.[46] Although LeT's mission is focused regionally rather than globally, the two groups share a basic philosophy.[47] Incidents such as the recent arrest of a senior al-Qa'ida leader in a LeT safe house lend credence to the argument for LeT's affiliation with al-Qa'ida.[48] Although there are some undeniable connections between LeT and al-Qa'ida, evidence of a strong relationship between the two groups is limited. The connections between them tend to be abstract and tenuous, and the available evidence lacks solid and consistent links to illustrate an overall narrative for an affiliation.[49]

LeT's ties to the Pakistani government appear to be stronger than its ties to the al-Qa'ida network. LeT's relationship with the Pakistani government began in the 1990s when the Inter-Services Intelligence (ISI-P), Pakistan's intelligence agency, began providing LeT with support in exchange for the group's promise to target Hindus in the regions of Kashmir and Jammu and to train Muslim extremists in India.[50] By launching attacks in Kashmir and other parts of India, the group has served as a reliable proxy for the Pakistani government in its conflict with India.[51] The group's utility in this capacity has led the Pakistani government and the ISI-P to protect LeT in spite of growing international pressure to restrict the group's activity.[52] The group was officially banned in 2002, but the Pakistani government made few efforts to truly reign in LeT until a crackdown in 2005.[53]

In addition to this tacit support for LeT, there are also indications that the ISI-P has provided the group with funding and training. Intelligence gathered following the arrest of David Headley, a Pakistani-American member of LeT involved in the group's 2008 Mumbai attacks, showed significant involvement by the ISI-P in LeT's operations.[54] Headley claimed that each LeT member involved in the plot had an ISI-P handler assigned to him, and that several ISI-P leaders consulted on the plans for the attack. If this intelligence is accurate, it may further indicate cooperation between the ISI-P and LeT.[55]

These recent activities have prompted concerns that it is broadening its agenda to global jihad, which some argue will cause the group to strengthen its ties to al-Qa'ida. The group's 2008 attacks in Mumbai are the primary source of these concerns. In November 2008 a 10-man assault team carried out a series of bombings and shootings at two hotels, a café, a railway station, and a Jewish community center, killing 166 people.[56] These attacks were on a much larger scale and higher level of sophistication than previous LeT efforts that the group had previously displayed. All of the targets were popular either with foreign tourists or Mumbai's Jewish residents.[57] This connection to the West and the Jewish community is indicative of a desire to wage jihad against a broader international entity rather than remaining focused on India alone.[58] The attacks reflect the group's traditional focus on India but the targets' ties to Western society indicate there may be an underlying objective of jihad against the West as well.[59] It remains unclear whether this new agenda is definitively indicative of deepening ties to al-Qa'ida.

Although LeT has some ties to the al-Qa'ida network, the ties do not constitute a strong affiliation between the two groups. LeT's ties to the Pakistani government however, are very strong. The rising concern that LeT is expanding the aim of its jihadist activities is warranted in light of recent evidence, particularly the attack on Mumbai. There is a possibility that LeT's expansion could strengthen its affiliation with al-Qa'ida.[60] As LeT's goals become more international in scope, its agenda increasingly overlaps with al-Qa'ida's. Also, increased terrorist activity in Pakistan and India could bring LeT into contact with more al-Qa'ida leaders and operatives. LeT, though lacking a concrete affiliation with al-Qa'ida at this time, has the potential to become stronger both in its own right and as an ally of al-Qa'ida.

Taliban

Following the Soviet invasion of Afghanistan in the 1980s, the mujahideen split along tribal lines vaulting Afghanistan into civil war. A group of students educated at madrassas on the Durand Line viewed this infighting as a direct result of the mujahideen's corruption and reliance on Western support. In this power vacuum came the Taliban, who pledged to restore order to the chaos which engulfed Afghanistan after the Soviet withdrawal.[61] The Taliban emerged in 1994 when it began working with the ISI-P as a security force for a convoy that traveled between Pakistan and Central Asia.[62] This support from ISI-P allowed the Taliban to branch out and gain control of Kandahar, which it used as its base to expand further into Afghanistan. This consolidation of power culminated in its takeover of Kabul in 1996.[63] The Taliban today is primarily made up of Afghan Pashtun tribesmen who have found refuge in neighboring Pakistan.[64]

After taking over the capital, the Taliban ruled Afghanistan from 1996-2001, acting as the de facto national government.[65] Though the Taliban considered itself to be the legitimate government of Afghanistan, only Pakistan, Saudi Arabia, and the UAE recognized its authority; the UN refused recognition of the Taliban internationally.[66] The Taliban maintained control until 2001, when the US and its allies invaded Afghanistan following the September 11 attacks, forcing the Taliban out of power. At the time of the invasion, the Taliban was ruling over 95% of the country.[67] Since 2001, the Taliban has become a non-state terrorist organization that continues to attack NGO workers, government officials, civilians, police, and coalition forces.

The Taliban's strict, anti-modern ideology is a hybrid of a literal following of the Quran, known as sharia law, and Pashtun tribal values, which rely on a strict following of the Pashtunwali, the code of conduct that outlines model behavior and how a society should function.[68] This is an ultra-orthodox ideology and is common among extremist groups such as al-Qa'ida and the Haqqani Network.[69] It does not allow women to work or attend school, and carries out amputations and public executions as punishment for violations of Islamic law.[70] The Taliban also seeks a broader goal, the removal of international forces from Afghanistan. While the Taliban governed Afghanistan, it spread its ideology with the intent to form the purest Islamic state in the world.[71]

Since the Taliban lost power in Afghanistan, the organization's hierarchical structure has disintegrated. Currently, Mullah Mohammad Omar is the leader; he acted as head of state when the Taliban ruled Afghanistan. Surrounding him is his Quetta Council, a group of his closest advisors that derives its name from its founding in the city of Quetta, Pakistan. Today the Quetta Council, specifically Mullah Abdul Qayyum Zakir, runs the Taliban both in Afghanistan and abroad.[72]

The Taliban is now split into three groups. The first group is members of the senior leadership, headed by Mullah Muhammad Omar, who live in Pakistan and are rumored to be under the protection of the ISI-P.[73] On May 23, 2011, Omar suffered a heart attack in Pakistan and the ISI-P rushed him to a hospital where he received treatment and was released a few days later. When this information reached Western news and intelligence outlets, the Taliban confirmed that Omar had been moved to Afghanistan and was alive and well there.[74]

The second group is the fighting commanders in Afghanistan. Since the Taliban are spread out over such a large territory, these fighting commanders work as generals, guiding a coalition of operatives in small-scale missions. They receive orders from Mullah Muhammad Omar or Mullah Abdul Qayyum Zakir and carry out their assignments accordingly.

The third group is commonly referred to as the "infantry" or the "militia." This group is the largest faction of the Taliban. It is armed, willing to fight for the Taliban, and opposes the new government.[75]

After being deported from Sudan in 1994, bin Laden formed a closer relationship with Mullah Muhammad Omar and found refuge in Afghanistan.[76] In return for sheltering bin Laden within its borders, the Taliban used bin Laden's connection with Ariana Airlines, the national airline of Afghanistan, to transport its people, money, and drugs internationally. Bin Laden provided the necessary logistical support for the Taliban; and in return, Omar provided safe haven for bin Laden so he would not be extradited to Saudi Arabia.[77] After the 9/11 attacks, the Taliban's support of Usama bin Laden made it a target of the US and prompted the US-led invasion that culminated in the overthrow of the Taliban on December 22, 2001.[78]

Following the invasion, the Taliban began distancing itself from al-Qa'ida, and the two groups only dealt with each other through third parties.[79] Because of the longtime friendship between Mullah Muhammad Omar and Usama bin Laden, the groups maintained a functioning relationship; however, they primarily used each other's services for logistical reasons. When they did plan or carry out attacks together, they usually worked with Gulbuddin Hikmatyar, a former mujahideen faction leader who maintained his relationship with Omar and bin Laden from their past fighting the Soviet invasion of Afghanistan.[80] The US labeled Hikmatyar's organization, the Hikmatyar Faction, a "Specially Designated Global Terrorist," on February 19, 2003 as a result of its activities with the Taliban and al-Qa'ida.[81]

The Taliban initially struggled following its loss of power, but recently it has been the focus of international attention following many deadly attacks in Afghanistan. According to the UN, in 2009 the Taliban was responsible for 76% of civilian deaths in Afghanistan.[82] This statistic furthers the notion that the Taliban continues to be a legitimate and formidable threat to peacekeeping efforts in Afghanistan.

The Taliban has begun using innocent civilians as bait to lure US troops towards IEDs, a tactic that has had tragic success.[83] Since May 2010, 16 IEDs have been planted in girls' schools, often strapped to children who have been kidnapped by the Taliban.[84] The killing of civilians came to the forefront again on July 24, 2011, when the Taliban hung an 8-year-old boy as punishment for his father's refusal to surrender to them.[85] These types of killings have hurt the Taliban's recruiting efforts and have cost it significant power and influence.

Today it is estimated that the insurgents control 4% of Afghanistan, encompassing 13 of 364 districts.[86] The Taliban has named "shadow governors" in 33 of 34 of Afghanistan's provinces, but these leaders have no influence and most provinces in northern Afghanistan were assessed as having minimal Taliban presence. While the Taliban may have a presence throughout the country, it has little to no real power in Afghanistan today, which is a vast improvement from the outset of the war.

Ansar al-Islam

Ansar al-Islam began to solidify in 2001, when various leaders from Kurdish Islamic factions discussed the idea of creating an "alternate al-Qa'ida base in Northern Iraq" while meeting with leaders of al-Qa'ida. Supposedly between $300,000 and $600,000 of al-Qaida "seed money," along with donations from Saudi Arabia, was used to activate the group.[87] Its founding name was Jund al-Islam, and it "declared jihad against secular and other political parties in Iraqi Kurdistan deemed to have deviated from the true path of Islam" after its official formation on September 1, 2001.[88] The formation of Ansar al-Islam occurred when Jund al-Islam merged with a splinter group from the Islamic Movement in Kurdistan.

Since the group's creation, there have been two main leaders. The first, believed to have been the founder of the organization, was Mullah Krekar. He has taken up residence in Norway since the 1990s, living as a refugee. Krekar was accused of sending funds from Norway to various terrorist organizations within Iraq. In 2002, Norway revoked Krekar's refugee status because the government believed that he had traveled to Iraq to fund and plan with these terrorist organizations. Norway had sought to deport him based on these allegations; but has yet to implement this measure because "Norwegian law… prohibits the country from exporting a refugee back to a country where the death penalty will be inflicted upon the accused."[89] It was then that Abu Abdullah al-Shafii, also known as Warba Holiri al-Kurdi, took over as the leader of Ansar al-Islam. He was arrested on May 3, 2010 by Iraqi Security Forces along with seven other members of the group as a part of several security operations in Mansour and Adhamiyah.[90]

The organization follows rigid Salafi ideology, and its founding declaration states that "…jihad in Iraq has become an individual duty of every Muslim after the infidel enemy attacked the land of Islam," and its members "…derive their jihad program and orders from the instructions of the holy Koran and the Prophet Muhammad's Sunnah."[91] In addition to this ideology, regions that are under the organization's control must follow "strict Taliban-like law," which is reflected through decrees issued by leaders that illustrate their strict interpretations and harsh punishments.[92] Ansar al-Islam's goal is to convert Iraq into a separate Islamic state, specifically, "to achieve in Iraq an Islamic country where Islam and its people are 'strong,' without the influence of Western cultures, and to expel Western influence from the homeland."[93]

Ansar al-Islam is located mainly in northern and central Iraq. It is not usually known for operating outside Iraq; however, there was some suspicion that the group may have been involved in a foiled plan to attack a NATO summit meeting in Istanbul in June 2004. In addition, there are some analysts who believe that the organization recruited members from Italy and that it has received logistical support in the past from Iran and Syria. They suspect that Iran provides assistance in the form of harboring militants within Iran, as well as providing a safe route for fighters to cross into Iraq.[94]

Since the formation of Ansar al-Islam members have carried out some sporadic attacks. The modus operandi includes assassination attempts against individuals who collaborate with foreign forces in Iraq. In addition, Ansar al-Islam directs suicide and car bomb attacks at Shi'a mosques, Christian churches, and Kurdish political meetings with the specific intention to kill civilians.[95]

There are four notable attacks since the group formed, although no attacks have been reported since 2005. Beginning in September 2001, shortly after the organization declared its existence, it ambushed and killed 42 fighters of the Patriotic Union of Kurdistan (PUK). The next attack followed three years later, on February 1, 2004, which is considered to be Ansar al-Islam's major attack. It was carried out during the Muslim festival Eid al-Adha when suicide bombers gained access to the PUK and Kurdistan Democratic Party (KDP) headquarters. 109 people were killed, including KDP Deputy Prime Minister Sami Abdul Rahman.[96] In December of the same year, Ansar al-Islam carried out another suicide bombing at a US military dining facility in Mosul, Iraq, in which 22 soldiers were killed.[97] The last known attack by the organization was in January 2005, when it assassinated Sheik Mahmoud Finjan, who was an assistant to senior Shi'a cleric Grand Ayatollah Ali al-Sistani.[98]

Asbat al-Ansar

Asbat al-Ansar, also known as the League of Followers or the Partisans' League, is a Sunni extremist group based primarily in Lebanon.[99] The group commands roughly 300 fighters primarily based in the Palestinian refugee camp Ayn al-Hilwah in southern Lebanon.[100] Asbat al-Ansar has a safe haven in the refugee camp out of reach of the Lebanese government, allowing it to bring in new members from people who have been "alienated" by larger Palestinian groups such as Hezbollah and al-Fatah.[101]

The group evolved in the 1990s from an Iranian-backed network called Ansarallah, formed by Hisham Shraydi.[102] Upon Shraydi's sudden assassination in 1991, successor Abd al-Karim al-Saadi, also known as Abu Mohjin, instigated a "sweeping reorientation in the group's religious identification" which included "stamping it with a Salafist character it did not originally have."[103] The group's leader was sentenced to death in absentia for murdering a Muslim cleric in 1994, and in his absence his brother, Haytham 'Abd Al-Karim Al Sa'di (aka Abu Tariq), took control of the group.[104]

The group's ideology centers on Salafism and is characterized by a strong opposition to Israel, the US, and the West, and to certain religious groups including Shi'a, Christians, and Druze.[105] Salafism in this context is used to justify the use of violence against civilians in order to achieve the group's goals.[106] The group's main mission has been debated; according to a Congressional Research Service (CRS) report in 2004, the group aims to establish an Islamic state in Lebanon by eliminating influences from the West and other religions. Some have claimed that there is little evidence to suggest that this was its intention, considering the actual attacks only inflicted "material damage and did not pose a threat to the state."[107]

Asbat al-Ansar has been able to carry out successful attacks in Lebanon and the surrounding area mainly using small bombs and grenades against civilian targets.[108] Asbat has conducted attacks against the state including the murder of four Lebanese judges in 1999 and the bombing of a customs building. [109] Asbat continued attacks on Lebanon after receiving funds from Usama bin Laden in 2000. In an attack on the Russian embassy in Lebanon, Asbat members killed a police officer and "used rocket-propelled grenades to show solidarity with Chechen rebels."[110] The circumstances of these attacks, and the fact that the group has not conducted attacks outside of Lebanon, support the characterization of Asbat's main goal as the formation of an Islamic state in Lebanon. In 2000, Asbat member Mahir al-Sa'di was sentenced to life imprisonment in absentia for a plot to assassinate former US Ambassador Statterfield. The plot coordinated by al-Sa'di and Abu Muhammad al-Masri, the head of the al-Qa'ida unit in the 'Ayn al Hilwah refugee camp.[111] In 2002 the group implemented plots against the US, killing American missionary Bonnie Penner, who was stationed in Sidon, and attacking US restaurants around the country.[112] Members of Asbat have been linked to the Katyusha rocket attacks on Israel and have fought against the Multi-National Forces in Iraq beginning in 2005, according to reports about the deaths of Asbat members in the region in 2006.[113] As reported in 2007, the group supported the struggle in Iraq and Afghanistan, while also plotting against Lebanese security and institutions.[114] In 2008 the Lebanese government charged Mu'ammar al-Aqami with plotting attacks on American fast food chains in 2002 and 2003.[115]

Although Asbat al-Ansar issued a statement after 9/11 praising bin Laden, the group denied all links to al-Qa'ida.[116] However, Asbat al-Ansar reportedly met with al-Qai'da emissary Salah Hajir in 2002 to "discuss future cooperation" between the groups.[117] According to sources in 2004, the main connection between al-Qa'ida and Asbat al-Ansar "hinge[d]" on Bilal Khazal, who formed a "linchpin" between Asbat al-Ansar and al-Qa'ida through a Lebanese group known as the Tripoli cell.[118] Khazal reportedly provided funds for the Tripoli cell, many members of which also belonged to and acted for Asbat al-Ansar.[119] Asbat al-Ansar was listed in 2005 as an active al-Qa'ida affiliate, though the extent of its cooperation and involvement in al-Qa'ida's operations was not reported.[120] The US Department of State maintains that Asbat al-Ansar has close ties to al-Qa'ida due to the proximity of the 'Ayn al-Hilwah refugee camp to al Qa'ida's command post and its strategic position to promote and expand al-Qa'ida's objectives in Lebanon.[121] On October 6, 2001, the UN listed the group as associated with al-Qa'ida, Usama bin Laden, or the Taliban because of its participation in funding and in planning actions on behalf of al Qa'ida, including Abu Musab al-Zarqawi's millennium plot aimed at Westerners and Christians in Jordan.[122] This was also seen in June 2007, when Lebanese authorities detained a cell of al-Qa'ida in Iraq extremists who claimed to have trained with members of Asbat al-Ansar and planned to attack the UN Interim Forces in Lebanon.[123]

The Egyptian Islamic Jihad

The Egyptian Islamic Jihad (EIJ), or al-Jihad, as it was first called, is an Islamic militant organization that formed in the 1970s, which combined forces with al-Qa'ida in 2001.[124] EIJ remains a separate entity and functions under the larger umbrella network of al-Qa'ida.[125] At its inception, the group had ties to the Muslim Brotherhood, though it eventually moved in a separate direction when the Brotherhood continued denouncing the practice of violence.[126] EIJ aims to overthrow the Egyptian government because it opposes any sort of Western influence, especially secularism and support for Israel.[127] EIJ has not committed an attack within the borders of Egypt since 1993.[128] While non-violence against the Egyptian government may cause people to believe the organization has moved away from its original goal, the EIJ remains a group focused on change within the country. For example, members of the organization released a statement in February 2011 supporting the protests throughout Egypt and called for the elimination of President Mubarak's regime.[129]

This organization has carried out or been associated with a number of attacks on high-level Egyptian officials, and US, and Israeli targets:

Successful: Attacks carried out by EIJ include the assassination of President Anwar Sadat in 1981 and the bombing of the Egyptian embassy in Islamabad, Pakistan, in 1995, which left 16 dead and 60 wounded.[130] In comparison to other terrorist organizations, EIJ is believed to have carried out the most attacks against the US in the past two decades, both by themselves and in conjunction with al-Qa'ida.[131]

Failed: EIJ has also taken part in several attacks that ended in failure. These include the attempted assassinations of Egyptian Prime Minister Atef Sedky and Interior Minister Hassan al-Alfi in 1993 and the attempted assassination of President Mubarak in 1995 during his visit to Ethiopia.[132] It was also linked to the attempted bombing of the US Embassy in Albania in 1998.[133]

Affiliated attacks: Since its affiliation with al-Qa'ida began in 2001, EIJ has had a role in several large-scale attacks. These attacks include those of September 11th, the attack on the *USS Cole*, and the East Africa embassy bombings.[134] A number of the September 11th hijackers were members of the EIJ, as was Mohammed Atta, the orchestrator of the group, and Ayman al-Zawahiri, EIJ's leader.[135]

The alliance between the EIJ and al-Qa'ida came about when the original EIJ became fragmented as a result of increasing crackdowns by the Egyptian authorities. Of the two factions that resulted, al-Zawahiri's group flourished, while the other faction, led by Abbud al-Zumar, slowly disintegrated, in part due to Zumar and other member's imprisonment.[136]

Throughout the 1980s, al-Zawahiri made several trips to Afghanistan, where he was captivated by the motivation displayed by the mujahideen. Inspired by the mujahideen and preempted by the government crackdown that the EIJ was facing in Egypt, Zawahiri uprooted his organization and moved it into the mountains of Afghanistan. There, they trained with the mujahideen and formed into cells that could survive separately from one another, much like the cells of al-Qa'ida.[137]

Starting in 1998, the EIJ received funding from al-Qa'ida, and the groups officially joined forces in 2001 when they issued a joint fatwa titled, "World Islamic Front against Jews and Crusaders."[138] This fatwa proclaimed war against Israel, the Jewish community, and the entire Western world, and justified the killing of Americans and their allies.[139] Since the formation of this alliance, al-Zawahiri has been considered number two in al-Qa'ida's ranks, and he was appointed the leader of the organization following the death of bin Laden in May 2011.[140]

Islamic Army of Aden

The Islamic Army of Aden (IAA), also known as the Aden-Abyan Islamic Army (AAIA), is a Sunni Islamic extremist group based out of southern Yemen, particularly in Aden and Abyan.[141] The group splintered off from the Yemini Islamic Jihad in 1996 and declared its independence as an army under the leadership of Yemeni Shabwah commander Zain al-Abidin al-Mihdar, also known as Abu Hassan.[142] The group's name derives from an "apocryphal hadith" that claims in the last days of earth "an army will arise from Aden-Abyan to fight for victory in God's name and God will grant them success."[143] The IAA centers its mission around performing jihad to "establish God's rule in the land of faith and wisdom, which was corrupted by the ruling, unjust and renegade gang [the Yemeni government]."[144] However, the IAA was not a prominent group until it issued public communiqués outlining its mission in 1998.[145] The IAA's goals include overthrowing the secular Yemeni government, establishing an Islamic state in Yemen, and promoting the mission of Usama bin Laden. While al-Qa'ida and the IAA do not have many formal links, they have historically upheld the same ideological goals, which have allowed them to collaborate on certain terrorist acts.

The IAA is composed of Yemeni and Arab militants who fought against the Soviets in 1989.[146] Bin Laden is suspected to have recruited many of the Yemeni militants to Afghanistan through his family connections to the country.[147]

Motivated by bin Laden's 1998 fatwa that "sanctioned the killing of Americans and Britons," the IAA issued a message threatening foreigners visiting or living in Yemen and claiming that these persons were "infidels and propagators of atheist, corrupt and vicious ideals" who hindered the development and success of Yemen as an Islamic land.[148] The small group had initially forged links to small al-Qa'ida training camps and provided logistics for al-Qa'ida attacks.[149] The IAA became more involved in international terrorism by working with al-Qa'ida in an attempt to bomb British and American embassies in Yemen and, in the aftermath of the operation's failure, holding Western tourists hostage in exchange for imprisoned IAA members.[150] In 1998, the IAA captured 16 Western tourists, four of whom were killed in the Yemeni government's rescue operation which was successful in capturing IAA founder and leader Abu Hassan.[151] The government believed that the ideology and success of the group was directly linked to Abu Hassan, and that with his death the group would also dissolve.[152]

The IAA continued its acts of terror after 1998 under the leadership of Khalid Abd al-Nabi, who led the group until 2003 when he surrendered to Yemeni authorities. He was subsequently released from custody and not charged for his actions.[153] The IAA claimed responsibility for the successful suicide attack against the *USS Cole* in October 2000, when a boat filled with explosives rammed the ship while it was refueling in Aden harbor.[154] The collision killed 17 sailors aboard the ship, and incurred about $250 million in damages.[155] Actual involvement by the IAA is disputed due to the "sophisticated" nature of the attack. The men arrested in the attack all claimed to have been trained by bin Laden in Afghanistan, and evidence suggests that most of the funding and planning for the attacks were not local endeavors.[156] However, al-Qa'ida allowed the IAA to "underscore" its efforts in the attack.[157] Less than a day after the attack on the Cole, the IAA attacked the British embassy in Sana'a; an IAA member threw a grenade that "by ill luck hit a diesel generator, which created a substantial explosion."[158] In September 2001, the IAA's assets were frozen by the US and the group was "designated for sanctions."[159] In October of 2002, the IAA claimed responsibility for bombing the MV Limburg in the Yemeni Port of Aden, stating it was in retaliation for the execution of IAA leader for his role in capturing Western tourists in 1998.[160] One person was killed and 90,000 barrels of oil were lost in the attack, which occurred on the "first anniversary of the US military campaign in Afghanistan against al-Qaida and the Taliban."[161]

The counterterrorism efforts of Yemeni officials between 2003 and 2006 reduced the size and operational effectiveness of the IAA, including the foiling of two attacks intended for embassies in Sana'a in 2003.[162] However, there were suspicions of the IAA's reemergence in 2003 following its attack against a medical convoy in the Abyan Governorate and the pardoning of IAA leader Khalid Abd al-Nabi.[163] Despite the Yemeni government's undulating crackdowns on terrorism in recent years, the group persists with an estimated 30 core members.[164] IAA's active engagement in terrorism appears to have dwindled in recent years, with the latest terror activity occurring in 2006 when two IAA members were arrested on the "suspicion of travel[ing] to Iraq to fight foreign forces."[165] According to Janes', the IAA has "limited organizational and operational capacities" essentially meaning that the IAA's "firm rhetoric has not been translated into a corresponding level of action."[166] Government officials claimed the IAA was defunct in 2006, stating "the Aden-Abyan Army does not exist. Khalid Abd al-Nabi turned himself in [to authorities] in the past, and was then pardoned by President Ali Abdullah Saleh. He now lives as an average citizen and owns a farm."[167] However, this statement contrasts with an interview conducted in 2008 with Khalid al-Nabi, who indicated that he continues to follow the IAA's ideological beliefs and practices, and stated that the Abyan Governorate is "ready for the emergence of IAA."[168] Notwithstanding, there is no recent evidence to show that the IAA has taken measures to rebuild itself, though the deteriorating role of law creates an environment ripe for groups who have attempted to form bonds with al-Qa'ida in the past.

Hezbollah

Hezbollah and al-Qa'ida, despite their theological differences and local versus global scopes, have a mutually beneficial relationship best exemplified by their connections to Iran and shared operations targeting their Western enemies. They are united by their hate for America and Israel, but have conflicting interests in other areas, for example in Iraq, where sectarian violence pits Sunni against Shi'a.[169]

The leaders of both movements have publicly criticized one another. Hezbollah's leader Hassan Nasrallah has "...expressed disapproval of Usama bin Laden's methods and called the Taliban 'the worst, the most dangerous thing that this Islamic revival has encountered.'"[170] The feeling is mutual; al-Qa'ida is believed to have plotted Nasrallah's failed assassination, and al-Qa'ida's Abu Musab al-Zarqawi has described Hezbollah as a "...shield protecting the Zionist enemy against the strikes of the mujahideen in Lebanon."[171]

These harsh words are based on important divides such as al-Qa'ida's disregard for killing Muslim civilians, al-Qa'ida's Sunni following as contrasted with Hezbollah's Shi'a constituents, and Hezbollah's ability to work within the government structure versus al-Qa'ida's complete opposition to regularization.[172]

Former Lebanese Prime Minister Fuad Siniora claimed that al-Qa'ida "does not have an indigenous presence in Lebanon. What the country faces instead is a fabricated threat by Damascus and its intelligence services that is intended to destabilize Lebanon and restore Syrian hegemony."[173] Hezbollah, however, believes that Sunnis within Lebanon are bringing al-Qa'ida to Lebanon in order to destabilize Hezbollah.[174]

Al-Qa'ida and Hezbollah share an anti-Israel mission. Al-Qa'ida leader Ayman al-Zawahiri has explained Hezbollah's fight against Israel during 2006 by stating, "We cannot just stand idly by while we see all these shells fall on our brothers in Gaza and Lebanon."[175]

Analysts have noted that al-Qa'ida advocates a war between Israel and Hezbollah in order to create a proxy war between the US and Iran, and the Muslim world at large, in order to annihilate Israel.[176] Regardless of the jihadists' sectarian identities, al-Qa'ida recognizes that they are waging the same war on the Israeli front.

Usama bin Laden had a great deal of respect for Hezbollah-affiliated terrorists, such as Imad Mugniyeh, and sought their help to generate attacks as devastating as Hezbollah's attacks on American targets abroad.[177] The groups' affinity for each other is, therefore, not ideological, but based on their mutual enemies of Israel and the US. In an interview, two Lebanese Sunni men of the Salafist belief (the same doctrine followed by al-Qa'ida's Azzam and Hamas's Yassin), Abu Anas and Basim al Kanj, explained their acceptance of Hezbollah: "We differ in our beliefs but we agree on fighting Israel... Israel is the enemy. We can settle our differences later." [178]

Beyond sharing Israel as an enemy, Hezbollah may share al-Qa'ida's broader goals, as indicated by FBI alerts to law enforcement agencies to be aware of Hezbollah operatives attempting to enter the US.[179] Shared goals have led the two groups to perform jihad together and could form the basis for future collaboration, possibly on American targets inside or outside US borders.[180] Hezbollah's "intelligence gathering activities have been seen by some officials as contingency planning," which could signal its more global intentions should either group wish to launch attacks in the US.[181]

Iran has served as a safe haven for al-Qa'ida terrorists and has actively supported Hezbollah both financially and with weaponry.[182] Iran and Hezbollah have been implicated in joint attacks on the Israeli embassy in Buenos Aires in 1992 and the Asociación Mutual Israelita Argentina (AMIA) Jewish cultural center bombing there two years later.[183]

Evidence indicates that al-Qa'ida leaders used Iran as a hideout after 9/11, although al-Qa'ida leaders such as al-Adel state that this "coordination" [with Iranians] was "...not made with the Iranian government..." but "...with sincere individuals who were hostile to the Americans and the

Israelis," implying that the al-Qa'ida-Iran marriage was formed on the same basis as the al-Qa'ida-Hezbollah union.[184] On July 28, 2011, the US Department of the Treasury issued a report saying that Iran was being used to funnel funds to al-Qa'ida, likely with the knowledge of Iranian officials, an accusation that Iran denies. As a result of this new information, the US imposed sanctions against six individuals who are involved in the transfer of money from throughout the Middle East to al-Qa'ida's leadership in Pakistan.[185] Following the strong historic division between Sunni al-Qa'ida and Shi'a Iran, "any cooperation between Al Qaeda and Iran against the US has been limited and cautious."[186] Yet Iran, as a state sponsor of terror, views the US as a larger threat to its regime than al-Qa'ida.

The two groups have had a long working relationship in terms of training and arms supplies. Several al-Qa'ida members received training in Hezbollah's Lebanese camps. Hezbollah also supported al-Qa'ida "with explosives and training in exchange for money and manpower."[187] Al-Qa'ida is believed to have had ties to Iranian-backed terror groups including Hezbollah dating back to its time in Sudan.[188]

The 9/11 Commission Report also noted bin Laden's respect for Hezbollah's Imad Mugniyah, as mentioned above, and that bin Laden sought out his help with training allegedly because he wanted to replicate terrorist attacks organized by Hezbollah in Lebanon in the early 1980s.[189] The bombings of the US embassies in Kenya and Tanzania in 1998 are perhaps the best-known product of al-Qa'ida and Hezbollah's joint efforts. Ali Mohamed, an al-Qa'ida operative, testified that he had set up a meeting between Mugniyah and bin Laden in Sudan to collaborate on the operation.[190]

Following the terrorist acts in Nairobi, Kenya and Dar es-Salaam, Tanzania, Iran was accused of aiding bin Laden and al-Qa'ida in the execution of the attacks and of aiding Hezbollah in supporting al-Qa'ida's efforts.[191] The 9/11 Commission concluded that Iran and Hezbollah provided "tactical expertise" essential to al-Qa'ida's successful execution of this operation.[192]

Hamas

Hamas is not directly linked to al-Qa'ida. The two groups are primarily connected by their ideological roots, and also through individuals, organizations, and governments that interact with Hamas and al-Qa'ida.

Palestinian Abdullah Azzam developed the principles jihad and istishhad (martyrdom) as essential components of al-Qa'ida and Hamas's programs.[193] Early in his career, Azzam was a member of the Muslim Brotherhood and worked with bin Laden in the Services Office, the organization that later developed into al-Qa'ida.[194] Azzam served as an ideologue, mentor, and father figure for bin Laden.[195] Theologically, Azzam was the one who gave bin Laden his understanding of jihad and istishhad, which continued to guide him and al-Qa'ida over the decades.[196] This same conception of jihad and istishhad was instrumental in the forming of Hamas's charter. Bin Laden provided Azzam with financial backing for his movements. Al-Qa'ida still memorializes Azzam by carrying out attacks in his name.[197] Bin Laden listed Azzam and Hamas founder Ahmed Yassin as important individuals who shaped his fundamental understanding and beliefs.[198]

While Azzam's activities with bin Laden were criticized for "abandoning" the Palestinian cause, he was later involved with Hamas, supporting its doctrine and finances. Azzam believed Hamas was a "spearhead in the religious confrontation against the Jews in Palestine."[199] He even wrote a book about Hamas, titled *Hamas: The Historical Roots and the Charter*.[200] Hamas, in turn, was influenced by him, respected his views, and, upon his death, labeled him a martyr. Usama bin Laden stated in an interview with Al Jazeera in December of 1998 that Azzam was involved with Hamas even during the first intifada.[201]

There are, of course, large differences between al-Qa'ida and Hamas despite their birth in similar ideologies. Hamas signed a ceasefire with Israel, a deal that the current al-Qa'ida leadership condemned as "selling out."[202] As a result of disagreements over strategy, their only recent positive, public exchange occurred when Hamas seized control of the Gaza strip. On this occasion, al-Qa'ida leadership offered Hamas congratulations and the wish that under Hamas's tutelage, Islamic law would be instituted in the Gaza strip.[203]

Muslim Brotherhood member Ahmed Yassin founded Hamas as the Brotherhood's militant group in the Occupied Territories.[204] As mentioned above, Yassin was praised by bin Laden as an influential thinker. Abdullah Azzam was also a member of the Muslim Brotherhood, an ideological mentor for al-Qa'ida founder Usama bin Laden, and, as mentioned above, inspired Hamas's interpretation of jihad and martyrdom in the same way as he did for al-Qa'ida, which became two of its premier tenets. Azzam in turn endorsed al-Qa'ida despite differences on concepts such as Hamas's notion of territorial nationalism, something Azzam rejected.[205]

Al-Fatah has also accused Hamas of having links to al-Qa'ida, but their accusations could be purely political rumors rather than fact.[206] Such statements could be effective in discrediting Hamas based on the following PEW report:

"While views of Hamas and Hezbollah are mixed, al-Qa'ida receives overwhelmingly negative ratings in nearly all [Muslim] countries... More than nine-in-ten (94%) Muslims in Lebanon express negative opinions of al-Qa'ida, as do majorities of Muslims in Turkey (74%), Egypt (72%), Jordan (62%), and Indonesia (56%)."[207]

Notes and Bibliographic References

1. Gartenstein-Ross, Daveed. "The Strategic Challenge of Somalia's Al-Shabaab." *Middle East Quarterly*, 16. No. 4 (Fall 2009): 25-36. *http://www.meforum.org/2486/somalia-al-shabaab-strategic-challenge*.

2. Anti-Defamation League, "Al Shabaab." 2011. *http://www.adl.org/terrorism/symbols/al_shabaab.asp*.

3. Rollins, John. Congressional Research Service, "Al Qaeda and Affiliates: Historical Perspective, Global Presence, and Implications for U.S. Policy." February 5, 2010. *http://assets.opencrs.com/rpts/R41070_20100205.pdf*.

4. *Ibid*. 2.

5. *Ibid*. 2.

6. Pike, John. Global Security, "Background Briefing by Senior Administration Officials on Al Shabaab Terrorist Organization." August 23, 2001. *http://www.globalsecurity.org/military/library/news/2010/07/mil-100714-whitehouse01.htm*; and *Ibid*. 2.

7. *Ibid*. 2.

8. *Ibid*. 1.

9. Hanson, Stephanie. Council on Foreign Relations, "Al Shabaab." July 28, 2010. *http://www.cfr.org/somalia/al-shabaab/p18650*.

10. *Ibid*. 2.

11. *Ibid*. 9.

12. *Ibid*. 2.

13. *Ibid*. 9.

14. *Ibid*. 2.

15. Saine, Cindy. Voice of America, "Somalia Terror Group Accused of Recruiting Muslim Americans." *http://www.voanews.com/english/news/Somali-Terror-Group-is-Recruiting-Muslim-Americans-says-US-Lawmaker-126286888.html*.

16. Thomas, Pierre. ABC News, "Feds Probing Possibly Minn. Terror Group." November 25, 2008. *http://abcnews.go.com/TheLaw/story?id=6331697&page=1*.

17. Stratfor Global Intelligence, "Somalia: Implications of the Al Qaeda-Al Shabaab Relationship.".

18. U.S. Department of State, "Country Reports on Terrorism 2009." Aug 5, 2010. *http://www.state.gov/s/ct/rls/crt/2009/140900.htm*.

19. *Ibid.* 2.

20. *Ibid.* 18.

21. *Ibid.* 18.

22. *Ibid.* 2.

23. *Ibid.* 2.; and *Ibid.* 6.

24. *Ibid.* 2.

25. *Ibid.* 9.; and *Ibid.* 6.; and *Ibid.* 2.

26. *Ibid.* 9.

27. *Ibid.* 2.

28. *Ibid.* 9.

29. *Ibid.* 1.; and *Ibid.* 9.

30. *Ibid.* 1.; and *Ibid.* 9.

31. *Ibid.* 2.

32. *Ibid.* 9.

33. *Ibid.* 1.

34. *Ibid.* 9.

35. Council on Foreign Relations, "Al-Qaeda." December 30, 2009. *http://www.cfr.org/terrorist-organizations/al-qaeda-k-al-qaida-al-qaida/p9126*.

36. *Ibid.* 1.

37. *Ibid.* 18.

38. *Ibid.* 1.

39. *Ibid.* 9.

40. Bennet, Brian. *Los Angeles Times*, "Al Qaeda's Yemen Branch Has Aided Somalia Militants." July 18, 2011. *http://articles.latimes.com/2011/jul/18/world/la-fg-bin-laden-somalia-20110718*.

41. Bajoria, Jayshree. Council on Foreign Relations, "Lashkar-e-Taiba (Army of the Pure)" January, 2010. *http://www.cfr.org*.

42. Tankel, Stephen. New America Foundation, "Lashkar-e-Taiba: Past Operations and Future Prospects." 2010. *http://newamerica.net/sites/newamerica.net/files/policydocs/Tankel_LeT_0.pdf*.

43. *Ibid.* 41.; and Kahn, Jeremy. "The Next al Qaeda?" *Newsweek*, Aug 26, 2010. *http://www.newsweek.com/2010/02/25/the-next-al-qaeda.html*.

44. *Ibid*. 42.
45. Chalk, Peter. "Lashkar-e-Taiba's Growing International Focus and Its Links with al-Qaeda." *Terrorism Monitor*. 8 No. 30 (July 2010). *http://www.jamestown.org/programs/gta/single/?tx_ttnews%5Btt_news%5D=36683&tx_ttnews%5BbackPid%5D=26&cHash=fc945260f6*.
46. Anti-Defamation League, "International Terrorist Symbols Database." *http://www.adl.org/terrorism/symbols/lashkaretaiba.asp*.
47. *Ibid*. 43.
48. *Ibid*. 45.
49. *Ibid*. 45.
50. Inter-Services Intelligence (ISI-P) is referenced throughout the chapter as ISI-P to distinguish it from the previously noted group, the Islamic State of Iraq; *Ibid*. 41.
51. *Ibid*. 42.
52. *Ibid*. 42.
53. *Ibid*. 41.; and *Ibid*. 42.
54. *Ibid*. 42.
55. *Ibid*. 42.
56. *Ibid*. 42.
57. *Ibid*. 42.
58. *Ibid*. 45.
59. *Ibid*. 45.
60. *Ibid*. 43.
61. CNN, "Taliban's History in Afghanistan." December 8, 2010. *http://www.cnn.com/2010/WORLD/asiapcf/12/07/taliban.explainer/index.html*.
62. *Ibid*. 61.
63. Bruno, Greg and Eben Kaplan. Council on Foreign Relations, "The Taliban in Afghanistan." August 3, 2009. *http://www.cfr.org/afghanistan/taliban-afghanistan/p10551*.
64. State Department: Bureau of South and Central Asian Affairs, "Background Note: Afghanistan." December 6, 2010. *http://www.state.gov/r/pa/ei/bgn/5380.htm*.
65. *Ibid*. 64.
66. *Ibid*. 63.
67. International Council on Security and Development, "Eight Years after 9/11 Taliban Now Have a Permanent Presence in 80% of Afghanistan." September 10, 2009. *http://www.icosgroup.net/2009/media/media-press-releases/eight_years_after_911/*.
68. *Ibid*. 67.

69. Katzman, Kenneth. Congressional Research Service, "Afghanistan: Post-Taliban Security, and U.S. Policy." June 3, 2011. *http://www.fas. org/sgp/crs/row/RL30588.pdf*.

70. *Ibid*. 67.

71. *Ibid*. 63.

72. Moreau, Ron. "America's New Nightmare." *Newsweek*, July 25, 2009. *http://www.newsweek.com/2009/07/24/america-s-new-nightmare.html*.

73. Tait, Paul. Reuters, "Afghan Taliban Say Leader Mullah Omar 'Safe and Sound.'" May 23, 2011. *http://www.reuters.com/article/2011/05/23/ us-pakistan-omar-idUSTRE74M0O220110523*.

74. *Ibid*. 73.

75. *Ibid*. 73.

76. Braun, Stephen and Judy Pasernak. *Los Angeles Times*, "Long Before Sept. 11, Bin Laden Aircraft Flew Under the Radar." November 18, 2001. *http://articles.latimes.com/2001/nov/18/news/mn-5593*.

77. *Ibid*. 76.

78. *Ibid*. 63.

79. *Ibid*. 69.

80. *Ibid*. 69.

81. *Ibid*. 69.

82. United Nations Assistance Mission in Afghanistan, "Afghan Civilian Casualties Rise 31 Per Cent in First Six Months of 2010." *http:// unama.unmissions.org/Default.aspx?tabid=1741&ctl=Details&mid= 1882&ItemID=9955*.

83. McCarthy, Terry. CBS News, "IED Attack Kills Two Marines." May 14, 2010. *http://www.cbsnews.com/8301-503543_162-20005019- 503543.html*.

84. *Ibid*. 83.

85. Global Post, "Afghan Insurgents Hang 8-Year-Old in Helmand." July 24, 2011. *http://www.globalpost.com/dispatch/news/regions/asia-paci fic/afghanistan/110724/afghanistan-insurgents-militants-taliban-boy- helmand*.

86. *Ibid*. 69.

87. International Institute for Counter-Terrorism, "Ansar al-Islam; Jund al Islam." *http://212.150.54.123/organizations/orgdet.cfm?orgid=96*.

88. Gregory, Kathryn. Council on Foreign Relations, "Ansar al-Islam (Iraq, Islamists/Kurdish Separatists), Ansar al-Sunnah." November 5, 2008. *http://www.cfr.org/iraq/ansar-al-islam-iraq-islamistskurdish- separatists-ansar-al-sunnah/p9237*.

89. *Ibid*. 88.

90. Official Website of US Forces- Iraq, "Suspected Leader of Ansar Al-Islam, 7 Criminal Associates Arrested." May 3, 2010. *http://www.usf-iraq.com/news/press-releases/suspected-leader-of-ansar-al-islam-7-criminal-associates-arrested.*

91. *Ibid*. 88.

92. *Ibid*. 87.

93. *Ibid*. 88.

94. *Ibid*. 88.

95. *Ibid*. 88.

96. *Ibid*. 88.

97. National Counterterrorism Center, "Ansar al-Islam (AI)." *http://www.nctc.gov/site/groups/ai.html.*

98. *Ibid*. 88.

99. U.S. Department of State, "Terrorist Organizations: Country Reports on Terrorism." April 30, 2007. *http://www.state.gov/s/ct/rls/crt/2007/103714.htm.*

100. Globalsecurity.org, "Asbat al-Ansar." *http://www.globalsecurity.org/military/world/para/asbatalansar.htm.*

101. National Consortium for the Study of Terrorism and Responses to Terrorism, "Terrorist Organization Profile: Asbat al-Ansar." *http://www.start.umd.edu/start/data_collections/tops/terrorist_organization_profile.asp?id=4639.*

102. *Ibid*. 101.

103. Gambil, Gary C. "Islamists Groups in Lebanon." *Middle East Review of International Affairs*. 11. No. 4 (December 2007).

104. Australian National Security, "Asbat al-Ansar." March 20, 2009. *http://www.ag.gov.au/agd/WWW/nationalsecurity.nsf/Page/What_Governments_are_doing_Listing_of_Terrorism_Organisations_Asbat_al-Ansar.*

105. CDI, "Terrorism Project: Asbat al Ansar." November 25, 2002. *http://www.cdi.org/terrorism/terrorist-groups.cfm.*

106. *Ibid*. 105.

107. Cronin, Audrey Kurth. CRS Report for Congress, "Foreign Terrorist Organization." February 6, 2004. *http://www.fas.org/irp/crs/RL32223.pdf*; and *Ibid*. 103.

108. *Ibid*. 107.

109. *Ibid*. 103.

110. *Ibid*. 105.

111. *Ibid.* 99.
112. *Ibid.* 107.
113. United Nations, "Security Council Committee Established Pursuant to Resolution 1267 (1999) Concerning Al-Qaida and the Taliban and Associated Individuals and Entities." October 6, 2001.
114. *Ibid.* 113.
115. *Ibid.* 104.
116. Schanzer, Jonathan. *Al-Qaeda's Armies*, (New York: Washington Institute for Near East Policy, 2005).
117. *Ibid.* 116.
118. *Ibid.* 107.
119. *Ibid.* 107.
120. *Ibid.* 69.
121. *Ibid.* 99.
122. *Ibid.* 113.; *Ibid.* 116.
123. *Ibid.* 113.
124. Fletcher, Holly. Council on Foreign Relations, "Egyptian Islamic Jihad." May 2008. *http://www.cfr.org/egypt/egyptian-islamic-jihad/p16376.*
125. PBS Frontline, "Background: al Qaeda, Inside the Terror Network." *http://www.pbs.org/wgbh/pages/frontline/shows/network/alqaeda/indictment.html.*
126. *Ibid.* 124.
127. *Ibid.* 124.
128. US State Department, "Background Information on Foreign Terrorist Organizations." October 1999. *http://www.state.gov/s/ct/rls/rpt/fto/2801.htm.*
129. Jihad Watch, "Egyptian Islamic Jihad Calls for 'Elimination of the Pharaoh and His Lackeys.'" February 2011. *http://www.jihadwatch.org/2011/02/egyptian-islamic-jihad-calls-for-elimination-of-the-pharaoh-and-his-lackeys----in-statement-issued-f.html.*
130. The Mackenzie Institute, "Al-Jihad, Egyptian Islamic Jihad (Jihad Group, Jihad Organization)." *http://www.mackenzieinstitute.com/profiles/Al-Jihad.html.*
131. *Ibid.* 124.
132. *Ibid.* 130.
133. Keats, Anthony. CDI, "In the Spotlight: Al-Jihad (Egyptian Islamic Jihad)." September 2002. *http://www.cdi.org/terrorism/aljihad.cfm.*
134. *Ibid.* 133.

135. BBC, "Investigating Terror Organisations." *http://news.bbc.co.uk/hi/english/static/in_depth/world/2001/war_on_terror/investigation_on_terror/organisation_2.stm.*

136. *Ibid*. 133.

137. *Ibid*. 133.

138. Anti-Defamation League, "Egyptian Islamic Jihad and the Formation of Al Qaeda." July 2009. *http://www.adl.org/main_Terrorism/Ayman+al-Zawahiri.htm?Multi_page_sections=sHeading_3.*

139. *Ibid*. 138.

140. CNN, "Al-Zawahiri Appointed al Qaeda's New Leader, Jihadist Websites Say." June 2011. *http://articles.cnn.com/2011-06-16/world/al.qaeda.new.leader_1_al-zawahiri-al-qaeda-statement-counterterrorism-official?_s=PM:WORLD.*

141. Parliament of Australia Joint Committee, "Chapter 2 The Listing: Islamic Army of Aden." November 1, 2007. *http://www.aph.gov.au/house/committee/pjcis/grouped/report/chapter2.pdf.*

142. Johnsen, Gregory D. "The Resiliency of Yemen's Aden-Abyan Islamic Army." *Terrorism Monitor.* 4 No. 14 (July 13, 2006). *http://www.jamestown.org/programs/gta/single/?tx_ttnews%5Btt_news%5D=838&tx_ttnews%5BbackPid%5D=181&no_cache=1.*

143. *Ibid*. 142.

144. Bodansky, Yossef. *Bin Laden: The Man Who Declared War on America*, (Prima Lifestyles, 2001), 374.

145. *Ibid*. 141.

146. Henley, John and Andrew Clark. *The Guardian*, "Debris Points to Terrorist Attack on Tanker." October 11, 2002. *http://www.guardian.co.uk/world/2002/oct/11/alqaida.yemen.*

147. *Ibid*. 146.

148. *Ibid*. 144.

149. Schanzer, Jonathan. Foreign Policy Research Institute, "Yemen's War on Terror." 2004. *http://www.humansecuritygateway.com/documents/WINEP_YemensWarOnTerror.pdf.*

150. *Ibid*. 144.

151. *Ibid*. 141.

152. *Ibid*. 142.

153. Novak, Jane. World Press, "Al Qaeda Escape in Yemen: Facts, Rumors and Theories." February 16, 2006. *http://www.worldpress.org/Mideast/2267.cfm.*

154. GlobalSecurity.org, "Homeland Security: *USS Cole* bombing." October 11, 2006. *http://www.globalsecurity.org/security/profiles/uss_cole_bombing.htm*.

155. *Ibid*. 154.

156. Whitaker, Brian. *The Guardian*, "Yemen bombers hit UK embassy." October 14, 2000. *http://www.guardian.co.uk/world/2000/oct/14/israel.alqaida*.

157. *Ibid*. 149.

158. *Ibid*. 156.

159. U.S. State Department, "Appendix C: Background Information on Other Terrorist Groups, State Department." *http://www.state.gov/documents/organization/31947.pdf*.

160. *Ibid*. 146.

161. *Ibid*. 146.

162. *Ibid*. 141.

163. *Ibid*. 142.

164. *Ibid*. 142.

165. Parliament of Australia, "Parliamentary Joint Committee on Intelligence and Security Committee Activities (Inquiries and Reports) Review of the Re-Listing of Ansar al-Sunna, JeM, LeJ, EIJ, IAA, AAA and IMU as Terrorist Organizations." 2007. *http://www.aph.gov.au/house/committee/pjcis/grouped/report.htm*.

166. *Ibid*. 141.

167. *Ibid*. 142.

168. *Ibid*. 165.

169. Kaplan, Eben. Council on Foreign Relations, "The Al-Qaeda-Hezbollah Relationship." August 14, 2006. *http://www.cfr.org/terrorist-organizations/al Qa'ida-hezbollah-relationship/p11275*.

170. *Ibid*. 169.

171. *Ibid*. 169.

172. Saab, Bilal. The Brookings Institution, "It's al Qaeda, Stupid!" January 18, 2008. *http://www.brookings.edu/opinions/2008/0118_terrorism_saab.aspx*.

173. *Ibid*. 172.

174. *Ibid*. 172.

175. Kaplan, Eben. Council on Foreign Relations, "New Fears of a Terror Alliance." August 14, 2006. *http://www.cfr.org/terrorist-organizations/new-fears-terror-alliance/p11280*.

176. *Ibid*. 172.

177. *Ibid.* 169.
178. Rosen, Nir. New America Foundation, "Al Qaeda in Lebanon." January/February 2008. *http://www.newamerica.net/node/9132.*
179. *Ibid.* 175.
180. *Ibid.* 169.
181. *Ibid.* 169.
182. Joscelyn, Thomas. *The Long War Journal*, "Analysis: Al Qaeda's Interim Emir and Iran." May 18, 2011. *http://www.longwarjournal. org/archives/2011/05/analysis_al_qaedas_i.php.*
183. Rother, Larry. *The New York Times*, "Defector Ties Iran to 1994 Bombing of Argentine Jewish Center." November 7, 2003. *http://www. nytimes.com/2003/11/07/world/defector-ties-iran-to-1994-bombing-of-argentine-jewish-center.html?scp=3&sq=argentina,%20Jewish,%20 bombing&st=cse*; and Australian Government, "Hizballah External Security Organisation." November 8, 2010. *http://www.ag.gov.au/ agd/WWW/nationalsecurity.nsf/Page/What_Governments_are_doing_ Listing_of_Terrorism_Organisations_Hizballah_External_Security_ Organisation.*
184. *Ibid.* 182.
185. Warrick, Joby. *The Washington Post*, "US Accuses Iran of Aiding al-Qaeda." July 28, 2011. *http://www.washingtonpost.com/world/national-security/us-accuses-iran-of-aiding-al-qaeda/2011/07/28/gIQARUPxfI_ story.html.*
186. Cooper, Helene. *The New York Times*, "Treasury Accuses Iran of Aiding al Qaeda." July 28, 2011. *http://www.nytimes.com/2011/07/29/ world/29terror.html?_r=1&scp=1&sq=al%20qaeda,%20iran&st=cse.*
187. *Ibid.* 169.
188. *Ibid.* 182.
189. *Ibid.* 182.
190. *Ibid.* 172.
191. NEFA Foundation, "Joyce Auma Ombese Abur, et al, Plaintiffs, versus Republic of Sudan, et al Defendants." November 22, 2005. *http:// www.nefafoundation.org/newsite/file/FeaturedDocs/Abur_v_Sudan_ FourthAmComplaint.pdf.*
192. *Ibid.* 182.
193. Maliach, Asaf. Institute for National Strategic Studies, "Abdullah Azzam, al-Qaeda, and Hamas: Concepts of Jihad and Ishtihhad." October 2010. 81. *http://www.inss.org.il/upload/(FILE)1298359986.pdf.*

194. Bajoria, Jayshree. Council on Foreign Relations, "Al-Qaeda Backgrounder." *http://www.cfr.org/terrorist-organizations/al Qa'ida-k-al-qaida-al-qaida/p9126.*

195. National Consortium for the Study of Terrorism and Responses to Terrorism, "Terrorist Organization Profile: al Qaeda." *http://www.start. umd.edu/start/data_collections/tops/terrorist_organization_profile. asp?id=6.*

196. *Ibid.* 193.

197. Riedel, Bruce. The Brookings Institution, "Al Qaeda's Post 9-11 Surge." September 9, 2010 *http://www.brookings.edu/opinions/2010/0909_ terrorism_riedel.aspx.*

198. Blanchard, Christopher M. Council on Foreign Relations, "CRS Report: Al Qaeda's Evolving Ideology." January 13, 2006. *http://www. cfr.org/terrorism/crs-report-al Qa'idas-evolving-ideology/p9827.*

199. *Ibid.* 193.

200. *Ibid.* 193.

201. *Ibid.* 193.

202. Byman, Daniel L. The Brookings Institution, "How to Handle Hamas." September/October 2010. *http://www.brookings.edu/articles/2010/0825_ hamas_byman.aspx.*

203. *Ibid.* 193.

204. National Consortium for the Study of Terrorism and Responses to Terrorism, "Terrorist Organization Profile: Hamas." *http://www.start. umd.edu/start/data_collections/tops/terrorist_organization_profile. asp?id=49.*

205. *Ibid.* 193.

206. Kershner, Isabel. *The New York Times*, "Abbas Accuses Hamas of Aid to al Qaeda." July 11, 2007. *http://query.nytimes.com/gst/fullpage.htm l?res=9807E4DB113EF932A25754C0A9619C8B63.*

207. PEW Research Center, "Muslim Publics Divided on Hamas and Hezbollah." December 2, 2010. *http://pewresearch.org/pubs/1814/ muslim-public-opinion-hamas-hezbollah-al Qa'ida-islam-role-in-politics-democracy.*

CHAPTER 7

Selected US Individuals with Alleged al-Qa'ida Connections

Methods and Scope

The threat of foreign affinity terrorism has increased significantly in the years following the 9/11 attacks. Foreign affinity terrorism, more commonly known as *homegrown terrorism* is loosely defined as an act of terror committed by a citizen of the host country but inspired by terrorist forces abroad. More specifically, for the purpose of this report, it is a role adopted by certain US citizens and permanent residents who consider themselves members of a distinct national "Diaspora," or as belonging to a broader, global ethnic, racial, or religious community, but whose loyalties lie with radical "foreign-affinity" strategic objectives sanctified by extremism and violence.[1]

This selected list of al-Qa'ida-linked foreign affinity terrorists chronicles plots, arrests, and attacks in the US since 9/11. Each of the following entries briefly summarizes the accused perpetrators' citizenship information, date of birth, arrest date, conviction date, sentence and sentencing date, the charges and relevant citations to the US Code, current status, and general background with other biographical information. In addition, selected case citations are included for cases that have been reported in a Federal Reporter. Where cases have not yet been reported but slip opinions are available, citations to those slip opinions have been included, as well as the WestLaw and/or Lexis number associated with the case by the WestLaw and/or LexisNexis online research services. Where court documents have been referred to for individuals with currently open cases, citations directly to the appropriate document, rather than to the entire case, are included. Additionally, the individuals must have targeted or plotted against the US in some form and been connected to al-Qa'ida through direct or indirect means, such as training or inspiration, respectively. Open-source information for these cases was collected from government sources, think-tank reports, court proceedings, commercial news entities and other media.

101

48 Case Studies of Selected US al-Qa'ida Connections

NOVEMBER 2001— JOHN WALKER LINDH

John Walker Lindh
AKA: Abu Sulayman al-Irlandi and Sulayman al-Faris.
Citizenship: US.
DOB: February 9, 1981.
Arrest: May 8, 2002. Captured on November 24, 2001, in Mazar-e-Sharif, Afghanistan.
Conviction: (US District Court for the Eastern District of Virginia) As part of an agreement reached on July 15, 2002, Lindh pled guilty to two counts: to supplying services to the Taliban army, and to a criminal information charge that he carried a rifle and two hand grenades while fighting against the US-backed Northern Alliance. As part of the plea deal, the government dropped all other counts in a lengthy criminal indictment, including one of the most serious charges—conspiracy to kill US nationals. CIA officer Johnny Michael Spann was killed in the Mazar-e-Sharif uprising. In this plea bargain, the US agreed not to treat Lindh as an enemy combatant.
Sentence: 20 years federal imprisonment.
Status: Indicted on February 5, 2002, and incarcerated until May 23, 2019, at the Federal Correction Institute (FCI) in Terre Haute, Indiana.
Cases: *U.S. v. Lindh,* 227 F. Supp. 2d 565 (E.D.Va. 2002); 2002 U.S. Dist. LEXIS 20863, October 4, 2002.
Charges: Conspiracy to murder US nationals (18 U.S.C. § 2332(b)); Conspiracy to provide material support & resources to foreign terrorist organizations (18 U.S.C. § 2339B); Providing material support & resources to foreign terrorist organizations (18 U.S.C. §§ 2339B & 2); Conspiracy to contribute services to al-Qa'ida (31 C.F.R. §§ 595.205 & 595.204 & 50 U.S.C. § 1705(b)); Contributing services to al-Qa'ida (31 C.F.R. §§ 595.204 & 595.205, 50 U.S.C. § 1705(b) & 18 U.S.C. § 2); Conspiracy to supply services to the Taliban (31 C.F.R. §§ 545.206(b) & 545.204 & 50 U.S.C. § 1705(b)); Supplying services to the Taliban (31 C.F.R. §§ 545.204 & 545.206(a), 50 U.S.C. § 1705(b), 18 U.S.C. § 2); Using and carrying firearms and destructive devices during crimes of violence (18 U.S.C. §§ 2 & 924(c)).
Links to al-Qa'ida: Received training at a camp associated with al-Qa'ida, attended a lecture by Usama bin Laden.

Background:

John Walker Lindh was born in Washington, DC, in 1981 to an affluent Irish Catholic family.[2] His family relocated to Marin County in California when he was ten years old, and he attended an elite alternative school focusing on individual development.[3] In 1997, Lindh converted to Islam, and in 1998 he traveled to Yemen for 9 months to study Arabic.[4] He returned to Yemen again on February 1, 2000, to continue his studies, but relocated to northern Pakistan and enrolled in a conservative madrassa.[5] While in Pakistan, Lindh joined the Harakat-ul Majahedeen-Al Almi, a militant Islamic group fighting in Kashmir.[6] Lindh became disillusioned with the group after 24 days of military training and joined the ranks of the Taliban instead.[7] From there he was sent to an al-Qa'ida training camp for 7 weeks, where he met with Usama bin Laden prior to the events of 9/11.[8] Lindh was sent to the front lines of the battle between the Taliban and the US-backed Northern Alliance, near Mazar-e-Sharif, where he remained following the 9/11 attacks.[9] During the US bombardment, he fled 100 miles on foot to Konduz, Afghanistan, where he was taken prisoner and sent back to a prison near Mazar-e-Sharif.[10] He was among 500 other Taliban fighters involved in the battle of Qala-i-Jangi, a prison revolt that lasted 6 days.[11] Following the battle, Western forces discovered his identity and took him into US military custody. Lindh was interrogated on the *USS Bataan* before being flown back to the US where he was tried in a civilian court.[12]

MAY 2002— DIRTY BOMB PLOT

Jose Padilla

AKA: Ibrahim, Abu Abduallah the Puerto Rican, Abu Abdullah al-Muhajir.
Citizenship: US.
DOB: October 18, 1970.
Arrest: May 8, 2002, on suspicion of plotting a radioactive bomb ("dirty bomb") attack. He was detained as a material witness pursuant to a warrant issued by the Chief Judge of the Southern District of New York in connection with a grand jury investigation of the terrorist attacks of 9/11. Padilla was designated an enemy combatant on June 9, 2002, (by executive order to Secretary Donald Rumsfeld), detained by the Department of Defense and transferred to the high security Naval Consolidated Brig, Charleston, South Carolina. On January 3, 2006, he was transferred to Miami, Florida, to face criminal conspiracy charges.

Conviction: Pled guilty on August 16, 2007, to conspiring to kill people in an overseas jihad and to funding and supporting overseas terrorism (no "dirty bomb" allegations).

Sentence: 17 years, 4 months in prison on January 22, 2008.

Status: Indictment issued on November 22, 2005, and incarcerated until March 23, 2021 at ADX Florence Supermax Prison in Florence, Colorado.

Cases: *Padilla ex rel. Newman v. Bush*, 233 F.Supp.2d 564 (S.D.N.Y.2002) ("Padilla I"); *Padilla v. Rumsfeld*, 352 F.3d 695 (2d Cir. 2003); *Rumsfeld v. Padilla*, 542 U.S. 426 (2004); *Padilla v. Hanft*, 423 F.3d 386 (4th Cir. 2005); *U.S. v. Padilla*, 2006 U.S. Dist. LEXIS 63248 (S.D. Fla. 2006); *Padilla v. Yoo,* 633 F. Supp. 2d 1005, 1012 (N.D. Cal. 2009).

Charges: Conspiracy to murder U.S. nationals (18 U.S.C. § 2332(b)); Conspiracy to provide material support to terrorists (18 U.S.C. § 2339B); Providing material support to terrorists (18 U.S.C. § 2339(a)).

Links to al-Qa'ida: extensive connections with al-Qa'ida. He received training from them and became involved with a plan to build a "dirty bomb."

Background:

Jose Padilla was born on October 18, 1970, in New York, but moved to Chicago, Illinois when he was five years old. He was affiliated with a street gang, the Latin Kings, in his formative years, and was arrested five times between 1985 and 1991. Before turning 18, he served a 3-year sentence in a juvenile detention facility for armed robbery, attempted armed robbery, and aggravated battery. In 1991, he was arrested following a road rage incident in Florida and was charged with two counts of aggravated assault, one count of using a firearm in the commission of a felony, and one count of carrying a concealed firearm. He spent 303 days in jail and was sentenced to an additional year of probation before being released in 1992.[13] Between 1992 and 1994, Padilla married and converted to Islam. He changed his name to Ibrahim and yearned to take Arabic courses and study the Quran.[14] By 1998, he wanted to immerse himself in Arabic and Islam by moving to Egypt to teach English and conduct religious studies. While in Egypt, he divorced his American wife and married an Egyptian girl, then began to travel throughout the Middle East and frequently to Pakistan and Afghanistan.[15] In 2001, American Intelligence was tipped off to his association with al-Qa'ida following the interrogation of Abu Zubaydah, an al-Qa'ida leader in US custody.[16] In 2002, he was observed by the CIA in Zurich, Switzerland, who monitored several calls he made to Pakistan.[17] On May 8, 2002,

Padilla flew to Chicago and was immediately apprehended by FBI agents on suspicion of attempting to detonate a dirty-bomb within the US.[18]

OCTOBER 2002— BUFFALO SIX/LACKAWANNA CELL

Cases: *U.S. v. Goba*, 220 F. Supp. 2d 182, 184 (W.D.N.Y. 2002).

Charges: Conspiracy to provide material support and resources to a foreign terrorist organization (18 U.S.C. § 2339B); Providing material support to al-Qa'ida (18 U.S.C. § 2339B).

Background:

A group of seven men from a tight-knit community of Yemeni-Americans in Lackawanna, New York (south of Buffalo), traveled to an al-Qa'ida training camp together to train for jihad months before the 9/11 attacks. The seven men were: Mukhtar al-Bakri, Sahim Alwan, Yasein Taher, Jaber Elbaneh, Faysal Galab, Shafal Mosed, and Yahya Goba.

Kamal Derwish recruited the young men in Lackawanna; he inspired and taught them the principles of jihad and eventually brought them to Afghanistan. Kamal Derwish moved into a relative's house in the city in 1998. He was no stranger to the area, having been born in Buffalo in 1973, but had spent most of his years in Saudi Arabia. Prior to moving back to the US, he attended training camps in Afghanistan, fought with Muslims in Bosnia, and was jailed in Saudi Arabia for extremist activities.[19]

The first group of men—Yasein Taher, Faysal Galab, and Shafel Mosed— flew to Afghanistan together, followed by the other three two weeks later. With the help of Kamal, the group made up a cover story for the trip, saying that they were going to Pakistan for religious study with Tablighi Jamaat.[20]

At the guesthouse in Kandahar, they viewed al-Qa'ida propaganda videos with footage of the *USS Cole* bombing and speeches by Usama bin Laden. When they traveled to the training camp, they were made to stay in tents outside the gates until the previous group left.[21] They experienced a regimen of military training and exercises, ate meagerly, and slept four to five to a tent. The men from Lackawana received weapons training (both small arms and anti-tank weaponry), explosives training (both high-explosive and incendiary), and tactical training (concealment and camouflage) and met with Usama bin Laden.[22] According to the groups' plea bargains, both bin Laden and Ayman al-Zawahiri visited the camp together to speak with the recruits. During this appearance, bin Laden gave a speech about an alliance with Egyptian Islamic Jihad and "anti-US and anti-Israel sentiments."[23]

An anonymous note was given to the FBI about the Lackawanna six while they attended the training camp, with special agent Edward Needham in charge of the case. Some of the group, having returned to the US (some returned immediately, others returned after traveling throughout the Middle East, and Jaber Elbaneh and Kamal Derwish remained) were immediately put under surveillance by the FBI. The Bureau became immediately concerned when Mukhtar al-Bakri traveled to Bahrain to be married, and sent a suspicious e-mail back to the States titled "Big Meal." On September 11, 2002, FBI agents questioned al-Bakri in Bahrain, where he was initially uncooperative about his trip to Pakistan. Later, he became more open and disclosed details about the trip, including the number of people at the training camp, roughly 200.[24]

The men were arrested in September 2002 and indicted in October of that year. The six men eventually struck plea bargains and pled guilty (the case never went to trial). The Anti-Terrorism and Effective Death Penalty Act of 1996 (Pub. L. No. 104-132, 110 Stat. 1214, (aka AEDPA)) gave the federal court in Buffalo jurisdiction over the case, thereby allowing the men an opportunity to retain and speak with counsel. They were sentenced from seven to ten years for providing material support to al-Qa'ida.[25] The seventh man, Jaber Elbaneh, stayed behind in Afghanistan, and eventually flew to Yemen when news of the others' arrests became public. Elbaneh was arrested and jailed in Sana'a in 2004, but escaped in 2006. He was tried in absentia in 2007, and finally jailed for 10 years in 2008 after he turned himself in.[26]

On November 2, 2002, it was reported by the Yemeni news agency that Kamal Derwish had been killed by a drone strike. Everyone else in the group has pled guilty to material support of a foreign terrorist organization and is serving between seven to ten years in prison. The timing of the case (days after the anniversary of 9/11), and harshness with which the media reported it, have aroused suspicion regarding the level of danger that the group of men actually posed. Arguably, the US was just beginning to understand this type of homegrown extremism.[27]

Mukhtar al-Bakri
Citizenship: Born in Yemen, naturalized US citizen.
DOB: 1981.
Arrest: Captured on September 10, 2002, in Manama, Bahrain.
Conviction: (Western District of New York) for providing material support to al-Qa'ida.
Sentence: 10 years imprisonment.
Status: Incarcerated until July 2, 2011, at the FCI, Terre Haute, Indiana.
Link to al-Qa'ida: Recruited by Kamal Derwish; attended al-Farooq training camp in Afghanistan and met personally with Usama bin Laden.

Sahim Alwan
Citizenship: US.
DOB: 1972.
Arrest: September 13, 2002, in Lackawanna, New York.
Conviction: Providing material support to al-Qa'ida.
Sentence: 9.5 years imprisonment; sentenced on December 17, 2003.
Status: Projected release date December 23, 2010, from the FCI, Terre Haute, Indiana.
Links to al-Qa'ida: Recruited by Kamal Derwish; attended al-Farooq training camp in Afghanistan and met personally with Usama bin Laden.

Faysal Galab
Citizenship: US.
DOB: 1976.
Arrest: September 13, 2002, in Lackawanna, New York.
Conviction: Providing material support to al-Qa'ida.
Sentence: 7 years imprisonment in December 2003.
Status: Incarcerated until April 29, 2008, at the FCI in Terre Haute, Indiana.
Links to al-Qa'ida: Recruited by Kamal Derwish; attended al-Farooq training camp in Afghanistan and met personally with Usama bin Laden.

Shafal Mosed
Citizenship: US.
DOB: 1978.
Arrest: September 2002.
Conviction: Providing material support to al-Qa'ida.
Sentence: 8 years imprisonment, in December 2003.
Status: Believed to reside at a federal halfway house in New York.

Links to al-Qa'ida: Recruited by Kamal Derwish; attended al-Farooq training
camp in Afghanistan and met personally with Usama bin Laden.

Yasein Taher
Citizenship: US.
DOB: 1978.
Arrest: September 2002.
Conviction: Providing material support to al-Qa'ida.
Sentence: 8 years imprisonment, in December 2003.
Status: Incarcerated at the FCI in Terre Haute, Indiana.
Links to al-Qa'ida: Recruited by Kamal Derwish; attended al-Farooq training
camp in Afghanistan and met personally with Usama bin Laden.

Yahya Goba
Citizenship: US.
DOB: 1977.
Arrest: September 2002.
Conviction: Providing material support to al-Qa'ida.
Sentence: 10 years imprisonment, in December 2003.
Status: now under federal protection, living under new name/identity, location
undisclosed.
Links to al-Qa'ida: Supervised by Kamal Derwish; attended training camp
in Afghanistan; met with Usama bin Laden.

Jaber Elbaneh
AKA: Jaber A. Elbanelt, Jaben A. Elbanelt, Jabor Elbaneh, Abu Jubaer,
Jubaer Elbaneh, Jubair.
Citizenship: Yemen (non-US).
DOB: 1966.
Arrest: Jaber Elbaneh turned himself in to Yemeni authorities on May 20,
2007.
Conviction: Charged with providing material support to al-Qa'ida; conspiracy
Status: Currently detained in Yemen.
Links to al-Qa'ida: Supervised by Kamal Derwish; attended training camp
in Afghanistan; met with Usama bin Laden.

OCTOBER 2002— PORTLAND SEVEN CELL

Cases: *Hawash v. Thomas*, 2008 U.S. Dist. LEXIS 73821 (D. Or. Sept. 23, 2008)
   Hawash v. Thomas, 2008 U.S. Dist. LEXIS 112522 (D. Or. July 22, 2008);
   U.S. v. Battle, 2007 U.S. Dist. LEXIS 83951 (D. Or. Nov. 9, 2007); *U.S.
   v. Patrice Lumumba Ford*, 2007 U.S. App. LEXIS 122,*; 216 Fed. Appx.
   652; *U.S. v. Jeffrey Leon Battle, et al*, Indictment. No. CR-02-399 HA.
Charges: 18 U.S.C. § 2384: Conspiracy to Levy War Against the US ("seditious
   conspiracy"). 18 U.S.C. § 2339B: Conspiracy to Provide Material Support
   & Resources to al-Qaida. 50 U.S.C. § 1705(b); 31 C.F.R. §§ 545.204,
   545.206(b), 595.204, 595.205: Conspiracy to Contribute Services to
   al-Qa'ida and the Taliban. 18 U.S.C. § 924(c)(1)(A)(iii): Possessing
   Firearms in Furtherance of Crimes of Violence.
Background:
   Six of the seven members of the "Portland Seven" were native-born US
   citizens. They were indicted in October 2002 on charges of conspiracy
   to wage war against the US, providing material support to al-Qa'ida,
   conspiracy to provide services to al-Qa'ida and the Taliban, and possession
   of firearms in furtherance of crimes of violence.[28] They planned to
   enter Afghanistan through China to join the Taliban. However, they had
   improper documentation and were thus denied entry.[29] The group also
   conspired to target Jewish schools and synagogues in the Portland area.
   Ford and Battle were sentenced to 18 years; Lewis was sentenced to 3
   years; Muhammad Ibrahim Bilal received eight years; Ahmed Ibrahim
   Bilal received 10 years, and Hawash was sentenced to seven years.[30]

Habis Abdulla al-Saoub
AKA: Abu Tarek.
Citizenship: Jordan.
DOB: November 19, 1965.
Arrest: n/a.
Conviction: n/a.
Sentence: n/a.
Charges: Conspiracy to levy war against the US, conspiracy to provide
   material support and resources to al-Qa'ida, conspiracy to contribute
   services to al-Qa'ida and the Taliban, and possessing firearms in
   furtherance of crimes of violence. The FBI offered a $5 million reward
   for his capture.
Status: Killed by Pakistani forces in October 2003.

Links to al-Qa'ida: Attempted to join al-Qa'ida and fight against the US in Afghanistan.

Background:

Habis Abdulla al Saoub fought against the Soviets in Afghanistan during the 1980s. He lived in Peshawar, Pakistan, until 1993, when he immigrated to the US. He worked as a parking lot attendant, computer assembler, and auto mechanic.

Maher "Mike" Hawash

Citizenship: US, but born in Palestine.

DOB: 1964.

Arrest: March 20, 2003.

Conviction: Conspiring to aid the Taliban in fighting against US forces and their allies in Afghanistan.

Sentence: In August 2003, Hawash surprised his supporters by pleading guilty to one charge in exchange for a reduced sentence. Prosecutors agreed to drop charges of conspiring to levy war against the US and conspiring to provide material support for terrorism. He was given seven years imprisonment.

Status: Released from prison in 2009.

Links to al-Qa'ida: Conspired to aid the Taliban's fight against the US in Afghanistan.

Background:

Hawash was born in the West Bank in 1964, but his family was displaced in 1967 during the Six Day War.[31] The family lived in Kuwaiti refugee camps before being allowed to return. Despite this upheaval at a young age, Maher excelled in school and was granted a scholarship to study at the University of Texas in Arlington, Texas. After earning degrees in engineering and computer science, he became a US citizen and took a job at Compaq Computer Corporation in Houston, Texas. In 1992, he was hired by Intel Corporation, and moved to Portland, Oregon. In Oregon, he lived a largely secular life. He met Lisa Ryan, a Christian by birth, and they were married in 1995. Four years into their marriage, they had a daughter together.

In 2000, Hawash's father passed away and Hawash returned to his Muslim faith to cope with the loss.[32] He became a regular at Masjed as-Saber, a more fundamentalist mosque in Portland, and took part in a pilgrimage to Mecca, Saudi Arabia. After 9/11, Hawash became radicalized further;

and on October 24, 2001, he flew to Hong Kong, where he planned to meet five others from his mosque and travel to Afghanistan to join the Taliban forces there.[33] However, they faced difficulty obtaining visas to travel through Pakistan, and Hawash and another returned to the US without ever entering Afghanistan.

Jeffrey Leon Battle

AKA: Ahmad Ali, Abu Isa.

Citizenship: US.

DOB: 1971.

Arrest: October 4, 2002.

Conviction: Conspiracy to levy war against the US.

Sentence: Sentenced after pleading guilty to seditious conspiracy and levying war against the US. He had two years added to his sentence for refusing to testify before a grand jury. In total, he was given 18 years imprisonment.

Status: Serving 18 years in prison.

Links to al-Qa'ida: Conspired to aid the Taliban's fight against the US in Afghanistan.

Background:

Battle is a former member of the US Army Reserves and lived in Portland, Oregon. He received his military discharge in January 2001. In late 2001, he attempted to enter Pakistan from China, with the goal of traveling to Afghanistan to join the Taliban and fight against US and allied soldiers there.[34] However, he was unable to do so, and returned to the US, where he was later arrested.

Patrice Lumumba Ford

AKA: Lumumba, Larry Jackson.

Citizenship: US.

DOB: 1971.

Arrest: October 4, 2002.

Conviction: Ford refused to cooperate with the government and was sentenced after pleading guilty to seditious conspiracy and levying war against the US and coalition forces.

Sentence: 18 years federal prison.

Charges: Conspiracy to levy war against the US.

Status: Currently serving US Penitentiary, Florence, CO.

Links to al-Qa'ida: Planned to aid the Taliban's fight against the US in Afghanistan.

Background:

Ford was born and raised in the US. In 1989, he entered Morehouse College in Atlanta, Georgia, but dropped out and returned to his home town of Portland, Oregon. There, he enrolled in Portland State University. While pursuing a Chinese and International Studies major, Ford had the opportunity to spend three semesters studying in China; it was there that he converted to Islam.[35] After returning to the US, he was an intern in Mayor Vera Katz's international relations office, first in 1998, and again in 1999. He returned to China on another internship, and then spent a further year there through Johns Hopkins University. There, he married a non-Muslim Chinese woman, Chunlin-Xie, and brought her back to Portland. On September 29, 2001, a sheriff's deputy found Ford and five others in a gravel pit, wearing turbans and shooting paper targets with rifles and pistols. On October 20, 2001, Ford flew to China. He allegedly planned to enter Afghanistan to support the Taliban against the US.[36]

Muhammad Ibrahim Bilal

Citizenship: US, Saudi Arabian descent.

DOB: 1980.

Arrest: October 4, 2002.

Conviction: Conspiracy to aid the Taliban and federal weapons charges.

Sentence: 8 years imprisonment on February 9, 2004.

Status: Released in September 2009.

Links to al-Qa'ida: Conspired to aid the Taliban's fight against the US in Afghanistan.

Background:

Bilal was born in the US and was arrested in Michigan, where he had been living with his sister. Many of his relatives, including his parents and most of his 16 siblings, live in Saudi Arabia.

Ahmed Ibrahim Bilal

Citizenship: US, Saudi Arabian descent.

DOB: 1978.

Arrest: October 6, 2002, in Malaysia.

Conviction: Conspiracy to aid the Taliban and federal weapons charges, convicted in 2003.

Sentence: 10 years imprisonment.

Status: Serving time in the Federal Correction Institute in Terre Haute, Indiana.

112

Links to al-Qa'ida: Conspired to aid the Taliban's fight against the US in Afghanistan.

Background:

Ahmed Bilal turned himself in to security officials at an Islamic university in Malaysia, where he had been studying. The university turned him over to Malaysian authorities, who then deported him to the US.

October Martinique Lewis

AKA: Khadijab.

Citizenship: US.

DOB: 1977.

Arrest: October 4, 2002.

Conviction: Pled guilty to six counts of money laundering and providing financial support to six men who conspired to help Islamic radicals fighting US and coalition forces in Afghanistan.

Sentence: 3 years in a federal prison.

Status: Released.

Links to al-Qa'ida: Transferred money to men who were attempting to join the fight against the US.

Background:

Lewis is the ex-wife of Jeffrey Leon Battle, and wired him money when he was overseas intending to join the Taliban in Afghanistan. She is said to have been cognizant of Battle's intentions at the time.[37]

JUNE 2002 — YASER ESAM HAMDI

Yaser Esam Hamdi

Citizenship: US.

DOB: September 26, 1980.

Arrest: Captured in late 2001 in Afghanistan, turned over to US troops.

Conviction: n/a.

Sentence: n/a.

Status: Hamdi was relocated in April 2002 from Guantanamo Bay to the stateside Navy Brig in Norfolk, Virginia. He was held there as an "enemy combatant" and released to Saudi Arabia in 2004.

Cases: *Hamdi v. Rumsfeld*, 296 F.3d 278 (4th Cir. 2002).

Charges: Authorization for Use of Military Force, Pub. L. No. 107-40, 115 Stat. 224 (Sept. 18, 2001). 28 U.S.C. § 2241: Writ of habeas corpus. Geneva Convention Relative to the Treatment of Prisoners of War, Aug. 12,

1949, 6 U.S.T. 3316, 75 U.N.T.S. 135. 18 U.S.C. § 4001(a): Limitation on detention; control of prisons.

Links to al-Qa'ida: Accused of fighting against the US in Afghanistan.

Background:

Yaser Esam Hamdi was born in Louisiana to a Saudi family. His father was employed by an oil company. Hamdi's family returned to Saudi Arabia when he was young, and Hamdi spent much of his life there. He was a student at King Fahd University of Petroleum and Minerals until 2001, when he crossed into Afghanistan to train in a Taliban camp in Kunduz province.[38]

At the end of that year, he was captured in Afghanistan and transferred into American custody. He was held at Guantanamo Bay, Cuba, until he was determined to be an American citizen; after which he was transferred to Norfolk, Virginia, and Charleston, South Carolina.[39] He was held as an enemy combatant in solitary confinement for approximately three years, but no charges were ever filed against him.[40] For most of this time, Mr. Hamdi was not allowed access to a defense lawyer.

In the Supreme Court case *Hamdi v. Rumsfeld,* the court ruled in favor of Mr. Hamdi in June 2004. The decision curbed the Executive Branch's power to indefinitely hold and interrogate detainees deemed "enemy combatants." In September 2004, Mr. Hamdi was released after an agreement with the Justice Department to deport him to Saudi Arabia, where he would accept certain travel restrictions, renounce his American citizenship, give up his right to sue the government for his detention, and not engage in terrorism.[41]

MAY 2003 — OHIO MALL PLOT

Cases: *U.S. v. Faris*, 162 Fed. Appx. 199 (4th Cir. 2005), *U.S. v. Abdi*, 498 F. Supp. 2d 1048 (S.D. Ohio 2007).

Charges: 18 U.S.C. §§ 371, 2339B: Conspiracy to provide material support to a foreign terrorist organization, 18 U.S.C. § 2339A: Providing material support to a foreign terrorist organization, 18 U.S.C. § 956: Conspiracy to provide material support to terrorists with the knowledge or intent that his support would be used to carry out a violation.

Background:

> This three-man cell, led by al-Qa'ida operative and truck driver Iyman Faris, made plans to blow up a shopping mall in Columbus, Ohio. Faris was arrested in 2003, while Nuradin Abdi was arrested in 2004, both on charges of giving material support to al-Qa'ida.[42] The third man, Christopher Paul, was arrested in 2007, for conspiracy to provide material support to terrorists, but not in connection with the mall plot. While talks were underway about this mall plot, Iyman Faris was simultaneously on direct assignment for Khalid Sheikh Mohammed for al-Qa'ida target selection in the US.[43] Faris is connected to another Khalid Sheikh Mohammed-directed plot, for which he collected materials to bomb the Brooklyn Bridge in New York and derail trains in Washington, DC.[44] Faris also allegedly attended an al-Qa'ida training camp in 2000. Faris was sentenced to 20 in prison, and Abdi was given 10 years.

Iyman Faris

AKA: Mohammad Rauf.

Citizenship: naturalized US (born in Kashmir, Pakistan).

DOB: June 4, 1969.

Arrest: Captured in March 2003.

Charges: Conspiracy; Providing material support to al-Qa'ida.

Conviction: Conspiracy; Providing material support to al-Qa'ida.

Sentence: 20 years imprisonment.[45]

Status: Serving sentence at Florence ADMAX, Florence, Colorado.

Links to al-Qa'ida: Trained with al-Qa'ida operatives and supported al-Qa'ida missions.

Background:

> Iyman Faris, otherwise known as Mohammad Rauf, was born in Pakistan and moved to the US in 1994. Mr. Faris married an American woman in 1995 and became a naturalized American citizen at the end of 1999; he was employed as a licensed truck driver and permitted to transport and access hazardous materials.[46] He trained with al-Qa'ida in Afghanistan in 2000 and met Usama bin Laden.[47] In a 2002 meeting with senior al-Qa'ida officials, he was directed to investigate the feasibility of severing the Brooklyn Bridge's cables using gas cutters and derailing trains.[48] He conducted his mission and concluded that an attack on such targets was unlikely to be successful, which he signaled by messaging the al-Qa'ida leader "The weather is too hot."[49] After an FBI investigation, Mr. Faris was arrested for conspiracy and providing material support to al-Qa'ida. He pled guilty to the charges and was convicted.

Nuradin Abdi

Citizenship: Somalia.

DOB: 1982.

Arrest: November 28, 2003.

Charges: Planned to blow up a shopping mall in Columbus and conspired with Ayman Faris, Christopher "Kenyatta" Paul, and others to carry out the bombing. He was also charged with fraud and misuse of documents for falsely applying for asylum in the US.

Conviction: July 31, 2007, on one count of conspiring to support terrorists. Because of the plea, the other charges against him were dropped.

Sentence: 10 years imprisonment followed by deportation to Somalia.

Status: Imprisoned in a federal penitentiary in Marion, IL.

Links to al-Qa'ida: Engaged in terrorist training and conspired to perform terrorist acts.

Background:

Nuradin Abdi was a Somali who entered the US on a false passport in 1995 and entered illegally again from Canada two years later.[50] Mr. Abdi was granted asylum in the US in January 1999 based on false statements, which was then revoked in January 2003.[51] In 1999, Mr. Abdia trained in Ethiopia in "radio usage, guns, guerilla warfare, and bombs," although he claimed on immigration paperwork that he was traveling to Germany to visit family and then to Saudi Arabia for religious reasons.[52] He conspired with Christopher Paul and Iyman Faris to bomb a shopping mall in Ohio.[53]

Christopher "Kenyatta" Paul

AKA: Abdulmalek Kenyatta.

Citizenship: US.

DOB: March 1, 1964.

Arrest: April 11, 2007.

Charges: Conspiring to support terrorists; conspiring to use a WMD and providing support to terrorists.

Conviction: In a plea agreement for planning terrorist attacks.

Sentence: 20 years imprisonment.

Status: Imprisoned at the FCI in Terre Haute, Indiana.

Links to al-Qa'ida: al-Qa'ida member who trained with the organization and plotted attacks.

Background:

Paul was originally born "Paul Kenyatta Laws," but changed his name to Abdulmalek Kenyatta in 1989, and then to Christopher Paul in 1994. Ten different aliases were listed on his original indictment.[54] Paul graduated from Worthington High School in Ohio in 1983, and converted to Islam in the late 1980s. He joined al-Qa'ida in the early 1990s and traveled to Pakistan and Afghanistan to receive weapons training. Paul became a trusted member of al- Qa'ida, and traveled across numerous countries on their behalf.[55]

Paul was investigated over the next four years as he traveled to at least eight countries on three continents. Although specifics were never given, Paul had a list of targets including US embassies. On April 16, 1999, Paul traveled to Germany and engaged in bomb training with a small cell. When Paul returned to the US, he stocked up with battle materials, such as night vision goggles. He also transferred money to his contact in Germany from a US banking institution.[56] Paul has a wife and a 13-year old daughter who is home-schooled.[57]

Paul was officially arrested and indicted on April 11, 2007. On June 3, 2008, Paul accepted a plea deal and pled guilty to planning terrorist attacks in the US and in Europe.[58] The US government made a deal to dismiss two counts of the indictment on the condition that Paul plead guilty to the charge of conspiracy to use WMD.[59] Paul's guilty plea confirmed that between 1993 and 1995, he traveled to war-zones in the Balkans to fight. He also led military training at an Ohio state park at the request of al-Qa'ida officials.[60] Between 1999 until 2000, he was involved in an intricate conspiracy to deploy a weapon of mass destruction. After pleading guilty, Paul was sentenced to 20 years in prison on February 26, 2009.[61]

JUNE 2003— NORTHERN VIRGINIA JIHAD CELL

Cases: *U.S. v. Royer et al.*, Indictment, US District Court, Eastern District of
  Virginia.
Charges: 18 U.S.C. § 371: Conspiracy; 18 U.S.C. § 960: Commencing an
  Expedition Against a Friendly Nation; 18 U.S.C. § 924(b): Receipt of
  Firearm or Ammunition with Cause to Believe a Felony will be Committed
  Therewith; 18 U.S.C. § 924(g): Acquisition of Firearm after Arrival from

Foreign Country with Intent to Engage in Crime of Violence; 18 U.S.C. § 924(h): Transfer of a Firearm for Use in a Crime of Violence; 18 U.S.C. § 924(o): Conspiracy to Possess and Use a Firearm in Connection with a Crime of Violence;18 U.S.C. § 1001(a): False Official Statement 18 U.S.C. § 924(c): Using a Firearm in Connection with a Crime of Violence.

Background:

On June 27, 2003, 11 men (including nine US citizens) were indicted for conspiring to train for and commit violent jihad overseas. They planned to use US passports "in order to travel more easily" to target Indian interests abroad. [62] Some went to Pakistan to train with the LeT, a Kashmiri separatist group.[63] Later on, Randall Royer and Masoud Khan were charged with conspiring to wage war against the US and conspiring to provide material support to al-Qa'ida and the Taliban.[64]

Randall Royer

AKA: Ismail.

Citizenship: US.

DOB: 1973.

Arrest: July 2003.

Conviction: On two-counts: using and discharging a firearm during and in relation to a crime of violence; and carrying an explosive during the commission of a felony. He entered guilty pleas in the US District Court for the Eastern District of Virginia. Under the terms of their plea agreements, both Royer and al-Hamdi were required to cooperate fully with the government in the prosecution of other individuals associated with the Virginia jihad network.

Sentence: 20 years.

Status: Indicted on July 23, 2003, for conspiring to engage in terrorist activities. Held in US Penitentiary Florence ADMAX.

Links to al-Qa'ida: Helped others enter LeT camps.

Background:

Randall Royer converted to Islam in St. Louis just after the 1992 Rodney King riots in Los Angeles. When Royer left St. Louis to study at American University in Washington, DC, he also worked for the nation's largest Muslim civil rights group, the Council on American-Islamic Relations (CAIR). In 1994, he quit college for a semester to enlist with Bosnian forces warring with the Serbians. Royer acknowledged that he helped other jihadists gain entry to the LeT training camp following a meeting on September 16, 2001.[65]

Masoud Ahmad Khan
Citizenship: US.
DOB: 1970.
Arrest: June 2003.
Conviction: On June 15, 2004, of conspiracy to levy war against the US and conspiracy to contribute services to the Taliban.
Sentence: Life imprisonment.
Status: Serving life in prison at US Penitentiary in Marion, IL.
Links to al-Qa'ida: Conspired to fight against the US and support al-Qa'ida and the Taliban.

Hammad Abdur-Raheem
Citizenship: US.
Conviction: Guilty.

Donald Thomas Surratt
Citizenship: US.
Conviction: Guilty.

Caliph Basha Ibn Abdur-Raheem
Citizenship: US.
Conviction: Guilty.

Mohammed Aatique
Citizenship: Pakistani national with H-1 visa.
Conviction: Guilty.

Yong Ki Kwon
Citizenship: US, born in South Korea.
Conviction: Guilty.

Sabri Benkhala
Citizenship: US.
Conviction: Acquitted of involvement, but found guilty on lesser charges of perjury, obstruction of justice, and making false statements to the FBI.[66]

Seifullah Chapman
Citizenship: US.
Conviction: Guilty.

Khwaja Mahmood Hasan
Citizenship: US, born in Pakistan.
Conviction: Guilty.

Ibrahim Ahmed
Citizenship: Yemen, non-resident US alien.
Conviction: Guilty.

JUNE 2003— GEORGE W. BUSH ASSASSINATION PLOT

Ahmed Omar Abu Ali
Citizenship: US.
DOB: 1981.
Arrest: June 2003.
Conviction: In 2005, for providing material support to the al-Qa'ida terrorist
    network, and for conspiracy to assassinate President George W. Bush.[67]
Sentence: 30 years imprisonment; re-sentenced in November 2009 to life in
    prison.[68]
Charges: Two counts of providing material support to terrorists, two counts of
    providing material support to al-Qa'ida, one count of contributing goods
    and services to al-Qa'ida, one count of receiving services from al-Qa'ida,
    conspiracy to assassinate the president, conspiracy to hijack an aircraft,
    and conspiracy to destroy an aircraft.
Status: Imprisoned at ADX, Florence, Colorado.
Cases: *U.S. v. Ahmed Omar Abu Ali*, 2011 U.S. App. LEXIS 2058 (4th Cir.
    2011).
Charges: USA PATRIOT Act (18 U.S.C. §2339B); 18 U.S.C. § 1751: conspiracy
    to assassinate the President; 49 U.S.C. § 46502(a)(2): conspiracy to
    commit aircraft piracy.
Background:
    Ali was born in 1981 in Houston, Texas, and raised in Falls Church,
    Virginia. He attended the Islamic Saudi Academy in Alexandria, and
    in 1999 began the electrical engineering program at the University of
    Maryland. He prayed at the Dar al-Hijrah Islamic Center in Falls Church,
    Virginia, the same mosque where Anwar al-Awlaki was an imam.[69] In
    the spring of 2000, Ali left the University of Maryland for the Islamic
    University of Medina in Saudi Arabia in order to study Islamic theology.
    While there, he met Zubayr al-Rimi and Ali Faqasi al-Ghamdi and acted
    as a senior staff member of the Dar al-Hijrah Center.[70]

Ali communicated to co-conspirators sometime in September 2002 that he wished to join al-Qa'ida as a "planner of terrorist operations like Muhammad Atta."[71] Between 2002 and 2003, he engaged in various activities for and with members of al-Qa'ida, including receiving cash payments to purchase items like cell phones and laptops; discussing the possibility of Ali leading an al-Qa'ida cell in the US; and undergoing explosives, document forgery, and weapons training.[72] Ali also discussed a plot to assassinate President George W. Bush by shooting from close range or remotely detonating a car bomb.[73]

Investigators alleged that Ali made contact with al-Qa'ida while studying at the Islamic University of Medina after they discovered incriminating items inside his Falls Church home.[74] Ahmed Omar Abu Ali was arrested in Saudi Arabia in June 2003 but was not transferred to US custody until February 2005. In Saudi Arabia, he signed confessions and made statements admitting to a plot against President George W. Bush and to having ties to an al-Qa'ida cell. He was extradited to the US in February 2005. The case turned the judiciary's focus upon the US "Extraordinary Rendition" program.[75]

2004— AHMED COUSINS

Cases: *U.S. v. Khaleel Ahmed*, 2008 U.S. Dist. LEXIS 106364 (N.D. Ohio Dec. 31, 2008); *U.S. v. Zubair Ahmed,* 2008 U.S. Dist. LEXIS 100084 (N.D. Ohio Nov. 21, 2008); *U.S. v. El-Hindi, 2009*, U.S. Dist. LEXIS 80988 (N.D. Ohio May 15, 2009); *U.S. v. Mohammad Zaki Amawi, Marwan Othman El-Hindi, Wassim I. Mazloum, Zubair A. Ahmed, and Khaleel Ahmed*. The US District Court for the Northern District of Ohio, Western Division. Superseding indictment, February 7, 2007.

Charges: 18 U.S.C. § 956: Conspiracy to kill and maim individuals outside the US, including members of the US military serving in Iraq and Afghanistan; 18 U.S.C. § 2339A: Conspiracy to provide material support to a terrorist organization.

Background:

Zubair and Khaleel Ahmed, both American citizens from Chicago, traveled to Egypt in May 2004 "with the intent of engaging in acts that would result in the murder or maiming of US military forces in Iraq or Afghanistan."[76] When the cousins returned to the US in July 2004, they solicited and received weapons and counter-surveillance training from an individual in Cleveland, Ohio.[77]

As part of the conspiracy, the Ahmed cousins began to communicate in codes to conceal their intent to damage American military targets and kill personnel.[78] They also purchased firearms, visited a firing range, learned about gunsmithing, and distributed various weapons manuals and videos of attacks on American military targets.[79]

Zubair Ahmed
Citizenship: US.
DOB: 1979.
Arrest: February 2007.
Conviction: In US District Court for the Northern District of Ohio, of one count of conspiracy to provide material support or resources to terrorists.
Sentence: 10 years imprisonment on July 12, 2010.
Status: Imprisoned.
Links to al-Qa'ida: Conspired to kill US military forces overseas.

Khaleel Ahmed
Citizenship: US.
DOB: 1977.
Arrest: February 2007.
Conviction: In US District Court for the Northern District of Ohio, of one count of conspiracy to provide material support or resources to terrorists.
Sentence: On July 12, 2010, to 8 years and 4 months imprisonment.
Status: Imprisoned.
Links to al-Qa'ida: Conspired to kill US military forces overseas.

JULY 2005 — FOLSOM PRISON PLOT

Cases: *U.S. v. Kevin James*, U.S. District Court for the Central District of California, October 2004.
Charges: 18 U.S.C. § 2384: Conspiracy to Levy War Against the US.
Background:
   In 1997 while incarcerated in a California State Prison in Sacramento, Kevin James, a converted Muslim, founded Jam'iyyat Ul-Islam Is-Saheeh (JIS), meaning "Assembly of Authentic Muslims." James preached a jihadist message that it was the duty of Muslims to target and kill infidels

and recruited other prison inmates to join his cause.[80] James allegedly admired Usama bin Laden, and cited al-Qa'ida as his inspiration for establishing JIS[81]

Levar Washington was born in South Los Angeles. At an early age he became involved in gang activity and ultimately ended up in the custody of the California Youth Authority. Washington converted to Islam while serving time in Corcoran State Prison for robbery.[82] He was later incarcerated at High Desert State Prison, and was placed under tight security because of his violent behavior.[83] Washington reportedly met Kevin James in prison around 2004.[84]

In 2004, Washington pledged himself to James "until death by martyrdom," and James tasked Washington with establishing a JIS cell outside the prison and recruiting new members and bomb experts.[85] Washington was paroled in December 2004, and quickly recruited two alleged accomplices, Gregory Patterson and Hamad Samana, at his mosque in Inglewood, California.[86] The mosque's imam later expressed his surprise at Washington's extreme anti-American sentiment.[87]

Washington, Patterson, and Samana began to research potential targets on the Internet, including the Los Angeles Israeli Consulate, El Al Airlines, various synagogues, and American military recruitment centers.[88] Between May and July of 2005, they robbed gas stations in Southern California to procure funds for firearms and other weapons.[89] When Washington was arrested in connection with the robberies, the police found a bulletproof vest and jihadist materials in his apartment, and the addresses of potential targets like the Los Angeles International Airport El Al ticket counter.[90]

Kevin James
AKA: Shakyh Shahaab Murshid.
Citizenship: US.
DOB: 1976.
Arrest: July 5, 2005.
Charges: Conspiracy to levy war against the US Government through terrorism; conspiracy to kill members of the US Government uniformed services; conspiracy to kill foreign officials; interference with commerce by robbery; conspiracy to possess and discharge firearms in furtherance

of crimes of violence; using and carrying a firearm in connection with a crime of violence; aiding and abetting.[91]

Conviction: December 14, 2007, of conspiracy to levy war against the US through terrorism.

Sentence: 16 years in federal prison.[92]

Status: Imprisoned in Federal Correction Institute, Terre Haute, Indiana.

Links to al-Qa'ida: al-Qa'ida and Usama bin Laden were his inspirations for creating Jam'iyyat Ul-Islam Is-Saheeh.

Levar Washington

AKA: Abdur Rahman.

Citizenship: US.

DOB: 1980.

Arrest: July 5, 2005, for armed robbery.

Charges: Conspiracy to levy war against the US Government through terrorism; conspiracy to kill members of the US government uniformed services; conspiracy to kill foreign officials; interference with commerce by robbery; conspiracy to possess and discharge firearms in furtherance of crimes of violence; using and carrying a firearm in connection with a crime of violence; aiding and abetting.[93]

Conviction: Conspiracy to levy war against the US through terrorism; conspiracy to possess and discharge firearms. Washington was sentenced to 22 years in prison on August 25, 2008, on related robbery and weapons charges.[94]

Sentence: 22 years imprisonment.

Status: Imprisoned in US Penitentiary, Lewisburg, Pennsylvania.

Links to al-Qa'ida: Pledged loyalty to James' al-Qa'ida inspired group.

Gregory Patterson

Citizenship: US, born in Pakistan.

DOB: 1984.

Arrest: July 5, 2005, for armed robbery.

Charges: Conspiracy to levy war the against the US Government through terrorism; conspiracy to kill members of the US Government uniformed services; conspiracy to kill foreign officials; interference with commerce by robbery; conspiracy to possess and discharge firearms in furtherance of crimes of violence; using and carrying a firearm in connection with a crime of violence; aiding and abetting.[95]

Conviction: Of conspiring to levy war against the US through terrorism and conspiring to possess and discharge firearms.[96]

Sentence: In July 2008 to 12.5 years in prison.[97]

Status: Imprisoned.

Links to al-Qa'ida: Planned attacks for al-Qa'ida inspired group.

Hammad Samana

Citizenship: US, born in Pakistan.

DOB: 1984.

Arrest: August 2, 2005.

Charges: Conspiracy to levy war against the US Government through terrorism; conspiracy to kill members of the US government uniformed services; conspiracy to kill foreign officials; interference with commerce by robbery; conspiracy to possess and discharge firearms in furtherance of crimes of violence; using and carrying a firearm in connection with a crime of violence; aiding and abetting.[98]

Conviction: Ruled mentally unfit to stand trial.[99]

Status: Receiving care at a federal prison facility as of 2008.[100]

Links to al-Qa'ida: Planned attacks for al-Qa'ida-inspired group.

SEPTEMBER 1, 2004 — PLOT TO BOMB CHICAGO FEDERAL COURTHOUSE

Gale Nettles

Citizenship: US.

DOB: 1940.

Arrest: August 5, 2004.

Conviction: September 2002, of attempting to bomb a federal government building.

Sentence: September 15, 2005, to 160 years imprisonment.

Status: Deceased.

Cases: *In re Nettles*, 394 F.3d 1001 (7th Cir. 2005); *U.S. v. Nettles*, 400 F. Supp. 2d 1084, 1086 (N.D. Ill. 2005).

Charges: 18 U.S.C. §§ 844(f)(1) and 844 (i): Attempting to damage and destroy a federal building by a fire or explosion; 18 U.S.C. § 2339A: Attempting to provide material support to terrorism; 18 U.S.C. § 471: Fraudulently making, forging and counterfeiting US Federal Reserve Notes; 18 U.S.C. § 473: Selling, exchanging, transferring, and delivering false, forged, counterfeited, and altered US Federal Reserve Notes, with the intent that the same be passed, published and used as true and genuine.

Links to al-Qa'ida: Believed he was contacting an al-Qa'ida operative who turned out to be an informant.

Background:

Gale Nettles was a native US citizen who was apprehended by the FBI following a sting operation. Nettles had plotted to destroy the Everett McKinley Dirksen Federal Building while serving a counterfeiting sentence in a Mississippi federal prison.[101] Nettles had discussed his plot with fellow inmates who notified the authorities about his intentions. The FBI began surveillance on Nettles following his release from prison. Several sting operations incriminated him, culminating in his arrest in August of 2004.[102]

FEBRUARY 2004— RYAN ANDERSON

Ryan Gibson Anderson

AKA: Amir Abdul Rashid.

Citizenship: US.

DOB: 1978.

Arrest: February 12, 2004.

Conviction: Pled not guilty by reason of insanity, offering the defense of bipolar disorder and Asperger's syndrome. The defense also claimed entrapment by the US government.

Sentence: Found guilty by a military jury on September 3, 2004. Anderson was demoted to the rank of private, given a dishonorable discharge, and was sentenced to life imprisonment with a possibility of eligibility for parole.[103]

Status: Imprisoned.

Cases: Unknown.

Charges: Five counts of attempting to aid and to provide intelligence to the enemy.

Links to al-Qa'ida: Sought to join al-Qa'ida, supported the organization with intelligence.

Background:[104]

Ryan Anderson lived in Everett, Washington, and graduated from Washington State University in 2002 with a degree in Middle Eastern military history. He had converted to Islam several years earlier and adopted the name Amir Abdul Rashid. After graduation, he enlisted with the Washington National Guard and was a member of a tank crew. He earned the rank of specialist.

Anderson was caught when an amateur anti-terrorist Internet monitor, Shannen Rossmiller, who was also a city judge in Montana, alerted the FBI of her suspicions. The FBI, US Army, and Department of Justice participated in a sting operation monitoring Anderson's activities in chat rooms and on Islamist Jihad websites.

Anderson was videotaped offering sketches of M1A1 and M1A2 tanks, a computer disk with his identifying information and photo, and information about US Army weapons systems, including the exact round needed to penetrate armored Humvees, to persons he believed to be al-Qa'ida operatives. Anderson was also caught on surveillance tape stating, "I wish to desert from the US Army. I wish to defect from the US. I wish to join al-Qa'ida, train its members, and conduct terrorist attacks."[105]

APRIL 2004— MOHAMMED BABAR

Mohammed Junaid Babar
Citizenship: US, born in Pakistan.
DOB: 1975.
Arrest: April 2004.
Conviction: Pled guilty on June 3, 2004.
Sentence: Released on parole in 2008 after 4.5 years imprisonment due to time served on account of his cooperation.[106,107]
Status: Indicted on June 3, 2004; sentence reduced in December 2010.
Cases: *U.S. v. Babar*, 04-CRIM 528 in US District Court, S.D.N.Y.
Charges: Five counts of providing, and conspiring to provide, money and supplies to al-Qa'ida terrorists fighting in Afghanistan against the US, and the Northern Alliance. 18 U.S.C. §§ 2339A, 2339B, 2, and 3238. 50 U.S.C. § 1705(B). 31 CFR §§ 595.204, and 595.205.
Links to al-Qa'ida: Provided supplies to al-Qa'ida members in Pakistan, met with al-Qa'ida officials, trained Mohammad Sidique Khan.
Background:
Babar moved to the US from Pakistan when he was 2 years old.[108] He attended an all-boys military boarding school on Long Island. Babar later attended St. Johns University in New York where he studied pharmacology before dropping out. Babar joined a number of groups,

including the al-Muhajiroun. Babar's mother was working in the World Trade Center on the 9th floor and survived the 9/11 terrorist attacks.

Within one week after the attacks, Babar decided to move to Pakistan to fight against the US in Afghanistan.[109] Over 2 1/2 years, he supplied high-ranking al-Qa'ida officials in South Waziristan with money, sleeping bags, night-vision goggles, socks and ponchos. While in Pakistan, Babar founded a training camp where Mohammad Sidique Khan learned to make the bombs that were used in the July 7, 2005, transportation attacks on the metro and bus in the UK.[110] Babar also met with numerous high-ranking al-Qa'ida members, including Abdul Hadi and Omar Sheikh.

Babar admitted to assisting Mohammad Sidique Khan and having knowledge of other terrorist plots in the UK. He was also the star witness in the 2006 Crevice trial against six men charged with planning to blow up several targets in Britain, including nightclubs and shopping centers.[111] Babar had been providing support to the cell during their planning. Babar also testified in the case against Momin Khawaja in Ottawa, Canada, in 2008.

On December 10, 2010, at a hearing in the US District Court for the Southern District of New York, Docket No. 04 Cr. 0528, the court released Babar based on time served (4 1/2 years) with supervised probation for 10 years and a $500 payment to the court. The government supported the case for a reduced sentence based on Babar's exceptional cooperation and testimony used in several other terrorist cases. The early release and sentence reduction has caused much speculation about Babar's actual involvement with the US Intelligence Community, and scrutiny from the British who hold Babar responsible for the July 7, 2005, bombings.[112] Babar now lives freely in the US.

MAY 2005— RONALD GRECULA

Ronald Allen Grecula
Citizenship: US.
DOB: Currently 74 years old.
Arrest: May, 2005.
Conviction: Pled guilty on September 21, 2006 to violating 18 U.S.C. §
   2339B; count two was dismissed.

Sentence: Five years in federal prison without parole, and three years of supervised release following prison.

Status: Indicted on June 16, 2005; superseding indictment on August 8, 2006; Grecula was released January 5, 2010.

Cases: *U.S. v. Grecula*, Criminal Docket No. H-05-257-S, US District Court for the Southern District of Texas.

Charges: Attempting to provide material support and resources to al-Qa'ida; 18 U.S.C. §§ 2339B and 2; additionally charged with distribution of a controlled substance. 21 U.S.C. §§ 841(a)(1), 841(b)(1)(c), and 846.

Links to al-Qa'ida: Met with agents posing as al-Qa'ida members to discuss supplying them with bombs to be used in the US.

Background:

Between April and May 2005, Grecula was involved in negotiations with an undercover FBI agent whom he believed to be a member of al-Qa'ida. Grecula attempted to build and sell an explosive device.[113] He also made comments pertaining to his ability to train pilots for al-Qa'ida missions. On May 20, 2005, Grecula arrived in Houston, Texas, to attend a meeting with the people he presumed to be al-Qa'ida members.[114] Grecula met with the undercover agents for an hour in an AmeriSuites Hotel and was videotaped indicating that he was willing to build and sell an explosive device to be used by al-Qa'ida against Americans. During a search of his residence, a mercury switch and lithium nitrate were discovered.[115]

JUNE 23, 2006 — SEAS OF DAVID CELL, AKA LIBERTY CITY SEVEN

Cases: *U.S. v. Batiste*, Not Reported in F.Supp.2d, 2007 WL 5303053, S.D.Fla., November 07, 2007 (NO. 06-20373-CR).

Arrest: All men arrested on June 23, 2006, during an FBI raid on an abandoned warehouse in Liberty City, Miami, which was used as a meeting spot for the group.

Indicted: June 22, 2006, in the US District Court for the Southern District of Florida in Miami.

Charges: Violation of 18 U.S.C. § 2339A, 18 U.S.C. § 844(n), 18 U.S.C. § 2384; The indictment charged the defendant with four counts: 1: conspiracy to provide material support to a foreign terrorist organization, namely al-Qa'ida (18 U.S.C.§2339A(b)(1)); 2: conspiracy to provide material support and resources to terrorists (18 U.S.C. §2339A(b)(1)); 3: conspiracy to maliciously damage and destroy property by means of an explosive (18

U.S.C. §844(n)); and 4: conspiring to levy war against the government of the US (18 U.S.C. §2384).

Background:

Beginning in November 2005, Batiste was in contact with FBI informants posing as al-Qa'ida members. Batiste told the informants that he was planning on building an Islamic Army in order to wage jihad against the US. He expressed interest in attending al-Qa'ida training for his "soldiers" in order to wage a full ground war and "kill all the devils we can."[116] Batiste and his co-conspirators attempted to receive support from al-Qa'ida in their mission to blow up the former Sears Tower in Chicago.[117] In another meeting, Batiste provided the informant with a list of materials needed for his plot to take down the Sears Tower, including radios, binoculars, bullet proof vests, firearms, vehicles, and $50,000 cash.[118]

In 2006, Batiste, Patrick Abraham, Naudimar Herrera, Burson Augustin, Lyglenson Lemorin, and Rothschild Augustine met with an FBI informant believing the individual was a member of al-Qa'ida, where they swore allegiance to the terrorist group.[119] As a group, they vowed to destroy FBI buildings in the US and provided the informant with photos of Miami's FBI building, photos and video of the James Lawrence King Federal Justice Building, federal courthouse buildings, the Federal Detention Center, and the facilities of the Miami Police Department.[120]

The FBI acknowledged that the group never had any actual contact with al-Qa'ida members. Many people criticized the police for their infiltration and eventual arrest of the men. The men were all unemployed, semi-employed, or even homeless; and seemed to be very unlikely to be capable of actually following through with any of their ideas.[121] The deputy director of the FBI described the group's plot as more "… aspirational than operational."[122] The group's ideology came from a mix of Christianity, Judaism, and Islam, but the Bible was the text they studied most.[123] The strongest evidence for the government's case came from paid informants working for the FBI.

Narseal Batiste
AKA: Brother Naz, Prince Manna.
Citizenship: US.
DOB: 1974.

Conviction: On all four counts.

Sentence: 162 months in prison, followed by 35 years of supervised release

Status: In prison, expected release date is March 25, 2018.

Links to al-Qa'ida: Swore allegiance and solicited support from al-Qa'ida.

Patrick Abraham

AKA: Brother Pat.

Citizenship: Illegal US Immigrant from Haiti.

DOB: 1967 in Haiti.

Conviction: On counts 1, 2, and 3.

Sentence: 112.5 months in prison, followed by 15 years of supervised release.

Status: to be released August 20, 2014.

Links to al-Qa'ida: Swore allegiance to al-Qa'ida.

Stanley Grant Phanor

AKA: Brother Sunni, Sunny.

Citizenship: US legal resident from Haiti.

DOB: 1975, arrived in the US legally in 1996.

Conviction: On counts 1 and 2.

Sentence: 96 months in prison, followed by 15 years of supervised release.

Status: Imprisoned, expected release date is April 30, 2016.

Links to al-Qa'ida: Swore allegiance to al-Qa'ida.

Rothschild Augustine

AKA: Brother Rot.

Citizenship: US.

Conviction: On counts 1 and 2.

Sentence: 84 months in prison, followed by 10 years of supervised release

Status: Imprisoned.[124]

Links to al-Qa'ida: Swore allegiance to al-Qa'ida.

Burson Augustin

AKA: Brother B.

Citizenship: US.

DOB: 1985.

Conviction: On counts 1 and 2.

Sentence: 72 months in prison, followed by 10 years of supervised release.

Status: Imprisoned, expected release in September 2012.

Links to al-Qa'ida: Swore allegiance to al-Qa'ida.

Naudimar Herrera
AKA: Brother Naudy.
Citizenship: US Citizen.
DOB: 1984.
Status: Acquitted on May 12, 2009.
Links to al-Qa'ida: n/a.[125]

Lyglenson Lemorin
AKA: Brother Levi, Brother Levi-El.
Citizenship: US permanent resident from Haiti since 1993.
DOB: 1975 in Haiti, family moved to the US in 1986.
Acquitted: December 13, 2007.
Released: December 14, 2007.
Status: Acquitted, deported to Haiti January 20, 2011.[126]
Links to al-Qa'ida: n/a.

MARCH 3, 2006— NORTH CAROLINA SUV ATTACK

Mohammed Reza Taheri-Azar
Citizenship: US, born in Iran.
DOB: May 5, 1983.
Arrest: March 3, 2006 after turning himself in to police following his attack.
Conviction: Pled guilty on August 12, 2008, to nine counts of attempted first-
degree murder.[127]
Sentence: August 8, 2008, to 33 years imprisonment.
Status: Indicted on May 1, 2006, currently imprisoned.
Cases: *State of North Carolina v. Taheri-Azar, Mohammed Reza*, 06-CRS
51275.
Charges: Nine counts of assault with a deadly weapon with intent to kill or
inflicting serious injury; 18 U.S.C. § 2332.
Links to al-Qa'ida: Admired Mohammad Atta.
Background:
On March 3, 2006, Taheri-Azar drove a rented Jeep Cherokee through
a crowded area known as "The Pit" on the campus of the University
of North Carolina in Chapel Hill, North Carolina. The Pit is an area
busy with pedestrian traffic and also a popular meeting spot for student
organizations. The barricades, which normally prevent vehicular traffic
from entering the area, were absent on that day. Taheri-Azar drove the
Jeep at a speed of 40-45 miles per hour, striking nine pedestrians. Six

of those struck were taken to the hospital for treatment. None of those struck was seriously injured.[128]

Taheri-Azar drove from the scene of the attack to a nearby city road and called 911 to turn himself in.[129] He told authorities that his reasons for the attack were outlined in a letter that would be found in his bedroom. Taheri-Azar then waited for authorities to arrive to take him into custody. In the letter, Taheri-Azar outlined that he wanted to punish the US for its immoral activities around the world and avenge the deaths of Muslims worldwide. In another letter, Taheri-Azar stated that he wanted to follow in the footsteps of one of his role-models, Mohamed Atta. During the trial, Taheri-Azar claimed to be happy for the chance to share the law of Allah.[130]

Taheri-Azar was said to have been a serious and often talkative student in the classroom. He was briefly president of the psychology club at the University of North Carolina. Fellow Muslims described him as unorthodox in his practice of Islam; he would not pray in Arabic nor pray in the direction of Mecca. Taheri-Azar dropped out of college for a small period of time before returning to finish his degree. In a letter, he explained that he wanted to show the world that "Allah's servants are very intelligent."[131] Taheri-Azar also wrote that he originally intended to purchase a handgun for the act, but was unable to. Taheri-Azar also responded to a news station's request for an interview. In the letter Taheri-Azar wrote:

> *Allah gives permission in the Koran for the followers of Allah to attack those who have raged war against them, with the expectation of eternal paradise in case of martyrdom and/or living one's life in obedience of all of Allah's commandments found throughout the Koran's 114 chapters...*[132]

JULY 28, 2006—JEWISH FEDERATION OF GREATER SEATTLE SHOOTING

Naveed Afzal Haq
Citizenship: US.
DOB: September 23, 1975.
Arrest: July 28, 2006.

Conviction: Found guilty, pled not guilty by reason of insanity.

Sentence: On January 14, 2010, sentenced to life without parole plus 120 years.

Status: Imprisoned.

Cases: *State of Washington v. Haq*; No. 06-1-06658-4 SEA.

Charges: Murder in the first degree with a firearms, RCW (A.32.030(1)(a), RCW 9.41.010; Malicious harassment with a firearm, RCW 9A.36.080(1) (a)(b) or (c); Burglary in the first degree with a firearm, RCW 9A.52.020, RCW 10.95.020(11)(c); Attempted murder in the first degree with a firearm, RCW 9A.28.020; Unlawful imprisonment with a firearm, malicious harassment with a firearm, RCW 9.94A.510(3).

Links to al-Qa'ida: No known links.

Background:

Although Haq's family was active within the Muslim community, and his father established the city's local Islamic center, Haq was never an open or devout Muslim. In 2005, Haq was baptized as a Christian and disavowed Islam. Haq stopped attending his Bible groups several months later. Several weeks before the shooting, Haq met with a senior member of his father's Islamic center. Haq had graduated from high school and enrolled in dentistry school at the University of Pennsylvania, where he later dropped out. He then got his degree in electrical engineering from Washington State University but never held steady employment, and was unemployed at the time of the shooting.[133] Haq was arrested for indecent exposure in 2006 at a mall in Kennewick, Washington, where he also stood on a fountain and harassed women at a make-up counter. At the time of the shooting, Haq was not known to be in contact with any friends and was taking medication for bi-polar disorder.

On July 28, 2006, Haq gained access to the Jewish Federation of Greater Seattle building after holding a thirteen-year-old girl hostage and forcing her to ask to be buzzed into the building. After entering the building, Haq began shooting while yelling that he was "… a Muslim American, angry at Israel."[134] Haq shot six women, killing one and critically injuring another. The shooting came a day after the FBI had warned Jewish organizations nationwide to be on alert after Hezbollah leaders in Lebanon and al-Qa'ida's second in command urged that the war raging in the Middle East be carried to the US .[135] Haq reportedly told operators in a 911 call during the shooting, "These are Jews. I want these Jews to get out."[136] He also demanded that the US leave Israel.[137] Haq eventually told the 911 operator that he would surrender, and left the federation building with his hands on his head; and he was arrested immediately.

MARCH 2006— GEORGIA MEN PLOT ATTACK

Cases: *U.S. v. Ahmed*, Not Reported in F.Supp.2d, 2009 WL 1370936, N.D.Ga., May 14, 2009 (NO. 1:06-CR-0147WSDGGB); *U.S. v. Sadequee*, Slip Copy, 2009 WL 3785566, N.D.Ga., November 10, 2009 (NO. 1:06-CR-147-WSD).

Charges: Conspiracy to provide material support to terrorists, providing and attempting to provide material support to terrorists, conspiracy to provide material support to a designated foreign terrorist organization, and attempting to provide material support to a designated foreign terrorist organization, 18 U.S.C. §§ 956, 2332b, 2339A(a), 2, and 2339B(a) (1); Making materially false statements in connection with an ongoing federal terrorism investigation, 18 U.S.C. § 1001.

Background:

Syed Haris Ahmed immigrated to the US at age 12 and became a citizen in 2003. Ehsanul Islam Sadequee was born in Fairfax, Virginia. Both were students who had grown up in the Atlanta, Georgia, area.[138] In March 2005, Ahmed and Sadequee travelled to Toronto, Canada, to meet with Fahim Ahmad, Jahmaal James, and another person who were all targets of ongoing FBI terrorism investigations. The group had met online to discuss Islam and hypothetical attacks against the US.[139] Ahmed and Sadequee were believed to have been inspired by the film *Paradise Now*, and were thought to be inquiring whether they would be able to hide out in Canada after an attack was made on the US. The group discussed what they believed to be suitable places in the US for a terrorist attack, including army bases and oil refineries.

In April 2005, after Ahmed and Sadequee's visit to Canada, the two men recorded what are described as "casing" videos of the Washington, DC area, including the Capitol, World Bank headquarters, and fuel storage tanks. The men sent the videos to their co-conspirators in Canada and to Younis Tsouli.[140]

In July 2005, Ahmed travelled to Pakistan to study in an Islamic religious school and then to obtain paramilitary training with the purpose of engaging in future terrorist acts. Ahmed intended to learn and fight with

LeT. While in Pakistan, Ahmed met with Aabid Hussein Khan to seek help with his plan to obtain paramilitary training. Ahmed was unable to obtain paramilitary training and returned to the US in August 2005.[141] He was questioned at the airport about other foreign travels and made false statements to the authorities about his trip to Canada and Pakistan.

In August 2005, Sadequee travelled to Bangladesh to wed, continue his schooling, and obtain training for terrorist activities. He was questioned at the airport and made false statements about his previous trip to Canada, stating that he had traveled to Canada by himself and had stayed with an aunt. Sadequee concealed a visitor's map of the DC area in his luggage, which included all the potential targets that the men had videotaped in April.[142] While both men were away, they continued to have contact with each other and other terrorist conspirators, including Tsouli and Mirsad Bektasevic.

In June of 2006, a series of raids took place in Toronto, Canada, which resulted in the arrest of 18 people (the "Toronto 18") for terrorist activities, including Fahim Ahmad and Jahmaal James.[143] Ahmed and Sadequee's ties to the Canadian group helped lead to the arrest of the Toronto 18.

Ehsanul Islam Sadequee

AKA: Shifa.

Citizenship: US.

DOB: July 30, 1986.

Arrest: April 17, 2006, in Bangladesh.

Conviction: Convicted on all counts August 2009, pled not guilty.

Sentence: In December 2009, sentenced to 17 years imprisonment with 30 years of supervised release after his prison term. During that period, he will have no access to the Internet.

Status: Imprisoned, to be released January 9, 2021. Extradited on April 20, 2006. Sealed indictment issued on March, 23, 2006, a superseding indictment on July 19, 2006, and another superseding indictment followed on December 9, 2008.[144]

Links to al-Qa'ida: Sought terror training in Bangladesh.

Syed Haris Ahmed

AKA: Haris.

Citizenship: US, born in Pakistan.

DOB: 1984.

Arrest: March 23, 2006.

Conviction: Pled not guilty and waived his right to a jury trial, convicted on June 9, 2009.

Sentence: In December 2009, sentenced to 13 years in prison followed by 30 years of supervised release, during which the Internet may not be accessed.

Status: Imprisoned, to be released July 19, 2017. Sealed indictment issued on March, 23, 2006, a superseding indictment on July 19, 2006, and another superseding indictment followed on December 9, 2008.[145]

Links to al-Qa'ida: Intended to train and fight with LeT.

JUNE 5, 2005 — CALIFORNIA TERROR CASE

Cases: *U.S. v. Hayat, 2005,* Case number MAG-05-0161 PAN.

Charges: Providing material support to terrorists in violation of 18 U.S.C. § 2339A; Making false statements in violation of 18 U.S.C. § 1001.

Background:

Hamid Hayat grew up in Lodi, California, where his father Umer was an ice cream truck driver.[146] The family returned to Pakistan every few years to visit; and when Hamid was in sixth grade, he was sent to live with his grandparents in Pakistan to receive religious education. Hamid returned to the US almost 10 years later, and lived with his family in Lodi. In 2002, Hamid became friends with Naseem Khan, who, unknown to Hamid, was an FBI informant for the Pakistani-Muslim community. Although Khan's focus was on two other men who were imams at the local mosque, his recorded conversations with Hamid were used by the FBI as evidence of Hamid's jihadist activities.

Between March and August of 2003, Hamid Hayat had made statements to Khan regarding his belief in violent jihad and that participation in jihad was required of every Muslim. He indicated that he had knowledge of jihadist training camps and that he had planned to receive training in such a camp after Ramadan. Between October 2003 and November

2004, Hamid lived in Pakistan while his mother received medical care.[147] During this time, Hamid also attended a jihadi training camp linked to al-Qa'ida with the intent of returning to America to commit acts of terrorism. On May 30, 2005, on a flight returning to the US, Hamid's plane was re-routed to Japan where he was questioned by the FBI. Hamid concealed the fact that he had attended a jihadist training camp. He was questioned again on June 3 and 4, and continued to conceal the fact that he had attended the training camp in Pakistan.[148] On June 4, 2005, during a taped interview, Hamid Hayat admitted to agents that he had attended a jihadist training camp in 2000 for a few days, and again attended a jihadist training camp in Pakistan during 2003 and 2004 for 3-6 months. He also admitted to returning to the US in order to wage violent jihad. FBI agents also recovered a scrapbook filled with articles from extremist groups in Pakistan that supported Usama bin Laden, the Taliban, and espoused anti-American beliefs. Hamid also had in his possession books written by Masood Azhar discussing the concept of violent jihad.[149]

Umer Hayat had previously made false statements to the FBI in 2003 while traveling to Pakistan. Umer had claimed to be carrying $10,000 out of the US, but was actually carrying over $28,000.[150] In 2005, Umer falsely told the FBI that he had no knowledge of jihadist training camps in Pakistan, and that Hamid had never attended a jihadist training camp.

Hamid Hayat
Citizenship: US.
DOB: September 10, 1983.
Arrest: June 5, 2005.
Conviction: Convicted on April 25, 2006, in a jury trial of one count of providing material support to a terrorist organization and three counts of making false statements to the FBI in an ongoing terrorist investigation.
Sentence: 24 years of imprisonment as of September 10, 2007.
Status: Imprisoned, projected release date May 5, 2026. Indicted June 7, 2005, superseding indictment issued on September 22, 2005.
Links to al-Qa'ida: Attended an al-Qa'ida-linked jihad training camp.

Umer Hayat
Citizenship: US, born in Pakistan.
DOB: January 5, 1958.
Arrest: June 7, 2005.

Conviction: Pled guilty on May 31, 2006, to one count of making a false statement to the FBI in April 2003.

Sentence: Time served and three years of supervised release on August 25, 2006.

Status: Free, released after being sentenced to time served August 25, 2006.[151] Indicted June 7, 2005, superseding indictment issued on September 22, 2005.

Links to al-Qa'ida: Son spent two years in an affiliated training camp, about which he made false statements to the FBI.

DECEMBER 8, 2006— ILLINOIS BOMB PLOT

Derrick Shareef

AKA: Talib Abu Salam Ibn Shareef.

Citizenship: US.

DOB: 1984.

Arrest: December 8, 2006.

Conviction: Pled guilty.

Sentence: 35 years imprisonment on September 30, 2008.

Status: Incarcerated until June 6, 2037 at Greenville, Illinois FCI, indicted January 4, 2007.

Cases: *U.S. v. Shareef*, 2011 U.S. Dist. LEXIS 51305 (N.D. Ill. May 13, 2011); *U.S. v. Aguilar-Huerta*, 576 F.3d 365 (7th Cir. Ill. 2009).

Charges: Attempting to damage and destroy, by means of fire or an explosive, any property used in interstate or foreign commerce, 18 U.S.C. § 844(i); Attempting to use a weapon of mass destruction against persons and property within the US, 18 U.S.C. § 2332a(a)(2)(D).

Links to al-Qa'ida: In 2003, Derrick lived with Hassan Abu Jihaad for seven months. Jihaad was a former Navy sailor found guilty of giving information to al-Qa'ida.

Background:

Derrick Shareef is an Islamic convert who, in December of 2006, was arrested for planning to set off several hand grenades in garbage cans in Rockford, Illinois.[152] Shareef was discovered after he confided to an FBI informant, William "Jameel" Chrisman, that he wanted to pursue violent jihad against the US. Shareef and the Chrisman discussed several targets before deciding on the Cherry Vale Shopping Center in Rockford, Illinois. Shareef visited the mall multiple times with Chrisman, and planned to

139

meet with another undercover FBI officer to exchange stereo equipment for four hand grenades and a handgun.[153]

On December 8, 2006, Shareef was apprehended by the FBI for attempting to commandeer the weapons. Shareef's al-Qa'ida connection comes from a seven-month stay with a former Navy sailor, Hassan Abu-Jihaad, who was found guilty of giving information to al-Qa'ida. The men roomed together in Phoenix, Arizona, where they discussed violent jihad. Shareef's family believes this is when Derrick turned to violence against the US.[154]

Shareef was originally indicted on January 4, 2007, and pled guilty on November 28, 2007, to one charge of attempting to use a weapon of mass destruction.[155] Shareef later withdrew his guilty plea, only to withdraw the withdrawal on September 27, 2008.[156] On September 30, 2008, Derrick Shareef was sentenced to 35 years imprisonment for attempting to use a weapon of mass destruction.[157]

JUNE 1, 2007— JOHN F. KENNEDY INTERNATIONAL AIRPORT PLOT

Russel Defreitas
AKA: Mohammed.
Citizenship: US, born in Guyana.
DOB: 1944.
Arrest: June 3, 2007.
Conviction: Pled guilty on June 29, 2010 to lesser charges in hopes of escaping life imprisonment.
Sentence: Life imprisonment on February 17, 2011.
Status: Incarcerated for life at Terre Haute, Indiana FCI, indicted June 2, 2007.
Cases: *U.S. v. Defreitas*, 2011 U.S. Dist. LEXIS 9052 (E.D.N.Y. Jan. 31, 2011); *U.S. v. Defreitas*, 701 F. Supp. 2d 297 (E.D.N.Y. 2010).
Charges: Conspiracy to attack public transportation system, 18 U.S.C. § 2332f; Conspiracy to destroy a building by fire or explosive, 18 U.S.C. § 844(n); Conspiracy to attack aircraft and aircraft materials,18 U.S.C. § 32; Conspiracy to destroy international airport facilities, 18 U.S.C. § 37; Conspiracy to attack a mass transportation facility, 18 U.S.C. § 1992(a)(10); Surveillance of mass transportation facility, 18 U.S.C. § 1992(a)(8).

Links to al-Qa'ida: Defreitas had sought help from at least one operative al-Qa'ida member during one of his many trips to the Caribbean.

Background:

Defreitas was indicted on June 28, 2007, along with three other men, for plotting to blow up major supply tanks and pipelines at John F. Kennedy International Airport in New York.[158] Steven Francis, an FBI informant, testified that he and Defreitas drove around the oil tanks to scope out the targets, and he had recorded Defreitas on camera saying that he had been eyeing the tanks for years. Defreitas also used satellite images from the Internet to scope out the targets at JFK Airport. This cell of four men and their planned hit never made it past the planning stages.[159] The other three men in the cell were Adbel Nur from Guyana, Abdul Kadir from Guyana, and Kareem Ibrahim of Trinidad. All of the men were Shi'a Muslims.

Defreitas immigrated to the US in 1972, and settled down with his wife, rearing one daughter. Defreitas is now estranged from both his wife and daughter, and he has spent much of his life in poverty in Brooklyn, New York, despite being a talented saxophone player. Defreitas was a former employee at JFK, where he worked as a cargo handler.[160] Defreitas was the mastermind behind the JFK plot, and he recruited the others to join him.[161] The group sought further help from other militant Muslims; and on one of many trips back and forth from Trinidad and Tobago, Defreitas attempted to seek help from at least one al-Qa'ida operative in the Caribbean.[162]

Defreitas was officially arrested on June 1, 2007, in New York, and the next day, June 2, 2007, all four men involved were charged with the conspiracy. All four of the cell members pled guilty on June 29, 2010, in hopes of escaping life imprisonment; each count held a maximum of 15 years. Defreitas was convicted on all six charges by a federal jury on August 3, 2010. On February 17, 2011, Defreitas was sentenced to life in prison on all six counts in the indictment.[163]

JUNE 1, 2009— LITTLE ROCK MILITARY RECRUITMENT CENTER ATTACK

Abdulhakim Mujahid Muhammad
AKA: Carlos Bledsoe.

Citizenship: US.

DOB: 1985.

Arrest: June 2009.

Conviction: After a mental evaluation, Muhammad's trial began on July 18, 2011; while he initially pled not guilty to all counts, he later wrote a letter to the presiding judge informing him that he wanted to plead guilty; however, by law he cannot plead guilty to a state, capital murder offense.

Sentence: n/a.

Status: Awaiting trial. He was originally arrested and charged on June 2, 2009, but was indicted again on April 26, 2010, for crimes he committed while detained.

Cases: *State of Arkansas v. Abdulhakim Mujahid Muhammad.*

Charges: Capital murder, A.C.A. § 5-10-101; 16 Counts of terrorist activities, A.C.A. § 5-54-205; the second set of charges included aggravated assault, A.C.A. § 5-13-204; terroristic threatening, A.C.A. § 5-13-301.

Links to al-Qa'ida: Personally stated that he had been in contact with al-Qa'ida in Yemen; specifically with Anwar al-Awlaki.

Background:

Carlos Bledsoe was raised as a Baptist in Memphis, Tennessee. He was arrested for possession of brass knuckles just before his eighteenth birthday. At the end of his freshman year at Tennessee State in Nashville, he was found to be in possession of an SKS rifle, two shotguns, a switchblade, and some marijuana. Bledsoe later admitted that he was involved in gangs, yet he was given a plea deal of probation to escape the possible 14-year sentence. After that, Bledsoe started to study religion. He became Sunni Muslim in 2004 and dropped out of school in 2005.[164]

Bledsoe changed his name to Abdulhakim Mujahid Muhammad and planned to move to Yemen in 2007 to study Arabic. Muhammad taught English in Yemen, studied Arabic at the City Institute in Sana'a, and married after one year there. He was arrested for overstaying his visa, and his case was complicated because he had fake Somali papers in his possession. The Yemeni government eventually deported Muhammad in January 2009. After his deportation, he worked in Little Rock, Arkansas, at one of his father's businesses (driving a sightseeing van out of the Hilton) to make money to bring his wife over from Yemen.[165,166]

Upon his return, Muhammad was becoming increasingly incensed about US involvement in both Afghanistan and Iraq. On June 1, 2009, Muhammad opened fire at a military recruitment center in Little Rock, killing Pvt. William Long, 23, and injuring Pvt. Quinton Ezeagwula, 18. At first, Muhammad pled not guilty, stating that jihad justified his actions. On January 12, 2010, Muhammad wrote to the presiding judge that he wanted to plead guilty and that he had fired several rounds at the privates with the intent to kill them. He also admitted that he would have killed more people if they had been in the parking lot, and that he was linked to AQAP.[167] It is claimed that this is the first homegrown terrorist case linked to AQAP, namely through Anwar al-Awlaki.[168]

Since being arrested on June 2, 2009 and after eighteen appearances in court, jury selection was set for July 18, 2011, in this case. Previous trials in February and June of 2011 had been postponed due to mental evaluations and because Muhammad has had difficulties getting along with his defense counsel.[169] Muhammad was also charged with aggravated assault and terrorist threats for attempting to stab one jail deputy and threatening to kill another on April 26, 2010.[170] Although the FBI had been following Muhammad after his return from Yemen in 2009, the federal government is giving deference to the State of Arkansas in jurisdiction, due to the state capital murder case pending against Muhammad.

NOVEMBER 2008 — LONG ISLAND TRANSIT PLOT "THE AMERICAN AL-QA'IDA"

Bryant Neal Vinas
AKA: Bashir al-Amriki, Ibrahim, Ben Yameen al-Kanadee.
Citizenship: US.
DOB: December 4, 1983.
Arrest: November 2008.
Conviction: Pled guilty to all charges on January 28, 2009.
Sentence: n/a.
Status: Awaiting sentencing, indicted November 14, 2008.
Cases: *U.S. v. Bryant Neal Vinas.*
Charges: Conspiracy to murder US citizens, 18 U.S.C. § 2332(b)(2); Providing information to a terrorist organization, 18 U.S.C. § 2339B; Receiving "military-type" training from al-Qa'ida, 18 U.S.C. § 2339D.

Links to al-Qa'ida: Traveled overseas to Pakistan and Afghanistan to join al-Qa'ida in March of 2008.

Background:

Bryant Neal Vinas was raised as a Catholic in Long Island, New York. A son of divorced parents, Vinas decided to enter the US military at the age of 18 instead of attending college. Around 2006, at the age of 22, Vinas converted to Islam and started going by the name Ibrahim, although he later had multiple aliases. Vinas was remembered as a kind, quiet individual by the imam at the local mosque that Vinas visited four to five times a week.[171] Soon after converting, Vinas began to adopt more violent jihadist ideas towards the US. Vinas worked as a truck driver before leaving home in 2007 to travel to Pakistan and Afghanistan.[172] He joined al-Qa'ida forces in March of 2008, and was eventually arrested in Peshwar, Pakistan, in November of that year.

Vinas was handed over to US authorities in January of 2009.[173] He had previously been indicted by the US on November 14, 2008, and pled guilty to the charges on January 28, 2009.[174] Part of the material support that Vinas lent to al-Qa'ida was information regarding the New York City transit system and the Long Island Railroad, which were under a high terrorism alert in late 2008. Vinas also admitted to firing missiles at US forces while a member of al-Qa'ida in Afghanistan in 2008. However, much of Vinas' case remains sealed by the government since he agreed to assist counterterrorism forces abroad and domestically on a number of cases. Currently, he is being held in an undisclosed location in New York under the eye of the Marshal's service.[175]

JULY 27, 2009— THE BOYD TERRORIST GROUP OF NORTH CAROLINA

Cases: *U.S. v Daniel Patrick Boyd, Hysen Sherifi, Anes Subasic, Zakariya Boyd, Dylan Boyd, Jude Kenan Mohammad, Mohammad Omar Aly Hassan, Ziyad Yaghi.*

Charges: Conspiracy to provide material support to terrorists, 18 U.S.C. § 2339A; Conspiracy to murder, kidnap, maim and injure persons, 18 U.S.C. § 956(a); Receiving firearms through interstate commerce, 18 U.S.C. § 924(b); Possession of a firearm in furtherance of crime of violence, 18 U.S.C. § 924(c); Knowing sale of firearms to a convicted felon, 18 U.S.C.

§ 922(d)(1); False statement, 18 U.S.C. § 1001; Attempting to murder military personnel.

Background:

Upon entering Boyd's home with a SWAT team, evidence of cash transactions, coded conversations, and stockpiled weapons was discovered. Boyd also lied about his numerous trips overseas to Kosovo, Israel, and Jordan.[176] Besides Boyd's sons, the other suspects are Anes Subasic, 33; Mohammad Omar Aly Hassan, 22; Ziyad Yaghi, 21; Hysen Sherifi, 24; and Jude Kenan Mohammad, 22. There was initially doubt as to whether these men were involved in practicing jihad against the US, since the only outward sign of suspicion had been military training expeditions in Virginia and North Carolina.[177] However, in September of 2009, it was discovered that the terrorist cell was plotting to attack the Marine base at Quantico, Virginia.

Daniel Boyd

AKA: Saifullah Abu Laith.

Citizenship: US.

DOB: 1970.

Arrest: July 27, 2009.

Conviction: Pled guilty on February 9, 2011.

Sentence: n/a.

Status: Awaiting sentencing, initially indicted July 22, 2009, superseding indictment issued on September 24, 2009.

Links to al-Qa'ida: While it has not been extremely clear whether Boyd is officially linked to al-Qa'ida, his ideology is aligned with the group, and it is believed that he trained with al-Qa'ida operatives while overseas. He has spread extremist literature glorifying Usama bin Laden.[178]

Background:

Daniel Patrick Boyd was born one of five boys to a former US Marine in 1970. His mother and father divorced in 1977, and his mother remarried an American Muslim from Washington, DC, a lawyer named William Saddler. Boyd converted to Islam after he graduated from high school in Alexandria, Virginia. Boyd married his high school sweetheart, Sabrina, who apparently converted to Islam hours before their wedding occurred. The Boyds moved to Pakistan in 1989 to help the Afghan rebels fight against the Soviets, but Boyd and his brother were arrested by the Pakistanis in 1991 on charges of stealing 80,000 rupees from a bank. They were sentenced to have their right hands and left feet cut off; but through some maneuvering the State Department convinced Pakistan to disallow the convictions.[179]

The Boyds returned to North Carolina, where they settled down in Willow Springs, where they raised three boys. The youngest son, Luqman, died in a car crash in 2007; but Boyd focused all of his religious attentions on his other sons, Dylan and Zakaria. Soon after Luqman's death, the Boyds parted from the local mosque due to the radicalization of their religious ideals. The FBI began following Boyd in 2006, in part because of his growing arsenal of weapons and because of frequent training trips to rural Virginia with his recruits.[180]

Boyd was initially indicted on July 22, 2009, and arrested five days later on July 27. However, a superseding indictment took place on September 24, 2009, after the information about the Quantico base attack had been fleshed out. On February 9, 2011, Boyd pled guilty to two of the superseding charges: conspiring to provide material support and conspiring to murder, kidnap, and maim people in a foreign country. The rest of the charges were dropped in the guilty plea agreement.[181]

Zakaria Boyd
AKA: Zak.
Citizenship: US.
DOB: January 27, 1989.
Arrest: July 27, 2009.
Conviction: Pled guilty on June 7, 2011.
Sentence: Sentencing date not set yet; could face 15 years in prison
Status: Awaiting sentencing, initial indictment on July 22, 2009, superseding indictment on September 24, 2009.
Links to al-Qa'ida: Through his father, Daniel Patrick Boyd.
Background:
The second oldest son of Daniel Boyd, Zakaria entered a guilty plea on Tuesday, June 7, 2011, to the federal charge of providing material support to terrorists. Zakaria became the second member of this group to plead guilty, following his father. Zakaria could face up to 15 years in prison.[182]

Dylan Boyd
AKA: Mohammad.
Citizenship: US.
DOB: 1987.
Arrest: July 27, 2009.
Conviction: n/a.
Sentence: n/a.
Status: Trial was scheduled to begin during September 2011, indicted on July 22, 2009, superseding indictment issued on September 24, 2009.
Links to al-Qa'ida: Through his father.
Background:
The oldest son of Daniel Boyd, Dylan Boyd, graduated from West Johnston High School in 2005 and attended North Carolina State University for two years, studying psychology. He lived with his parents at the time of his arrest, but was married to Zenat Boyd, who is currently pregnant. He was introduced to fellow cell member Ziyad Yaghi in college.[183] Dylan was awaiting trial in September 2011.[184]

Ziyad Yaghi
Citizenship: US, born in Jordan.
DOB: January 22, 1988.
Arrest: July 27, 2009.
Conviction: n/a.
Sentence: n/a.
Status: Initial indictment on July 22, 2009, superseding indictment issued on September 24, 2009.
Links to al-Qa'ida: Through Daniel Boyd.

Hysen Sherifi
Citizenship: US, born in Kosovo.
DOB: August 24, 1984.
Arrest: July 27, 2009.
Conviction: n/a.
Sentence: n/a.
Status: Awaiting trial, initially indicted on July 22, 2009; superseding indictment issued on September 24, 2009.[185]
Links to al-Qa'ida: Through Daniel Boyd.

Background:

Sherifi moved to the US in 1999 to avoid the civil war in Kosovo. Although Sherifi lived in Raleigh with his family, his pregnant wife still remains in Kosovo; and he had hoped to rejoin her. He traveled to Kosovo in 2008 to pursue violent jihad. When he returned, he followed Daniel Boyd on military training expeditions, and was involved in the plan to attack the Quantico military base.[186]

Mohammad Omar Aly Hassan

Citizenship: US.

DOB: May 15, 1987.

Arrest: July 27, 2009.

Conviction: n/a.

Sentence: n/a.

Status: Awaiting trial, initially indicted on July 22, 2009, superseding indictment issued on September 24, 2009.

Links to al-Qa'ida: Through Daniel Boyd.

Background:

Hassan graduated from Cary High School in Raleigh, North Carolina, and was living there at the time of his arrest. He also attended North Carolina State University, majoring in sociology. He was engaged to be married at the time of his arrest. He traveled to Israel to pursue violent jihad, but his attempts there failed. Hassan has a criminal history that includes charges for assault in 2004, assault on his fiancée in 2007, and false imprisonment charges in 2009 that landed him in jail.[187]

Anes Subasic

Citizenship: US, born in Bosnia.

DOB: 1966 or 1967.

Arrest: July 27, 2009.

Conviction: n/a.

Sentence: n/a.

Status: Awaiting trial, initially indicted on July 22, 2009, superseding indictment issued on September 24, 2009.

Links to al-Qa'ida: Through Daniel Boyd.

Background:

Subasic emigrated from Bosnia in the 1990s because of the civil war there. He was living with his father in Holly Springs, North Carolina, at the time of his arrest, and had filed for bankruptcy under Chapter 7 in 2007. His bankruptcy case was later dismissed. Subasic engaged in the study of assassination and purchased sniper rifle equipment. He had multiple- coded conversations with Daniel Boyd about sending warriors abroad for violent jihad.[188]

Jude Kenan Mohammad
Citizenship: US.
DOB: November 4, 1988.
Arrest: n/a.
Conviction: n/a.
Sentence: n/a.
Status: At large, initially indicted on July 22, 2009, superseding indictment issued on September 24, 2009.
Links to al-Qa'ida: Through connection to Daniel Boyd.
Background:

Kenan's father is from the Pakistani town of Dara Adam Khel, which is not far from Peshawar. His mother is an American who converted from Catholicism to Islam. His parents met in the 1980s in New York, and ended up having four girls and one boy—Jude Kenan. He converted to Islam as a teenager. As Boyd's and the rest of the group's intentions became more clear, the suspicion that Boyd had an accomplice in Kenan grew.[189]

Kenan's father still lives in Pakistan, and it is possible he is helping his son evade the law. In 2008, Kenan claimed he was visiting Pakistan to visit his father, but the FBI believes the visit was for violent jihad. Kenan was arrested in October 2008 in Pakistan for attempting to enter the terrorist-laden tribal region. After failing to show up for his court date on September 5, 2009, it is now believed he is on the run somewhere in Pakistan.[190] Kenan is on the FBI's wanted list.[191]

SEPTEMBER 18, 2009— ATTEMPTING TO JOIN TERRORIST ORGANIZATIONS OVERSEAS

Betim Kaziu
Citizenship: US.
DOB: 1988.
Arrest: 2009.

Conviction: n/a.

Sentence: n/a.

Status: Awaiting trial, indicted September 18, 2009.

Cases: n/a.

Charges: Conspiracy to commit murder in a foreign country 18 U.S.C. § 956(a); Conspiracy to provide material support to terrorists, 18 U.S.C. 2339A.

Links to al-Qa'ida: Allegedly attempted to join al-Shabaab, an organization affiliated with al-Qa'ida.

Background:

> Kaziu was born and raised in Brooklyn, New York. Kaziu was one of four siblings who dropped out of high school (he later achieved his high school equivalency diploma). Around the age of 18, he became fascinated by religion and the concept of the devotion of one's life to God. Kaziu told his family he was going to Egypt to study Arabic, and also notified them that he was traveling to Macedonia and Kosovo to see distant relatives. In 2009, Kaziu was arrested with three other men in Kosovo under suspicion that they were going to engage in terrorist activities.[192] Kaziu had flown first to Cairo, Egypt, out of JFK International Airport on February 19, 2009.

> Cairo was merely Kaziu's first stop, as he then attempted to join al-Shabaab in Somalia; and he was planning to travel to Iraq, Afghanistan, Pakistan, and the Balkans in order to engage in violent jihad against US forces.[193] Kaziu was indicted by the US government on September 18, 2009, and faces up to a maximum of 15 years in prison.[194] A trial date was set for July 5, 2011.

SEPTEMBER 19, 2010— NEW YORK CITY SUBWAY BOMB PLOT

Cases: *U.S. v. Zazi*, 2010 U.S. Dist. LEXIS 67595 (E.D.N.Y. June 28, 2010);

Charges: Conspiracy to use WMD, 18 U.S.C. § 2332(a)(2); Conspiracy to commit murder in a foreign country 18 U.S.C. § 956(a); Providing material support to a foreign terrorist organization 18 U.S.C. § 2339B; Conspiracy to obstruct justice, 18 U.S.C. § 1512(k); Obstruction of justice, 18 U.S.C. § 1512(c); Witness tampering, 18 U.S.C. § 1512(b)(3); Obstruction of justice, 18 U.S.C. § 1519; Obstruction of justice 18 U.S.C. § 1503(a); Materially false statements, 18 U.S.C. § 1001(a)(2); Making materially false statements in matter involving terrorism, 18 U.S.C. 1001(F); Conspiracy to provide material support to a foreign terrorist organization, 18 U.S.C. § 2339B(1); Receiving military-type training from a foreign terrorist organization, 18 U.S.C. § 2339D(a); Conspiracy to commit an act of terrorism transcending national boundaries, 18 U.S.C. § 2332b(c); Attempting to commit an act of terrorism transcending national boundaries, 18 U.S.C. § 2332b(a)(1)(A); Use of destructive device, 18 U.S.C. § 924(c)(1)(A)(i); Conspiracy to use a destructive device, 18 U.S.C. § 924(c)(1)(B)(ii).[195]

Najibullah Zazi
AKA: Salahuddin.
Citizenship: US, born in Afghanistan.
DOB: 1985.
Arrest: September 2009.
Conviction: Pled guilty on February 22, 2010, to all three superseding charges after initially pleading not guilty.
Sentence: Awaiting sentencing.
Status: Indicted September 24, 2009.
Links to al-Qa'ida: Pled guilty to receiving weapons training from al-Qa'ida and to providing material support to the terrorist organization; he also planned an attack on behalf of al-Qa'ida targeting the New York City subway.
Background:
    Zazi moved from Afghanistan to Pakistan when he was seven years old, and then to the US in 1999. Zazi used his Pakistani wife as an excuse to travel back and forth from Pakistan to the US in 2007 and 2008. Beginning in 2009, Zazi was a shuttle driver for the Denver International Airport, and lived in Aurora, Colorado.

    In September 2009, Zazi drove to New York and attempted to rent a U-Haul on September 10. Zazi had his car and computer searched by the authorities during his trip. There are recorded calls to his father, Mohammad Wali Zazi, and to Ahmed Weis Afzali, two co-conspirators. In these calls Zazi expressed his concern that the authorities were watching his actions. Zazi was arrested on September 19, 2009, and subjected to three days of questioning, in which he admitted to receiving weapons training from al-Qa'ida in Pakistan in 2008.[196]

151

Zazi was officially indicted on September 24, 2009, and charged with receiving bomb-making instructions in Pakistan, buying bomb-making materials, and traveling to New York in connection with the planned subway bombing. Upon his initial arrest, the State of Colorado had jurisdiction over Zazi, but in light of his plans to attack the New York City subway, the US District Court for the Eastern District of New York will hear the case.

Initially, Zazi pled not guilty on September 29, 2009. Further evidence gathered by law enforcement showed that Zazi had bought large amounts of chemicals from beauty stores, such as nail polish for its acetone, with which he planned to create a bomb. Nine pages of notes on Zazi's computer were dedicated to the making of triacetone triperoxide (TATP). He bought much of the chemicals in Denver, and checked into a hotel suite in Aurora, Colorado. The suite had a stove which was later found to have acetone residue on the vent above. After he became suspicious that the authorities were monitoring him, Zazi immediately bought a plane ticket and flew back from New York to Denver, two days before his rental car was due back.[197]

On February 22, 2010, Zazi pled guilty to superseding charges, including conspiracy to use WMD against persons or property in the US, conspiracy to commit murder in a foreign country, and providing material support to al-Qa'ida. It is believed that Zazi had personal contact with senior al-Qa'ida officials as well. Part of Zazi's plea deal provided for him to lend support to ongoing cases and investigations both domestically and abroad. Zazi's sentencing date was scheduled for June 24, 2011, but it could have been delayed again because Zazi has been cooperating with ongoing investigations, including one against his father.[198]

Mohammed Wali Zazi

Citizenship: US, born in Afghanistan.

DOB: 1955.

Arrest: September 2009.

Conviction: n/a.

Sentence: n/a.

Status: Originally indicted on October 8, 2009; superseding indictment on November 29, 2010, currently awaiting trial.

Links to al-Qa'ida: Through conspiracy to help his son evade authorities in order to carry out al-Qa'ida terrorist attacks.

Background:

Zazi resided in Colorado when he was arrested for helping his son plot a terrorist attack on the New York City Subway. Zazi pleaded not guilty to the charges on February 17, 2010, and the next day he was released from custody after posting $50,000 bail. Zazi was allowed to return to Aurora, Colorado, under the condition of house arrest.[199] In November 2010, Zazi was indicted again on charges of witness tampering and lying to the FBI in efforts to cover up the bomb plot. Zazi's trial had been set to take place in July 2011, and his own son could be called as a possible witness against him.[200]

Ahmed Weis Afzali

Citizenship: US, born in Afghanistan.

DOB: 1972.

Arrest: September 19, 2009.

Conviction: Pled guilty on March 4, 2010.

Sentence: Sentenced on April 8, 2010, to time served and given 90 days to leave the country.

Status: Released from prison and living abroad.

Links to al-Qa'ida: Attempted to cover up Najibullah Zazi's connection to al-Qa'ida.

Background:

Afzali was an imam in Queens, New York. Afzali and both Zazis were the first three men indicted together in the planned New York subway bombing. Afzali was contacted by the FBI on September 10, and was asked questions about his knowledge of Najibullah and Zarein Ahmedzay, whom he had known since they were teenagers. A day later, on September 11, 2009, Afzali contacted Zazi and warned him that the authorities were watching. After the FBI later interrogated Afzali on September 13, he denied that he had tipped off Zazi about the FBI's suspicions.

Afzali pled guilty to lying to the FBI, which carries a maximum sentence of eight years if it is connected with a terrorist investigation. His sentencing hearing was on April 8, 2010.[201] On that day, Afzali was sentenced to time served; and as part of his guilty plea deal, he was ordered to leave the US within 90 days.[202]

Zarein Ahmedzay

Citizenship: US, born in Afghanistan.

DOB: 1985.

Arrest: January 8, 2010.

Conviction: Pled guilty on April 23, 2010.

Sentence: Faces possible life sentence.

Status: Awaiting sentencing, indicted February 24, 2010, and previously indicted on January 8, 2010.

Links to al-Qa'ida: Through Najibullah Zazi.

Background:

> Ahmedzay was a fellow high school student with Najibullah Zazi, and accompanied both Zazi and another high school friend, Adis Medunjanin, on a trip to Pakistan to join the Taliban in 2008. However, two al-Qa'ida operatives intercepted them and stated that their abilities would better serve the cause back in the US through suicide bombings. Ahmedzay and his two accomplices received both weapons training and bomb-making tutorials from al-Qa'ida operatives in Pakistan. In his statements in court, Ahmedzay stated that the attack on the subway in New York was planned for September 14-16 of 2009.[203]

> Ahmedzay had previously pled not guilty in January 8, 2010, and then pled not guilty again to more serious charges on February 25, 2010. The more serious charges included attempting to use WMD and making false statements to the FBI. Finally, on April 23, 2010, Ahmedzay pled guilty to the three terrorism charges, which carry a maximum sentence of life in prison. A former New York taxi driver, Ahmedzay was to meet with Zazi on September 10, 2009, to assemble the bombs, and then set off three coordinated explosions on a date between September 14 and 16.[204]

Adis Medunjanin

Citizenship: US, born in Bosnia.

DOB: 1985.

Arrest: January 8, 2010.

Conviction: n/a.

Sentence:n/a.

Status: Awaiting trial, indicted February 24, 2010, previously indicted on January 8, 2010.

Links to al-Qa'ida: Through Zazi.

Background:

Medunjanin attended high school with Najibullah Zazi and Ahmedzay. He was the third man who was to participate in the New York City Subway suicide bombings. Medunjanin arrived in the US in 1994 from Bosnia, and became a naturalized US citizen in 2002.[205] Medunjanin was charged in the same superseding indictment as Ahmedzay on February 25, 2010, and followed his comrade by pleading that he was not guilty. Medunjanin again pled not guilty to another superseding indictment on July 7, 2010.[206] Medunjanin, like the elder Zazi, is fighting the charges, although a new trial date has not been set.

Adnan el-Shukrijimah

AKA: Adnan G. El Shukri Jumah, Abu Arif Ja'far Al-Tayar, Jaffar Al-Tayyar.
Citizenship: Naturalized US Citizen.
DOB: August 4, 1975.
Arrest: n/a.
Conviction: n/a.
Sentence: n/a.
Status: At large, indicted July 2010.
Links to al-Qa'ida: Key al-Qa'ida operative for whose capture the US has offered $5 million.
Background:

El-Shukrijimah lived much of his life in Florida and New York. His father was an imam in New York before the family moved to Florida in the mid-1990s. It was there that el-Shukrijimah began to favor radicalized Islam. El-Shukrijimah worked numerous odd-jobs so that he could afford to attend a small college in South Florida, where he studied chemistry and improved his English.

Authorities believe that el-Shukrijimah has risen to a key position in the al-Qa'ida group, beginning his ascent as a dishwasher at training facilities. It was discovered that el-Shukrijimah was the mastermind behind the New York City Subway terrorist plot, directing the plot from Pakistan and persuading Zazi, Ahmedzay, and Medunjanin to sacrifice themselves as suicide bombers. The government believes el-Shukrijimah to be the equivalent to the chief of operations for al-Qa'ida, and they believe he is extremely dangerous to the US, as evidenced by the $5 million reward for his capture.

SEPTEMBER 23, 2009—FINDLEY FEDERAL BUILDING BOMB PLOT

Michael Finton

AKA: Talib Islam.

Citizenship: US.

DOB: 1980.

Arrest: September 24, 2009.

Conviction: Pled guilty to use of a weapon of mass destruction against property owned by the US, 18 U.S.C. 2332a(a) on May 9, 2011.

Sentence: 28 years imprisonment on May 9, 2011.

Status: Indicted October 7, 2009, imprisoned.

Cases: *U.S. v. Finton*, 2010 U.S. Dist. LEXIS 134659.

Charges: Attempting to murder a federal officer or employee, 18 U.S.C. 1114(3); Attempting to use a weapon of mass destruction against property owned by the US, 18 U.S.C. 2332a(a).

Link to al-Qa'ida: Finton believed he was working with low-level al-Qa'ida operatives when he was performing his terrorist acts.

Background:

Finton converted to Islam while he was serving an Illinois jail sentence from 2001 to 2006 for aggravated robbery and aggravated battery. Finton listed his hometown as Visalia, California, on his MySpace page, although he attended high school in Warren, Michigan. Finton traveled to Saudi Arabia in 2008, and stayed there about a month. That trip, coupled with letters speaking of dying a martyr that were found in his car, alerted the authorities. FBI agents, posing as low-level al-Qa'ida operatives, befriended Finton. This relationship culminated with his attempt to park a vehicle he thought was filled with explosives outside of the Paul Findley Federal Building in Springfield, Illinois, on September 23, 2009. At the time, Finton was working as a fry cook at Seals Fish & Chicken in Decatur, Illinois.

Finton was described by coworkers and neighbors as a mild-mannered, friendly man. However, they also noted he had passionate, unwavering feelings about strict Islam. Finton's goal was to bring down the US government; and although he occasionally expressed feelings that he was being set up, he decided that it was worth the risk to see the American government's downfall.[207]

On May 9, 2011, Michael Finton pled guilty to the charge of attempting to use a weapon of mass destruction against US property. Finton admitted to parking a van at a corner near the federal building, and then to getting out of the van and into another car with an undercover officer to use a cell phone that he thought would detonate the bomb. The location and type of attack were both ideas created by Finton. Finton was sentenced to 28 years in prison on May 9.[208]

AUGUST 5, 2010 INDICTMENT— 14 SOMALI-AMERICANS

Cases: *U.S. v Ahmed Ali Omar, et al.*
Charges: Soliciting others to threaten violence 18 U.S.C. § 373; Possession of a firearm in furtherance of crime of violence, 18 U.S.C. § 924(c); Conspiracy to murder, kidnap, maim and injure persons abroad, 18 U.S.C. § 956(a)(1); False statements to a federal agent investigating an offense involving domestic terrorism , 18 U.S.C. § 1001(a) (2); Use and attempted use of a US passport issued and designed for the use of another, to facilitate an act of international terrorism, 18 U.S.C. § 1544; Conspiring to provide material support to terrorists, 18 U.S.C. § 2339A(a); Providing material support to terrorists, 18 U.S.C. § 2339B; use and attempted use of a US passport issued and designed for the use of another, to facilitate an act of international terrorism, 18 U.S.C. § 2.

Abdikadir Ali Abdi
Citizenship: US, born in Somalia.
DOB: 1991.
Arrest: n/a.
Conviction: n/a.
Sentence: n/a.
Status: Indicted August 5, 2010.
Link to al-Qa'ida: Providing material support to al-Shabaab.
Background:
Abdi is a Somali-American who grew up in Hopkins, Minnesota, a suburb of Minneapolis. He departed the US for Somalia on November 3, 2008, with Abdisalan Ali and other young Somali men to join al-Shabaab.[209]

Abdisalan Hussein Ali
Citizenship: US, born in Somalia.
DOB: 1989.

Arrest: n/a.
Conviction: n/a.
Sentence: n/a.
Status: Indicted August 5, 2010.
Link to al-Qa'ida: Providing material support to al-Shabaab.
Background:

> Ali was a few months old when his family fled Somalia and sought refuge in Kenya. Ali and his family arrived in Seattle in 2000 and later settled in Minneapolis, Minnesota. Ali sold sneakers out of his locker at Edison High School to help support his family, was elected president of the Somali Student Association, and worked at a law firm called Briggs & Morgan. He studied Chemical Engineering and was pursuing the pre-Med track at the University of Minneapolis when he was wrongly accused of robbing a local Subway sandwich shop. Although the charges were later dropped, Ali was left bitter, and he left for Somalia on November 3, 2008.[210]

Amina Ali
Citizenship: US, born in Somalia.
DOB: 1977.
Arrest: August 5, 2010.
Conviction: n/a.
Sentence: n/a.
Status: Indicted August 5, 2010, awaiting trial.
Link to al-Qa'ida: Allegedly helped finance al-Shabaab.
Background:

> Ali is a resident of Rochester, Minnesota. She is charged with 12 counts of providing material support to terrorists. The Department of Justice alleged that Ali raised money for the terrorist group al-Shabaab under the pretense that the funds were going to the poor. In an opinion dated June 21, 2011, a federal judge in Minnesota upheld Ali's indictment.[211] It is alleged that 12 money transfers to al-Shabaab were made between September 17, 2008, and July 19, 2010. If convicted, Ali faces 15 years on the conspiracy charge, as well as an additional 15 years for each instance of material support. Ali's trial is set for October 3, 2011.

Hawo Mohamed Hassan

Citizenship: US.

DOB: 1948.

Arrest: August 5, 2010.

Conviction: n/a.

Sentence: n/a.

Status: Awaiting trial, indicted August 5, 2010, indictment upheld June 21, 2011.

Link to al-Qa'ida: Allegedly helped finance al-Shabaab.

Background:

Hassan lived in Rochester, Minnesota, and raised funds for al-Shabaab by canvassing door-to-door and conducting teleconferences across the US and Canada. Hassan was indicted and arrested on August 5, 2010. Her indictment was upheld by a federal judge in Minnesota on June 21, 2011. Her jury trial is scheduled to begin on October 3, 2011.[212]

Farah Mohamed Beledi

Citizenship: US.

DOB: 1984.

Arrest: n/a.

Conviction: n/a.

Sentence: n/a.

Status: Deceased in a suicide attack.

Link to al-Qa'ida: Participated in attacks with al-Shabaab.

Background:

Beledi immigrated to the US in 1996 when he was 12. Beledi was a gang member and convicted criminal in St. Paul; he served a year in prison for stabbing a man in the neck at a Central High School soccer game. He became more religious and began regularly attending the same mosque as the Minnesotan defectors to Somalia.[213]

Beledi was last spotted crossing the border from the US into Mexico on October 8, 2009, with Abdiweli Yassin Isse and Cabdulaahi Ahmed Faarax. He intended to travel to Mexico City. It is assumed these men were instrumental in recruiting young Somali men in the Minneapolis area to join al-Shabaab.[214] The FBI recently confirmed that Beledi had killed two African Union peacekeepers and himself in a suicide bombing attack in Mogadishu.[215]

Cabdulaahi Ahmed Faraax, a.k.a. Adaki

Citizenship: US, born in Somalia.

DOB: 1977.[216]

Arrest: n/a.

Conviction: n/a.

Sentence: n/a.

Status: Presumed dead, indicted August 5, 2010.

Link to al-Qa'ida: Participated in attacks with al-Shabaab.

Background:

> Faraax was initially charged in October 2009, but that indictment was later superseded by an August 5, 2010, indictment that included 14 Somali-Americans. It is believed that Faraax traveled to Somalia to fight in 2007. Upon his return to Minneapolis, he spoke of brotherhood and violent jihad, and attempted to recruit other Somali-Americans to fight jihad in Somalia. Faraax was last seen with Beledi and Isse at the Mexican border on October 8, 2009. The FBI recently confirmed that Faraax joined Beledi in the suicide bombing in Mogadishu that killed two others, and Faraax is now believed to be dead.[217]

Abdiweli Yassin Isse

AKA: Farhan.

Citizenship: US, born in Somalia.

DOB: 1984.

Arrest: n/a.

Conviction: n/a.

Sentence: n/a.

Status: at large, indicted August 5, 2010.

Link to al-Qa'ida: Material support for al-Shabaab.

Background:

> Isse was charged in the same October 2009 and August 2010 indictments as Faraax. Isse and Faraax both recruited jihadists to fight against the Ethiopians, and Isse raised money to support jihadists traveling to fight. Isse was last seen on the Mexican border with Beledi and Faraax, and is believed to be abroad and at large.[218]

Omar Hammami

AKA: Abu Mansour al Amriki.

Citizenship: US.

DOB: May 6, 1984.

Arrest: n/a.

Conviction: n/a.

Sentence: n/a.

Status: Indicted August 5, 2010, at large.

Link to al-Qa'ida: Material support to al-Shabaab.

Background:

Hammami was born to a Southern Baptist woman named Debra and a Syrian immigrant named Shafik. Hammami was raised in Daphne, Alabama, a town with a population of about 19,000. Hammami, his older sister Dena, and his parents lived a life that resembled that of many typical American families. Answering to "Omie," Hammami enjoyed hunting, reading, and playing soccer. Hammami and his sister always seemed to have their feet in two camps: one foot was with their mother in attending Sunday service at the local Baptist church, and the other was with their father, a devout Muslim who installed quotes from Islamic writing on the walls around the house instead of paintings or pictures. Hammami was exceptionally smart and often short tempered.

Starting in eighth grade, Hammami began using mushrooms and marijuana with his older sister, who was rebelling against their strict Muslim father. Dena eventually moved out at the age of 16 to live with a friend, but she and Hammami always remained close. Hammami became popular at his high school, playing sports, and dating a popular girl. He was even elected sophomore class president. Yet Hammami internally struggled over whether to become a Christian or Muslim. He had voluntarily been baptized at an early age, yet trips to Damascus with his family had offered other religious options.

Soon after a trip to Damascus when he was 16, Hammami became more religious. He began to feel guilty if he smoked a cigarette, he wouldn't hold his girlfriend's hand anymore, and he and his mother constantly debated about religion. By his junior year, Hammami had begun praying openly during school, attempting to convert his classmates, and lashing out at other students and teachers. Hammami skipped his senior year and enrolled early at the University of South Alabama. There he became

161

president of the Muslim Student Association and found a new mentor in a man named Tony Sylvester, who had converted to Islam in his 20s, moved to Alabama with his wife and six children to find an Islamic job, and was a prominent member of the fundamentalist Salafi movement.

Shafik ordered Hammami to move out of the house as a result of Hammami's radical beliefs. Although Hammami denounced violent jihad, his religious beliefs were similar to those of his father. In December of 2002, Hammami dropped out of college, stating that he could not bear to be near women anymore. Hammami soon followed a friend he had converted to Toronto, where he wanted to seek a wife. His friend set Hammami up with his sister-in-law; and two months after they began dating, they were married. The two friends and their families moved to Alexandria, Egypt, in order to live in a Muslim land, but they found it to be too secular, which prompted Hammami's friend to leave.

Soon thereafter, Hammami met fellow American convert Daniel Moldonado, and the two became fast friends. They were transfixed by the al-Shabaab's activities in Somalia, mostly against the Christian country of Ethiopia. By late 2006, Hammami was a member of al-Shabaab, fighting to institute a new Islamic state in Somalia. Since then, Hammami has risen in the ranks of the al-Shabaab due to his intelligence, computer prowess, and linguistic skills. It was rumored that Hammami was dead at one point from a suicide bombing; but as recently as bin Laden's death, Hammami released propaganda promising retaliation against the US. He was indicted on August 5, 2010.[219]

Jehad Serwan Mostafa
AKA: Ahmed, Emir Anwar, Awar.
Citizenship: US.
DOB: 1982.
Arrest: n/.
Conviction: n/a.
Sentence: n/a.
Status: Indicted August 5, 2010, presumed alive in Somalia.
Link to al-Qa'ida: Material support to al-Shabaab.
Background:
  Mostafa, a native of San Diego, California, was charged with three counts of providing material support to terrorists, namely al-Shabaab in

Somalia. It is believed that Mostafa left the US in 2005, and is currently in Somalia. Little is known about Mostafa's life in California, other than that he studied at the University of California at San Diego, had a license to be a security guard for the Bureau of Security and Investigative Services, and worked at an auto business from 2002 until 2004.[220] People who knew Mostafa called him quiet, polite, mild-mannered, and friendly. The imam at the local mosque where Mostafa prayed also stated that Mostafa got married to a woman in the mosque. Although he couldn't recall her name, he remembered she was Somali. Mostafa also claimed to be a believer that Islam was a religion of peace and love.[221]

Khalid Mohamud Abshir
Citizenship: US, born in Somalia.
DOB: 1983.
Arrest: n/a.
Conviction: n/a.
Sentence: n/a.
Status: Indicted August 5, 2010, at large.
Link to al-Qa'ida: Allegedly trained with al-Shabaab.
Background:
> Abshir was a naturalized US citizen who resided in Minneapolis, Minnesota. He allegedly persuaded four other individuals to accompany him to Somalia to engage in violent jihad.[222]

Ahmed Ali Omar
Citizenship: US, born in Somalia.
DOB: 1986.
Arrest: n/a.
Conviction: n/a.
Sentence: n/a.
Status: Indicted August 5, 2010, at large.
Link to al-Qa'ida: Material support to al-Shabaab.
Background:
> Omar graduated from Edison High School in 2004, and was one of five men who allegedly left Minneapolis, Minnesota, in 2007 for Somalia in order to engage in violent jihad. Omar is still at large.[223]

Mohamed Abdullahi Hassan

Citizenship: US, born in Somalia.
DOB: 1989.
Arrest: n/a.
Conviction: n/a.
Sentence: n/a.
Status: Indicted August 5, 2010, at large.
Link to al-Qa'ida: Material support to al-Shabaab.
Background:
> Hassan lived in Minneapolis, Minnesota, and allegedly left for Somalia in August 2008 a year before he was to graduate from Roosevelt High School. Hassan remains at large.[224]

Zakaria Maruf

Citizenship: US, born in Somalia.
DOB: 1980.
Arrest: n/a.
Conviction: n/a.
Sentence: n/a.
Status: Indicted August 5, 2010, deceased.
Link to al-Qa'ida: Material support to al-Shabaab.
Background:
> Maruf was a graduate of Edison High School in Minneapolis, Minnesota. After graduation, he became involved with street gangs and crime. People who knew him growing up recall an angry man with little intellect.[225] Some reports indicate that Maruf was an influential recruiter for al-Shabaab. In July 2009, Maruf was one of two Somali-Americans killed fighting in Mogadishu. In an interview with a Somali radio station prior to his death, Maruf expressed his love for Allah and desire to fight the enemies of Allah.[226]

Mustafa Salat

Citizenship: US, born in Somalia.
DOB: 1990.
Arrest: n/a.
Conviction: n/a.
Sentence: n/a.
Status: Indicted August 5, 2010, at large.
Link to al-Qa'ida: Material support to al-Shabaab.

Background:

Salat left St. Paul, Minnesota for Somalia in August of 2008, one year before he was set to graduate from Harding High School.[227] Salat remains at large, presumably in Somalia as part of al-Shabaab.

MAY 2007— FORT DIX PLOT

Cases: *U.S. v. Abdullahu*, 2007 U.S. Dist. LEXIS 45593; *U.S. v. Shnewer*, 2008 U.S. Dist. LEXIS 112001.

Charges: Conspiring to commit an offense against the US in affecting commerce in firearms and ammunition by illegal aliens, 18 U.S.C. §§922(g)(5) and 2; Conspiracy to murder members of the US military, 18 U.S.C. 1114; Possession of firearms in furtherance of a crime of violence, 18 U.S.C. § 924(c)(1)(A)(i), (ii); Possession of machine guns; Possession of firearms by an alien; Aiding and abetting the possession of firearms by aliens, 18 U.S.C. §§ 922(g)(5), 922(o), 1117 & 2.[228-231]

Agron Abdullahu
Citizenship: US, born in Kosovo.
DOB: September 23, 1982.
Arrest: May 7, 2007.
Conviction: Pled guilty.
Sentence: 20 months.
Status: Released March 2009.
Link to al-Qa'ida: Influenced by Usama bin Laden.
Background:

Abdullahu and his family fled Kosovo in 1999 for America. When US law enforcement officers learned that Abdullahu and five others undertook a military training mission in the Pocono Mountains on January 3, 2006, they began surveillance of the individuals. The group trained again in the Poconos in February 2007. It was alleged that Abdullah had amassed weapons for the group, as the Dukas brothers were in the US illegally without green cards. Abdullahu was arrested on May 7, 2007, at his residence in Williamstown, New Jersey.[232]

On October 31, 2007, Abdullahu accepted a plea deal and pled guilty to conspiracy to provide firearms to three illegal aliens. Abduallahu admitted to knowing that the Dukas brothers were in the US illegally, but he stated that he had had a mental breakdown and been seeing a psychiatrist. The six men also admitted to being influenced and motivated by the ideologies of Usama bin Laden.[233] The charge to which Abdullahu pled guilty carries a 5-year maximum sentence; but on March 31, 2008, Abdullahu received a 20-month prison sentence. His plea deal did not require him to testify in the trials of the other five individuals.[234]

Serdar Tatar
Citizenship: US Resident, born in Turkey.
DOB: July 19, 1983.
Arrest: May 8, 2007.
Conviction: Guilty of conspiracy.
Sentence: 33 years.
Status: Imprisoned.
Link to al-Qa'ida: Influenced by Usama bin Laden.
Background:

The Tatar family immigrated to the US in 1992. Tatar's father opened an upscale pizzeria in Cherry Hill, New Jersey, several miles from the gates of Fort Dix. Tatar attended Cherry Hill High School. Although he never graduated; he later earned his equivalency diploma.[235] Tatar resided in Philadelphia, Pennsylvania, at the time of his arrest and worked at a 7-Eleven. He had applied for jobs with the police forces in Philadelphia and Oakland, California.

Tatar's father's business gave the six plotters the perfect Trojan horse in which to enter Fort Dix. The initial plans were for the men to be in a pizza delivery truck, mimicking a pizza delivery. Tatar had delivered pizza to Fort Dix many times before as a delivery man for his father. Once inside Fort Dix, the men planned to open fire upon soldiers. Tatar admitted to providing a map of Fort Dix to his comrades for planning purposes.[236]

On October 20, 2008, the trial for the plotters began without Abdullah. On December 22, 2008, the five men were found guilty of conspiracy but not of attempted murder. On January 1, 2009, Tatar appealed to have his conviction overturned on the basis that providing a map of Fort Dix did not implicate him in the conspiracy. Tatar's appeal was denied; and on April 30, 2009, he was sentenced to 33 years in prison. The judge believed that Tatar was less radical than the others and that he could be rehabilitated, and thus he received a lesser penalty than life imprisonment.

As of May 23, 2011, the five Fort Dix men have reportedly appealed their convictions and sentences again, claiming that their discussions about violent jihad were just harmless religious debates.[237]

Mohamad Ibrahim Schnewer

Citizenship: US.
DOB: April 28, 1985.
Arrest: May 8, 2007.
Conviction: Guilty.
Sentence: Life plus 30 years imprisonment.
Status: Imprisoned.
Link to al-Qa'ida: Influenced by Usama bin Laden.
Background:

> Schnewer was born in Jordan, but spent most of his life in Cherry Hill, New Jersey. At the time of his arrest, he was a taxi cab driver in Philadelphia, Pennsylvania. Schnewer was enrolled at Camden Community College, but dropped out of school in order to earn money. It is believed that he was the driving force behind the Fort Dix plot, even suggesting and scoping out other targets, including the White House. Schnewer is married to the youngest sister of the Duka brothers. In government recordings made prior to his arrest on May 7, 2007, Schnewer was the most outspoken of the plotters.[238]

Schnewer shared the same trial and sentencing dates as Tatar. Schnewer received the harshest sentence of the plotters: life imprisonment for the first count, and thirty years for the four remaining weapons charges.[239]

The Duka Brothers

Cases: *U.S. v. Mohamad Ibrahim Shnewer, Dritan Duka, Eljvir Duka, Shain Duka, Serdar Tatar, and Agron Abdullahu*
Charges: Conspiracy to murder members of the US military; Possession of machine guns; Possession of firearms by an alien
Background:

> In 1984, the Duka brothers entered the US through a crossing near Brownsville, Texas, allowing them to live illegally in the US for over 20 years. An investigation was looking into whether they were smuggled into the country.[240] The three brothers are ethnic Albanians from the former

Yugoslavia who ran a roofing company in Cherry Hill, New Jersey. All three were given life terms, with Dritan and Shain getting added 30-year sentences.[241]

Dritan Duka
Citizenship: Ethnic Albanian, in the US illegally.
DOB: 1978.
Arrest: May 8, 2007.
Conviction: Guilty.
Sentence: Life plus 30 years imprisonment.
Status: Imprisoned.
Link to al-Qa'ida: Inspired by Usama bin Laden.

Eljvir Duka
Citizenship: Ethnic Albanian, in US illegally.
DOB: 1983.
Arrest: May 8, 2007.
Conviction: Guilty.
Sentence: Life imprisonment.
Status: Imprisoned.
Link to al-Qa'ida: Inspired by Usama bin Laden.

Shain Duka
Citizenship: Ethnic Albanian, in US illegally.
DOB: Jan. 21, 1981.
Arrest: May 8, 2007.
Conviction: Guilty.
Sentence: Life plus 30 years imprisonment.
Status: Imprisoned.
Link to al-Qa'ida: Inspired by Usama bin Laden.

JANUARY 21, 2007— FIRST US CITIZEN CHARGED WITH AIDING SOMALI TERRORISTS

Daniel Joseph Maldonado
AKA: Daniel Aljughaifi.
Citizenship: US.
DOB: 1980.
Arrest: January 21, 2007.

Conviction: Guilty, pled guilty.

Sentence: 10 years imprisonment.

Status: Imprisoned.

Cases: *U.S. v. Daniel Joseph Maldonado.*

Charges: Conspiracy to use WMD outside of the US, 18 U.S.C. §2332a(b); Receiving military training from a foreign terrorist organization 18 U.S.C. §2339D.

Link to al-Qa'ida: Trained and consorted with al-Qa'ida members in Somalia.

Background:

Maldonado grew up in New Hampshire and Massachusetts. He converted to Islam in the early 2000s, and he moved to Houston, Texas, in 2005. He traveled to Egypt on November 24, 2005, and then to Somalia in November of 2006. Maldonado admitted to receiving weapons training in Somali terrorist camps where he visited, discussed, and trained with al-Qa'ida operatives and members.[242]

In Somalia, Maldonado became good friends with Omar Hammami of al-Shabaab. Maldonado also attempted to contact Tarek Mehanna in Massachusetts, a fellow Muslim whom Maldonado had met at their local mosque. Maldonado discussed violent jihad with both men, and they expressed pleasure over the 9/11 attacks and the killing of Americans who interfere with the Islamic faith.[243]

Maldonado was originally arrested by the Kenyan government on January 21, 2007, when he attempted to flee to Somalia. He was returned to the US, where he was officially charged on February 13, 2007. Maldonado pled guilty in Texas on April 19, 2007, and was sentenced to 10 years in prison on July 20, 2007, for receiving weapons training from a terrorist organization.[244]

APRIL 30, 2010— TWO BROOKLYN MEN CHARGED WITH AIDING AL-QA'IDA

Cases: *U.S. v Wesam el-Hanafi and Sabrihan Hasanoff.*

Charges: Conspiracy to provide material support to a foreign terrorist organization, 18 U.S.C. §2339; Providing and attempting to provide material support to a foreign terrorist organization; Conspiracy to make and receive a contribution of funds, goods, or services to and for the benefit of al-Qa'ida; Making and receiving a contribution of funds, goods, or services to and for the benefit of al-Qa'ida[245]

Wesam el-Hanafi

Citizenship: US.

DOB: 1977.

Arrest: April 30, 2010.

Conviction: n/a.

Sentence: n/a.

Status: awaiting trial, indicted April 30, 2010, superseded by an indictment on September 14, 2010.

Link to al-Qa'ida: Trained by and supported al-Qa'ida.

Background:

El-Hanafi was born in Brooklyn, New York, and lived there at the time of his arrest and indictment on April 30, 2010. El-Hanafi worked as a computer engineer for Lehman Brothers. In February 2008, he allegedly traveled to Yemen to meet with two senior al-Qa'ida operatives. It was then that el-Hanafi swore allegiance, trained with, and accepted missions from al-Qa'ida. In May 2008, el-Hanafi met with an unidentified co-conspirator in New York. Under his tutelage, the co-conspirator swore allegiance to al-Qa'ida. Around this time, el-Hanafi also purchased software that enabled him to speak securely with various individuals over the Internet.

In June 2008, el-Hanafi gave the co-conspirator specific assignments. In April 2009, he bought seven Casio watches on behalf of al-Qa'ida to be used for homemade explosive devices. El-Hanafi was originally charged with one count of conspiracy to provide material support to a foreign terrorist organization, which carries a maximum sentence of 15 years. But on September 14, 2010, the US issued a superseding indictment against el-Hanafi and Sabirhan Hasanoff.[246] The superseding indictment added charges of providing material support to terrorists, conspiracy to make and receive contributions for the benefit of terrorists, and making and receiving goods for the benefit of terrorists. If convicted on all counts, el-Hanafi faces up to 70 years in prison.[247] Both men were arrested in Dubai, arraigned in Virginia, and will now face trial in New York.

Sabirhan Hasanoff

Citizenship: US and Australia.

DOB: 1976.

Arrest: April 30, 2010.

Conviction: n/a.

Sentence: n/a.

Status: Awaiting trial.

Link to al-Qa'ida: Hasanoff planned to join al-Qa'ida and commit terrorist acts on its behalf.

Background:

At the time of his arrest and arraignment, Hasanoff worked as an accountant for PricewaterhouseCoopers International. Both Hasanoff and el-Hanafi allegedly provided technical, computer systems expertise to al-Qa'ida in attempts to improve the terrorist organization's Internet structure. This allowed the government to charge the men with violating the International Emergency Economic Powers Act.[248]

In May 2008 after el-Hanafi returned from Yemen, he and Hasanoff met with an unidentified co-conspirator multiple times to discuss plans to join al-Qa'ida and carry out al-Qa'ida tasks. Hasanoff had previously received $50,000 from the co-conspirator to finance his terrorist activity. Hasanoff traveled to New York in August 2008 to perform specific terrorist tasks that were given him by al-Qa'ida and el-Hanafi.[249] Both of these men had college degrees, impressive jobs, and families. Future trial dates are currently unknown.

NOVEMBER 21, 2010— MISSOURI-MINNESOTA AL-SHABAAB FUND

Cases: *U.S. v Yusuf, Mohamud Abdi.*[250]

Charges: Conspiracy to provide material support to a foreign terrorist organization, 18 U.S.C. §2339B(a)(1); providing material support to a designated foreign terrorist organization, 18 U.S.C. §2339B(a); Conspiracy to structure monetary transactions 31 U.S.C. §5324; Immigration Fraud 18 U.S.C. §1015(a); Conspiracy to structure monetary transactions, 31 U.S.C. §5324.[251]

Mohamud Abdi Yusuf

Citizenship: US, born in Somalia.

DOB: n/a.

Arrest: November 1, 2010.

Conviction: n/a.

Sentence: n/a.

Status: Indicted October 21, 2010.

Link to al-Qa'ida: Financial support of al-Shabaab.

Background:

> Yusuf was originally arrested on November 1, 2010, after a federal indictment was filed on October 21, 2010, for the charges above. Yusuf faces up to 15 years in prison and $250,000 in fines for each material support charge, and five years and $250,000 for the conspiracy charge.[252] Yusuf allegedly cooperated with Abdi Mahdi Hussein, an employee at a licensed remittance company, in order to mask their financial donations to al-Shabaab. The funding provided by Hussein, Yusuf, and a third man from Kenya named Duwayne Mohamed Diriye, was designated to fund weapons procurement for al-Shabaab.[253]

> Between February 2008 and July 2009, Yusuf was at work getting money to send to al-Shabaab. Yusuf and his co-conspirators discussed their transactions in coded language, and Yusuf was able to raise funds both inside and outside the Eastern District of Missouri, where the trial will be held.[254]

Abdi Mahdi Hussein

Citizenship: US, born in Somalia.

DOB: n/a.

Arrest: November 2, 2010.

Conviction: n/a.

Sentence: n/a.

Status: Indicted.

Link to al-Qa'ida: Financial support of al-Shabaab.

Background:

> Hussein was working at a licensed remittance company in Minneapolis, Minnesota, when he was arrested on November 2, 2010. He is named in the same indictment as the Kenyans Diriye and Yusuf. He faces up to 5 years in prison and up to $250,000 in fines. Both Hussein and Yusuf made their first court appearances on November 3, 2010.[255]

MARCH 26, 2010— CHICAGO TAXI DRIVER ACCUSED OF AIDING AL-QA'IDA

Raja Lahrasib Khan
Citizenship: US, born in Pakistan.
DOB: 1953.
Arrest: March 26, 2010.
Conviction: Pled not guilty.
Sentence: n/a.
Status: Indicted, awaiting trial.
Cases: *U.S. v Khan, Raja Lahrasib*.[256]
Charges: Providing material support or resources to a designated foreign terrorist organization.
Link to al-Qa'ida: Accused of conspiring to support al-Qa'ida.
Background:

Khan is a US citizen from Pakistan who was naturalized in 1988. At the time of his arrest, he worked as a Chicago, Illinois, taxi driver, and had allegedly discussed plans to attack a major sports stadium, although the government said no such attack was imminent. Khan was indicted on March 25, 2010, and he was taken into custody on the following day.[257]

Khan, who resided on the upper north side of Chicago, apparently sent $950 overseas, with $300 of it meant to make its way to an al-Qa'ida-linked group. Khan had also planned to meet his son in Chicago to receive $700 more, which he planned to give to an al-Qa'ida operative himself for weapons and other supplies. Khan openly admitted in taped phone calls that he had plans to bomb a US stadium, and that America "should pay."[258]

On April 5, 2010, Khan pled not guilty to charges that he conspired to send al-Qa'ida material support, namely money. Both counts carry maximum sentences of 15 years in prison and fines of $250,000 each. On April 20, 2011, Khan's trial date was tentatively set for November 7, 2011.

OCTOBER 2009— MASSACHUSETTS RESIDENT SEEKS TO JOIN AL-QA'IDA

Tarek Mehanna

Citizenship: US.

DOB: 1983.

Arrest: November 10, 2008, and October 21, 2009.

Conviction: n/a.

Sentence: n/a.

Status: Awaiting trial; scheduled for October 2011.

Cases: *U.S. v. Mehanna*, 669 F.Supp.2d 160, 18 Nov. 2009 (Allowing government's motion for detention, denying defendant's motion for release); 2011 WL 796400 (Denial of defendant's motions for release on bail, for bill of particulars, and for discovery.).

Charges: Material support to designated terrorist organization, 18 U.S.C. §2339B; Material support to terrorists, 18 U.S.C. §2339A; Conspiracy to kill in a foreign country, 18 U.S.C. §956; Conspiracy, 18 U.S.C. §371; Making false statements, 18 U.S.C. §1001(a)(2) & (3).

Link to al-Qa'ida: Self-motivated, allegedly attempted to join al-Qa'ida.

Background:

Tarek Mehanna is an American citizen of Egyptian descent. He received a doctorate in pharmacology in 2008 and planned to travel to Saudi Arabia to practice as a pharmacist.[259] According to the "Free Tarek Mehanna" website, Mehanna is described as "...humble, reserved, warm, peaceful, charismatic, knowledgeable, and dedicated."[260]

Mehanna was arrested on November 10, 2008, for a violation of 18 U.S.C. §2331(1), knowingly and willfully making a materially false and fraudulent statement to the FBI in connection with an investigation involving international and domestic terrorism. He was released on bail, and was arrested again on additional charges on October 21, 2009.[261]

The charges in his current indictment include providing material support to a terrorist organization, providing material support to terrorists, conspiracy, conspiracy to kill in a foreign country, and making false statements. If convicted, he will be required to forfeit all assets related to proceeds traceable to the crime or other property up to the value of such property.[262] He was indicted along with Ahmad Abousamra, another

American citizen from Massachusetts who is believed to be currently living in Syria.

One of the key points of the indictment against Mehanna involves his translation from Arabic to English of the book *39 Ways to Serve and Participate in Jihad*, and his ambition to be the "media wing" of al-Qa'ida.[263] Mehanna maintains that translating *39 Ways* was not material support to terrorism, but was rather an exercise of protected First Amendment speech.[264]

The indictment and opinions also refer to a trip to Yemen in 2004 with Abousamra and an individual who is now a government informant. The trip was allegedly an attempt on the part of the three men to train in a terrorist training camp, although none of the men underwent training.[265] The translation of *39 Ways* and the attempt to enroll in terrorist training were cited by the Magistrate Judge as reasons for denying Mehanna's release on bail.[266]

Mehanna has a support network based around the website "FreeTarek.com" and its associated Facebook, Twitter, and YouTube pages. The website solicits donations for his defense. Included on the website are letters to and from Mehanna, along with samples of Mehanna's artwork from prison, where he is in solitary confinement.[267]

His most recent hearing was a status hearing held on June 13, 2011, and his trial was scheduled for October 2011.

NOVEMBER 5, 2009—FORT HOOD SHOOTING

Major Nidal Malik Hasan
Citizenship: US.
DOB: September 8, 1970.
Arrest: November 5, 2009.
Conviction: n/a.
Sentence: n/a.
Status: Awaiting interlocutory decision by Ft. Hood commanding officer as of May 19, 2011.
Cases: Court Martial.
Charges: Unknown.

Link to al-Qa'ida: Corresponded with Anwar al-Awlaki.
Background:

In a 14 minute-long attack, Major Hasan opened fire with a high-powered pistol at a deployment processing facility at Fort Hood, Texas, on November 5, 2009. Twelve military personnel and one civilian contractor were killed before Major Hasan was shot and disabled by a local civilian law enforcement officer.[268] He is now paralyzed from the waist down.[269]

Major Hasan graduated from Army medical school and later completed his residency and became a psychiatrist. He sought advice from the imam at the Texas mosque he attended about counseling fellow Muslim soldiers about serving in Iraq or Afghanistan and killing other Muslims.[270] Major Hasan had also sought an early discharge from the Army, but gave up on the idea because of the Army's policy at the time of recruiting more Muslim soldiers. Reports indicate that Major Hasan, who had never before been deployed, had a difficult time reconciling with the idea that he might be deployed to Iraq or Afghanistan to assist in what he believed was a war against Islam.[271]

His parents died of cancer in 1997 and 2001, after which Major Hasan turned to Islam for comfort. He worshipped in the Falls Church, Virginia, mosque where Anwar al-Awlaki served as imam, and later carried on a six-month email correspondence with the cleric. Al-Awlaki was also linked with the shooting at Fort Dix.[272]

The civilian attorney for Major Hasan declined to put on a defense at the preliminary hearing because he said he had been denied access to certain internal military reports.[273] The colonel presiding at the hearing determined that there was enough evidence to try Major Hasan by court-martial on thirteen counts of premeditated murder and 32 counts of attempted premeditated murder. The colonel cited the presence of an "aggravating factor" to support the death penalty as an option attaching to a conviction.[274]

The commander of Fort Hood can determine the aspects of the court-martial, and whether the case will be considered as a capital case or not. There is no deadline for that decision.[275]

NOVEMBER 2009— SOMALI-AMERICAN TERROR CHARGES

Mahamud Said Omar

Citizenship: US Permanent Resident, born in Somalia.

DOB: n/a.

Arrest: November 8, 2009.

Conviction: n/a.

Sentence: n/a.

Status: Indicted, extradited to US.

Cases: *U.S. v. Mahamud Said Omar.*

Charges: Conspiracy to kill, kidnap, maim, or injure in a foreign country, 18 U.S.C. §956(a) (1); Material support to terrorists, 18 U.S.C. §2339A (a); Material support to a designated terrorist organization, 18 U.S.C. §2339B.

Link to al-Qa'ida: Allegedly funded al-Qa'ida affiliate group al-Shabaab.

Background:

Mahamud Said Omar was arrested in the Netherlands on November 8, 2009, under an indictment dated August 20, 2009.[276] He was charged with providing material support to terrorists, conspiracy to provide material support to terrorists, conspiracy to provide material support to a foreign terrorist organization, and conspiracy to kill, kidnap, maim, and injure. The Dutch Supreme Court approved the US request for extradition in February 2011.[277]

Omar allegedly visited a safe house for al-Shabaab, and provided them with money for the purchase of AK-47 assault rifles. He also travelled to Somalia in 2008, when the indictment alleges that he was providing support to al-Shabaab. Omar's brother, however, insists that the 2008 trip was for Omar's marriage.[278]

Nine other individuals are listed in Omar's indictment as co-conspirators: Shirwa Ahmed, Salah Osman Ahmed, Kamal Said Hassan, Ahmed Ali Omar, Abdifatah Isse, Khalid Mohamud, Zakaria Maruf, Mohamed Abdullahi, and Mustafa Ali Salat. Each of these individuals flew out of Minneapolis and connected to Somalia. Omar, however, was captured in Amsterdam, boarding a flight returning to Minneapolis.[279]

APRIL 2010— YOUNG MAN TARGETED "SOUTH PARK" CREATORS

Zachary Adam Chesser

AKA: Abu Talhah al-Amrikee, Abuu Talxah al-Amrikii.

Citizenship: US.

DOB: December 22, 1989.

Arrest: July 21, 2010.

Conviction: Pled guilty.

Sentence: 25 years in prison on February 24, 2011.

Status: Indictment waived, currently serving 25 years at US Penitentiary, Marion, Illinois.

Cases: *U.S. v. Zachary Adam Chesser.*

Charges: 18 U.S.C. § 875(c) Communicating Threats; 18 U.S.C. § 373 Soliciting Others to Threaten Violence; 18 U.S.C. § 2239B Material Support to Terrorists.

Link to al-Qa'ida: Conducted correspondence with Anwar al-Awlaki.

Background:

> Chesser pled guilty in the Eastern District of Virginia to charges, including making threats against Trey Parker and Matt Stone, the creators of the Comedy Central animated program *South Park*.[280] The program depicted the prophet Muhammad in several of its episodes, which is forbidden by Muslim teaching. Chesser also corresponded with Anwar al-Awlaki.[281]

> Chesser posted to certain jihadist websites and on his own YouTube channel entitled "LearnTeachFightDie."[282] After allegedly deciding to travel to Yemen to join al-Shabaab, Chesser was arrested while attempting to board a flight to Uganda with his newborn son.

> In exchange for his plea, the government agreed, *inter alia*, to cease the prosecution of his wife.[283] He received 25 years imprisonment out of a possible maximum of 30 years.[284]

MAY 2010— FINANCING AND COMMUNICATIONS WITH AL-QA'IDA

Khalid Ouazzani

Citizenship: US, born in Morocco.

DOB: December 17, 1977.

Arrest: February 2010.

Conviction: Pled guilty, May 2010.

Sentence: n/a.

Status: Awaiting Sentencing. Faces up to 65 years and $1,000,000 fine plus restitution.

Cases: *U.S. v. Khalid Ouazzani.*

Charges: Bank fraud (18 U.S.C. §1344); Money laundering (18 U.S.C. §1956 &18 U.S.C. §1957); Interstate fraud (18 U.S.C. §2314); False statement to government agency (18 U.S.C. §1001).

Link to al-Qa'ida: Provided funds to al-Qa'ida from the sale of his business.

Background:

Ouazzani pledged an oath of allegiance to al-Qa'ida in June 2008 and conspired to provide material support until February 2010.[285] Ouazzani, a naturalized US citizen, waived his right to a jury trial and pled guilty to conspiracy to provide material support to a terrorist organization, and to an indictment returned under seal. The sealed indictment contained five counts concerning bank fraud.[286]

As the owner of a used auto parts business, Ouazzani pledged to make a payment to al-Qa'ida, which he did through an intermediary.

Included in the guilty plea were charges unrelated to terrorism. Only the information to which Ouazzini pled guilty contained charges of conspiracy to provide material support. The February 2010 indictment contained only charges pertaining to taking out a bank loan against his business and then using those funds to purchase a home in the United Arab Emirates.

MARCH 2010— NEW JERSEY MAN ARRESTED IN YEMEN

Sharif Mobley

Citizenship: US.

DOB: January 19, 1984.

Arrest: March 2010.[287]

Conviction: n/a.

Sentence: n/a.

Status: Pending Trial in Yemen.

Cases: Unknown.

Charges: Murder, Membership in AQAP.

179

Link to al-Qa'ida: Motivated by preaching of Anwar al-Awlaki.
Background:

Sharif Mobley, the son of two US citizens, grew up in New Jersey and attended Islamic school. He worked at nuclear power plants in New Jersey between 2002 and 2008, and volunteered as an Election Day worker during a New Jersey gubernatorial election in 2004.[288] He married a Philadelphia native, Nzinga Saba Islam, in 2005, had a child in 2007, and moved to Newark, Delaware.

Unlike the New Jersey mosques he attended in his youth, the Newark mosque was mainly comprised of immigrants. At the Newark mosque, he assisted other Muslims in arranging pilgrimages to the Middle East and listened to CD recordings of Anwar al-Awlaki. His wife recalled her impression of al-Awlaki only as a popular preacher.[289]

The family travelled to Yemen and briefly returned to the US following complications in Islam's pregnancy.[290] They began preparations to leave Yemen for the US in late 2009 after the attempted bombing by Umar Farouk Abdulmutallab, and were questioned by the FBI while Mobley attempted to get additional pages for his passport in order to have room for an exit visa.

Mobley was arrested by Yemeni police in January 2010 on reports of his allegedly being linked to AQAP.[291] He complained of injury and was hospitalized. While in the hospital, he befriended and prayed with the two guards assigned to him. At one point, one guard left his gun unattended while washing and the other guard left. Mobley proceeded to lead police on a three-hour shootout and siege on the sixth floor of the hospital, which ended with Mobley injured and two hospital guards dead and a third wounded.[292]

Mobley was charged with murder of a police officer, a capital offense. He is currently awaiting trial in Yemen.[293]

JUNE 2010—OPERATION ARABIAN KNIGHT

Cases: *U.S. v. Almonte*, 10-cr-594, and *U.S. v. Alessa*, 10-mj-8109, U.S. District Court, District of New Jersey (Newark).

Charges: Conspiracy to commit murder in a foreign country, 18 U.S.C. §956(a)(1).

Background:

Alessa and Almonte were arrested while attempting to board different international flights at John F. Kennedy International Airport on June 5, 2010. The FBI titled the four-year surveillance operation "Operation Arabian Knight," after a name Alessa used for himself online and a group called the "Arabian Knights" to which he had belonged in his youth.[294]

Alessa grew up in Bergen, New Jersey, and briefly attended Islamic school before transferring to public school where he was repeatedly in trouble with the school authorities. After 9/11, some of his neighbors recall the family flying the Palestinian flag instead of the American flag. Alessa was well known for his jihadist leanings.[295]

Almonte converted to Islam in 2004 against his father's wishes. He was known for appearing at the 2008 Israel Day parade in New York City with a sign reading "Death to all Juice (*sic*)." [296]

The two attempted to enter Iraq to fight against US forces in 2007. They failed in their attempt and were upset with their inability to join the mujahideen. Authorities credited Anwar al-Awlaki with inspiring the men to violent jihad. They were on their way to joining al-Shabaab at the time of their arrests.[297] Both men pled guilty on March 3, 2011, and could face life in prison.[298]

Mohamed Mahmood Alessa
Citizenship: Dual US and Jordan.
DOB: ca. 1990.
Arrest: June 5, 2010.
Conviction: Pled guilty March 3, 2011.
Sentence: Pending.
Status: Awaiting sentencing (as of July 2011).
Links to al-Qa'ida: Attempted to join al-Qa'ida affiliate al-Shabaab.

Carlos Eduardo Almonte
AKA: Omar.
Citizenship: Dual; US and Dominican Republic.
DOB: ca. 1986.
Arrest: June 5, 2010.
Conviction: Pled guilty March 3, 2011.

Sentence: Pending.

Status: Awaiting sentencing (as of July 2011).

Links to al-Qa'ida: Attempted to join al-Qa'ida affiliate al-Shabaab.

AUGUST 2010— CHICAGO MAN VOLUNTEERS TO JOIN AL-QA'IDA

Shaker Masri

Citizenship: US.

DOB: 1985.

Arrest: August 3, 2010.

Conviction: n/a.

Sentence: n/a.

Status: Awaiting Trial.

Cases: *U.S. v. Shaker Masri*.

Charges: 18 U.S.C. §2339B(a)(1), Providing Material Support to a Designated Terrorist Organization;18 U.S.C. §2339A, Providing Material Support to Terrorists.

Link to al-Qa'ida: Allegedly attempted to join al-Shabaab and encouraged others to join jihad.

Background:

Masri is a US citizen who worked at a nonprofit organization translating the Quran into English.[299] As part of an FBI investigation, a confidential source was placed near Masri. Masri encouraged the source to watch "martyrdom videos" and listen to speeches by leaders of al-Qa'ida, including Anwar al-Awlaki.[300]

Masri informed the FBI source that he intended to travel to participate in violent jihad, and did not anticipate that he would live to the age of 30. Masri wanted to travel to Somalia or Afghanistan, and he planned to obtain a part-time job in order to afford travel arrangements.[301] He attempted to persuade a woman in London to pay for a trip to see her, and from there to travel to Jordan and Somalia. Masri later communicated to her that he intended to travel to Merca, a city in Somalia under the control of the al-Qa'ida-affiliated group al-Shabaab.[302] Masri was arrested on August 3, 2010.

MAY 30, 2010— MATERIAL SUPPORT TO AL-QA'IDA IN THE ARABIAN PENINSULA

Barry Walter Bujol, Jr.

Citizenship: US.

DOB: 1981.

Arrest: May 30, 2010 in Houston, Texas.

Conviction: n/a.

Sentence: n/a.

Status: Indicted on June 3, 2010, US District Court, Southern District of Texas. Currently awaiting trial without bail in Houston, Texas (as of June 29, 2011).

Cases: *U.S. v. Bujol, No.* 4:10-CR-00368, 2010 WL 2286923 (S.D. Tex. June 3, 2010).

Charges: (1) Attempting to provide material support or resources to designated foreign terrorist organizations (18 U.S.C. § 2339B); (2) Aggravated identity theft (18 U.S.C. §1028A(a)(2)).

Link to al-Qa'ida: E-mail correspondence with Anwar al-Awlaki starting in 2008; Confidential Human Source (FBI informant) posing as al-Qa'ida member.[303]

Background:

Barry Walter Bujol, Jr. was born to a Baptist family but converted to Islam with his wife around 2006. Neighbors stated that Bujol and his wife "...kept to themselves and never caused any trouble." and it was a shock for Bujol's family members when they found out he was arrested on terror charges.[304] Bujol was arrested in Texas twice for driving with a suspended license and was also arrested in New Jersey for driving with a suspended license during an unsuccessful attempt to travel to the Middle East. A month after being denied the right to board a plane in Houston, Texas, Canadian authorities denied him permission to pass through a Detroit border crossing.

The FBI Joint Terrorism Task Force started monitoring Bujol in early 2008 and determined in the summer of 2008 that Bujol was communicating with Anwar al-Awlaki via e-mail.[305] Al-Awlaki provided Bujol with a document entitled *42 Ways of Supporting Jihad*, and Bujol asked al-Awlaki how he could help fund overseas fighters.

After being contacted by an FBI informant whom Bujol thought was an al-Qa'ida agent, Bujol agreed to carry money and materials, including cell phones, prepaid telephone calling cards, global positioning system equipment, and sensitive US military weapons publications.[306] In a sting operation, Bujol was arrested after boarding a ship that was to start his journey to Yemen.

The federal judge in charge of Bujol's case, Judge David Hittner, has written an order precluding Bujol from filing any pleadings or documents on his own behalf because he is represented by counsel. This preclusion order came after a self-filed motion disclosed information deemed sensitive to the government's investigation.[307] If convicted, Bujol faces up to 20 years in prison.

JULY 2010— AMERICAN CITIZEN PUBLISHES ENGLISH-LANGUAGE JIHAD MAGAZINE

Samir Khan
Citizenship: US and Saudi Arabia.
DOB: 1986.
Arrest: n/a.
Conviction: n/a.
Sentence: n/a.
Status: Killed September 30, 2011, in a drone strike along with Anwar al-Awlaki.[308]
Cases: n/a.
Charges: No indictment yet, federal grand jury convened.
Link to al-Qa'ida: Communicated with Anwar al-Awlaki before leaving for Yemen to join AQAP.
Background:
Born in Riyadh, Saudi Arabia, Khan moved with his family to Queens, New York, in 1993 at the age of seven, and then to Charlotte, North Carolina, with his family in 2004. While living in Queens as a teenager, Khan is reported to have attended meetings of the Islamic Thinkers Society, a nonviolent group that promotes Islam by leafleting in New York.

Khan began promoting Islam on his personal blog in 2001 out of his parents' house. He created a number of different blogs over the next several years, changing service providers frequently as citizen watchdog groups reported his activities. While living in America, Khan authored one of the most popular English language sites promoting violent jihad, what *The New York Times* called "...a kind of Western relay station for the multimedia productions of violent Islamic groups."[309]

When Khan was still living with his parents in North Carolina, his father arranged two interventions in which elders from the local Muslim community attempted to disabuse him of his violent beliefs. According to the man who hosted the meetings, "Samir had very few friends around here...he was clearly going down the wrong path. And we tried to talk to him about that."[310]

Intelligence officials believe that Anwar al-Awlaki then invited Khan to Yemen and sponsored him to join AQAP and publish *Inspire* magazine.[311] Khan left for Yemen on a round-trip ticket in October 2009 but never returned. In the first issue of *Inspire*, Khan wrote a four-page article that detailed his reasons for fleeing America and joining AQAP in Yemen. There have been seven issues of *Inspire* to date, all thought to be edited by Samir Khan in Yemen.

A federal grand jury convened in Charlotte, North Carolina, in August of 2010 to consider evidence against Samir Khan. He was still publishing *Inspire* for AQAP in Yemen when he was killed by a drone strike in September 2011.

MAY 19, 2010— ALASKAN COUPLE CREATES JIHADIST HIT-LIST

Cases: *U.S. v. Rockwood*, No. 3:10-cr-00061-RRB (D. Alaska); *U.S. v. Rockwood*, 3:10-cr-00060-RRB (D. Alaska).
Charges: False Statements to a Federal Agent investigating an Offense Involving Domestic Terrorism (18 U.S.C. § 1001(a)(2)).
Background:
Paul Rockwood and his wife converted to Islam between 2001 and 2002 in Virginia.[312] There, Rockwood became a strict adherent to al-Awlaki's ideology and became convinced that it was his religious responsibility to kill anyone who desecrated Islam.

He moved to King Salmon, Alaska, in 2006 and began researching individuals as potential targets and methods for his mission.[313] Rockwood is known to have read al-Awlaki's works while residing in King Salmon, including *Constants on the Path to Jihad* and *44 Ways to Support Jihad*. During this time, Rockwood began researching explosive components, the design of remote triggering devices, and the construction of IEDs for delivery through the mail or by a courier.[314]

In late 2009, Rockwood started to share his ideas about committing violent acts against the enemies of Islam; and by 2010, Rockwood had a formalized list containing more than 15 specific targets.[315] In April 2010, Rockwood gave the written target list to his wife Nadia, who took the list to Anchorage, where it was eventually obtained by the FBI Joint Terrorism Task Force.[316] FBI agents interviewed Paul Rockwood on May 19, 2010, and it was at this time that he denied creating the list, knowing the purpose of the list, and ever having a list of names.

Paul Gene Rockwood

Citizenship: US.

DOB: 1975.

Arrest: May 19, 2010.

Conviction: Pled guilty.

Sentence: Filed August 16, 2010; 8 years in prison followed by 3 years of supervised release; plea deal is contingent on wife's plea deal of five years of probation to be served outside the US.

Status: Indicted July 21, 2010, serving 8 years in federal prison in Alaska (as of 6/29/11).

Link to al-Qa'ida: self-radicalized, known to have read Anwar al-Awlaki's works, including *Constants on the Path to Jihad* and *44 Ways to Jihad*.

Nadia Rockwood

Citizenship: Dual US and UK.

DOB: 1974 or 1975.

Arrest: May 19, 2010.

Conviction: Plea filed on August 16, 2010.

Sentence: 5 years probation to be served outside the US.

Status: Indicted July 21, 2010, serving probation in UK and fighting court battle to visit the US to see husband and have kids spend time in the US (as of 6/29/11).

Links to al-Qa'ida: Inspired by the teachings of Anwar al-Awlaki.

OCTOBER 26, 2010— DC METRO STATION BOMB PLOT

Farooque Ahmed

Citizenship: US, born in Pakistan.

DOB: n/a.

Arrest: October 27, 2010.

Conviction: Pled guilty to the first 2 counts, and the third count was dropped.

Sentence: 23 years in prison followed by 50 years of supervised release.

Status: Indicted October 26, 2010; serving sentence in federal prison in Virginia (as of 6/29/11).

Cases: *U.S. v. Ahmed*, No. 1:10 cr 413 (October 26, 2010) Indictment (2010 WL 4788451 (E.D. Va.); *U.S. v. Ahmed*, No. 1:10 413 (April 11, 2011) Plea Agreement (2011 WL 1348599 (E.D. Va.)).

Charges: (1) Attempting to provide material support to a designated foreign terrorist organization (18 U.S.C. § 2339B); (2) Collecting information to assist in planning a terrorist attack on a transit facility (18 U.S.C. § 1992(a)(8)); (3) Attempting to provide material support to terrorists (18 U.S.C. § 2339A).

Link to al-Qa'ida: Communicated and planned attacks with FBI agents posing as al-Qai'da members.

Background:

From April 2010 until his arrest in October 2010, Ahmed was in contact with what he believed were members of al-Qa'ida, but who were actually undercover FBI operatives. Despite attempts to contact militants abroad, Ahmed had no known contact with al-Qa'ida or its affiliates.[317]

On May 15, 2010, during a meeting with an undercover FBI operative, Ahmed agreed to carry out surveillance at a local hotel and at the Arlington National Cemetery Metro station. After performing the surveillance, he delivered a USB stick with a video to a person he believed was an al-Qa'ida member. Again, on September 28, 2010, Ahmed provided another USB stick with further pictures of Metro stations.[318] Ahmed also gave the undercover officers advice on where to plant explosives as a result of his surveillance.

Ahmed was caught in the sting operation and arrested on October 25, 2010. During subsequent searches of his home, police found three guns and a copy of the biography of Anwar al-Awlaki.[319] According to authorities, the public was never in danger because the FBI was aware of Ahmed's activities, monitored him throughout the entire process, and arrested him before he could cause any harm.[320]

OCTOBER 2010— NEWBURGH FOUR: NY SYNAGOGUE BOMB PLOTS

Cases: *U.S. v. Cromitie*, No. 09 Cr. 558(CM), slip op. May 10, 2011 (2011 WL 1842219).

Charges: (1) Conspiracy to use WMD within the US (18 U.S.C. § 2332a(a) (2)(C)); (2)-(4) Attempting to use WMD within the US (18 U.S.C. § 2332a(a) (2)(C)); (5) Conspiracy to acquire and use anti-aircraft missiles (18 U.S.C. §§ 2332g(a) (1), (b) (1), (b)(4), (b)(5), and (c) (1)); (6) Attempting to acquire and use anti-aircraft missiles (18 U.S.C. §§ 2332g(a) (1), (b) (1), (b) (4), (b)(5), and (c)(1)); (7) Conspiracy to kill officers and employees of the US (18 U.S.C. §§ 1114 and 1117); (8) Attempting to kill officers and employees of the US (18 U.S.C. §§ 1114 and 2).

Background:

On May 20, 2009, the FBI and NYPD arrested a four-man homegrown terror cell. They had planned to shoot down a cargo plane en route to Iraq or Afghanistan with surface-to-air guided missiles, while simultaneously using their cell phones to detonate car bombs parked at two synagogues in the Bronx. Unbeknownst to the men, their operation was an FBI sting, and the explosives and weaponry provided by the FBI were totally inert.[321]

The men were petty criminals, three American-born and one Haitian immigrant, who were all jailhouse converts to Islam, with a vague understanding of radical Islam, looking for retribution for the hardships of their lives.[322] Led by Cromitie, the cell found the outlet of jihad justified as vengeance for the "killing of Muslim brothers and sisters in Muslim countries," and blamed all the world's problems on the Jews.[323]

The FBI had been monitoring the cell for over a year after being tipped off by an informant. The group had no ties to any terrorist organization. They believed they were linked to al-Qa'ida operatives; however, the operatives were undercover FBI agents.[324]

James Cromitie
Citizenship: US.
DOB: December 24, 1964.
Arrest: May 20, 2009.
Conviction: Guilty, October 2010.
Sentence: 25 years in prison.
Status: Imprisoned.
Link to al-Qa'ida: Attempted to contact al-Qa'ida, but operatives were
    actually FBI agents.[325]

David Williams
Citizenship: US.
DOB: February 9, 1981.
Arrest: May 20, 2009.
Conviction: Guilty, October 2010.
Sentence: 25 years in prison.
Status: Imprisoned.
Link to al-Qa'ida: Attempted to contact al-Qa'ida, but operatives were
    actually FBI agents.

Onta Williams (no relation to David)
Citizenship: US.
DOB: June 29, 1976.
Arrest: May 20, 2009.
Conviction: Guilty, October 2010.
Sentence: 25 years in prison.
Status: Imprisoned.
Link to al-Qa'ida: Attempted to contact al-Qa'ida, but operatives were
    actually FBI agents.

Laguerre Payen
Citizenship: US, born in Haiti.
DOB: September 24, 1981.
Arrest: May 20, 2009.
Conviction: Guilty, October 2010.
Sentence: 25 years in prison.
Status: Imprisoned.
Link to al-Qa'ida: Attempted to contact al-Qa'ida, but operatives were
    actually FBI agents.[326]

NOVEMBER 26, 2010 — SOMALI-AMERICAN ATTEMPTS VEHICLE BORNE IED ATTACK IN PORTLAND

Mohamed Osman Mohamud

Citizenship: US, born in Somalia.

DOB: 1991.

Arrest: November 26, 2010.

Conviction: Pretrial motions ongoing with a 15-day jury trial set for April 10, 2012, in Portland before Judge Garr M. King.

Sentence: If convicted, Mohamud faces a maximum sentence of life in prison.

Status: Indicted November 29, 2010, awaiting trial (as of 6/29/11).

Cases: *U.S. v. Mohamud*, No. 10-CR-475-KI, Indictment, WL 4814683 (D.Or.) November 29, 2010.

Charges: (1) Attempting to use a weapon of mass destruction (18 U.S.C. § 2332a(a)(2)(A)).

Link to al-Qa'ida: Contacted suspected terrorists in Pakistan.

Background:

> Mohamud is a naturalized US citizen who lived in Corvalis, Oregon, and dropped out of Oregon State University on October 6, 2010. He was born in Somalia, but graduated from Westview High School in Beaverton, Oregon.[327]

> FBI officials began their surveillance of Mohamud in August 2009 and saw that he was in contact with an unindicted suspected terrorist currently living in Pakistan.[328] He was put on the no-fly list after e-mailing suspected terrorists and discussing the possibility of flying to Pakistan to engage in violent jihad.[329] Mohamud was prevented from boarding a flight to Alaska on June 10, 2010, at which point he was interviewed by the FBI and a sting operation began.

> On June 23, an undercover agent e-mailed Mohamud pretending to be an associate of Mohamud's friends in Pakistan. The undercover agent first met with Mohamud on July 30.[330] Over the next several months, Mohamud planned the details of the bombing, which was to include a VBIED at a downtown Portland Christmas tree-lighting ceremony. Mohamud and an undercover FBI agent drove a van with a fake bomb to the downtown location, but when Mohamud dialed a code into a cell phone that he thought would serve as a detonator, police arrested him instead.[331]

Mohamud occasionally attended services at the Salman Al-Farisi Islamic Center of Corvallis, Oregon, which was set on fire on November 28, 2010. Authorities have linked the arson to Mohamud's failed bombing attempt, but the FBI is still investigating. If convicted of the single count of attempt to use a weapon of mass destruction, Mohamud faces up to life in prison.[332]

DECEMBER 8, 2010— BALTIMORE VEHICLE BORNE IED BOMB PLOT

Antonio Martinez
AKA: Muhammad Hussain.
Citizenship: US.
DOB: September 14, 1989.
Arrest: June 30, 2011.
Conviction: Pled not guilty.
Sentence: n/a.
Status: Indicted December 8, 2010, US District Court, District of Maryland. Currently held without bail, no trial date set yet (as of 6/29/11).
Cases: *U.S. v. Martinez*, No. 10-4761 JKB, December 8, 2010, 2010 WL 4970016 (D.Md.) (Trial Pleading).
Charges: (1) Attempted murder of federal officers/employees (18 U.S.C. § 1114(3); (2) Attempted use of a weapon of mass destruction against property owned, leased or used by the US (18 U.S.C. §2332a(a)(3)).[333]
Link to al-Qa'ida: Inspired by al-Awlaki.
Background:

In early October 2010, the FBI began monitoring Martinez after several public Facebook posts. After a confidential source began a relationship with Martinez in early October, the FBI recorded a series of conversations in which Martinez identified an Armed Forces recruiting center as his intended target.[334] After this, Martinez was introduced to an undercover officer who Martinez thought would help him.

During the course of planning the attack, Martinez told the undercover officer that al-Awlaki was an inspiration, and a public Facebook post by Martinez read "I love Sheikh Anwar al Awlaki for the sake of ALLAH."[335] He also told the undercover officer in early November that his goal was to become a martyr, but that he needed training. After Mohamed Osman Mohamud was arrested in Portland on November 26, 2010, Martinez expressed hesitation over his plans, but ultimately decided to complete the bombing.[336]

Notes and Bibliographic References

1. Yonah Alexander, *Terrorists in Our Midst*, (Santa Barbara, CA: Praeger, 2010).

2. BBC, "Profile: John Walker Lindh." 2002. *http://news.bbc.co.uk/2/hi/americas/1779455.stm*.

3. *Ibid*. 2.

4. CNN, "John Walker Lindh Profile." 2001. *http://www.cnn.com/CNN/Programs/people/shows/walker/profile.html*.

5. *Ibid*. 4.

6. *Ibid*. 4.

7. *Ibid*. 4.

8. *Ibid*. 2.

9. *Ibid*. 4.

10. *Ibid*. 2.

11. Perry, Alex. "Inside the Battle at Qala-I-Jangi." *TIME Magazine*, December 1, 2001. *http://www.time.com/time/magazine/article/0,9171,1001390,00.html*.

12. *Ibid*. 4.

13. CNN, "Dirty Bomb Suspect's Criminal Record." June 11, 2002. *http://edition.cnn.com/2002/US/06/11/muhajir.background/index.html*.

14. Sontag, Deborah. *The New York Times*, "Terror Suspect's Path from Streets to Brig." April 25, 2004. *http://www.nytimes.com/2004/04/25/us/terror-suspect-s-path-from-streets-to-brig.html?pagewanted=6&src=pm*.

15. Kelley, Jack, and Donna Leinwand. *USA Today*, "U.S. Citizen Arrested in 'Dirty Bomb' Plot." June 11, 2002. *http://www.usatoday.com/news/nation/2002/06/10/terror-arrest.htm*.

16. *Ibid*. 15.

17. *Ibid*. 14.

18. *Ibid*. 14.

19. Purdy, Matthew and Lowell Bergman. *The New York Times*, "Where the Trail Led: Inside the Lackawanna Case." October 12, 2003. *http://www.nytimes.com/2003/10/12/nyregion/where-trail-led-between-evidence-suspicion-unclear-danger-inside-lackawanna.html?ref=mukhtaralbakri&pagewanted=all*.

20. *Ibid*. 19.
21. *Ibid*. 19.
22. United States Department of Justice, "Mukhtar al-Bakri Pleads Guilty to Providing Material Support to al Qaeda." May 19, 2003. *http://www.justice.gov/opa/pr/2003/May/03_crm_307.htm*.
23. *Ibid*. 22.
24. *Ibid*. 22.
25. Temple-Raston, Dina. *The Washington Post*, "Enemy Within? Not Quite." September 9, 2007. *http://www.washingtonpost.com/wp-dyn/content/article/2007/09/07/AR2007090702049.html*.
26. AL-Haj, Ahmed. *USA Today*, "FBI Most Wanted Terror Suspect Jailed in Yemen." May 19, 2008. *http://www.usatoday.com/news/world/2008-05-19-649772150_x.htm*.
27. *Ibid*. 25.
28. FindLaw, "Oregon Terror Cell Case." October 3, 2002. *http://news.findlaw.com/legalnews/us/terrorism/cases/index.html*.
29. Global Jihad, "Portland Seven." May 9, 2008. *http://www.globaljihad.net/view_page.asp?id=1101*.
30. *Ibid*. 29.; and FBI Portland Field Office, "FBI'S Joint Terrorism Task Force Arrests Four on Terrorism Charges, Two Others Who Were Indicted Are Now Fugitives." October 4, 2002.
31. Howlett, Deborah. Star-Ledger, "The Two Sides of One Law, the Two Lives of One Man." July 24, 2005. *http://web.archive.org/web/20070503154313/http://www.nj.com/news/ledger/index.ssf?/news/ledger/stories/patriotact/partthree.html*.
32. *Ibid*. 31.
33. *Ibid*. 31.
34. CNN, "First Court Appearance for 3 of 6 Linked to al Qaeda Ties." October 4, 2002. *http://articles.cnn.com/2002-10-04/us/oregon.fbi.alqaeda_1_al-qaeda-ties-muhammad-ibrahim-bilal-habis-abdulla-al-saoub?_s=PM:US*.
35. Budnick, Nick. Willamette Week, "The Making of a 'Terrorist.'" October 16, 2002. *http://www.wweek.com/portland/article-1377-the_making_of_a_terrorist.html*.
36. *Ibid*. 35.
37. U.S. Department of Justice, "October Martinique Lewis Pleads Guilty to Money Laundering Charges in Portland Cell Case." September 26, 2003. *http://findarticles.com/p/articles/mi_pjus/is_200309/ai_3199387328/*.

38. Brinkley, Joel and Eric Lichtblau. *The New York Times*, "U.S. Releases Saudi-American It Had Captured in Afghanistan." October 12, 2004. *http://www.nytimes.com/2004/10/12/international/middleeast/12hamdi.html?ref=yaseresamhamdi.*

39. *Ibid.* 38.

40. Lichtblau, Eric. *The New York Times*, "U.S., Bowing to Court, to Free 'Enemy Combatant.'" Sept 23, 2004. *http://www.nytimes.com/2004/09/23/politics/23hamdi.html?pagewanted=2&_r=2*; and Brinkley, Joel. *The New York Times*, "Deportation Delayed for 'Enemy Combatant.'" October 1, 2004. *http://www.nytimes.com/2004/10/01/politics/01hamdi.html?ref=yaseresamhamdi.*

41. *Ibid.* 38.

42. The NEFA Foundation, "The Columbus Mall Plot." August 2007. *http://www.nefafoundation.org/miscellaneous/ColumbusMall_Plot.pdf.*

43. *Ibid.* 42.

44. U.S. Department of Justice, "Iyman Faris Sentenced for Providing Material Support to al-Qaida." October 28, 2003. *http://www.justice.gov/opa/pr/2003/October/03_crm_589.htm.*

45. *Ibid.* 44.

46. Thomas, Pierre, George Zonders, and Jason Ryan. ABC News, "Ohio Terrorist Talking to FBI." June 20, 2003. *http://abcnews.go.com/US/story?id=90546&page=1.*

47. U.S. Department of Justice, "Iyman Faris Sentenced for Providing Material Support to al-Qaida." October 28, 2003. *http://www.justice.gov/opa/pr/2003/October/03_crm_589.htm*; and Defense Human Resources Activity, "Other Case Summaries: Iyman Faris-Reactivated Veteran." *http://www.dhra.mil/perserec/adr/counterterrorism/casesummaries.htm.*

48. Arena, Kelli and Terry Frieden. CNN, "Ashcroft: Ohio Trucker Admits Terror Ties." June 19, 2003. *http://articles.cnn.com/2003-06-19/justice/alqaeda.plea_1_qaeda-plea-agreement-plea-deal?_s=PM:LAW.*

49. *Ibid.* 48.

50. Johnston, David. *The New York Times*, "Somali is Accused of Planning a Terror Attack at a Shopping Center in Ohio." June 15, 2004. *http://www.nytimes.com/2004/06/15/national/15terror.html?scp=4&sq=Nuradin%20Abdi&st=cse.*

51. *Ibid.* 50.

52. U.S. Department of Justice, "Ohio Man Sentenced to Ten Years Imprisonment for Conspiracy to Provide Material Support to Terrorists."

Nov 27, 2007. *http://www.justice.gov/opa/pr/2007/November/07_ nsd_944.html*.

53. MSNBC, "Man Allegedly in al-Qaida Plot to Bomb Ohio Shopping Mall." June 15, 2004. *http://www.msnbc.msn.com/id/5209103/ns/us_ news-security/t/man-allegedly-al-qaida-plot-bomb-ohio-shopping- mall/#.TqrLGpsUqso*.

54. CBS News, "Ohio Man Indicted on Terrorism Charges." Feb 11, 2009. *http://www.cbsnews.com/stories/2007/04/12/terror/main2675595.shtml*.

55. Flutty, John. The Columbus Dispatch, "Worthington Man Gets 20 Years in Terrorist Plot." February 26, 2009. *http://www.freerepublic. com/focus/news/2194730/posts*.

56. U.S. Department of Justice, "Ohio Man Pleads Guilty to Conspiracy to Bomb Targets in Europe and the United States." June 3, 2008. *http:// www.justice.gov/opa/pr/2008/June/08-nsd-492.html*.

57. *Ibid*. 54.

58. Anti-Defamation League, "Criminal Proceedings in 2009." March 9, 2010. *http://www.adl.org/main_Terrorism/american_ muslim_extremists_criminal_proceedings.htm?Multi_page_ sections=sHeading_3*.

59. Global Jihad, "Christopher 'Kenyatta' Paul." *http://www.globaljihad. net/view_page.asp?id=1630*.

60. *Ibid*. 56.

61. *Ibid*. 58.

62. Global Jihad, "Virginia Terror Network." *http://globaljihad.net/view_ page.asp?id=547*.

63. Arena, Kelli, Kevin Bohn, and Terry Frieden. CNN, "Feds Charge 11 Men with Conspiracy in Overseas Jihad." June 27, 2003. *http://www. cnn.com/2003/US/06/27/terror.arrests/index.html?iref=allsearch*.

64. Bohn, Kevin. CNN, "'Virginia Jihad' Suspects Charged with Plotting to Fight U.S." September 26, 2003. *http://articles.cnn.com/2003-09-25/ justice/virginia.terror.suspects_1_virginia-jihad-seifullah-chapman- hammad-abdur-raheem?_s=PM:LAW*.

65. U.S. Department of Justice, "Two Defendants in Virginia Jihad Case Plead Guilty to Weapons Charges, Will Cooperate with ongoing Investigation." January 16, 2004.

66. *Ibid*. 62.

67. Markon, Jerry. *The Washington Post*, "VA Man's Sentence Increased to Life in Terror Plot." July 28, 2009. *http://www.washingtonpost.com/ wp-dyn/content/article/2009/07/27/AR2009072701384.html*.

68. Redman, Justine. CNN, "Al Qaeda Conspirator Re-Sentenced to Life." July 27, 2009. *http://articles.cnn.com/2009-07-27/justice/terrorism. resentencing_1_ahmed-omar-abu-ali-al-qaeda-resentenced?_ s=PM:CRIME.*

69. Dao, James and Eric Lichtblau. *The New York Times*, "Case Adds to Outrage for Muslims in Northern Virginia." February 27, 2005. *http:// www.nytimes.com/2005/02/27/national/nationalspecial3/27terror.html.*

70. Global Jihad,"Ahmed Omar Abu Ali." February 6, 2008. *http:// www.globaljihad.net/view_page.asp?id=932.*

71. U.S. Department of Justice, "Virginia Man Returned to the United States to Face Charges of Providing Material Support to al-Qaida." February 22, 2005. *http://www.justice.gov/opa/pr/2005/February/05_ crm_072.htm.*

72. *Ibid.* 71.

73. *Ibid.* 71.

74. *Ibid.* 70.

75. Markon, Jerry. *The Washington Post*, "Falls Church Man's Sentence in Terror Plot is Increased to Life." July 28, 2009. *http:// www.washingtonpost.com/wp-dyn/content/article/2009/07/27/ AR2009072701384.html.*

76. U.S. Department of Justice, "Chicago Cousins Plead Guilty to Conspiracy to Provide Material Support to Terrorists." January 15, 2009. *http://www.investigativeproject.org/documents/case_docs/762.pdf.*

77. *Ibid.* 76.

78. *Ibid.* 76.

79. *Ibid.* 76.

80. U.S. Department of Justice, "Four Men Indicted on Terrorism Charges Related to Conspiracy to Attack Military Facilities, Other Targets." August 31, 2005. *http://www.justice.gov/opa/pr/2005/August/05_ crm_453.html.*

81. Ross, Brian. ABC News, "Terror Plot Hatched in California Prison." August 16, 2005. *http://abclocal.go.com/kgo/story?section=news/ state&id=3356111.*

82. Marquez, Jeremiah. Associated Press, "Four Indicted in Alleged Terror Plot against LA-Area Targets." September 1, 2005. *http://web.archive. org/web/20060815233005/http://sfgate.com/cgi-bin/article.cgi?f=/n/ a/2005/08/31/state/n143135D24.DTL.*

83. PBS Online, "Homegrown: Islam in Prison." April 2007. *http:// www.pbs.org/weta/crossroads/about/show_homegrown_film.html.*

84. *Ibid.* 83.
85. *Ibid.* 82.
86. *Ibid.* 83.
87. *Ibid.* 81.
88. *Ibid.* 80.
89. *Ibid.* 80.
90. *Ibid.* 83.
91. PBS Online, "America at a Crossroads: US District Court for the Central District of California October 2004 Grand Jury." October 2004. *http:// www.pbs.org/weta/crossroads/incl/JIS_Indictment.pdf.*
92. *Ibid.* 80.
93. *Ibid.* 91.
94. Anti-Defamation League, "Two Sentenced in Los Angeles Terror Plot against Jewish Institutions." August 26, 2008. *http://www.adl.org/ main_Terrorism/los_angeles_sentenced.htm.*
95. *Ibid.* 91.
96. *Ibid.* 94.
97. *The New York Times,* "California: 12 Year Sentence in Terrorism Plot." July 22, 2008. *http://query.nytimes.com/gst/fullpage.html?res=9C0CE FDC143FF931A15754C0A96E9C8B63.*
98. *Ibid.* 91.
99. Murr, Andrew. The Daily Beast, "Thwarting Terror." December 15, 2007. *http://www.newsweek.com/2007/12/14/thwarting-terror.html.*
100. Mrozek, Thom. U.S. Attorney's Office in the Central District of California, "Press Release: Man Involved in Domestic Terrorism Plot Targeting Military and Jewish Facilities Sentenced to 22 years." June 23, 2008. *http://www.justice.gov/usao/cac/Pressroom/pr2008/085.html.*
101. Nichols, Terry. CNN, "Chicago Man Arrested in Alleged Bob Plot." 2004. *http://articles.cnn.com/2004-08-05/us/chicago.arrest_1_bomb-plot-timothy-mcveigh-truck-bomb?_s=PM:US.*
102. Anti-Defamation League, "Man Sentenced to 160 Years for Plot to Bomb Chicago Courthouse." 2006. *http://www.adl.org/learn/extremism_in_the_news/Anti_Government/gale_nettles_plot_12306.htm?LEARN_Cat=Extremism&LEARN_SubCat=Extremism_in_the_News.*
103. Sanders, Eli. *The New York Times,* "Guardsman Given Life in Prison for Trying to Help al Qaeda." September 4, 2004. *http://www.nytimes. com/2004/09/04/national/04soldier.html?scp=2&sq=%22Amir%20 Abdul%20Rashid%22&st=cse.*

104. Global Jihad, "Ryan Gibson Anderson." July 26, 2009. *http://www.globaljihad.net/view_page.asp?id=1634*; and Defense Personnel Security Research Center, "2000-2004." *http://www.dhra.mil/perserec/espionagecases/2000-04.htm*.

105. *Los Angeles Times*, "Guardsman's Terrorism Case Hearing Begins." May 13, 2004. *http://articles.latimes.com/2004/may/13/nation/na-hearing13*.

106. Malik, Shiv. *The Guardian*, "Mohammed Junaid Babar Left Prison Still Advocating Violence." March 9, 2011. *http://www.guardian.co.uk/world/2011/mar/09/mohammed-junaid-babar-prison-violence*.

107. Malik, Shiv. *The Guardian*, "Jihadi Who Helped Train 7/7 Bomber Freed by US after just Five Years." February 13, 2011. *http://www.guardian.co.uk/uk/2011/feb/13/jihadi-train-7-7-bomber-freed*.

108. Global Jihad, "Mohammed J. Babar." May 12, 2007. *http://www.globaljihad.net/view_page.asp?id=192*.

109. Hays, Tom. ABC News, "New Yorker May be Link to London Attacks." July 19, 2005. *http://web.archive.org/web/20060219055413/http://abcnews.go.com/US/wireStory?id=953171*.

110. Rashbaum, William K. and Ravi Somaiya. *The New York Times*, "British Anger over Release of Babar, Linked to 2005 Bombings." February 15, 2011. *http://www.nytimes.com/2011/02/16/world/europe/16babar.html*.

111. Malik, Shiv. *The Guardian*, "The al-Qaida Supergrass and the 7/7 Questions that Remain Unanswered." February 13, 2011. *http://www.guardian.co.uk/uk/2011/feb/14/al-qaida-supergrass-77-questions*.

112. *Ibid*. 111.

113. Rice, Harvey and Renee Lee. *The Houston Chronicle*, "Experts Doubt Suspect's Superbomb would Work." May 25, 2005. *http://www.chron.com/news/houston-texas/article/Experts-doubt-suspect-s-superbomb-would-work-1502240.php*.

114. Lozano, Juan. CBS News, "Texas Tall Tales, or Terror Plot?" September 10, 2009. *http://www.cbsnews.com/stories/2005/05/27/terror/main698157.shtml*.

115. Investigative Project on Terrorism, "United States of America v. Ronald Allen Grecula." August 8, 2006. *http://www.investigativeproject.org/documents/case_docs/336.pdf*.

116. United States Attorney's Office, "Liberty City Defendants Sentenced on Terror-Related Charges." November 20, 2009. *http://www.justice.gov/usao/fls/PressReleases/091120-04.html*.

117. *Ibid*. 116.

118. Laughlin, Meg and Tamara Lush. *St. Petersburg Times*, "Feds: Hatred of U.S. Fueled Plots." June 24, 2006. *http://www.sptimes. com/2006/06/24/State/Feds__Hatred_of_US_fu.shtml.*

119. Weaver, Jay. *Miami Herald*, "Fate of Remaining 'Liberty City Seven' Defendants Now up to Appeals Court." August 23, 2011. *http:// www.miamiherald.com/2011/08/23/2371841/fate-of-remaining-liberty-city.html.*

120. Griffen, Drew et al. CNN, "Indictment: Suspects Wanted to 'Kill All the Devils We Can.'" June 24, 2006. *http://www.cnn. com/2006/US/06/23/miami.raids/index.html.*

121. "Miami Arrests: Seas of David." *The Economist*, June 29, 2006. *http://www.economist.com/node/7117914?story_id=7117914.*

122. *Ibid.* 121.

123. *Ibid.* 121.

124. United States Immigration and Customs Enforcement, "Liberty City Defendants Sentenced to Federal Prison on Terror-related Charges." 2009. *http://www.ice.gov/news/releases/0911/091120miami.htm.*

125. U.S. Department of Justice, "Leader of Liberty City Six Convicted on All Counts..." May 12, 2009. *http://www.justice.gov/usao/fls/ PressReleases/090512-01.html.*

126. Weaver, Jay and Trenton Daniel. *Miami Herald*, "Acquitted Haitian Defendant in Liberty City Seven Terror Case is Deported." January 20, 2011. *http://www.miamiherald.com/2011/01/20/2026227/acquitted-haitian-defendant-in.html.*

127. North Carolina Department of Correction, "Offender Public Information: Mohammed R. Taheriazar." *http://webapps6.doc.state. nc.us/opi/viewoffender.do?method=view&offenderID=0943499&sear chLastName=Taheri-Azar&listurl=pagelistoffendersearchresults&lis tpage=1.*

128. Global Jihad, "Mohammed Reza Taheri-Azar." August 3, 2009. *http:// www.globaljihad.net/view_page.asp?id=1645.*

129. Eyewitness News, "Taheri-Azar Writes to Eyewitness News." March 14, 2006. *http://abclocal.go.com/wtvd/story?section=news/ local&id=3992674.*

130. *Ibid.* 129.

131. Taheri-Azar, Mohammed. *Herald-Sun*, "Mohammed Taheri-Azar's Letter to Police." March 24, 2006. *http://www.investigativeproject. org/documents/case_docs/248.pdf.*

132. *Ibid.* 129.

133. FOX News, "1 Killed, 5 Wounded in Seattle Jewish Center Shooting." 2006. *http://www.foxnews.com/story/0,2933,206172,00.html*.

134. *Ibid*. 133.

135. *The Seattle Times*, "Once inside He Immediately Started Firing." July 29, 2006. *http://seattletimes.nwsource.com/html/localnews/2003160576_shootingweb29.html*.

136. Jihad Watch, "11 New Charges Filed in Jewish Federation Shootings; Defendant Pleads Insanity." May 30, 2007. *http://www.jihadwatch.org/2007/05/11-new-charges-filed-in-jewish-federation-shootings-defendant-pleads-insanity.html*.

137. *Ibid*. 135.

138. U.S. Department of Justice, "Ehsanul Islam Sadequee Faces Up to 60 Years in Federal Prison." August 12, 2009. *http://www.justice.gov/opa/pr/2009/August/09-nsd-790.html*.

139. Hayes, Ashley. CNN, "Georgia Men get Lengthy Prison Time for Supporting Terrorists." December 14, 2009. *http://articles.cnn.com/2009-12-14/justice/terror.sentence_1_terrorist-sadequee-and-ahmed-syed-haris-ahmed?_s=PM:CRIME*.

140. *Ibid*. 138.

141. *Ibid*. 139.

142. Federal Bureau of Investigation, "Terrorism Defendants Sentenced." December 14, 2009. *http://www.fbi.gov/atlanta/press-releases/2009/at121409a.htm*.

143. *Ibid*. 142.

144. Federal Bureau of Prisons, "Inmate Locator: Ehsanul Islam Sadequee." *http://www.bop.gov/iloc2/InmateFinderServlet?Transaction=NameSearch&needingMoreList=false&FirstName=ehsanul&Middle=&LastName=sadequee&Race=U&Sex=U&Age=&x=70&y=16*.

145. *Ibid*. 144.

146. PBS Frontline, "The Enemy Within: Hayat Family Slides." *http://www.pbs.org/wgbh/pages/frontline/enemywithin/etc/pop1.html*.

147. Investigative Project on Terrorism, "United States of America v. Hamid Hayat and Umer Hayat." September 22, 2005. *http://www.investigativeproject.org/documents/case_docs/176.pdf*.

148. United States Department of Justice, "Hamid Hayat Sentenced to 24 Years in Connection with Terrorism Charges." September 10, 2007. *http://www.justice.gov/opa/pr/2007/September/07_nsd_700.html*.

149. *Ibid*. 148.

150. *Ibid*. 148.

151. *Ibid.* 148.
152. The Heritage Foundation, "39 Terrorist Plots Against the U.S. Foiled Since 9/11." 2011. *http://www.heritage.org/Multimedia/ InfoGraphic/2011/05/39-terror-plots-against-the-US.*
153. U.S. Department of Justice, "United States of America v. Derrick Shareef." November 29, 2006. *http://www.justice.gov/usao/iln/ indict/2006/us_v_shareef.pdf.*
154. Global Jihad, "Derrick Shareef." 2009. *http://www.globaljihad.net/ view_page.asp?id=1642.*
155. United States Department of Justice, "Shareef Sentenced to 35 Years in Prison for Foiled Plot to Bomb Shopping Mall During Holiday Season." September 30, 2008. *http://www.justice.gov/opa/pr/2008/ September/08-nsd-872.html.*
156. *Ibid.* 154.
157. *Ibid.* 155.
158. NYPD Counter Terrorism Bureau, "Threat Analysis – JFK Airport/ Pipeline Plot." June 2, 2007. *http://www1.nefafoundation.org/ miscellaneous/FeaturedDocs/NYPD_JFKPlot.pdf.*
159. Global Jihad, "The JFK Terror Cell." 2007. *http://www.globaljihad. net/view_page.asp?id=422id=422.*
160. *Ibid.* 159.
161. United States Attorney's Office, "Russel Defreitas Sentenced to Life in Prison for Conspiring to Commit Terrorist Attack at JFK Airport." February 17, 2011. *http://www.fbi.gov/newyork/press-releases/2011/ russell-defreitas-sentenced-to-life-in-prison-for-conspiring-to- commit-terrorist-attack-at-jfk-airport.*
162. BBC, "Life Sentence for Russel Defreitas in JFK Bomb Plot." February 17, 2011. *http://www.bbc.co.uk/news/world-us-canada-12499345.*
163. *Ibid.* 161.
164. Goetz, Kristina. *Knox News*, "Muslim Who Shot Soldier in Arkansas Says He Wanted to Cause More Death." November 13, 2010. *http:// www.knoxnews.com/news/2010/nov/13/muslim-who-shot-solider- arkansas-says-he-wanted-ca/.*
165. CNN, "Obama 'Saddened' by Attack on Recruiters." June 4, 2009. *http:// articles.cnn.com/2009-06-04/justice/obama.arkansas.shooting_1_ quinton-ezeagwula-white-house-yemeni-embassy?_s=PM:CRIME.*
166. Dao, James. *The New York Times*, "A Muslim Son, a Murder Trial, and Many Questions." February 16, 2010. *http://www.nytimes. com/2010/02/17/us/17convert.html?pagewanted=1.*

167. CNN, "Arkansas Recruiting Center Killing Suspect: 'This was a Jihadi Attack.'" January 27, 2010. *http://www.cnn.com/2010/CRIME/01/22/arkansas.recruiter.shooting/index.html?iref=storysearch*.

168. FOX News, "Family of Suspect in Arkansas Military Center Shooting Says Gov't Knew He was Dangerous." *http://politics.foxnews.mobi/quickPage.html?page=23877&content=52722649&pageNum=-1*.

169. Goins, David. FOX News, "Muhammad Ready for July Trial after Final Hearing." June 13, 2011. *http://www.fox16.com/news/local/story/Muhammad-ready-for-July-trial-after-final-hearing/p-hpiofCT0KsT7QwhRKV0w.cspx*.

170. Anti-Defamation League, "Criminal Proceedings: A Timeline of U.S. Terror Cases." March 9, 2010. *http://www.adl.org/main_Terrorism/american_muslim_extremists_criminal_proceedings.htm?Multi_page_sections=sHeading_2*.

171. Global Jihad, "Bryant Vinas Accused of Terror." July 23, 2009. *http://www.globaljihad.net/view_news.asp?id=983*.

172. *TIME Magazine*. "Bryant Neal Vinas: An American in Al-Qaeda." July 24, 2009. *http://www.time.com/time/nation/article/0,8599,1912512,00.html*.

173. *Ibid*. 171.

174. Ryan, Jason and Pierre Thomas. ABC News, "Suburban New Yorker Charged With Being Al-Qaeda Fighter." July 22, 2009. *http://abcnews.go.com/US/story?id=8148473&page=1*.

175. *Ibid*. 172.

176. *The New York Times*, "Daniel Patrick Boyd." July 29, 2009. *http://topics.nytimes.com/topics/reference/timestopics/people/b/daniel_patrick_boyd/index.html*.

177. Ahlers, Mike. CNN, "No Bail for 'Jihad' Suspects despite Judge's Skepticism." August 5, 2009. *http://www.cnn.com/2009/CRIME/08/05/nc.terror.suspects/index.html*.

178. Walsh, Declan and Daniel Nasaw. *The Guardian*, "American Jihad or FBI Blunder? The Riddle of the 'North Carolina Taliban.'" September 3, 2009. *http://www.guardian.co.uk/world/2009/sep/03/carolina-taliban-jude-mohammad*.

179. Stephey, M.J. *TIME Magazine*, "Daniel Boyd: A Homegrown Terrorist?" July 30, 2009. *http://www.time.com/time/nation/article/0,8599,1913602,00.html*.

180. Johnson, Carrie and Spencer S. Hsu. *The Washington Post*, "Terror Suspect Daniel Boyd Seemed to Have Typical Suburban Life." July 29, 2009. *http://www.washingtonpost.com/wp-dyn/content/article/2009/07/28/AR2009072803193.html.*

181. *Ibid.* 58.

182. CNN, "North Carolina Man Pleads Guilty to Terrorism Conspiracy. June 8, 2011. *http://edition.cnn.com/2011/CRIME/06/08/north.carolina.terror.plot/*

183. WRAL.com, "Dylan Boyd." *http://www.wral.com/news/local/page/5674387/.*

184. Kouri, Jim. Examiner.com, "Homegrown Islamic Terrorist: Rep. King Proven Right by North Carolina Case." *http://www.examiner.com/law-enforcement-in-national/homegrown-islamic-terrorist-rep-king-proven-right-by-north-carolina-case?CID=examiner_alerts_article.*

185. FOX News, "5 NC Suspects in Terrorism Plot Plead Not Guilty." August 15, 2011. *http://www.foxnews.com/us/2011/08/15/5-nc-suspects-in-terrorism-plot-plead-not-guilty/.*

186. WRAL.com, "Hysen Sherifi." *http://www.wral.com/news/local/page/5674285/.*

187. WRAL.com, "Mohammad Omar Aly Hassan." *http://www.wral.com/news/local/page/5674405/.*

188. WRAL.com, "Anes Subasic." *http://www.wral.com/news/local/page/5674319/.*

189. *Ibid.* 178.

190. Global Jihad, "Jude Kenan Mohammad." April 8, 2009. *http://www.globaljihad.net/view_page.asp?id=1648.*

191. FBI, "Wanted by the FBI: Jude Kenan Mohammad." *http://www.fbi.gov/wanted/alert/jude-kenan-mohammad.*

192. Rivera, Ray. *The New York Times*, "Brooklyn Man is Accused of Trying to Aid Terrorists." September 24, 2009. *http://www.nytimes.com/2009/09/25/nyregion/25jihad.html.*

193. Bergen, Peter et al. New America Foundation and Syracuse University's Maxwell School of Public Policy, "Post 9/11 Jihadist Terrorism Cases Involving U.S. Citizens and Residents: An Overview." *http://www.peterbergen.com/services/print.aspx?id=461.*

194. U.S. Department of Justice, "Brooklyn Resident Indicted for Conspiracy to Commit Murder Overseas and Conspiracy to Provide Material Support to Terrorists." September 24, 2009. *http://www.justice.gov/usao/nye/pr/2009/2009sep24.html.*

195. FBI, "Wanted by the FBI: Adnan G. El-Shukrijumah." *http://www.fbi. gov/wanted/wanted_terrorists/adnan-g.-el-shukrijumah.*

196. Fletcher, Dan. *TIME Magazine*, "Terrorism Suspect Najibullah Zazi." September 22, 2009. *http://www.time.com/time/nation/ article/0,8599,1925270,00.html.*

197. Feyerick, Deborah. CNN, "Suspect Pleads Not Guilty in Alleged New York Bomb Plot." September 30, 2009. *http://www.cnn.com/2009/ CRIME/09/29/us.terror.probe/index.html?iref=storysearch.*

198. Banda, P. Solomon. *The Huffington Post*, "Najibullah Zazi's Family Believed to be Cooperating in Obstruction Case." January 20, 2011. *http://www.huffingtonpost.com/2011/01/20/najibullah-zazis-family- b_n_811492.html.*

199. Marzulli, John. *NY Daily News*, "Mohammed Wali Zazi, Father of Terror Suspect Najibullah Zazi, Free on Bail." February 18, 2010. *http:// articles.nydailynews.com/2010-02-18/news/27056591_1_najibullah- zazi-mohammed-wali-zazi-bomb-making.*

200. Banda, P. Solomon. Newsmax.com, "NY Subway Bomb Plotter Waiting in Wings as Witness." January 20, 2011. *http://www.newsmax. com/US/Terror/2011/01/20/id/383336.*

201. Rizzo, Jennifer. CNN, "Imam Pleads Guilty to Lying to Feds in Alleged Terror Plot." March 4, 2010. *http://www.cnn.com/2010/CRIME/03/04/ new.york.terror.plot/index.html?iref=allsearch.*

202. Marzulli, John. *NY Daily News*, "Imam Ahmad Afzali Linked to Najibullah Zazi NYC Subway Plot Dodges Jail Time but Must Leave Country." April 15, 2010. *http://articles.nydailynews.com/2010-04- 15/news/27061826_1_jail-time-subway-plot.*

203. Hays, Tom. *The Huffington Post*, "Zarein Ahmedzay: Al-Qaida Ordered Suicide Attack in NYC." April 24, 2010. *http://www.huffingtonpost. com/2010/04/24/zarein-ahmedzay-alqaida-o_n_550519.html.*

204. U.S. Department of Justice, "Zarein Ahmedzay Pleads Guilty to Terror Violations in Connection with Al-Qaeda New York Subway Plot." April 23, 2010. *http://www.justice.gov/opa/pr/2010/April/10-ag-473.html.*

205. Candiotti, Susan. CNN, "Taxi Driver Indicted in Connection with Alleged Terror Plot." January 9, 2010. *http://www.cnn.com/2010/ CRIME/01/08/new.york.terror.case/index.html?iref=allsearch.*

206. Anti-Defamation League, "Criminal Proceedings in 2010." March 9, 2010. *http://www.adl.org/main_Terrorism/american_muslim_extremists_ criminal_proceedings.htm?Multi_page_sections=sHeading_2.*

207. Johnson, Dirk. *The New York Times*, "Suspect in Illinois Bomb Plot 'Didn't Like America Very Much.'" September 27, 2009. *http://www.nytimes.com/2009/09/28/us/28springfield.html?pagewanted=1*.

208. U.S. Department of Justice, "Illinois Man Admits Plotting to Bomb Federal Courthouse and Is Sentenced to 28 Years in Prison." May 9, 2011. *http://www.justice.gov/opa/pr/2011/May/11-nsd-590.html*.

209. Global Jihad, "Minnesota al-Shabab Suspects 2007-2010." August 8, 2010. *http://www.globaljihad.net/view_page.asp?id=1946*.

210. *Ibid*. 209.

211. Cannon, Ellen. Examiner.com, "Minnesota Judge Upholds Indictments in Terror Case." June 22, 2011. *http://www.examiner.com/homeland-security-in-chicago/minnesoto-judge-upholds-indictments-terror-case*.

212. Seper, Jerry. *The Washington Times*, "14 Indicted in Plot to Aid Somali Terrorists." August 5, 2010. *http://www.washingtontimes.com/news/2010/aug/5/14-indicted-in-plot-to-aid-somali-terrorists/*.

213. Yuen, Lauren. Minnesota Public Radio, "Family IDs Minn. Man Allegedly Behind Somali Suicide Bombing." June 7, 2011. *http://minnesota.publicradio.org/display/web/2011/06/07/farah-beledi-minnesota-man-suicide-attack/*.

214. *Ibid*. 209.

215. Anti-Defamation League, "Al Shabaab's American Recruits." July 2011. *http://www.adl.org/NR/exeres/D0E7DF5A-46A1-47F9-8252-784E6AFBB52C,DB7611A2-02CD-43AF-8147-649E26813571,frameless.htm*.

216. *Ibid*. 215.

217. Global Jihad, "Cabdulaahi Ahmed Faarax." July 8, 2010. *http://www.globaljihad.net/view_page.asp?id=1943*.

218. *Ibid*. 209.

219. Elliot, Andrea. *The New York Times*, "The Jihadist Next Door." January 27, 2010. *http://www.nytimes.com/2010/01/31/magazine/31Jihadist-t.html?pagewanted=1&%2360&%2362&%2359*.

220. Moran, Greg. *The San Diego Union-Tribune*, "Former SD Man Among 14 Charged with Aiding Terror Group." August 5, 2010. *http://www.signonsandiego.com/news/2010/aug/05/san-diegan-among-those-charged-aiding-somalian-ter/*.

221. Davis, Kristina and Michael Stetz. *The San Diego Union-Tribune*, "Portrait of Terror Suspect with SD Ties Begins to Emerge." August 6, 2010. *http://www.signonsandiego.com/news/2010/aug/06/portrait-terror-suspect-sd-ties-begins-emerge*.

222. *Ibid.* 215.
223. *Ibid.* 215.
224. *Ibid.* 215.
225. Walsh, James. WardheerNews.com, "Court Records Detail Minnesota Somalis' Path to Terrorism." July 15, 2009. *http://wardheernews.com/ News_09/July/15_Court_records_detal_path_to_terrorism.html.*
226. Yuen, Laura. Minnesota Public Radio News, "Man Killed in Somalia May Have Recruited Others to Cause." July 13, 2009. *http://minnesota. publicradio.org/display/web/2009/07/13/maruf_profile/.*
227. *Ibid.* 215.
228. U.S. Department of Justice, "United States of America v. Agron Abdullahu." *http://www.justice.gov/usao/nj/Press/files/pdffiles/Older/ abdullahusupersedinginformation.pdf.*
229. U.S. Department of Justice, "United States of America v. Mohamad Ibrahim Shnewer." October 31, 2007. *http://www.justice.gov/usao/nj/ Press/files/pdffiles/Older/Indictment0605.pdf*
230. The Investigative Project on Terrorism, "US v Shnewer, Mohamad Ibrahim et al." *http://www.investigativeproject.org/case/223.*
231. *Ibid.* 229.
232. The Investigative Project on Terrorism, "United States of America v. Agron Abdullahu." May 16, 2007. *http://www.investigativeproject.org/ documents/case_docs/411.pdf.*
233. Graham, Troy. Philly.com, "First of Fort Dix Six Pleads Guilty but Agron Abdullahu Won't Testify Against Five Accused of Attack Plot." November 1, 2007. *http://articles.philly.com/2007-11-01/ news/25225782_1_attack-plot-agron-abdullahu-prison-and-eventual- deportation/2.*
234. Anti-Defamation League, "New Jersey Man Sentenced on Weapons Charge in Fort Dix Terror Plot." April 4, 2008. *http://www.adl.org/ main_Terrorism/abdullahu_sentenced.htm.*
235. Appezzato, John. NJ.com, "Suspect's Father: Arrest is 'Religious Persecution.'" May 8, 2007. *http://blog.nj.com/ledgerupdates/2007/05/ suspects_father_sons_arrest_is.html.*
236. CBS News, "Serdar Tatar." *http://www.cbsnews.com/2316-100_162- 2786025-5.html.*
237. Georgetown Law Center on National Security and the Law, "Five Muslim Immigrants Appeal NJ Terrorism Convictions in Deadly Fort Dix Plot." May 23, 2011. *http://www.securitylawbrief.com/*

main/2011/05/5-muslim-immigrants-appeal-nj-terrorism-convictions-in-deadly-fort-dix-plot.html.

238. Global Jihad, "Fort Dix Six." December 19, 2007. *http://www.globaljihad.net/view_page.asp?id=635.*

239. *Ibid.* 230.

240. Herridge, Catherine. FOX News, "Brothers Charged in Terror Plot Lived Illegally in U.S. for 20 Years." May 9, 2007. *http://www.foxnews.com/story/0,2933,270892,00.html.*

241. FOX News, "3 Brothers Convicted in Fort Dix Terror Plot Sentenced to Life in Prison." April 28, 2009. *http://www.foxnews.com/story/0,2933,518251,00.html.*

242. FOX News, "Maldonado Criminal Complaint." February 13, 2007. *http://www.foxnews.com/projects/pdf/Maldonado_Complaint.pdf.*

243. Anti-Defamation League, "Houston Terror Suspect Admits to Weapons Training in Somalia." February 8, 2010. *http://www.adl.org/main_Terrorism/maldonado_somalia.htm.*

244. Anti-Defamation League, "Criminal Proceedings in 2007." March 9, 2010. *http://www.adl.org/main_Terrorism/american_muslim_extremists_criminal_proceedings.htm?Multi_page_sections=sHeading_5.*

245. The Investigative Project on Terrorism, "United States of America v. Wesam el-Hanafi and Sabirhan Hasanoff." *http://www.investigativeproject.org/documents/case_docs/1371.pdf.*

246. U.S. Department of Justice, "Manhattan U.S. Attorney Charges Two Brooklyn Men with Conspiring to Provide Material Support to Al Qaeda." April 30, 2010. *http://www.justice.gov/usao/nys/pressreleases/April10/ehanafiandhasanoffindictmentpr.pdf.*

247. *Ibid.* 245.

248. Anti-Defamation League, "New Yorkers Charged with Providing Technical Assistance to Al Qaeda." September 20, 2010. *http://www.adl.org/main_Terrorism/hanafi_hasanoff_charged.htm.*

249. U.S. Department of Justice, "Manhattan U.S. Attorney Announces Additional Charges Against Two U.S. Citizen Alleged to Have Provided Material Support to Al Qaeda." September 14, 2010. *http://www.investigativeproject.org/documents/case_docs/1372.pdf.*

250. The Investigative Project on Terrorism, "USA v. Yusuf, Mohamud Abdi." *http://www.investigativeproject.org/case/499.*

251. *Ibid.* 250.

252. Harris, Joe. Courthouse News Service, "More Arrests in Alleged Terror Plot." November 4, 2010. *http://www.courthousenews.com/2010/11/04/31610.htm.*

253. CNN, "U.S. Charges Men with Funding Somali Extremists." November 3, 2010. *http://articles.cnn.com/2010-11-03/us/al.shabaab.indictments_1_indictment-states-foreign-terrorist-organization-material-support?_s=PM:US.*

254. U.S. Department of Justice, "Two Indicted in Missouri on Charges of Providing Material Support to a Terrorist Organization." November 3, 2010. *http://www.investigativeproject.org/documents/case_docs/1411.pdf.*

255. *Ibid.* 254.

256. U.S. Department of Justice, "Chicago Man Charged with Providing Material Support to Al Qaeda by Attempting to Send Funds Overseas." March 26, 2010. *http://www.investigativeproject.org/documents/case_docs/1205.pdf.*

257. *Ibid.* 256.

258. Global Jihad, "Raja Lahrasib Khan Arrested in Chicago." March 27, 2010. *http://www.globaljihad.net/view_news.asp?id=1432.*

259. Suddath, Claire. TIME, "Alleged U.S. Terrorist Tarek Mehanna." October 22, 2009. *http://www.time.com/time/nation/article/0,8599,1931521,00.html.*

260. The Tarek Mehanna Support Committee, "Free Tarek Mehanna." *http://www.freetarek.com.*

261. *Ibid.* 260.

262. The Investigative Project on Terrorism, "U.S. v Tarek Mehanna." *http://www.investigativeproject.org/case/282.*

263. *Ibid.* 262.

264. *Ibid.* 260.

265. Spitz, Julia. *The MetroWest Daily News*, "Spitz: Who is the Real Tarek Mehanna?" February 24, 2011. *http://www.metrowestdailynews.com/news/x889929739/Spitz-Who-is-the-real-Tarek-Mehanna.*

266. *Ibid.* 262.

267. *Ibid.* 260.

268. McKinley, James C. Jr. and James Dao. *The New York Times*, "Fort Hood Gunman Gave Signals before His Rampage." November 8, 2009. *http://www.nytimes.com/2009/11/09/us/09reconstruct.htm.*

269. McCloskey, Megan. *Stars and Stripes*, "Civilian Police Officer Acted Quickly to Help Subdue Alleged Gunman." November 8, 2009. *http://www.stripes.com/news/civilian-police-officer-acted-quickly-to-help-subdue- alleged-gunman-1.96218.*

270. *Ibid*. 269.
271. Blum, James. Bloomberg, "Hasan Called War on Terror an Attack on Islam Classmate Says." November 7, 2009. *http://www.bloomberg. com/apps/news?pid=newsarchive&sid=a0OrWS8lBtNg*.
272. *Ibid*. 286.
273. Zucchino, David. *Los Angeles Times*, "Lawyers for Ft. Hood Suspect Decline to Put on a Defense." November 16, 2010. *http://articles. latimes.com/2010/nov/16/nation/la-na-ft-hood-20101116*.
274. Zucchino, David. *Los Angeles Times*, "Army Colonel Recommends Trial, Death Penalty in Fort Hood Shooting." November 18, 2010. *http://articles.latimes.com/2010/nov/18/nation/la-na-1118-fort-hood-20101118*.
275. Keyes, Charley. CNN, "Lawyer for Alleged Fort Hood Shooter Makes Case for No Death Penalty." May 19, 2011. *http://www.cnn.com/2011/ CRIME/05/19/us.fort.hood.shooter.defense/index.html*.
276. U.S. Department of Justice, "Terror Charges Unsealed in Minneapolis Against Eight Men, Justice Department Announces." November 23, 2009. *http://www.justice.gov/opa/pr/2009/November/09-nsd-1267.html*.
277. Rubenfeld, Samuel. *The Wall Street Journal,* "Dutch High Court Backs Extradition for Terror Suspect to US." January 15, 2011. *http://blogs. wsj.com/corruption-currents/2011/02/15/dutch-high-court-backs-extradition-for-terror-suspect-to-us/*.
278. Yuen, Laura. Minnesota Public Radio News, "Family Members say Somali Suspect Lived 'Simple Life.'" November 24, 2009. *http:// minnesota.publicradio.org/display/web/2009/11/24/omar-profile/*.
279. The Investigative Project on Terrorism, "United States v. Omar." August 20, 2009. *http://www.investigativeproject.org/case/502*.
280. Bahrampour, Tara. *The Washington Post*, "Out of Suburbia, the Online Extremist." November 2, 2010. *http://www.washingtonpost.com/wp-dyn/content/article/2010/11/01/AR2010110107035.html*.
281. Ryan, Jason. ABC News, "American-Bred Terrorists Causing Alarm for Law Enforcement." July 22, 2010. *http://abcnews.go.com/WN/ suspected%20-american-terrorists-islamic-ties-causing-concern-law/ story?id=11230885*.
282. MacDonald, Gregg. *Fairfax Times*, "Fairfax County Man Accused of Link to Terrorist Group." July 28, 2010. *http://ww2.fairfaxtimes.com/ cms/story.php?id=1886*.
283. The Investigative Project on Terrorism, "United States v. Chesser." October 20, 2010. *http://www.investigativeproject.org/case/476*.

284. Cratty, Carol. CNN, "Man Who Threatened 'South Park' Creators Gets 25 Years in Prison." February 24, 2011. *http://articles.cnn.com/2011-02-24/justice/virginia.terror.sentence_1_online-threats-online-readers-maximum-sentence?_s=PM:CRIME.*

285. Federal Bureau of Investigation, "Al Qaeda Supporter Pleads Guilty to Supporting Terrorist Organization." May 19, 2010. *http://www.fbi.gov/kansascity/press-releases/2010/kc051910.htm.*

286. U.S. Department of Justice, "United States of America v Khalid Ouazzani." February 3, 2010. *http://www.justice.gov/usao/mow/news2010/ouazzani_indictment.pdf.*

287. Rozen, Laura. *Politico*, "American Terrorism Suspect Arrested in Yemen Worked for Nuclear Plants." March 11, 2010. *http://www.politico.com/blogs/laurarozen/0310/AP_American_terrorism_suspect_arrested_in_Yemen_worked_for_nuclear_plants.html.*

288. Geraghty, Jim. *The National Review*, "Jon Corzine Funded a Terrorist. Kind of." March 12, 2010. *http://www.nationalreview.com/campaign-spot/4834/jon-corzine-funded-terrorist-kind.*

289. Finn, Peter. *The Washington Post*, "The Post-9/11 Life of an American Charged with Murder." September 4, 2010. *http://www.washingtonpost.com/wp-dyn/content/article/2010/09/04/AR2010090403328.html.*

290. *Ibid.* 289.

291. Kasinof, Laura. *The Christian Science Monitor*, "Why Sharif Mobley is to be tried in Yemen and what it means for American Muslims." October 27, 2010. *http://www.csmonitor.com/World/Middle-East/2010/1027/Why-Sharif-Mobley-is-to-be-tried-in-Yemen-and-what-it-means-for-American-Muslims.*

292. *Ibid.* 289.

293. Reprieve, "Sharif Mobley." *http://www.reprieve.org.uk/cases/sharifmobley/.*

294. Fahim, Kareem and Karen Zraick. *The New York Times*, "Neighbors Saw Changes as Suspects Grew Up." June 7, 2010. *http://www.nytimes.com/2010/06/07/nyregion/07suspects.html.*

295. *Ibid.* 294.

296. Salazar, Carolyn and Chuck Bennett. *The New York Post*, "NJ Warrior Wannabe was Jihad Clod: Boss." June 10, 2010. *http://www.nypost.com/p/news/local/nj_warrior_wannabe_was_jihad_clod_eO6wMwKbjxHfUsainuFsyI?CMP=OTC-rss&FEEDNAME=.*

297. Rashbaum, William K. *The New York Times*, "Two Arrested at Kennedy Airport on Terror Charges." June 6, 2010. *http://www.nytimes.com/2010/06/07/nyregion/07terror.html.*

298. CBS News New York, "Two New Jersey Men Plead Guilty to Trying to Join Al-Shabab Terror Group Overseas." March 3, 2011. *http://newyork.cbslocal.com/2011/03/03/two-new-jersey-men-plead-guilty-to-trying-to-join-al-shabab-terror-group-overseas/.*

299. Goudie, Chuck and Ross Weidner. ABC News, "Feds: Chicago Man Wanted to Blow Up American Soldiers." August 4, 2010. *http://abcnews.go.com/Blotter/shaker-masri-feds-chicago-man-wanted-blow-american/story?id=11326655.*

300. Hammerman, Joel M. ABC News, "United States District Court Northern District of Illinois Eastern Division USA v. Shaker Masri." August 3, 2010. *http://dig.abclocal.go.com/wls/documents/Masri%20Complaint.pdf.*

301. *Ibid*. 300.

302. Rice, Ross. Federal Bureau of Investigation, "Chicago Man Arrested for Attempting to Provide Material Support to a Terrorist Organization." August 4, 2010. *http://www.fbi.gov/chicago/press-releases/2010/cg080410.htm.*

303. The *Wall Street Journal*, "United States v. Bujol." June 3, 2010. *http://online.wsj.com/public/resources/documents/BujolIndictment.pdf.*

304. Horswell, Cindy. *The Houston Chronicle*, "Al-Qaida Aid Charges Stun Hempstead Man's Family." June 4, 2010. *http://www.chron.com/news/houston-texas/article/Al-Qaida-aid-charges-stun-Hempstead-man-s-family-1712373.php.*

305. Allen, JoAnne. Reuters, "U.S. Indicts Texan for Trying to Aid Yemen Al Qaeda." June 3, 2010. *http://www.reuters.com/article/2010/06/04/us-security-qaeda-texas-idUSTRE65309020100604.*

306. *Ibid*. 303.

307. Schiller, Dane. *The Houston Chronicle*, "Former Prairie View Student Accused of Terrorism Not Going Quietly." June 23, 2011. *http://www.chron.com/news/houston-texas/article/Former-Prairie-View-student-accused-of-terrorism-2078461.php.*

308. Brown, Robbie and Kim Severson. *The New York Times*, "2nd American in Strike Waged Qaeda Media War." September 30, 2011. *http://www.nytimes.com/2011/10/01/world/middleeast/samir-khan-killed-by-drone-spun-out-of-the-american-middle-class.html?ref=samirkhan.*

309. Moss, Michael and Souad Mekhennet. *The New York Times*, "An Internet Jihad Aims at U.S. Viewers." October 15, 2007. *http://www.nytimes.com/2007/10/15/us/15net.html?pagewanted=all.*

310. Temple-Raston, Dina. National Public Radio, "Grand Jury Focuses on N.C. Man Tied to Jihad Magazine." August 18, 2010. *http://www.npr.org/templates/story/story.php?storyId=129263809.*

311. Stalinsky, Steven. MEMRI, "Issue V of 'Inspire,' The English-Language Magazine of Al-Qaeda in the Arabian Peninsula—A General Review." March 30, 2011. *http://www.memri.org/report/en/0/0/0/0/0/0/5155.htm.*

312. The Investigative Project on Terrorism, "Plea Agreement: United States v. Paul Rockwood." July 21, 2010. *http://www.investigativeproject.org/documents/case_docs/1348.pdf.*

313. Pemberton, Mary. *Anchorage Daily News*, "Man Who Compiled Hit List Sentenced to 8 Years in Prison." August 24, 2010. *http://www.adn.com/2010/08/23/1421397/man-who-compiled-hit-list-sentenced.html.*

314. The Investigative Project on Terrorism, "United States v. Paul Rockwood." August 16, 2010. *http://www.investigativeproject.org/documents/case_docs/1362.pdf.*

315. *Ibid.* 313.

316. The Investigative Project on Terrorism, "United States v. Nadia Rockwood." July 21, 2010. *http://www.investigativeproject.org/documents/case_docs/1345.pdf.*

317. Jabali-Nash, Naimah. CBS, "Farooque Ahmed Arrested in FBI Sting Operation, Allegedly Plotted to Bomb DC Metro Stations." October 27, 2010. *http://www.cbsnews.com/8301-504083_162-20020933-504083.html.*

318. BBC, "DC 'Bomb Plot' Man Tried to Contact Militants, FBI Says." October 28, 2010. *http://www.bbc.co.uk/news/world-us-canada-11646032.*

319. Cratty, Carol. CNN, "Accused Would-Be DC Metro Bomber Pleads Not Guilty in Federal Court." November 9, 2010. *http://articles.cnn.com/2010-11-09/justice/virginia.bomb.plot_1_qaeda-al-awlaki-speedy-trial?_s=PM:CRIME*; and TBD, "Farooque Ahmed Sentenced in Metro Bomb Plot." April 11, 2011. *http://www.tbd.com/articles/2011/04/plea-hearing-for-man-accused-of-metro-bomb-plot--58269.html.*

320. *Ibid.* 317.

321. Daly, Michael, Alison Gendar, and Helen Kennedy. NY Daily News, "FBI Arrest Four in Alleged Plot to Bomb Bronx Synagogues, Shoot Down Plane." May 20, 2009. *http://articles.nydailynews.com/2009-05-20/news/17924045_1_synagogues-car-bombs-cell-phones.*

322. Chiaramonte, Perry et al. *New York Post*, "Path to Radical Islam Began in Jails." May 22, 2009. *http://www.nypost.com/p/news/regional/item_6Aj75Jlg3pKKHbp11EaLHL;jsessionid=8F1DD38F560EF8463D61E F02DA8BC984.*

323. Roth, Zachary. TPM Muckraker, "The Newburgh Four—And The Government Mole Who Betrayed Them." May 22, 2009. *http:// tpmmuckraker.talkingpointsmemo.com/2009/05/the_newburgh_four_--_and_the_goverment_mole_who_be.php.*

324. Wilson, Michael. *The New York Times*, "In Bronx Bomb Case, Missteps Caught on Tape." May 21, 2009. *http://www.nytimes.com/2009/05/22/ nyregion/22plot.html?_r=1&hp=&pagewanted=all.*

325. Weiser, Benjamin and Andy Newman. *The New York Times*, "3 Men Sentenced to 25 Years in Synagogue Bomb Plot." June 29, 2011. *http:// cityroom.blogs.nytimes.com/2011/06/29/three-men-sentenced-to-25-years-in-synagogue-bomb-plot/.*

326. Dolmetsch, Chris and Bob Van Voris. Bloomberg, "New York Synagogue Bomb Plotter Laguerre Payen Sentenced to 25 Years." September 7, 2011. *http://www.bloomberg.com/news/2011-09-07/new-york-synagogue-bomb-plotter-laguerre-payen-sentenced-to-25-years.html.*

327. *USA Today*, "Oregon Bomb-Plot Suspect Wanted 'Spectacular Show.'" November 28, 2010. *http://www.usatoday.com/news/nation/2010-11-27-bomb-plot_N.htm.*

328. FOX News, "Somali-Born Teen Who Plotted Car Bombing Contacted Suspected Terrorist." November 27, 2010. *http://www.foxnews.com/ us/2010/11/27/feds-somali-born-teen-plotted-car-bombing-ore/.*

329. Brooks, Caryn. *TIME Magazine*, "Portland's Bomb Plot: Who Is Mohamed Mohamud? November 28, 2010. *http://www.time.com/time/ nation/article/0,8599,2033372,00.html.*

330. *Ibid.* 327.

331. *Ibid.* 329.

332. The Investigative Project on Terrorism, "U.S. v. Mohamud, Indictment." November 29, 2010. *http://www.investigativeproject.org/case/504.*

333. The Investigative Project on Terrorism, "U.S. v. Martinez." December 8, 2010. *http://www.investigativeproject.org/case/505.*

334. Cronk, Terri Moon. U.S. Department of Defense, "FBI Stops Attack on Maryland Recruitment Center." December 8, 2010. *http://www. defense.gov/news/newsarticle.aspx?id=62019.*

335. *Ibid.* 334.

336. Savage, Charlie and Gary Gatley. *The New York Times*, "Man Arrested in Bomb Plot in Maryland." December 8, 2010. *http://www. nytimes.com/2010/12/09/us/09bomb.html?scp=1&sq=Antonio%20 Martinez&st=cse.*

CHAPTER 8

Operation Neptune Spear and Beyond

The Hunt for bin Laden and the May 2, 2011 Raid

US intelligence services had been searching for Usama bin Laden since before the 9/11 attacks. US forces had been close to locating bin Laden during the attack on Tora Bora in late 2001, although bin Laden managed to elude capture and avoid US and Coalition forces then and for most of the past decade. While it was widely speculated that bin Laden was living in the mountainous area of the Afghanistan-Pakistan border, he was eventually found and killed in a walled compound in Abbotabad, Pakistan, a short distance from the Pakistani capital of Islamabad.

Intelligence on the likely whereabouts of bin Laden since Tora Bora began to emerge in the summer of 2010 while monitoring of one of bin Laden's couriers. The courier, Abu Ahmed al-Kuwaiti, first came to the attention of US officials when his name was mentioned during the interrogations of several al-Qa'ida associates in US custody, many of them at CIA-operated secret prison sites in Eastern Europe.[1] Officials came to suspect that the courier was a significant member of al-Qa'ida during the subsequent interrogation of Khalid Sheikh Mohammed, who attempted to obfuscate the courier's identity and importance in the organization in contrast with known information.[2]

The lead on the existence of a courier, al-Kuwaiti, close to bin Laden at first consisted only of his nom de guerre. This led to an intensive investigation by US intelligence agencies that eventually led them to bin Laden in Abbotabad. In 2005 the courier's family name was discovered, and his phone calls and emails were intercepted. This surveillance revealed his full name, Sheikh Abu Ahmed, a Pakistani who was born in Kuwait.[3] US intelligence's investigation of al-Kuwaiti coincided with a reorganization of intelligence assets and a refocusing of priorities and resources in South and Central Asia. Dubbed Operation Cannonball, the end result was, by 2005, an increase of CIA agents and assets in Pakistan who were able to follow up on the al-Kuwaiti lead.[4]

Officials monitoring al-Kuwaiti identified his car in Peshawar and were able to trace it to the Abbotabad compound.[5] With the compound now under scrutiny, the CIA began monitoring it from a nearby safe house.[6] US intelligence officials grew increasingly suspicious of the compound due to its high security walls, tinted windows, burned trash and other unusual measures used to maintain the privacy and anonymity of the occupants. Officials concluded that the compound was used to house a relatively senior official in the al-Qa'ida network, although it did not yet have a clear indication that it was bin Laden. After continuing its surveillance into 2011, it was able to advise the National Security Council, (NSC) which began planning military options against the compound, that they were "between 50% and 80%" certain that the house was occupied by bin Laden and several associates.[7]

Once it had been confirmed that bin Laden was likely to be residing in Abbotabad, the NSC began deliberating on the proper course of action, with President Obama chairing several meetings prior to the May 2nd raid.[8] The President's advisers were unable to reach a unanimous decision. The commander of the US military's Joint Special Operations Command, Vice Admiral William McRaven, was asked in February 2011 to plan a strike against the compound. He came up with three options: "a high-altitude bombing raid by B-2 bombers, a 'direct shot' with cruise missiles, or a helicopter assault using a team of US commandos." [9] The first two suggestions were ruled out due to unacceptable levels of collateral damage that would annihilate the compound and any bodies, leaving no verification that bin Laden had been killed.[10] A ground operation by American special forces would reduce the risk of civilian casualties and confirm bin Laden's presence at the compound, but carried several risks of its own. The raid would be deep in Pakistani territory, and would be considered a violation of Pakistani sovereignty, and a failure of the raid would likely precipitate a foreign policy crisis for the US. After much deliberation by the NSC, a raid by US Navy SEALS, who had been preparing for this operation for several months using a full replica of the compound, was given a green light.

Most importantly, and perhaps most controversially, the Pakistani government was not informed of the raid before being carried out. While the US and Pakistan had cooperated on previous intelligence and counter-terror efforts, the US had, in recent years, begun to suspect the reliability of the Pakistani government and the ISI-P. There was a general feeling among top US officials, including Secretary of State Hillary Clinton and Chairman of the Joint Chiefs Adm. Mike Mullen, that segments of the ISI-P had been cooperating with the Taliban, and may have even been aware of bin Laden's whereabouts.[11]

As a result of the mistrust of Pakistan, the military had to plan the raid around keeping the Pakistanis uninformed until as late in the operation as possible. They also had to plan for the potential failure of the raid and the Pakistani reaction. The helicopters that ferried the SEALs over the Pakistani border from Afghanistan flew low to the ground and were equipped with radar-deflecting and noise-reducing technology. The US had previously not acknowledged that such helicopters existed in order to avoid detection by Pakistani air defenses.[12] The SEALs had also built into their plan the possibility that they would have to engage the Pakistani military if discovered. In preparation for such a scenario they deployed two helicopters full of SEALs as a reserve force.[13]

In the early morning of Monday, May 2, Pakistani time, the SEAL team crossed into Pakistan; the team that was chosen for this mission was SEAL Team 6, which had been hunting for bin Laden in Afghanistan since 2001. There were 23 SEALs on two Black Hawk helicopters, along with an interpreter and a tracking dog. In addition, there were two dozen more SEALs in reserve. Originally, the two Black Hawks were to drop the SEALs off and leave within several minutes. One would hover above the compound, allowing the SEALs to descend into the courtyard. The other helicopter would hover above the roof to allow the team to fast rope down onto the building, and then put more SEALs outside to ensure a surprise attack. As a result of the intense heat, the helicopter pilot who was attempting to hover over the compound could not keep the aircraft steady and was forced to attempt to land. During the landing, the tail and rotor became caught on the compound's high walls rendering the aircraft unusable for the operation. After this misstep the second Black Hawk chose to land on the ground rather than attempt to hover. Before finishing the mission, the commandos blew up the damaged helicopter so that the technology inside would not be compromised.[14]

As the SEALs entered the compound, a firefight ensued as al-Kuwaiti fired on them from the guesthouse. He was killed, and his wife was killed in the crossfire. As the team reached the main building, the commandos blew open the front door and shot and killed the courier's brother, whom they believed had been preparing to fire on them. Bin Laden's son Khalid was also killed as the team made its way up the stairs. Bin Laden was found on the third floor with an AK-47 rifle and a Makarov pistol within arm's reach.

A SEAL shot him in the left eye and the chest, killing him. Bin Laden's wife was wounded while trying to attack one of the SEALs.[15]

The codeword "Geronimo" was announced following the operation to inform the President that the SEAL team had killed or captured Usama bin Laden. In order to verify that the remains were bin Laden's, a commander on the ground made a visual identification. Then a digital image was sent to the CIA, where it was processed through a facial recognition system. One of bin Laden's widows also identified the remains. When the remains reached Afghanistan, a DNA test was done and initial results showed a high correlation with the DNA on file that had been obtained by the Saudi government from members of the bin Laden family. Further DNA testing was done that provided "100 percent certainty" that the remains were bin Laden's.[16]

Overall, the operation took 38 minutes, 8 minutes longer than had been planned; the discrepancy in time was the result of the mechanical failure of one of the helicopters. In addition to bin Laden, his son, the owner of the compound, and several others were killed in the raid. The SEALs left the compound with several computer drives and other hardware, which would subsequently be searched for intelligence, as well as with bin Laden's body. He was buried at sea within twelve hours of his death, in accordance with Islamic tradition, depriving al-Qa'ida supporters of a potential burial shrine.[17]

Pakistan claimed the death of bin Laden "illustrates the resolve of the international community, including Pakistan, to fight and eliminate terrorism," though the incident exacerbated feelings of distrust and wariness between both nations.[18] The Pakistani government has stated since that "...the US had made 'an unauthorized unilateral action' that would not be tolerated in the future."[19] The Pakistani Foreign Office further stated "...such an event shall not serve as a future precedent for any state, including the US."[20]

Relations between the two nations' intelligence agencies have deteriorated considerably recently. According to former CIA officials, this distrust exists in part due to the relationship the ISI-P has with the Taliban[21] There is also the question of how Pakistani intelligence could not have known that bin Laden had been living in Abbottabad given that the compound is a very short distance away from a Pakistani Military base and the Pakistan Military Academy. Some individuals within the US believe that the Pakistani government sheltered bin Laden and was fully aware of his location. This lack of faith has in turn aroused suspicion by the Pakistanis. Senior Pakistani officials have said that the secrecy of the bin Laden raid illustrated a "deep distrust."[22]

Even though Pakistan vocalized its frustration and outrage over the US raid in Abbottabad, President Obama asserted that it should not have been unexpected. He stated that the US "believed the hunt for bin Laden transcends international borders and diplomatic boundaries ...Over the years, [he] [has] repeatedly made clear that [the] [US] would take action within Pakistan if we knew where bin Laden was."[23] Following the rise in tensions, there is much discussion within the US government about the future of relations with Pakistan. Rep. Ted Poe (R) of Texas wants legislation to be passed cutting off future aid to the Pakistan unless "the US State Department certifies that Pakistan was not 'providing sanctuary' to bin Laden." [24] Similarly, Sen. Frank Lautenberg (D) of New Jersey believes that current aid should be halted so that it can be determined if Pakistan is on the side of the US in the fight against terrorism.[25]

As of July 2011, the US decided to suspend $800 million in military aid to Pakistan.[26] This is about 40% of the $2 billion that the US gives to Pakistan annually in military aid, which includes funds for counterterrorism operations. Hasan-Askari Rizvi, a Pakistani political and defense analyst, explained the implications of such actions, "The Pakistani military has been the major supporter of the US in the region because it needed weapons and money. Now, when the US builds pressure on the military, it will lose that support."[27] While some believe that aid to Pakistan should stop immediately, others hold the view that the US needs to maintain relations with Pakistan, arguing that the US and Pakistan need to maintain their relationship to ensure the safety and access of transport routes to Afghanistan. In addition, Pakistan supposedly can sway certain Afghan insurgent commanders, which would be beneficial in ending the war in Afghanistan through a peace deal with the Taliban.[28]

While this may be the case, Islamabad is still seething over the raid and claims that the operation violated its sovereignty. As the US continues drone attacks within Pakistan and increases pressure on Pakistani officials to arrest militants within the country, Pakistan's parliament has passed a resolution condemning the US raids and has threatened to halt NATO supplies to Afghanistan. Additionally, it detained five CIA informants who passed on information to the CIA regarding the raid on bin Laden's compound.[29] As of late, Pakistan has been distancing itself from the US in dealing with intelligence and counterterrorism operations within Pakistan. In addition, the country is beginning to show restraint in granting visas to US intelligence officers, and it has threatened to place greater restrictions on drone flights.[30]

Al-Qa'ida in the Post-Usama bin Laden Era

The death of Usama bin Laden is a major milestone for the US and international community in the War on Terror. Usama bin Laden created al-Qa'ida and built it into the multinational terror organization that it is today. While emotionally and symbolically his death is significant, the extent to which his death affects the day-to-day operations of al-Qa'ida may not be as critical as hoped. His death, coinciding with the Arab Spring, should still be considered the biggest setback for al-Qa'ida in recent memory. In order for the organization to survive and remain relevant in the world today, there are several goals that it must accomplish. In the short term, al-Qa'ida's goal will be to reorganize its leadership, reassess its security, and survive the constant systematic elimination of its leadership. The intermediate goal is for Ayman al-Zawahiri to consolidate power and snuff out any opposition. The organization will likely attempt to conduct a major terrorist attack to prove the group's continued relevancy to the international community and the Muslim world. Al-Qa'ida's long-term goal is presumably to hijack the Arab Spring and use the popular discontent for the group's own purposes, ultimately achieving its overarching goals of the destroying Israel, removing Western influence from the region, and the instating a pan-Islamic caliphate.

The future of al-Qa'ida is subject to debate among terrorism experts, and there is no clear understanding of what the fate of the organization will be. Though there are many predictions, the most likely scenarios are: that al-Qa'ida was already on the decline, and decentralization will ultimately reduce the group's cohesiveness until the organization fades into obscurity; that al-Qa'ida's ability to evolve and reshape itself into a franchise organization will surmount the elimination of its central leadership; that al-Qa'ida has been consistently consolidating its power and creating strong international ties, making the organization far more powerful than it was before; or, finally, that the organization requires significant state support from countries like Iran to survive and this will ultimately result in al-Qa'ida gradually evolving into a state-terror organization.[31] What is irrefutable is that the group is still very dangerous and deserves constant harassment by the US and international forces.

The summer 2011 (1432) issue of al-Qa'ida's magazine *Inspire* predicts: "With the martyrdom of Shaykh Usama, the al Qaeda organization will only strengthen."[32] Yahya Ibrahim praised the deceased leader and endorsed the new leadership of Ayman al-Zawahiri. An article dedicated to bin Laden, titled "Sadness, Contentment, and Aspiration" denounces democracy as a force in the Muslim world and proclaims it incompatible with sharia.[33] It then promises that the Islamic umma will answer America's act with attacks against her interests.

Short-Term Goals

To survive the immediate future, al-Qa'ida's leadership must reassess its security. The killing of Usama bin Laden by US Special Forces already indicates a major security breach for the group. Additionally, the computers and files recovered from bin Laden's compound will likely shed light on al-Qa'ida's plans, secret locations, and inner workings. This poses a significant existential threat. Determining what information may have been compromised and responding appropriately are urgent needs to ensure survival.[34] The systematic elimination of al-Qa'ida leadership, such as the drone strike that killed Ilyas Kashmiri on June 4, 2011, is another existential threat to the organization.[35] Drone strikes and targeted killings by special operations must somehow be circumvented if al-Qa'ida's core is to survive. Communication is necessary for the reorganization of the network, but poses a large security risk. Analysts have observed, "No mode of communication is safe for the terrorist leaders. It is the line-level, individual instruments of al-Qa'ida's terrorist enterprise who seek martyrdom, not its general command."[36]

Intermediate Goals

Ayman al-Zawahiri has succeeded Usama bin Laden as leader of the al-Qa'ida organization, though there is evidence that this leadership faces considerable opposition from many of al-Qa'ida's members. Zawahiri and the interim leader Saif al-Adel are Egyptian and are not revered on the same religious level as those in al-Qa'ida who were born on the Arabian Peninsula (such as Usama bin Laden).[37] Al-Zawahiri has the potential to be a divisive force; while "bin Laden tried to transcend the divisions within the jihadist movement, Al-Zawahiri often exacerbated them, especially by his denunciations of rival jihadist groups."[38] He was involved in disputes with the Muslim Brotherhood and Hamas; furthermore, he is known to have broken under torture, which has eroded his credibility amongst his peers.[39] Under al-Zawahiri's leadership, "[R]ecruitment and fundraising may suffer as a result as wealthy donors give their money to other causes while impressionable youth take up more local fights."[40]

The intermediate goals of the organization must be to have al-Zawahiri consolidate power and gain the loyalty of the group.

Besides the internal difficulties of rearranging the leadership structure of al-Qa'ida, the organization also faces an even greater danger to its existence, irrelevancy. The Arab Spring should be considered a repudiation of everything al-Qa'ida stands for. The movement was not based on Islamic fundamentalism and most of the revolutions championed nonviolent methods. Revolutionaries included women, members of other religions, and secular forces. Certain revolutionary segments sought to establish democracy and not an Islamic autocracy. This rejection of al-Qa'ida principles threatens al-Qa'ida on a multitude of levels. Recruitment of new and younger members into the group could be affected as young Arabs have witnessed a legitimate alternative to al-Qa'ida's violence and suicide bombing. The Arab Spring promises tangible benefits that can be enjoyed in the present instead of al-Qa'ida's promise of benefits in the afterlife.[41].

In order for the organization to demonstrate its significance, it must initiate a substantial terror attack in retaliation for Usama bin Laden's death.[42] There have been some terrorist attacks committed by affiliated and allied terror groups, such as the May 17, 2011, suicide bombing in Charsadda, Pakistan by TTP, which killed 98 people.[43] Al-Qa'ida has also released videos and Internet statements calling on Muslims who are not directly affiliated with al-Qa'ida to conduct individual attacks all over the world.[44] In one statement, the names of 40 US citizens were listed as targets for Islamic jihadists; the list included pictures and asked for addresses in order to send mail bombs.[45] Al-Qa'ida has not yet executed a major retaliatory terror attack.

There is legitimate concern that al-Qa'ida may try to use a WMD or other unconventional attack in response to bin Laden's death. Speculation has arisen that al-Qa'ida may try to acquire a nuclear weapon or radiological material within Pakistan, especially after the May 23, 2011 attack on Pakistan's Mehran naval air base, which is only a few miles from a supposed nuclear weapon storage facility.[46] Al-Qa'ida has consistently described its intent to acquire a nuclear weapon; Usama bin Laden issued a statement in 1998 titled "The Nuclear Bomb of Islam," which calls on all Muslims to attempt to procure nuclear weapons to be used against the "enemies of Islam."[47] WikiLeaks documents record that Khalid Sheikh Mohammed told his interrogators at Guantanamo of plotting attacks on US nuclear power plants.[48] Any threat involving potential WMDs should be taken with the utmost seriousness and should be a principal concern of counterterrorism authorities.

Long-Term Goals

In the long term it is likely that al-Qa'ida will attempt to take advantage of the Arab Spring. Libya, in particular, is vulnerable to al-Qa'ida given the disorganized nature of the fighting against Muammar Qaddafi and the fact that eastern Libya has long been a source of insurgents fighting in Afghanistan and Iraq.[49] Currently, the eastern part of Libya is home to the Libyan Islamic Fighting Group, which "reportedly trained more than a thousand Libyan nationals in Afghan training camps before 9/11 and...was often thought of as the most lethal Islamist group in North Africa." Al Qa'ida has responded favorably to the rebels with "an unprecedented flurry of messages... in support of their [the rebels'] bid to bring down the hated Qaddafi regime."[50] There is already indication that al-Qa'ida is taking advantage of the chaos in North Africa; Thomas Sanderson of CSIS reported that AQIM was able to acquire several anti-aircraft missiles from Western militaries that were originally designated to support Libyan rebels.[51] He argues that AQIM is poised to take advantage of the current chaos in Libya by strengthening itself in the anarchical regions far removed from police forces. Zawahiri has expressed interest in the region and called on Muslims to help the rebels defeat both Qaddafi and NATO forces.[52] It is in al-Qa'ida's best interest to capitalize on the Muslim world's dissatisfaction and restlessness to shift the Arab Spring's goals away from democracy and towards theocracy. Ultimately, al-Qa'ida's long-term goals coincide with the original goals of the organization: creating a new Islamic caliphate, defeating Israel, purifying Muslim lands of Western cultural and military influence, and mandating sharia law.[53]

The Future of al-Qa'ida

Experts agree that the organization has evolved into a decentralized multifaceted institution. But their analyses differ on how this will affect the group as a whole; some experts believe that the organization is slowly dying, while others believe it is stronger than ever.

Usama bin Laden's death marks a milestone in combating al-Qa'ida. The systematic elimination of leadership and personnel from al-Qa'ida's ranks has significantly disrupted the organization's ability to function, much less mount an aggressive terror campaign. Moisés Naím of the Carnegie Endowment for International Peace articulates this point in his article "Is Al Qaeda Obsolete?" He suggests that al-Qa'ida was already on the decline and that decentralization has resulted in the organization being relegated to the roll of inspiring terrorism and training recruits. He observes that al-Qa'ida has become a pariah and that state support of the group has been severely handicapped by American military pressure.[54] He believes that al-Qa'ida is slowly being pushed to the fringes of legitimacy and that the Arab Spring will likely result in the end of the al-Qa'ida network as we know it.[55]

Naím is not alone in his prediction. Professors Leonard Binder, James Gelvin, and David Rapoport were featured in a publication that discussed bin Laden's death and the future of al-Qa'ida. They found that the organization has been severely hindered by international efforts, that the Arab Spring is a repudiation of al-Qa'ida, and that the organization is essentially finished and will slowly vanish over the next decade.[56]

Other experts, such as Brian Jenkins of RAND and Steve Coll of The New Yorker, also agree with the aforementioned prediction. They conclude that, with the charismatic bin Laden gone, al-Qa'ida has lost a very important and symbolic leader and that Zawahiri as his replacement will only serve to agitate the leadership within the group as well as prospective recruits.[57]

Many agree that with the deaths of Usama bin Laden and Illyas abu Kashmiri, al-Qa'ida has been deprived of two important leaders. While terror attacks by individuals who may be inspired by al-Qa'ida will still occur, large-scale international attacks, such as 9/11, will not. Al-Qa'ida will not likely recover from these blows, and it is only a matter of time before the leadership is rounded up or killed and the organization fades into obscurity.

Another prevailing thought on the future of al-Qa'ida is that decentralization has been a significant factor in the organization's survival and that it will be very difficult to completely eliminate the al-Qa'ida brand. Mohamad Bazzi, of the Council on Foreign Relations, suggests that al-Qa'ida is unlikely to be eradicated, and that it can effectively adapt to decentralized control by having individuals or small cells carry out attacks inspired by al-Qa'ida's message and methods disseminated over the Internet.[58] He believes that bin Laden's death will not impact an organization whose most successful attacks in the past few years were a result from the inspiration and not from the direct planning by al-Qa'ida core.[59]

The Senate Foreign Relations Committee hearing on "Al Qaeda, The Taliban & Other Extremist Groups in Afghanistan and Pakistan" featured several experts who discussed al-Qa'ida, the Taliban, and LeT. The witnesses doubted that al-Qa'ida would be destroyed in the near future. They explained that al-Qa'ida has engrained and intertwined with a multitude of other

Islamic terror groups, especially LeT in Pakistan. They argued that the death of bin Laden will not spell an end to the organization and that al-Qa'ida will continue to exist within its traditional stronghold on the border of Pakistan and Afghanistan.[60]

In addition, others predict that Pakistan and other countries will become bases for terrorists preferring cells rather than the Internet to execute their mission. Yemen, given its economic frustrations and unstable government is a home to AQAP. Somalia's al-Shabaab proclaims jihad against the government. None of these groups is likely to be deterred by the death of al-Qa'ida's leader.[61] In fact, "decapitation appears to be least effective in groups that are well-established, religious or relatively large."[62] Not only will non-al-Qa'ida groups continue to carry out attacks regardless of bin Laden's death, but, "intelligence agencies expect the various branches to attempt to prove their power by avenging his death, in particular in attacks against American targets."[63]

The House Committee on Foreign Affairs also concluded that al-Qa'ida is not dead and will likely not be destroyed quickly. The witnesses stated that the decentralized structure of al-Qa'ida has made it more resilient than it was before and that, given this resiliency, it will be difficult to eliminate the group entirely. The hearing described al-Qa'ida's goals of hijacking the popular discontent behind the Arab Spring and finding new areas in North Africa to exploit, given the anarchy of the region.[64] They also discussed how the traditional notions of terror groups are no longer valid, as many terror groups are interrelated, with members joining and switching between groups freely.[65] They concluded that al-Qa'ida was stronger than it was 10 years ago due to decentralization; expanding from 5 networks to 11 as well as expanding its membership by 50%.[66]

The last possibility that will be discussed here is a future for al-Qa'ida as a state sponsored organization. Following bin Laden's death, Iran could play a larger role in the organization. Despite deep religious differences between Shi'a Iran and Sunni al-Qa'ida, previous chapters discussed their cooperation based on mutual hatred of the US. Al-Qa'ida has had ties to Iranian-backed terror groups dating back to its time in Sudan, where it worked with Hezbollah.[67] Iran allowed senior al Qa'ida officials to take refuge there, including Atiyah Abd al-Rahman and Saif al-Adel.[68] Under pressure after 9/11, Iran made low-level arrests and disrupted some cells; however, it has continued to release high-ranking al-Qa'ida operatives from custody and let them travel, in violation of UN rules: "If al-Adel or any of the other senior figures were released, Iran would be in violation of a UN resolution and the US has made it clear that is unacceptable."[69]

Notes and Bibliographic References

1. Mazzetti, Mark, Helene Cooper, and Peter Baker. *The New York Times*, "Clues Gradually Led to the Location of Osama bin Laden." May 2, 2011. *http://www.nytimes.com/2011/05/03/world/asia/03intel.html?_r=1&scp=54&sq=bin%20laden&st=cse*.
2. *Ibid.* 1.
3. BBC, "Timeline: The Intelligence Hunt Leading to Bin Laden." May 6, 2011. *http://www.bbc.co.uk/news/mobile/world-south-asia-13279283*.
4. *Ibid.* 1.
5. *Ibid.* 1.
6. Miller, Greg. *The Washington Post*, "CIA Spied on Bin Laden from Safe House." May 5, 2011. *http://www.washingtonpost.com/world/cia-spied-on-bin-laden-from-safe-house/2011/05/05/AFXbG31F_story.html*.
7. Von Drehle, David. "Killing bin Laden: How the U.S. Finally Got its Man." *TIME Magazine*, May 20, 2011. *http://www.time.com/time/nation/article/0,8599,2069455,00.html*.
8. *Ibid.* 1.
9. *Ibid.* 3.
10. *Ibid.* 3.
11. *Ibid.* 3.
12. Drew, Christopher. *The New York Times*, "Attack on Bin Laden Used Stealthy Helicopter that had been a Secret." May 5, 2011. *http://www.nytimes.com/2011/05/06/world/asia/06helicopter.html?_r=1&scp=24&sq=bin%20laden&st=cse*.
13. Scherer, Michael. *TIME Magazine*, "Obama Pushed for 'Fight Your Way Out' Option in bin Laden Raid." May 3, 2011. *http://swampland.time.com/2011/05/03/obama-pushed-for-fight-your-way-out-option-in-bin-laden-raid/*.
14. Dozier, Kimberly. Siasat.pk, "Abbotabad Mission Details Revealed by USA: Osama bin Laden's Guns Found 'only after' US Navy SEALs Killed him." May 18, 2011. *http://www.siasat.pk/forum/showthread.php?66234-Abbotabad-Mission-details-revealed-by-USA-Usama-bin-Laden-s-guns-found-only-after-US-Navy-Seals-killed-him*.

15. Harnden, Toby. *The Telegraph*, "Osama bin Laden Dead: Wife was Shot in the Leg not Killed." May 3, 2011. *http://www.telegraph.co.uk/ news/worldnews/al-qaeda/8490814/Osama-bin-Laden-dead-wife- was-shot-in-the-leg-not-killed.html*.

16. MSNBC, "How the US Tracked Couriers to Elaborate bin Laden Compound." May 3, 2011. *http://www.msnbc.msn.com/id/42853221/ ns/world_news-death_of_bin_laden/t/how-us-tracked-couriers- elaborate-bin-laden-compound/*.

17. *Ibid*. 15.

18. Dwyer, Devin. ABC News, "Osama Bin Laden Killing: Pakistan Reacts Cautiously to U.S. Raid on its Soil." May 2, 2011. *http://abcnews. go.com/Politics/usama-bin-laden-killed-pakistan-reacts-cautiously- us/story?id=13507918#.TtekX7JFuso*.

19. Perlez, Jane and David Rhode. *The New York Times*, "Pakistan Pushes Back Against U.S. Criticism on Bin Laden." May 3, 2011. *http://www.nytimes.com/2011/05/04/world/asia/04pakistan. html?pagewanted=1&_r=1*.

20. *Ibid*. 19.

21. *Ibid*. 19.

22. *Ibid*. 19.

23. *Ibid*. 18.

24. Perkowski, Katie. *The Houston Chronicle*, "Ted Poe Introduces Legislation to Freeze Pakistan Aid if Leaders Knew bin Laden was there." May 3, 2011. *http://blog.chron.com/txpotomac/2011/05/ ted-poe-introduces-legislation-that-would-freeze-aid-to-pakistan-if- leaders-knew-bin-laden-was-there/*.

25. Shiner, Meredith. *Politico*, "Frank Lautenberg: Suspend Aid to Pakistan." May 2, 2011. *http://www.politico.com/news/ stories/0511/54131.html*.

26. Albritton, Chris and Zeeshan Haider. Reuters, "U.S. Aid Cut to Pakistan Could Hurt Economy." July 11, 2011. *http://www.reuters. com/article/2011/07/11/us-pakistan-usa-idUSTRE76A13S20110711*.

27. NPR, "U.S. Suspend $800 Million in Aid to Pakistan." July 10, 2011. *http://www.npr.org/2011/07/10/137746664/u-s-to-suspend-800- million-in-aid-to-pakistan*.

28. *The Guardian*, "US-Pakistan Relations 'At Turning Point' After Killing of Bin Laden, Warns Clinton." May 27, 2011. *http://www.guardian. co.uk/world/2011/may/27/clinton-zardari-us-pakistan-bin-laden*.

29. Schmitt, Eric and Mark Mazzetti. *The New York Times*, "Pakistan Arrests C.I.A. Informants in Bin Laden Raid." June 14, 2011. *http://www.nytimes.com/2011/06/15/world/asia/15policy.html?pagewanted=1&_r=1&ref=global-home*.

30. *Ibid*. 29.

31. House Committee on Foreign Affairs, "Future of al-Qaeda." May 24, 2011. *http://foreignaffairs.house.gov/hearing_notice.asp?id=1299*; and Joscelyn, Thomas. *The Long War Journal*, "Al Qaeda's Interim Emir and Iran." May 18, 2011. *http://www.longwarjournal.org/archives/2011/05/analysis_al_qaedas_i-print.php*.

32. *Inspire*. Summer 2011. 47.

33. *Ibid*. 32., 50.

34. Bergen, Peter. New America Foundation, "Egyptian Saif al-Adel Appointed Acting Leader of Al Qaeda." May 17, 2011. *http://www.newamerica.net/publications/articles/2011/egyptian_saif_al_adel_appointed_acting_leader_of_al_qaeda_51286* .

35. Crilly, Rob. *The Telegraph*, "Drone Strike Targets al-Qaeda 'Kingpin' Ilyas Kashmiri." June 4, 2011. *http://www.telegraph.co.uk/news/worldnews/asia/afghanistan/8556427/Drone-strike-targets-al-Qaeda-kingpin-Ilyas-Kashmiri.html*.

36. Jenkins, Brian Michael. RAND Corporation, "Al-Qaeda after Bin Laden." May 12, 2011. *http://www.rand.org/commentary/2011/05/12/NJ.html*.

37. *Ibid*. 36.

38. Byman, Daniel. The Brookings Institution, "Zawahiri's Big Challenge." May 12, 2011. *http://www.brookings.edu/opinions/2011/0512_al_qaeda_byman.aspx*.

39. *Ibid*. 38.

40. *Ibid*. 38.

41. Parvez, Tariq and Hassan Abbas. "The Future of Al-Qaeda." *Foreign Policy*, June 6, 2011. *http://afpak.foreignpolicy.com/posts/2011/06/06/the_future_of_al_qaeda*.

42. *Ibid*. 36.

43. *Dawn*, "Death Toll Climbs to 98 in Charsadda Suicide Attack." May 17, 2011. *http://www.dawn.com/2011/05/17/death-toll-climbs-to-98-in-charsadda-suicide-attack.html*.

44. Dienst, Jonathan. MSNBC, "Website Unveils al-Qaida Alleged US Hit List." June 17, 2011. *http://www.msnbc.msn.com/id/21134540/vp/43443514#43443514*.

45. *Ibid.* 44.
46. Rajghatta, Chidanand. *The Times of India*, "Pak Nuke Security in Focus Again After Naval Base Attack." May 23, 2011. *http://articl es.timesofindia.indiatimes.com/2011-05-23/us/29573575_1_nuclear-installations-nuclear-assets-pakistani-militant-attacks*; and Masood, Salman and David E. Sanger. *The New York Times*, "Pakistan's Military Faces New Questions after Raid." May 23, 2011. *http:// www.nytimes.com/2011/05/24/world/asia/24pakistan.html?smid=tw-nytimes&seid=auto*.
47. Allison, Graham. *Belfer Center for Science and International Affairs*, "Nuclear Terrorism Fact Sheet." April 2010. *http://belfercenter.ksg. harvard.edu/publication/20057/nuclear_terrorism_fact_sheet.html*.
48. Rizzo, Jennifer. CNN, "Wikileaks Papers Reveal Guantanamo Detainees' Talk of Post-9/11 Plots." May 12, 2011. *http://articles. cnn.com/2011-05-12/us/wikileaks.plots_1_terror-plots-wikileaks-documents?_s=PM:US*.
49. *Ibid.* 41.
50. Boucek, Christopher. Carnegie Endowment for International Peace, "Islamist Terrorist in Libya." May 11, 2011. *http://carnegieendowment. org/publications/index.cfm?fa=view&id=43951&solr_hilite=Usama*.
51. *Ibid.* 41.
52. Fuchs, Martina. Reuters, "Zawahiri Says Muslims Should Fight NATO in Libya." April 15, 2011. *http://www.reuters.com/article/2011/04/15/ us-libya-qaeda-idUSTRE73E1TH20110415*.
53. Blanchard, Christopher M. CRS Report for Congress, "Al Qaeda: Statements and Evolving Ideology." July 9, 2007. *http://www.fas.org/ sgp/crs/terror/RL32759.pdf*.
54. Naim, Moises. Carnegie Endowment for International Peace, "Is Al Qaeda Obsolete?" May 11, 2011. *http://www.carnegieendowment. org/publications/index.cfm?fa=view&id=43914*.
55. *Ibid.* 54.
56. UCLA Newsroom, "al-Qaeda after Bin Laden." May 4, 2011. *http:// newsroom.ucla.edu/portal/ucla/news-week-al-qaeda-after-bin-laden-202606.aspx*.
57. *Ibid.* 36.; and Coll, Steve. "Notes on the Death of Osama Bin Laden." *The New Yorker,* May 2, 2011. *http://www.newyorker.com/online/ blogs/newsdesk/2011/05/notes-on-the-death-of-usama-bin-laden. html%23ixzz1LD7FnG6O*.

58. Bazzi, Mohamad. *The National*, "Brand al Qa'eda Cannot be Killed as Easily as its Icon." May 3, 2011. *http://www.thenational.ae/ thenationalconversation/comment/brand-al-qaeda-cannot-be-killed-as-easily-as-its-icon?pageCount=0.*

59. *Ibid.* 58.

60. U.S. Senate Committee on Foreign Relations, "Al Qaeda, the Taliban & Other Extremist Groups in Afghanistan and Pakistan." May 24, 2011. *http://foreign.senate.gov/hearings/hearing/?id=805120d6-5056-a032-5247-313a14503d33.*

61. Raghavan, Sudarsan and Craig Whitlock. SFGate.com, "Al Qaeda's Leadership, Future Uncertain." May 3, 2011. *http://www. sfgate.com/cgi-bin/article.cgi?f=/c/a/2011/05/03/MNH81JASMM. DTL&type=printable.*

62. Jordan, Jenna. *The Chicago Tribune*, "Can al-Qaida Survive This?" May 3, 2011. *http://articles.chicagotribune.com/2011-05-03/news/ct-oped-0503-terrorists-20110503_1_qaida-al-qaida-hamas-leaders.*

63. Bar'el, Zvi. *Haaretz*, "Bin Laden May be Dead, but al-Qaida will Live On." May 2, 2011. *http://www.haaretz.com/news/international/bin-laden-may-be-dead-but-al-qaida-will-live-on-1.359389.*

64. *Ibid.* 41.

65. *Ibid.* 41.

66. *Ibid.* 41.

67. *Ibid.* 31.

68. *Dawn.* "Iran Could Play role in al Qaeda, Post-Bin Laden." May 19, 2011. *http://www.dawn.com/2011/05/19/iran-could-play-role-in-al-qaeda-post-bin-laden.html.*

69. *Ibid.* 68.

Appendices

1. Selected Electronic Political Communication from al-Qa'ida (October 2001— 2011)
2. US Indictment of Osama bin Laden (November 5, 1998)[1]
3. President Obama's Strategies
   A. Remarks by the President on Osama bin Laden (May 2, 2011)[2]
   B. "Ensuring al-Qa'ida's Demise" (Remarks by John Brennan on June 29, 2011)[3]
   C. National Strategy for Counterterrorism (June 2011)[4]
   D. Empowering Local Partners to Prevent Violent Extremism in the US (August 2011)[5]
4. Senate Select Committee on Intelligence and House Permanent Select Committee on Intelligence Joint Hearing to Mark the 10th Anniversary of 9/11 (September 13, 2011)
   A. The Honorable James R. Clapper, Director of National Intelligence[6]
   B. David H. Petraeus, Director of CIA[7]

Appendices

Appendix 1: Selected al-Qa'ida Electronic Political Communication

- Source: NBC Nightly News (video on YouTube)/PBS News Hour
  - Date Published: 7 October 2001
  - Available at: *http://www.youtube.com/watch?v=Q-St8s9RKEU; http://www.pbs.org/newshour/terrorism/international/ binladen_10-7.html*
  - Statement Title: Unknown
  - Document Title: Bin Laden Statement
  - Speaker: Usama bin Laden
  - Summary: Shortly before the first wave of American attacks against the capital of Afghanistan, bin Laden issued a statement declaring, "I want to tell the US and its people, I swear by God, by Allah, he who has praised the sky, that the US will not have peace." He goes on to say the Muslims have been blessed with destroying America, "Every Muslim after this event [should fight for his religion..."

- Source: BBC News
  - Date Published: 10 October 2001
  - Available at: *http://news.bbc.co.uk/2/hi/south_asia/1590559.stm*
  - Statement Title: Unknown
  - Document Title: "Al-Qaeda Threatens Fresh Terror Attacks"
  - Speaker: Sulaiman Abu Ghaith (Spokesman for al-Qa'ida)
  - Summary: In this message, Ghaith spoke highly of the September 11th attacks, saying there would be more of them to come, especially since the continuous air raids on Afghanistan "had opened a door that would never be closed." These attacks from both American and British troops served as justification for al-Qa'ida to continue the fight. He also went on to say, "There are thousands of the Islamic nation's youths who are eager to die just as the Americans are eager to live."

- Source: CNN
  - Date Published: 1 November 2001
  - Available at: *http://archives.cnn.com/2001/WORLD/asiapcf/central /11/01/ret.robertson.otsc/index.html*
  - Statement Title: Unknown
  - Document Title: Nic Robertson on bin Laden letter

- Speaker: Usama bin Laden
- Summary: In this letter, delivered to Al Jazeera, bin Laden calls upon the Pakistani people to stand up against their government, which has allied itself with America. He states, "Standing against wrong will strengthen Muslims' resolve." According to him, the war being fought is splitting the world into two sides: one believing in Christianity and the other Islam.

- Source: PBS News Hour & The NEFA Foundation
  - Date Published: 9 November 2001 (Released 13 December 2001)
  - Available at: *http://www.pbs.org/newshour/bb/terrorism/july-dec01/video_12-13a.html*
  - Statement Title: Unknown
  - Document Title: "Usama Bin Laden Claims Responsibility for the 9/11 Attacks"
  - Speaker: Usama bin Laden
  - Summary: In this 60 minute video, bin Laden, speaking to a room of supporters, talks about the success of September 11th, making it clear he was the mastermind behind the attacks. With very specific detail, he talks about how calculated the attacks were, such as the number of floors that would be directly impacted. He also mentions where he and his fellow men were at the exact time of the attack, saying they had known the attacks would take place on September 11th a week in advance. At one point he says, "This is all that we hoped for." Aside from discussion about the attack, the video depicts bin Laden at a site where a US helicopter crashed in southern Afghanistan.

- Source: CNN
  - Date Published: 27 December 2001
  - Available at: *http://edition.cnn.com/2001/WORLD/asiapcf/central/12/26/ret.bin.laden.statement/index.html*
  - Statement Title: Unknown
  - Document Title: "Bin Laden Calls Sept. 11 Attacks 'Blessed Terror'"
  - Speaker: Usama bin Laden
  - Summary: In this 34 minute video, bin Laden calls the September 11th attacks, "blessed terror" and accuses the West of hating the Islamic faith, "It's very clear that the West in general, and America

in particular, have an unspeakable hatred for Islam." Bin Laden also touches upon the bombing of an al-Qa'ida base and mosque in Khost, chastising the American troops for affecting the lives of civilians, "Those who claim to be humane and free, we have seen their real crimes."

- Source: CNN
  - Date Published: 9 October 2002
  - Available at: *http://articles.cnn.com/2002-10-09/world/otsc. mcvicar.zawahiri.tape_1_audiotape-bin-ayman-al-zawahiri?_ s=PM:WORLD*
  - Statement Title: Unknown
  - Document Title: "MicVicar on the al-Zawahiri Tape"
  - Speaker: Ayman al-Zawahiri
  - Summary: In this video, al-Zawahiri proudly asserts, "Neither America nor its allies have been able to harm the leadership of al Qaeda and the Taliban, including Mullah Mohammed Omar and Sheikh Osama bin Laden.... " This statement, along with an ominous threat directed at the US saying the country will not go "unpunished for its crimes," gives the impression the organization is succeeding in its fight against the West and will continue to attack those who denounce Islam.

- Source: BBC News
  - Date Published: 12 November 2002
  - Available at: *http://news.bbc.co.uk/2/hi/middle_east/2455845.stm*
  - Statement Title: Unknown
  - Document Title: "Bin Laden's Message"
  - Speaker: Usama bin Laden
  - Summary: In this statement, bin Laden accuses the American government of being gangsters and butchers, who are killing women, children, and elderly people. He says George Bush is the "pharaoh of this age" and he urges people to put as much distance between themselves and the White House as possible. He also justifies al-Qa'ida's attacks by saying, "You will be killed just as you kill, and will be bombed just as you bomb." In bin Laden's eyes it is unfair that the people of Iraq are being treated unjustly, while those in the West are enjoying stability and happiness.

- Source: BBC News
  - Date Published: 12 February 2003
  - Available at: *http://news.bbc.co.uk/2/hi/2751019.stm*
  - Statement Title: Unknown
  - Document Title: Bin Laden tape: Text
  - Speaker: Usama bin Laden
  - Summary: In this audio message, bin Laden talks about a number of important values, including showing good intentions, continuously preparing for jihad, and being mindful of the psychological warfare the Americans are using. He also questions the capability of the US and its allies in defeating the Muslim world, while trying to instill morale among the Muslim community, saying "…honest Muslims… should move, incite, and mobilize the [Islamic] nation…"

- Source: BBC News
  - Date Published: 16 February 2003
  - Available at: *http://news.bbc.co.uk/2/hi/not_in_website/syndication/monitoring/media_reports/2768873.stm*
  - Statement Title: "Sermon for the Feast of the Sacrifice"
  - Document Title: Bin Laden Tape Urges Jihad
  - Speaker: Usama bin Laden
  - Summary: In this 53 minute message, bin Laden blames both President Bush and British Prime Minister Tony Blair for attacking the Muslim world, accusing them both of using the war on terrorism as a cover-up for their true goal of destroying the Islamic religion. According to bin Laden, the true objective of both countries is to establish a "Jewish superstate", claiming the current events in Pakistan are foreshadowing what is to come throughout the rest of the region.

- Source: *Guardian* (UK)
  - Date Published: 8 April 2003
  - Available at: *http://www.guardian.co.uk/world/2003/apr/08/afghanistan.alqaida*
  - Statement Title: Unknown
  - Document Title: Latest Bin Laden Tape Urges Suicide Attacks
  - Speaker: Usama bin Laden
  - Summary: In this video, bin Laden urges Muslims to carry out suicide missions in Pakistan, Afghanistan, Bahrain, Kuwait, and

Saudi Arabia. He states, "…jihad against them is your duty." He also explains that those who cannot physically take up the fight must do so financially, as should women by providing fighters with food.

- Source: Afghanistan News
  - Date Published: 29 September 2003
  - Available at: *http://www.afghanistannewscenter.com/news/2003/september/sep302003.html*
  - Statement Title: Unknown
  - Document Title: "Al-Qaeda Number Two Calls on Pakistanis to Overthrow Musharraf."
  - Speaker: Ayman al-Zawahiri
  - Summary: In this audiotape, al-Zawahiri places blame on President Musharraf, saying he played a significant role in the US being able to dismantle the Taliban in Afghanistan. As a result of this alliance, the citizens of Pakistan should rise up against their traitorous leader. He also criticizes a portion of the Congressional report, written after September 11, because it dealt with prohibiting the Saudi Arabian government from printing the Koran, which speaks of attacks on both Christians and Jews.

- Source: NEFA Foundation & CNN World
  - Date Published: 4 January 2004
  - Available at: *http://articles.cnn.com/2004-01-05/world/binladen. tape_1_bin-laden-tape-audiotape-voice-of-osama-bin?_ s=PM:WORLD*
  - Statement Title: Unknown
  - Document Title: Usama Bin Laden Audiotape
  - Speaker: Usama bin Laden
  - Summary: In this audiotape, bin Laden talks about the importance of waging jihad and overthrowing regimes in the Middle East that are collaborating with the US. During his message he declared:

There can be no dialogue with occupiers except through arms… Islamic countries in the past century were not liberated from the Crusaders' military occupation except through jihad in the cause of God. Under the pretext of fighting terrorism, the West today is doing its utmost to tarnish jihad and kill anyone seeking jihad… Jihad is the path, so seek it.

- Source: CNN & MSNBC
  - Date Published: 15 April 2004
  - Available at: *http://edition.cnn.com/2004/WORLD/asiapcf/04/15/ binladen.tape/index.html*
  - Statement Title: Unknown
  - Document Title: "Europe: No Deal with Bin Laden"
  - Speaker: Usama bin Laden
  - Summary: In an audiotape delivered to Al Jazeera and Al-Arabiya, bin Laden offered European countries the opportunity to enter into a truce with al-Qa'ida, if they pulled their troops from the Islamic countries they were currently residing in. Caveats to this truce include the offer being on the table for only three months, and the exclusion of the US from any chance at a peace offering. Aside from this offer, bin Laden also threatened to take revenge on the US for the killing of Sheikh Ahmed Yassin, the founder of Hamas.

- Source: *The New York Times*
  - Date Published: 29 October 2004
  - Available at: *http://www.nytimes.com/2004/10/30/international/ middleeast/30qaeda.html?scp=1&sq=In%20Video%20 Message,%20Bin%20Laden%20Issues%20Warning%20to%20 US&st=cse*
  - Statement Title: Unknown
  - Document Title: "In Video Message, Bin Laden Issues Warning to US"
  - Speaker: Usama bin Laden
  - Summary: In his first video appearance in over a year, bin Laden again threatened the American people by warning that if they wanted to avoid another attack like September 11th, they needed to discontinue their attacks on the Muslim world. He stated, "Your security is not in the hands of Kerry or Bush or Al Qaeda; your security is in your own hands." While no direct threats were made, the surfacing of this video only four days before the Presidential election suggested the fate of America and the next President could be related to one another.

- Source: Fox News
  - Date Published: Was released 29 November 2004 (Believed to have been made in late October)

- Available at: *http://www.foxnews.com/story/0,2933,139885,00.html*
- Statement Title: Unknown
- Document Title: "Al-Zawahiri Vows to Keep Fighting US"
- Speaker: Ayman al-Zawahiri
- Summary: In this video, al-Zawahiri gives his opinion of the recent Presidential election, saying, "Vote [for] whoever you want, Bush, Kerry or the devil himself. This does not concern us. What concerns us is to purge our land [of] the aggressors." He offers the American people two options: They can either treat the Muslim world with respect or they can continue to be subjected to attacks until they change their policies.

- Source: MEMRI
  - Date Published: 7 December 2004
  - Available at: MEMRI
  - Statement Title: Unknown
  - Document Title: "Al-Qaeda Leader Ayman Al-Zawahiri's Interview to Al-Sahab"
  - Speaker: Ayman al-Zawahiri
  - Summary: In this interview, originally conducted on the 4th anniversary of September 11th, Zawahiri calls upon the American people to join Islam. He says all types of reform can be successful only if they take place through jihad. Zawahiri continues his tirade by accusing America of spreading corruption throughout the world rather than freedom.

- Source: *Guardian* (UK)
  - Date Published: 16 December 2004
  - Available at: *http://www.guardian.co.uk/world/2004/dec/16/alqa ida.saudiarabia1*
  - Statement Title: Unknown
  - Document Title: "New Bin Laden Tape Posted on Website"
  - Speaker: Usama bin Laden
  - Summary: In this audiotape, bin Laden expresses his happiness over the attack on the US Consulate in Saudi Arabia. He also criticizes the Saudi Arabian royal family, saying they and not "holy warriors" are the ones who are at fault for the current state of the country. He states, "The sins the regime committed are great...it practised injustices against the people, violating their rights, humiliating their

pride…" He demands change because in his opinion the country's elite has done nothing to rectify their wrongdoings.

- Source: CNN
  - Date Published 18 June 2005
  - Available at: *http://articles.cnn.com/2005-06-17/world/alzawahiri. video_1_bin-laden-deputy-zawahiri-qaeda?_s=PM:WORLD*
  - Statement Title: Unknown
  - Document Title: "Bin Laden Deputy Sends Message"
  - Speaker: Ayman al-Zawahiri
  - Summary: In his first message in four months, al-Zawahiri reiterates the importance of continuing to fight against the US because the Muslim world has the right to oversee what goes on in its region without the influence of foreign nations. He called for the removal of US embassies in Islamic countries because they were "meddling" in Middle Eastern affairs. During his tirade, he quoted from the Quran, with particular emphasis on this verse: "God said fight them and God will torture them through your hands." He also placed blame on the US for a lack of reform throughout the region saying, "We cannot imagine any reform while our land is occupied by the crusaders who are stationed on all our land, from end to end."

- Source: *Guardian* (UK)
  - Date Published: 5 August 2005
  - Available at: *http://www.guardian.co.uk/uk/2005/aug/05/politics. july7*
  - Statement Title: Unknown
  - Document Title: "A Chilling Message to Britons"
  - Speaker: Ayman al-Zawahiri
  - Summary: Four weeks after the July 7, 2005 bombings in London left 56 people dead, al-Zawahiri released this video proclaiming his approval of the attacks. Al-Zawahiri blamed British Prime Minister Tony Blair for the attacks, saying "policies brought you destruction in central London and will bring you more destruction." The US was also warned that if it continued to remain in the Middle East it would experience more death and destruction from al-Qa'ida. He also spoke of his disappointment in regards to the European nations ignoring the truce bin Laden had offered the previous year.

- Source: MEMRI
  - Date Published: 7 December 2005
  - Available at: MEMRI
  - Statement Title: Unknown
  - Document Title: "Al-Qaeda Leader Ayman Al-Zawahiri's Interview to Al-Sahab" (Part II)
  - Speaker: Ayman al-Zawahiri
  - Summary: The main focus of this interview, originally done on the 4th anniversary of September 11th, was to discuss the current state of al-Qa'ida. Zawahiri denounces Bush and says al-Qa'ida has not been eradicated, but is still a thriving base for the jihad. He goes further by saying Bush is not being forthcoming with the number of soldiers actually being killed in Afghanistan. He concludes with this statement, "If the only way to repel these thieves is by killing them, they should be killed without honor."

- Source: *Guardian* (UK)
  - Date Published: 20 February 2006
  - Available at: *http://www.guardian.co.uk/world/2006/feb/20/alqaida.terrorism*
  - Statement Title: "I Will Never Be Taken Alive"
  - Document Title: "Bin Laden: 'I Will Never Be Taken Alive'"
  - Speaker: Usama bin Laden
  - Summary: In this audiotape, bin Laden declares he will never be taken alive, but will instead live free. Throughout his speech he makes a comparison between Saddam Hussein and the US military in Iraq, calling the fight both barbaric and repressive. He is positive the jihad is growing in strength and mocks President Bush's belief that the conflict in Iraq ended in 2003. Finally, he criticizes the incorrect figures released by the Pentagon in regards to the number of American troops killed and injured during battle, as well as increases in suicide rates and a decrease in morale.

- Source: BBC News & CNN
  - Date Published: 29 April 2006
  - Available at: *http://news.bbc.co.uk/2/hi/middle_east/4957078.stm; http://edition.cnn.com/2006/WORLD/meast/04/28/zawahiri.tape/index.html?iref=allsearch*
  - Statement Title: "A Message to the People of Pakistan"

241

- Document Title: "Al-Zawahiri Praises Insurgents in Video"
- Speaker: Ayman al-Zawahiri
- Summary: In this 15 minute video, al-Zawahiri commends Iraqi fighters on their victories during the war, saying, "We praise Allah that three years after the Crusader invasion of Iraq, America, Britain, and their allies have achieved nothing but losses, disaster and misfortunes." Zawahiri urges the people of Pakistan to follow in Iraqi footsteps and overthrow their treacherous President Pervez Musharraf, who has been "taking bribes from the United States."

- Source: CNN
  - Date Published: 11 September 2006
  - Available at: *http://articles.cnn.com/2006-09-11/us/zawahiri.911_1 _zawahiri-al-qaeda-leader-ayman?_s=PM:US*
  - Statement Title: Unknown
  - Document Title: "Al Qaeda Releases 9/11 Anniversary Message"
  - Speaker: Ayman al-Zawahiri
  - Summary: On the fifth anniversary of September 11th, al-Zawahiri warns of new attacks in the works and again urges Muslims to step up the fight against the US and the West. He calls for an increase in defiance in Somalia and mentions all Muslims must take revenge on America in response to the imprisonment of Omar Abdel Rahman, a man known for his theology throughout the al-Qa'ida network.

- Source: CNN
  - Date Published: 5 May 2007
  - Available at: *http://articles.cnn.com/2007-05-05/world/al.qaeda. tape_1_al-zawahiri-al-qaeda-shiites?_s=PM:WORLD*
  - Statement Title: Unknown
  - Document Title: "Al Qaeda Video Taunts Bush, Iran, Shiites"
  - Speaker: Ayman al-Zawahiri
  - Summary: In this hour long video, al-Zawahiri focuses on an estimated timetable for pulling troops out of Iraq. Al-Zawahiri calls upon Allah, asking "…that they only get out of it after losing 200 to 300 hundred thousand killed, in order that we give the spillers of blood in Washington and Europe an unforgettable lesson…" Aside from this declaration, he encouraged Sunni Muslims to unite and spread Sharia throughout the land.

- Source: *The Washington Post*
  - Date Published: 8 September 2007
  - Available at: *http://www.washingtonpost.com/wp-dyn/content/article/2007/09/07/AR2007090700279.html*
  - Statement Title: "The Solution"
  - Document Title: "Bin Laden Predicts US Failure in Iraq"
  - Speaker: Usama bin Laden
  - Summary: This 25 minute video addressed the ongoing war in Iraq and the consequences that would ensue if the American people continued to oppress the Muslim world. He stated, "The blood of the Muslims will not be spilled with impunity." Husain Haqqani, an expert on Islamic terrorist groups, believed the purpose of this video was to increase morale within al-Qa'ida while simultaneously denouncing the US and its Western views.

- Source: Global Terror Alert/NEFA Foundation
  - Date Published: 20 September 2007
  - Available at: *http://www.globalterroralert.com/al-qaida-leaders/30-usama-bin-laden-qcome-to-jihad-a-speech-to-the-people-of-pakistanq.html*.
  - Statement Title: "Come to Jihad: A Speech to the People of Pakistan"
  - Document Title: Unknown
  - Speaker: Usama bin Laden
  - Summary: Again, the people of Pakistan were urged to take up the fight against President Pervez of Pakistan, this time by bin Laden himself. In this video, bin Laden claimed it was the duty of the Pakistani people to overthrow their President because his continued alliance with the US was against Islam, making violence against him justifiable.

- Source: *The Long War Journal*/NEFA Foundation
  - Date Published: 23 October 2007
  - Available at: *http://nefafoundation.org/index.cfm?pageID=44; http://www.longwarjournal.org/archives/2007/10/osama_bin_laden_on_t.php*
  - Statement Title: "A Message to the People of Iraq"
  - Document Title: "Osama bin Laden on the State of Iraq"
  - Speaker: Usama bin Laden

- Summary: In this video, bin Laden criticizes the failures of al-Qa'ida throughout Iraq, including the dividing of ranks, violation of al-Qa'ida laws, and ignorance towards God being the sole authority. He says those who have violated the law need to be punished, because while everybody makes mistakes only the best admit to them. Bin Laden's comments on al-Qa'ida provide insight into the problems the organization is facing within the borders of Iraq.

- Source: *The Guardian* (UK)
    - Date Published: 30 November 2007
    - Available at: *http://www.guardian.co.uk/world/2007/nov/29/ usa.afghanistan*
    - Statement Title: "Message to the Peoples of Europe"
    - Document Title: "Bin Laden: Europe Must Quit Afghanistan"
    - Speaker: Usama bin Laden
    - Summary: In this video, bin Laden calls upon European governments to end their cooperation with the US in Afghanistan, saying, "the American tide is ebbing," and "It is better for you to restrain your politicians who are thronging the steps of the White House." He reiterates his role in al-Qa'ida rather than the Taliban and criticizes both the US and European countries for their continuing attacks on Afghanistan. Shortly after this video was released, the Afghan government issued a statement denouncing bin Laden's comments and saying their people were not killed by NATO troops but by Islamic extremists.

- Source: The NEFA Foundation
    - Date Published: 14 December 2007
    - Available at: *http://nefafoundation.org/miscellaneous/ nefazawahiri1207-2.pdf*
    - Statement Title: "Annapolis: The Betrayal"
    - Document Title: "Two Statements by Dr. Ayman al-Zawahiri"
    - Speaker: Ayman al-Zawahiri
    - Summary: In this recording, al-Zawahiri condemns the Israeli-Palestinian peace summit that took place in Annapolis, Maryland. He urges the Palestinians to rethink who their true brothers are. He goes on by saying the West will not follow through with freeing Palestine, even though they are denouncing al-Qa'ida and terrorism.

- Source: The NEFA Foundation
  - Date Published: 16 December 2007
  - Available at: *http://nefafoundation.org/miscellaneous/ nefazawahiri1207-2.pdf*
  - Statement Title: "A Review of Events"
  - Document Title: "Ayman al-Zawahiri: 'A Review of Events'"
  - Speaker: Ayman al-Zawahiri
  - Summary: Only two days after condemning the Palestinians for taking part in peace talks with Israel, al-Zawahiri partook in an interview with as-Sahab; al-Qa'ida's official propaganda outlet. Highlights include Al-Zawahiri's praises for al-Qa'ida in Iraq; anybody who thought otherwise was foolishly attempting to put blame on the organization for the failures of American troops. While the most important transformation for the future is "...the emergence of the Mujahid vanguard of the Muslim Ummah as a power imposing itself on the world stage..."

- Source: The NEFA Foundation
  - Date Published: 3 January 2008
  - Available at: *http://nefafoundation.org/index.cfm?pageID=44*
  - Statement Title: "The Way to Frustrate the Conspiracies"
  - Document Title: "Usama Bin Laden: 'The Way to Frustrate the Conspiracies'"
  - Speaker: Usama bin Laden
  - Summary: In this audiotape, bin Laden's main focus is on calling upon insurgents in the Islamic State of Iraq to join the al-Qa'ida organization. He also makes a statement directed towards Palestine in which he says, "we will widen the scope of our jihad and we will not recognize Sykes-Picot borders...Blood for blood, destruction for destruction."

- Source: The NEFA Foundation
  - Date Published: 7 February 2008 & 27 February 2008
  - Available at: *http://nefafoundation.org/index.cfm?pageID=44*
  - Statement Title: Unknown
  - Document Title: "Shaykh Mustafa Abu al-Yazid 'Light and Fire an Announcement to the Ummah'" & "Dr. Ayman al-Zawahiri 'An Elegy to the Martyred Commander Abu al-Layth al-Libi'"

- Speaker: Shaykh Mustafa Aby al-Yazid (Al'Qa'ida leader in Afghanistan) & Ayman Al-Zawahiri
- Summary: In both of these videos, al-Yazid and al-Zawahiri each mourn and vow to avenge the death of Abu al-Laith al-Liby, a commander for al-Qa'ida. Al-Yazid declares in his speech, "[We] will not rest until they avenge him and realize his aspirations and hopes..." He goes further by saying the killing of a top level member of al-Qa'ida will not hinder jihad from continuing, but will instead be a motivator for strengthening the will to fight. Al-Zawahiri gives the same message in his video, saying "Every time a martyr falls, another martyr grabs the banner from him...nor has our blood been spilled without a response."

- Source: The NEFA Foundation
  - Date Published: 19 March 2008
  - Available at: *http://nefafoundation.org/index.cfm?pageID=44*
  - Statement Title: "May Our Mothers Be Bereaved of Us If We Fail to Help Our Prophet"
  - Document Title: "Usama Bin Laden 'May Our Mothers Be Bereaved of Us If We Fail to Help Our Prophet'"
  - Speaker: Usama bin Laden
  - Summary: In this audio recording, bin Laden denounces the cartoons, criticizing Islam, which were published in Denmark. He refuses to acknowledge their attempts at asserting free speech by saying, "If there is no check on the freedom of your words, then let your hearts be open to the freedom of our actions..."

- Source: The NEFA Foundation
  - Date Published: 21 March 2008
  - Available at: *http://nefafoundation.org/index.cfm?pageID=44*
  - Statement Title: "The Way for the Salvation of Palestine"
  - Document Title: "Usama Bin Laden 'The Way for the Salvation of Palestine'"
  - Speaker: Usama bin Laden
  - Summary: In this audiotape, bin Laden talks about reclaiming control of Palestine. He also urges al-Qa'ida members and supporters to welcome "brothers" from Palestine and allow them a place among the mujahideen in Iraq, saying "The mujahideen

246

coming from outside shall encounter their brothers within…and the Muslims shall delight in their clear victory."

- Source: The NEFA Foundation
  - Date Published: 21 April 2008 (Released April 17th)
  - Available at: *http://nefafoundation.org/index.cfm?pageID=44*
  - Statement Title: Unknown
  - Document Title: "Dr. Ayman al-Zawahiri 'On the Fifth Anniversary of the Invasion and Torture of Iraq'"
  - Speaker: Ayman al-Zawahiri
  - Summary: In this audio recording, al-Zawahiri claims Iraq is nearing victory and will soon become a "fortress of Islam." He believes Iraq will continue to play a key role in the war between Islam and the Western world, and because of this, people must continue to assist in the jihad. Furthermore, he sends out a warning to Muslims saying they must act sooner rather than later when taking up the fight.

- Source: The NEFA Foundation
  - Date Published: 22 May 2001
  - Available at: *http://nefafoundation.org/index.cfm?pageID=44*
  - Statement Title: "A Message to the People of the West from the Shaykh Usama Bin Laden: The Reasons for the Conflict on the Sixtieth Anniversary of the Israeli Conquest"
  - Document Title: "Usama Bin Laden 'A Message to the People of the West'"
  - Speaker: Usama bin Laden
  - Summary: In this new audio recording, bin Laden reiterates that the Palestinian issue is al-Qa'ida's main focus. He goes further by saying the Palestinian issue has been a motivating factor for his viewpoints since he was a young child. Then, in an attempt to justify al-Qa'ida's acts of terrorism, bin Laden claims "The real terrorism and the armed assaults are being carried out by a leader who is the most terrible instrument of war humanity has ever seen…" Finally, he states the Israelis are the real terrorists because they have killed many civilians including women and children.

- Source: The NEFA Foundation
  - Date Published: 29 May 2008
  - Available at: *http://nefafoundation.org/index.cfm?pageID=44*

- Statement Title: "A Message to the Islamic Nation"
- Document Title: "Usama bin Laden 'A Message to the Islamic Nation'"
- Speaker: Usama bin Laden
- Summary: In this audio recording, bin Laden targets Muslim youths and asks them to take up arms and defend their brothers in Palestine who are facing a great battle in the Gaza Strip. He firmly believes the only way to reach Palestine is to continue to wage jihad on the governments, including Egypt, surrounding the land of the Jews.

- Source: The NEFA Foundation
  - Date Published: 7 June 2008
  - Available at: *http://nefafoundation.org/index.cfm?pageID=44*
  - Statement Title: "On the Anniversary of the Disaster--A Call to Help Our People in Gaza"
  - Document Title: "New Zawahiri Recording 'Lift the Siege of Gaza'"
  - Speaker: Ayman al-Zawahiri
  - Summary: In this audio recording, al-Zawahiri reiterates bin Laden's message from May 2008, saying "the sons of the Islamic nation" must continue to rise up and fight against the countries surrounding Israel in order to join the battles going on in Palestine. He states, "…help your brothers in Gaza. Join in their battles…and if they start to break down the wall of betrayal, join them." He also addresses the Palestinians themselves, encouraging them to keep up the fight and not waver from their mission of establishing Islamic law in the land of Israel.

- Source: The NEFA Foundation
  - Date Published: 20 August 2008
  - Available at: *http://nefafoundation.org/index.cfm?pageID=44*
  - Statement Title: Unknown
  - Document Title: "Ayman al-Zawahiri 'To Pakistan Army and the People of Pakistan'"
  - Speaker: Ayman al-Zawahiri
  - Summary: In this audio message, al-Zawahiri focuses his attention on the Pakistani military, asking them to rise up against their President and the alliance he has formed with the US mentioning his own experiences with Pakistan, he states the only reason he is

speaking in English, or the language of the "enemies of Islam", is because of his unfamiliarity with Urdu.

- Source: The NEFA Foundation
  - Date Published: 8 October 2008 (Released October 3rd)
  - Available at: *http://nefafoundation.org/index.cfm?pageID=44*
  - Statement Title: "The Believer Isn't Stung from the Same Hole Twice"
  - Document Title: "Adam Gadahn 'The Believer Isn't Stung from the Same Hole Twice'"
  - Speaker: Adam Gadahn
  - Summary: In this video message, Gadahn criticizes the leadership of both the Pakistani government and military. Aside from these criticisms, he speaks of the imminent economic crisis in America, saying the reason for this meltdown is due to Americans "turning their backs on Allah's revealed laws, which forbid interest-bearing transactions, exploitation, greed, and injustice..." It is because of America's ignorance towards Allah that they are facing an economic catastrophe.

- Source: The NEFA Foundation
  - Date Published: 19 November 2008
  - Available at: *http://nefafoundation.org/index.cfm?pageID=44*
  - Statement Title: "On the Parting of Bush and the Arrival of Obama"
  - Document Title: "Dr. Ayman al-Zawahiri 'On the Parting of Bush and the Arrival of Obama'"
  - Speaker: Ayman al-Zawahiri
  - Summary: In this audio recording, Zawahiri sends a personal message to Obama, warning, "[a] heavy legacy of failure and crimes...awaits you." He also accuses the newly elected President of having the "same criminal American mentality towards the world and towards the Muslims." He encourages the President to remain cognizant of the jihad and reiterates that America is not facing individuals or organizations, but a movement that is responsible for "...shaking the pillars of the entire Islamic world."

- Source: The NEFA Foundation
  - Date Published: 10 December 2008
  - Available at: *http://nefafoundation.org/index.cfm?pageID=44*
  - Statement Title: "The Lions of Al-Azhar"
  - Document Title: "Dr. Ayman al-Zawahiri 'The Lions of Al-Azhar'"
  - Speaker: Ayman al-Zawahiri
  - Summary: In this interview, al-Zawahiri focuses on a number of different issues. First, in response to the embargo that was imposed on the Gaza strip, Egyptians must strike; this refusal to leave their homes will be a direct attack against Israel. Second, when asked about the common misconception made in regards to the link between America and the creation of al-Qa'ida, Zawahiri vaguely responds, saying, "My comment is the American Congress's official recognition of the falseness of the misconception in its report on the events of September 11th." Finally, he shares his viewpoints on the Presidential election, saying the fact that both candidates are in favor of assisting Israel solidifies America's stance towards Islam.

- Source: NEFA Foundation
  - Date Published: 6 January 2009
  - Available At: *http://nefafoundation.org//index.cfm?pageID=44*
  - Statement Title: "The Massacre of Gaza and the Siege of the Traitors"
  - Document Title: "Zawahiri Issues Orders to 'Strike Everywhere' in Revenge for Gaza"
  - Speaker: Ayman al-Zawahiri
  - Summary: This audio recording condemns the Israeli raids in Gaza and blames them on President Mubarak and President Obama. Because of this, al-Zawahiri calls on supporters to carry out revenge on American and Israeli targets.

- Source: NEFA Foundation
  - Date Published: 15 January 2009
  - Available At: *http://nefafoundation.org//index.cfm?pageID=44*
  - Statement Title: "A Call for Jihad to Stop the Gaza Assault"
  - Document Title: "Usama Bin Laden, ' A Call for Jihad to Stop the Gaza Assault'"

- Speaker: Usama bin Laden
- Summary: This audio recording by bin Laden calls on youth to take up arms and join the jihad against the Zionist-Crusader alliance. He also blames the Gaza raid on a declining US economy. Lastly, bin Laden requests donations from faithful Muslims.

- Source: NEFA Foundation
  - Date Published: 22 February 2009
  - Available At: *http://nefafoundation.org//index.cfm?pageID=44*
  - Statement Title: "From Kabul to Mogadishu"
  - Document Title: "New Zawahiri Audio, 'From Kabul to Mogadishu'"
  - Speaker: Ayman al-Zawahiri
  - Summary: This audio recording congratulates the Shebaab al-Mujahideen Movement in Somalia on recent victories.

- Source: NEFA Foundation
  - Date Published: 14 March 2009
  - Available At: *http://nefafoundation.org//index.cfm?pageID=44*
  - Statement Title: "Practical Steps to Liberate Palestine"
  - Document Title: "New Bin Laden Audio, 'Practical Steps to Liberate Palestine'"
  - Speaker: Usama bin Laden
  - Summary: In this audio recording, bin Laden asks "how long must our family in Palestine live in fear, while we enjoy security--albeit a false, temporary security?" He is speaking about why the situation in Gaza, or "the holocaust," as he refers to it, is further reason why Muslims need to detach themselves from the "hypocrites."

- Source: NEFA Foundation
  - Date Published: 19 March 2009
  - Available At: *http://nefafoundation.org//index.cfm?pageID=44*
  - Statement Title: "Fight On, Champions of Somalia"
  - Document Title: "New Bin Laden Audio 'Fight On, Champions of Somalia'"
  - Speaker: Usama bin Laden
  - Summary: This audio recording by the al-Qa'ida leader condemns "the decision of former Somali Islamic Courts Union (ICU) president

Shaykh Shareef to join in a peace initiative with the interim Somali government." It is bin Laden's opinion that he is abandoning his religion.

- Source: NEFA Foundation
  - Date Published: 24 March 2009
  - Available At: *http://nefafoundation.org//index.cfm?pageID=44*
  - Statement Title: "Crusade Sets Its Sights on the Sudan"
  - Document Title: "New Zawahiri Audio 'Crusade Sets Its Sights on the Sudan'"
  - Speaker: Ayman al-Zawahiri
  - Summary: This audio recording urges followers in Sudan to train and take up arms to prepare for a guerilla war, because the Sudanese regime will not be able to defend the Sudan.

- Source: NEFA Foundation
  - Date Published: 16 June 2009
  - Available At: *http://nefafoundation.org//index.cfm?pageID=44*
  - Statement Title: "Speech to the Pakistani Nation"
  - Document Title: "Usama Bin Laden 'Speech to the Pakistani Nation'"
  - Speaker: Usama bin Laden
  - Summary: In this audio recording, bin Laden states that President Obama "ha[s] instilled new seeds to increase the hatred and revenge towards America" and that US citizens should prepare themselves for the future.

- Source: NEFA Foundation
  - Date Published: 22 June 2009
  - Available At: *http://nefafoundation.org//index.cfm?pageID=44*
  - Statement Title: not available
  - Document Title: "Shaykh Mustafa Abu al-Yazid's Al-Jazeera Interview"
  - Speaker: Shaykh Mustafa Abu al-Yazid
  - Summary: In this interview, al-Yazid was asked about Pakistani nuclear weapons; he replied that, hopefully, the US would not obtain them, but rather the Muslims would have them and be able to use them against the US. In regards to Hezbollah, he said that it is not considered an Islamic Party and that its loyalty is with Iran; there is

no relationship between Hezbollah and al-Qa'ida. Lastly, regarding Iran, he said that it is "a state of hypocrisy and schism, and it is the state that appears Muslim and claims Islam but in fact it fights the Muslims."

- Source: MEMRI Jihad & Terrorism Threat Monitor Project
  - Date Published: 31 July 2009
  - Statement Title: "Somalia: The Summer Cloud Has Dispersed"
  - Document Title: "Abu Yahya Al-Libi Blasts Somali Government, Offers Advice to Somali Mujahideen."
  - Speaker: Abu Yahya Al-Libi
  - Summary: This 40 minute video offers advice to the mujahideen in Somalia, with an emphasis on remaining loyal to the fight against the westernized African government and Union troops. Al-Libi speaks of the dangerous munafiqun, who are Muslims who profess Islam, but are in fact disbelievers. These disbelievers and true Muslims must be separated from one another.

- Source: CNN World/MEMRI Jihad & Terrorism Threat Monitor Project
  - Date Published: 3 August 2009
  - Available at: *http://articles.cnn.com/2009-08-03/world/al.qaeda. video_1_al-zawahiri-al-qaeda-palestinian-state?_s=PM:WORLD*
  - Statement Title: "The Realities of Jihad and the Fallacies of Hypocrisy"
  - Document Title: "Ayman Al-Zawahiri: 'Obama Is Selling an Illusion; France Will Pay the Price for Its Hatred of Islam.'"
  - Speaker: Ayman Al-Zawahiri
  - Summary: In this 90 minute video, al-Zawahiri denounces President Obama's support for a Palestinian state, making statements such as "Obama wants a Palestinian state that works as a branch for the Israeli government," and "Israel is a crime that needs to be wiped out." He goes further by claiming the mujahideen have been victorious, and will not be deterred, in both Afghanistan and Iraq. Finally, he comments on the recent ban of burqas in France and declares France will pay for its hostility towards Islam.

- Source: Reuters
  - Date Published: 9 August 2009
  - Available at: *http://in.reuters.com/article/2009/08/28/idINIndia-42051620090828*
  - Statement Title: "Path of Doom"
  - Document Title: "Qaeda's Zawahiri Calls for Pakistani Jihad"
  - Speaker: Ayman Al-Zawahiri
  - Summary: In this 22 minute video, al-Zawahiri urges Pakistanis to struggle against the Americans and the Pakistani army. He declares, "People of Pakistan...back the jihad and mujahideen with your persons, wealth, opinion, expertise, information and prayers and by exhorting others to help them and preach their message."

- Source: NEFA Foundation
  - Date Published: 14 September 2009
  - Available At: *http://nefafoundation.org//index.cfm?pageID=44*
  - Statement Title: not available
  - Document Title: "Usama Bin Laden's 9/11 Message to the American People"
  - Speaker: Usama bin Laden
  - Summary: In this audio recording, bin Laden urges the US to stop supporting Israel and, in exchange, "offered to respond to this decision in accordance with sound and just principles; otherwise, it is inevitable that we will continue our war of extermination against you on all possible fronts."

- Source: NEFA Foundation
  - Date Published: 25 September 2009
  - Available At: *http://nefafoundation.org//index.cfm?pageID=44*
  - Statement Title: "A Message from Shaykh Usama bin Laden to the People of Europe"
  - Document Title: "Usama Bin Laden 'Message to the People of Europe'"
  - Speaker: Usama bin Laden
  - Summary: This audio recording asks Europe to cease its NATO partnership with the US or face the consequences.

- Source: Critical Threats
  - Date Published: 9 November 2009
  - Available at: *http://www.criticalthreats.org/yemen/christmas-day-attack-manifestation-aqap-shift-targeting-america*
  - Statement Title: Unknown
  - Document Title: "Christmas Day Attack: Manifestation of AQAP Shift Targeting America"
  - Speaker: Muhammad Ibn 'Abd Al-Rahman Al-Rashid (Commander of AQAP
  - Summary: This 20 minute video, released by AQAP, calls attention to the US and NATO, who are viewed as the enemies of Islam. AQAP also accuses the Shi'ites of being enemies because their collaboration with the Crusaders has turned them evil. This video urges Sunni Muslims to join the mujahideen who will protect them, as opposed to the regimes who only claim they can offer protection.

- Source: MEMRI Jihad & Terrorism Threat Monitor Project
  - Date Published: 14 November 2009
  - Statement Title: "The Ziama Mansouria Attack"
  - Document Title: "New AQIM Video: 'The Ziama Mansouria Attack'"
  - Speaker: Al-Qaeda in the Islamic Maghreb (AQIM)
  - Summary: This 25 minute video was part of a larger series produced by AQIM titled "In the Shade of the Swords." This video depicts the AQIM attack on a base in Jijel province in eastern Algeria, which took place on February 22, 2009. At least nine security guards were killed, along with one member of AQIM. The main purpose of this video was to serve as a propaganda tool for the organization.

- Source: MEMRI Jihad & Terrorism Threat Monitor Project
  - Date Published: 11 November 2009
  - Statement Title: "The [Islamic] State [of Iraq] –In Their Own Words"
  - Document Title: "Al-Qaeda in Iraq: 'The Salafi Movement Has Passed the Point Where It Can Be Wiped Out'; 'Nobody Can Stop the Banner of Islam from Rising over the Entire World'"

- Speaker: ISI
- Summary: This hour long video, originally posted on the Islamist forum Al-Faluja, combines narratives, video, and other sources to display the current situation playing out in Iraq. These stories are drawn from both Arab and foreign media outlets. Throughout the video an emphasis is placed on Iraqi security personnel, Sahwa forces, American administrators, and army commanders.

- Source: NEFA Foundation
  - Date Published: 20 November 2009
  - Available At: *http://nefafoundation.org//index.cfm?pageID=44*
  - Statement Title: "Blackwater and the Peshawar Bombings"
  - Document Title: "Mustafa Abu al-Yazid Blames Blackwater for Peshawar Bombings"
  - Speaker: Mustafa Abu al-Yazid
  - Summary: This video message states that "we totally reject these bombings which occur in Muslim marketplaces and amongst residents...we have nothing to do with them." Rather he blamed Blackwater, a US security company, for the bombings.

- Source: MEMRI Jihad & Terrorism Threat Monitor Project
  - Date Published: 9 December 2009
  - Statement Title: not available
  - Document Title: not available
  - Speaker: AQIM
  - Summary: This communiqué confirms that AQIM was responsible for the kidnappings of one French national and three Spanish nationals, the former being in Mali and the latter occurring in Mauritania. Ransom demands were not given, but it was indicated that they would be given at a later date.

- Source: MEMRI Jihad & Terrorism Threat Monitor Project
  - Date Published: 15 December 2009
  - Statement Title: "The Idol of Unity and Nationalism"
  - Document Title: not available
  - Speaker: Al-Zawahiri
  - Summary: This 25 minute video declares "the concepts of national unity as of little value and pointless, as opposed to religious unity and jihad for the sake of Allah, which [Zawahiri] said was the

only way Palestine would be liberated." He also "condemn[s] the representatives of nationalism" and calls them "'Arab Zionists' who are acting to serve Israel and the West against the jihad fighters from among their own people."

- Source: MEMRI Jihad & Terrorism Threat Monitor Project
  - Date Published: 12 December 2009
  - Statement Title: "The Mujahideen Don't Target Muslims"
  - Document Title: not available
  - Speaker: Adam Gadahn
  - Summary: This 17 minute video claims that the mujahideen is not responsible for bombings against innocent Muslims. Rather, Gadahn states that the CIA, Blackwater, Pakistani ISI-P, or India's Research and Development Wing are to be blamed in their attempts to frame jihadist groups.

- Source: MEMRI Jihad & Terrorism Threat Monitor Project
  - Date Published: 29 December 2009
  - Statement Title: "The Buds of Victory and the Breezes of Empowerment"
  - Document Title: not available
  - Speaker: Abu Yahya Al-Libi
  - Summary: This 20 minute video states that there is hope for the mujahideen because the US "has been defeated and humiliated in Afghanistan and in Iraq." Therefore, each day Muslims become closer to achieving the goal of worldwide Islamic rule.

- Source: MEMRI Jihad & Terrorism Threat Monitor Project
  - Date Published: 8 February 2010
  - Statement Title: "A Response to the Crusader Aggression"
  - Document Title: not available
  - Speaker: Sheikh Abu Sufyan Al-Azdi (known as "Sa'id Al-Shihri")
  - Summary: This 12 minute video condemns aerial bombings of al-Qa'ida strongholds in Yemen and urges Yemeni residents to respond by waging jihad against the Jews, Christians, and their allies.

- Source: MEMRI Jihad & Terrorism Threat Monitor Project
  - Date Published: 13 January 2010
  - Statement Title: not available
  - Document Title: "Yemen Government to United States: [We Are Ready to Submit] Our Neck for Slaughter Instead of Your Neck"
  - Speaker: Abu Yahya Al-Libi
  - Summary: In this article, al-Libi states that the US realizes that its reign as a superpower has come to an end, and that it will never achieve security through all of its counterterrorism measures. The article also accuses Yemen of collaborating with the US.

- Source: MEMRI Jihad & Terrorism Threat Monitor Project
  - Date Published: 25 February 2010
  - Statement Title: "Towards a Life of Honor"
  - Document Title: not available
  - Speaker: Al-Qa'ida in the Arabian Peninsula (AQAP)
  - Summary: This 24 minute video focuses on domestic Yemeni issues and urges Yemeni residents to "support implementation of the shari'a." The video is split into two parts, with the first criticizing corrupt President 'Ali' Abdallah Saleh and his regime. It goes on to criticize "the socialist leaders of the former South Yemen."

- Source: NEFA Foundation
  - Date Published: 7 March 2010
  - Available At: *http://nefafoundation.org//index.cfm?pageID=44*
  - Statement Title: "A Call to Arms"
  - Document Title: "Adam Gadahn, 'A Call To Arms'"
  - Speaker: Adam Gadahn
  - Summary: This 25 minute video first praises the Detroit and Khost attacks of December 2009 before praising the Fort Hood shooter, Nidal Hasan, as an exemplary figure. He then urges listeners to choose targets that will cause serious economic damage to a country, and that conventional weapons are not always necessary, as was true in the case of 9/11.

- Source: MEMRI Jihad & Terrorism Threat Monitor Project
  - Date Published: 9 March 2010
  - Statement Title: not available
  - Document Title: not available

- • Speaker: Abu 'Ubayda Yusuf
- • Summary: This 18 minute audio message argues that "Jews and Christians are trying to transform the Sahel and West African countries into a new front in the war on Islam with the secret aim of occupying them in the end." He also warns Sahel countries and West African countries to not help non-Muslims fight against fellow Muslims.

- • Source: NEFA Foundation
  - • Date Published: 6 May 2010
  - • Available At: *http://nefafoundation.org//index.cfm?pageID=44*
  - • Statement Title: "Quraidhah and America: A Breeding Ground for Treachery and a Fountain of Evil"
  - • Document Title: "Abu Yahya Al-Liby, 'Quraidhah and America: A Breeding Ground for Treachery and a Fountain of Evil'"
  - • Speaker: Abu Yahya al-Liby
  - • Summary: This communication argues that "America deserves to be fought and invaded in their own lands solely due to the crimes they have committed and continue to commit against the Muslims."

- • Source: MEMRI Jihad & Terrorism Threat Monitor Project
  - • Date Published: 16 May 2010
  - • Statement Title: "In Support of Sheikh Anwar Al-Awlaki"
  - • Document Title: not available
  - • Speaker: Nasir Abu Basir Al-Wuhayshi
  - • Summary: This 10 minute audio recording attacks the Obama administration for its supposed authorization of the killing of cleric Anwar Al-Awlaki. In addition, he urges Muslims, specifically US Muslims, to emigrate to jihad fronts and join with the fighting.

- • Source: MEMRI Jihad & Terrorism Threat Monitor Project
  - • Date Published: 25 May 2010
  - • Statement Title: not available
  - • Document Title: "Eulogy"
  - • Speaker: Ayman Al-Zawahiri
  - • Summary: This audio recording is a eulogy for Abu Omar Al-Baghdadi and Abu Hamza Al-Muhajir. However, most of the message condemns Iran and the Shi'ites of Iraq, whom he blames for the two deaths.

- Source: MEMRI Jihad & Terrorism Threat Monitor Project
  - Date Published: 3 June 2010
  - Statement Title: not available
  - Document Title: not available
  - Speaker: Abu Sufyan Al-Azdi
  - Summary: In this audio recording, Al-Azdi strongly suggests that all Muslims use any means necessary to free mujahideen prisoners in Saudi Arabia, even the women. He even goes as far as to say that it is "…both a collective duty and an individual religious duty of every Muslim."

- Source: MEMRI Jihad & Terrorism Threat Monitor Project
  - Date Published: 15 June 2010
  - Statement Title: not available
  - Document Title: not available
  - Speaker: Mustafa Abu Al-Yazid (aka Sa'id Al-Masri)
  - Summary: This 26 minute posthumous audio recording calls on listeners to carry out attacks within the US. In addition, he confirms that Pakistani jihad commander Ilyas Kashmiri is part of al-Qa'ida, heading up the organization's network in Kashmir. Lastly, Al-Yazid attempts to raise money for the organization, pleading that several operations cannot occur due to a lack of funding.

- Source: NEFA Foundation
  - Date Published: 21 June 2010
  - Statement Title: "Legitimate Demands Part 2: Barack's Dilemma"
  - Document Title: "Adam Gadahn, 'Legitimate Demands Part 2: Barack's Dilemma'"
  - Speaker: Adam Gadahn
  - Summary: This video was a direct address to President Obama with its main point being the reiteration of al-Qa'ida's demands of the US, including: "…complete troop withdrawal from Iraq, Afghanistan, and all other Muslim countries; complete disengagement from the Muslim world and an end to United States support for these countries' regimes; an imposition of Cuba-like restrictions on United States citizens' contacts with Israel, and the release of all Muslim prisoners." However, even though these demands were made, it seems that al-Qa'ida is aware that they cannot be met. Gadahn ends

the video by making a direct threat against the US by promising to carry out mass casualty attacks within the country.

- Source: MEMRI Jihad & Terrorism Threat Monitor Project
  - Date Published: early June 2010
  - Statement Title: not available
  - Document Title: not available
  - Speaker: Abu Sufyan Al-Azdi
  - Summary: In early June, Al-Azdi "…called upon Saudi mujahideen to abduct Saudi emirs, army commanders and officials, as well as Christians, in order to bargain for the release of imprisoned mujahideen." He "…urged the mujahideen to gather information, collect resources, and create cells to carry out the abductions."

- Source: MEMRI Jihad & Terrorism Threat Monitor Project
  - Date Published: 12 July 2010
  - Statement Title: not available
  - Document Title: "Interview with Ustad Ahmad Farooq"
  - Speaker: Ahmad Farooq
  - Summary: This is the second installment of the interview, the first having been released in November, 2009. In the first part of the interview, he argued that the wars in Pakistan and Afghanistan are both jihad rather than rebellions against an Islamic state. Secondly, he argued that there are two reasons for jihad against Pakistan: The government supports infidels, and it has not implemented Islamic sharia within the country.

- Source: MEMRI Jihad & Terrorism Threat Monitor Project
  - Date Published: 25 July 2010
  - Statement Title: not available
  - Document Title: documentary about a "martyrdom" attack
  - Speaker: not available
  - Summary: This 43 minute video documents an attack carried out on a military base in the Urgun district of Paktika province, near the Pakistani border, on May 21, 2010. There were four "martyrdom" attackers, who carried out "The Raid of the Two Martyred Sheikhs." The video also discusses the motivation in general for martyrdom attacks, and criticizes the Western media, specifically the BBC.

- Source: MEMRI Jihad & Terrorism Threat Monitor Project
  - Date Published: 8 August 2010
  - Statement Title: "We Will Not Surrender: We Will Be Victorious or Die"
  - Document Title: not available
  - Speaker: Abu Mus'ab 'Abd al-Wadoud
  - Summary: This 15 minute audio recording argues that "the Algerian regime's failure to achieve military victory is what led it to wage ideological warfare."

- Source: MEMRI Jihad & Terrorism Threat Monitor Project
  - Date Published: 2 October 2010
  - Statement Title: "Save Your Brothers in Pakistan"
  - Document Title: not available
  - Speaker: Usama bin Laden
  - Summary: This audio message by the leader of al-Qa'ida discusses the flooding in Pakistan and urges the relief effort to be increased. In his eyes, not enough has been done by the Pakistani government to help those in need.

- Source: NEFA Foundation
  - Date Published: 22 October 2010
  - Available At: *http://nefafoundation.org//index.cfm?pageID=44*
  - Statement Title: "The Arabs and Muslims: Between the Conferences of Desertion and the Individual Duty of Jihad"
  - Document Title: "Adam Gadahn: 'The Arabs and Muslims: Between the Conferences of Desertion and the Individual Duty of Jihad'"
  - Speaker: Adam Gadahn
  - Summary: In this video, Gadahn states that it is everyone's duty to defend Islam and Muslims and to participate in jihad against "criminals" such as the US and the Europeans, etc.

- Source: NEFA Foundation
  - Date Published: 8 November 2010
  - Available At: *http://nefafoundation.org//index.cfm?pageID=44*
  - Statement Title: not available
  - Document Title: "Dr. Ayman al-Zawahiri: 'Who Will Support Scientist Aafia Siddiqui?'"

- • Speaker: Ayman al-Zawahiri
- • Summary: In this audiotape, al-Zawahiri discusses revenge for the jailing of Dr. Aafia Siddiqui. He sent the message to the US, saying "be arrogant as you wish…the Islamic Ummah will respond strike for strike, and kill for kill, and destruction for destruction, and attack for attack."

- • Source: NEFA Foundation
  - • Date Published: 9 November 2010
  - • Available At: *http://nefafoundation.org//index.cfm?pageID=44*
  - • Statement Title: "To the French People"
  - • Document Title: "A Message from Usama Bin Laden to the French People"
  - • Speaker: Usama bin Laden
  - • Summary: This audiotape explains to the French why its citizens are being kidnapped. It is because France will not allow women to wear a jihab; therefore, capturing its citizens is retaliation.

- • Source: NEFA Foundation
  - • Date Published: 18 February 2011
  - • Available At: *http://nefafoundation.org//index.cfm?pageID=44*
  - • Statement Title: "Message of Hope and Glad Tidings to Our People in Egypt"
  - • Document Title: "Dr. Ayman al-Zawahiri: 'Message of Hope and Glad Tidings to Our People in Egypt'"
  - • Speaker: Ayman al-Zawahiri
  - • Summary: This message describes the situation in Egypt as a "deviation from Islam including…corruption, immorality, injustice, oppression and dependence." He sees the regime as oppressive rather than democratic, as it claims to be.

- • Source: NEFA Foundation
  - • Date Published: 24 February 2011
  - • Available At: *http://nefafoundation.org//index.cfm?pageID=44*
  - • Statement Title: "Message of Hope and Glad Tidings to Our People in Egypt Episode 2"
  - • Document Title: "Dr. Ayman al-Zawahiri: 'Message of Hope and Glad Tidings to Our People in Egypt, Episode 2'"

- • Speaker: Ayman al-Zawahiri
- • Summary: This message discusses recent operations that have been attributed to the mujahideen. Al-Zawahiri says that these operations are condemned by al-Qa'ida and Allah, regardless of who committed them.

- • Source: NEFA Foundation
  - • Date Published: 27 February 2011
  - • Available At: *http://nefafoundation.org//index.cfm?pageID=44*
  - • Statement Title: "Message of Hope and Glad Tidings to Our People in Egypt, Episode 3"
  - • Document Title: "Dr. Ayman al-Zawahiri: 'Message of Hope and Glad Tidings to Our People in Egypt, Episode 3'"
  - • Speaker: Ayman al-Zawahiri
  - • Summary: This message urges that the outrage resulting from the situations in Tunisia and Egypt should not be forgotten, so that it can fuel further uprisings.

- • Source: NEFA Foundation
  - • Date Published: 3 March 2011
  - • Available At: *http://nefafoundation.org//index.cfm?pageID=44*
  - • Statement Title: "Message of Hope and Glad Tidings to Our People in Egypt, Episode 4"
  - • Document Title: "Dr. Ayman al-Zawahiri: 'Message of Hope and Glad Tidings to Our People in Egypt, Episode 4'"
  - • Speaker: Ayman al-Zawahiri
  - • Summary: This message urges the Tunisian people "to 'continue' their 'Jihad and resistance until' they 'excise tyranny from' their 'land and until the flags of Islam, freedom, glory and justice begin fluttering over' their 'plains.'"

- • Source: NEFA Foundation
  - • Date Published: 14 April 2011
  - • Available At: *http://nefafoundation.org//index.cfm?pageID=44*
  - • Statement Title: "Message of Hope and Glad Tidings to Our People in Egypt, Episode 5"
  - • Document Title: "Dr. Ayman al-Zawahiri: 'Message of Hope and Glad Tidings to Our People in Egypt, Episode 5'"
  - • Speaker: Ayman al-Zawahiri

- Summary: This message has several sections which discuss different countries. The first section is regarding events in Libya, whereas the second section discusses Egypt. The third section has to do with Tunisia, and the final section has some concluding messages. Within the message, al-Zawahiri urges Egyptians to support and provide supplies to those protesting in Libya. In addition, he urges all individuals to fight against the US and NATO forces if they enter Libya.

- Source: NEFA Foundation
  - Date Published: 6 May 2011
  - Available At: *http://nefafoundation.org//index.cfm?pageID=44*
  - Statement Title: not available
  - Document Title: "Qa'ida al-Jihad Organization-General Command (al-Qaida): 'Statement Regarding the Defiant Battle and the Martyrdom of Sheikh Usama bin Laden--may Allah have mercy on him'"
  - Speaker: not available
  - Summary: This is the first official statement from al-Qa'ida regarding the death of Usama bin Laden. It states that "Sheikh Usama didn't build an organization to die with it and go away with it." It goes on to call "...our Muslim people in Pakistan...to rise and revolt to wash off this shame." The speaker also warned, "We warn the Americans regarding the mistreatment of the Sheikh's corpse...Any harm will be revisited many times."

- Source: NEFA Foundation
  - Date Published: 18 May 2011
  - Available At: *http://nefafoundation.org//index.cfm?pageID=44*
  - Statement Title: not available
  - Document Title: "Usama Bin Laden Final Audio Message: 'To the Muslim Ummah'"
  - Speaker: Usama bin Laden
  - Summary: This is the final audio message given by bin Laden and it was released after his death. It encourages and supports the revolutions in Tunisia, Egypt, and Libya. Bin Laden warns youth that they should not be hasty with their actions, but should rather seek the advice of those with expertise and experience before carrying out anything.

- Source: NEFA Foundation
  - Date Published: 19 May 2011
  - Available At: *http://nefafoundation.org//index.cfm?pageID=44*
  - Statement Title: not available
  - Document Title: "Statement from al-Fajr Media Center on the 'Martyrdom of the Lion Shaykh Usama bin Laden'"
  - Speaker: Fajr Media Center (al-Qa'ida online logistics agency)
  - Summary: This communiqué states: "We advise every Muslim to seize the opportunity...do not waste it, and do not consult anyone in killing the Americans and destroying their economy." The statement then encourages supporters "...to wage individual terrorism operations that have big results but which need only simple preparation."

- Source: NEFA Foundation
  - Date Published: 21 May 2011
  - Available At: *http://nefafoundation.org//index.cfm?pageID=44*
  - Statement Title: "Message of Hope and Glad Tidings to Our People in Egypt Episode 6"
  - Document Title: "Dr. Ayman al-Zawahiri: 'Message of Hope and Glad Tidings to Our People in Egypt, Episode 6'"
  - Speaker: Ayman al-Zawahiri
  - Summary: This is the sixth installment of al-Zawahiri's series, and warns Muslims in Libya to be careful regarding the NATO plan to turn Libya into a new Iraq. He warns that "NATO seeks to replace Gadhafi 'with one of their own stooges, who will assist them in stealing Libya's oil and resources.'" Therefore, he suggests that all Muslims continue collecting and storing weapons for the future.

- Source: NEFA Foundation
  - Date Published: 8 June 2011
  - Available At: *http://nefafoundation.org//index.cfm?pageID=44*
  - Statement Title: not available
  - Document Title: "Dr. Ayman al-Zawahiri: 'And the Noble Knight Dismounts'"
  - Speaker: Ayman al-Zawahiri
  - Summary: In this recorded message al-Zawahiri gives a eulogy for bin Laden.

- Source: NEFA Foundation
  - Date Published: 3 June 2011
  - Available At: *http://nefafoundation.org//index.cfm?pageID=44*
  - Statement Title: "Thou Are Held Responsible Only for Yourself"
  - Document Title: "As-Sahab Media: 'You Are Held Responsible Only for Thyself-Part 1'"
  - Speaker: Adam Gadahn
  - Summary: In this video, Gadahn supports "lone wolf" jihad. He advises that "...every brother who wants to work for this religion not to undertake any action before taking advantage of the wide range of resources available today on the Internet, particularly the various manuals, encyclopedias and courses which deal with the Mujahideen's operational and electronic security, and security in general."

- Source: NEFA Foundation
  - Date Published: 3 June 2011
  - Available At: *http://nefafoundation.org//index.cfm?pageID=44*
  - Statement Title: "Thou Are Held Responsible Only for Yourself Part 2"
  - Document Title: As-Sahab Media: "You Are Held Responsible Only for Thyself-Part 2"
  - Speaker: As-Sahab Media Foundation
  - Summary: This video was devoted to electronic jihad. According to As-Sahab, "Hacking on the Internet is one of the key pathways to Jihad, and we advise the Muslims who possess the expertise in the field to target the websites and the information networks of big companies and government agencies of the countries that attack Muslims."

- Source: NEFA Foundation
  - Date Published: 16 June 2011
  - Available At: *http://nefafoundation.org//index.cfm?pageID=44*
  - Statement Title: not available
  - Document Title: Statement Regarding the Succession in the Leadership of Qaida't al-Jihad
  - Speaker: al-Qa'ida General Command
  - Summary: This statement was regarding Ayman al-Zawahiri taking command of the organization. Along with the announcement,

General Command issued its support for the revolutions going on with the Muslim people. It further encourages all Muslims to continue to provide resistance until "full and anticipated change comes, which will not be achieved except by the Islamic Ummah's return to the Sharia of its Lord."

- Source: Reuters
  - Date Published: 8 August 2011
  - Available At: *http://www.reuters.com/article/2011/08/08/us-iraq-violence-qaeda-idUSTRE7776LE20110808*
  - Statement Title: not available
  - Document Title: Indeed, the Islamic State Will Remain
  - Speaker: Islamic State of Iraq Spokesman Abu Mohammed al-Adnani
  - Summary: This statement praised al-Qa'ida's new leader Ayman al-Zawahiri as a successor to Usama bin Laden. Al-Adnani also said that foreign fighters continue to join his cause, which remains strong. He then condemned the Awakening Council and called for them to give up their "satanic" ways in supporting the government.

- Source: Reuters
  - Date Published: 15 August 2011
  - Available At: *http://www.thememriblog.org/blog_personal/en/40113.htm*
  - Statement Title: not available
  - Document Title: not available
  - Speaker: Ayman al-Zawahiri
  - Summary: To begin Ramadan, al-Zawahiri calls on Muslims to engage in jihad against America to avenge the death of their former leader. The 12 minute video urged followers to: "Pursue America, which killed the 'Imam of the Mujahadeen' and threw his body into the sea and then captured his women and sons."

Appendix 2: US Indictment of Usama bin Laden

US DISTRICT COURT

SOUTHERN DISTRICT OF NEW YORK

US OF AMERICA

- V-

USAMA BIN LADEN,

a/k/a "Usamah Bin-Muhammad Bin-Laden,"
a/k/a "Shaykh Usamah Bin-Laden,"
a/k/a "Mujahid Shaykh,"
a/k/a "Abu Abdallah,"
a/k/a "Qa Qa,"

Defendant

COUNT ONE

Conspiracy to Attack Defense Utilities of the US

The Grand Jury charges:

Background: Al Qaeda

1. At all relevant times from in or about 1989 until the date of the filing of this Indictment, an international terrorist group existed which was dedicated to opposing non-Islamic governments with force and violence. This organization grew out of the "mekhtab al Khidemat" (the "Services Office") organization which had maintained (and continues to maintain) offices in various parts of the world, including Afghanistan, Pakistan (particularly in Peshawar) and the United States, particularly at the Alkifah Refugee Center - in Brooklyn. From in or about 1989 until the present, the group called itself "Al Qaeda" ("the Base"). From 1989 until in or about 1991, the group was headquartered in Afghanistan and Peshawar, Pakistan. In or about 1992, the leadership of Al

Qaeda, including its "emir" (or prince) USAMA BIN LADEN the defendant, and its military command relocated to the Sudan. From in or about 1991 until the present, the group also called itself the "Islamic Army." The international terrorist group (hereafter referred to as "Al Qaeda") was headquartered in the Sudan from approximately 1992 until approximately 1996 but still maintained offices in various parts of the world. In 1996, USAMA BIN LADEN and Al Qaeda relocated to Afghanistan. At all relevant times, Al Qaeda was led by its "emir," USAMA BIN LADEN. Members of Al Qaeda pledged an oath of allegiance to USAMA BIN LADEN and Al Qaeda.

2. Al Qaeda opposed the United States for several reasons. First, the United States was regarded as "infidel" because it was not governed in a manner consistent with the group's extremist interpretation of Islam. Second, the United States was viewed as providing essential support for other "infidel" governments and institutions, particularly the governments of Saudi Arabia and Egypt, the nation of Israel and the United Nations, which were regarded as enemies of the group. Third, Al Qaeda opposed the involvement of the United States armed forces in the Gulf War in 1991 and in Operation Restore Hope in Somalia in 1992 and 1993. In particular, Al Qaeda opposed the continued presence of American military forces in Saudi Arabia (and elsewhere on the Saudi Arabian peninsula) following the Gulf war. Fourth, Al Qaeda opposed the United States Government because of the arrest, conviction and imprisonment of persons belonging to Al Qaeda or its affiliated terrorist groups, including Sheik Omar Abdel Rahman.

3. Al Qaeda has functioned both on its own and through some of the terrorist organizations that have operated under its umbrella, including: the Islamic Group (also known as "al Gamaa Islamia" or simply "Gamaa't"), led by co-conspirator Sheik Oxar Abdal Rahman; the al Jihad group based in Egypt; the "Talah e Fatah" ("Vanguards of conquest") faction of al Jibad, which was also based in Egypt, Which faction was led by co-conspirator Ayman al Zawahiri ("al Jibad"); Palestinian Islamic Jihad and a number of Jihad groups in other countries, including Egypt, the Sudan, Saudi Arabia, Yemen, Somalia, Eritrea, Kenya, Pakistan, Bosnia, Croatia, Algeria, Tunisia, Lebanon, the Philippines, Tajikistan, Chechnya, Bangladesh, Kashmir and Azerbaijan. In February 1998, Al Qaeda joined forces with Gamaa't, Al Jihad, the Jihad Movement in Bangladesh and the "Jamaat ul Ulema e Pakistan" to issue a fatwah (an Islamic religious ruling) declaring war against American civilians

worldwide under the banner of the "International Islamic Front for Jibad on the Jews and Crusaders."

4. Al Qaeda also forged alliances with the National Islamic Front in the Sudan and with the government of Iran and its associated terrorist group Hezballah for the purpose of working together against their perceived common enemies in the West, particularly the United States. In addition, al Qaeda reached an understanding with the government of Iraq that al Qaeda would not work against that government and that on particular projects, specifically including weapons development, al Qaeda would work cooperatively with the Government of Iraq.

5. Al Qaeda had a command and control structure which included a majlis al shura (or consultation council) which discussed and approved major undertakings, including terrorist operations.

6. Al Qaeda also conducted internal investigations of its members and their associates in an effort to detect informants and killed those suspected of collaborating with enemies of Al Qaeda.

7. From at least 1991 until the date of the filing of this Indictment, in the Sudan, Afghanistan and elsewhere out of the jurisdiction of any particular state or district, USAMA BIN LADEN, a/k/a "Usamah Bin-Muhammad Bin-Laden," a/k/a "Shaykh Usamah Bin-Laden," a/k/a "Mujahid Shaykh," a/k/a "Abu Abdallah," a/k/a "Qa Qa," the defendant, and a co-conspirator not named as a defendant herein (hereafter "Co-conspirator") who was first brought to and arrested in the Southern District of New York, and others known and unknown to the grand jury, unlawfully, willfully and knowingly combined conspired, confederated and agreed together and with each other to injure and destroy, and attempt to injure and destroy, national-defense material, national-defense premises and national-defense utilities of the United States with the intent to injure, interfere with and obstruct the national defense of the United States.

Overt Acts

8. In furtherance of the said conspiracy, and to effect the illegal object thereof, the following overt acts, among others, were committed:

a. At various times from at least as early as 1991 until at least in or about February 1998, USAMA BIN LADEN, the defendant, met with Co-conspirator and other members of Al Qaeda in the Sudan, Afghanistan and elsewhere;

b. At various times from at least as early as 1991, USAMA BIN LADEN, and others known and unknown, made efforts to obtain weapons, including firearms and explosives, for Al Qaeda and its affiliated terrorist groups;

c. At various times from at least as early as 1991 USAMA BIN LADEN, and others known and unknown, provided training camps and guest houses in various areas, including Afghanistan and the Sudan, for the use of Al Qaeda and its affiliated terrorist groups;

d. At various times from at least as early as 1991, USAMA BIN LADEN, and others known and unknown, made efforts to produce counterfeit passports purporting to be issued by various countries and also obtained official passports from the Government of the Sudan for use by Al Qaeda and its affiliated groups;

e. At various times from at least as early as 1991, USAMA BIN LADEN, and others known and unknown, made efforts to recruit United States citizens to Al Qaeda in order to utilize the American citizens for travel throughout the Western world to deliver messages and engage in financial transactions for the benefit of Al Qaeda and its affiliated groups;

f. At various times from at least as early as 1991, USAMA BIN LADEN, and others known and unknown, made efforts to utilize non-Government organizations which purported to be engaged in humanitarian work as conduits for transmitting funds for the benefit of Al Qaeda and its affiliated groups;

g. At various times from at least as early as 1991, Co-conspirator and others known and unknown to the grand jury engaged in financial and business transactions on behalf of defendant USAMA BIN LADEN and Al Qaeda, including, but not limited to: purchasing land for training camps; purchasing warehouses for storage of items, including explosives; transferring funds between bank accounts opened in various names, obtaining various communications equipment, including satellite telephones and transporting currency and weapons to members of Al Qaeda and its associated terrorist organizations in various countries throughout the world;

h. At various times from in or about 1992 until the date of the filing of this Indictment, USAMA BIN LADEN and other ranking members of Al Qaeda stated privately to other members of Al Qaeda that Al Qaeda should put aside its differences with Shiite Muslim terrorist organizations, including the Government of Iran and its affiliated terrorist group Hezballah, to cooperate against the perceived common enemy, the United States and its allies;

i. At various times from in or about 1992 until the date of the filing of this Indictment, USAMA BIN LADEN and other ranking members of Al Qaeda stated privately to other members of Al Qaeda that the United States forces stationed on the Saudi Arabian peninsula, including both Saudi Arabia and Yemen, should be Attacked;

j. At various times from in or about 1992 until the date of the filing of this Indictment, USAMA BIN LADEN and other ranking members of Al Qaeda stated privately to other members of Al Qaeda that the United States forces stationed in the Horn of Africa, including Somalia, should be attacked;

k. Beginning in or about early spring 1993, Al Qaeda members began to provide training and assistance to Somali tribes opposed to the United Nations intervention in Somalia;

l. On October 3 and 4, 1993, members of Al Qaeda participated with Somali tribesmen in an attack on United States military personnel serving in Somalia as part of Operation Restore Hope, which attack killed a total of 18 United States soldiers and wounded 73 others in Mogadishu;

m. On two occasions in the period from in or about 1992 until in or about 1995, Co-conspirator helped transport weapons and explosives from Khartoum to Port Sudan for transshipment to the Saudi Arabian peninsula;

n. At various times from at least as early as 1993, USAMA BIN LADEN and others known and unknown, made efforts to obtain the components of nuclear weapons;

o. At various times from at least as early as 1993 USAMA BIN LADEN and others known and unknown, made efforts to produce chemical weapons;

p. On or about August 23, 1996, USAMA BIN LADEN signed and issued a declaration of Jihad entitled "Message from Usamah Bin-Muhammad Bin-Laden to His Muslim Brothers in the Whole World and Especially in the Arabian Peninsula: Declaration of Jihad Against the Americans Occupying the Land of the Two Holy Mosques; Expel the Heretics from the Arabian Peninsula" (hereafter the "Declaration of Jihad) from the Hindu Kush mountains in Afghanistan. The Declaration of Jihad included statements that efforts should be pooled to kill Americans and encouraged other persons to join the jihad against the American enemy";

q. In or about late August 1996, USAMA BIN LADEN read aloud the Declaration of Jihad and made an audiotape recording of such reading for worldwide distribution; and

r. In February 1998, USAMA BIN LADEN issued a joint declaration in the name of Gamaa't, Al Jihad, the Jihad movement in Bangladesh and the "Jamaat ul Ulema e Pakistan" under the banner of the "International Islamic Front for Jihad on the Jews and Crusaders," which stated that Muslims should kill Americans—including civilians—anywhere in the world where they can be found.

(Title 18, United States code, Section 2155(b).)

Appendix 3A: Remarks by the President on Osama bin Laden (May 2, 2011)

The White House
Office of the Press Secretary
For Immediate Release
May 02, 2011
Remarks by the President on Osama Bin Laden
East Room
11:35 P.M. EDT

THE PRESIDENT: Good evening. Tonight, I can report to the American people and to the world that the United States has conducted an operation that killed Osama bin Laden, the leader of al Qaeda, and a terrorist who's responsible for the murder of thousands of innocent men, women, and children.

It was nearly 10 years ago that a bright September day was darkened by the worst attack on the American people in our history. The images of 9/11 are seared into our national memory—hijacked planes cutting through a cloudless September sky; the Twin Towers collapsing to the ground; black smoke billowing up from the Pentagon; the wreckage of Flight 93 in Shanksville, Pennsylvania, where the actions of heroic citizens saved even more heartbreak and destruction.

And yet we know that the worst images are those that were unseen to the world. The empty seat at the dinner table. Children who were forced to grow up without their mother or their father. Parents who would never know the feeling of their child's embrace. Nearly 3,000 citizens taken from us, leaving a gaping hole in our hearts.

On September 11, 2001, in our time of grief, the American people came together. We offered our neighbors a hand, and we offered the wounded our blood. We reaffirmed our ties to each other, and our love of community and country. On that day, no matter where we came from, what God we prayed to, or what race or ethnicity we were, we were united as one American family.

We were also united in our resolve to protect our nation and to bring those who committed this vicious attack to justice. We quickly learned that the 9/11 attacks were carried out by al Qaeda—an organization headed by Osama bin Laden, which had openly declared war on the United States and was committed to killing innocents in our country and around the globe. And so we went to war against al Qaeda to protect our citizens, our friends, and our allies.

Over the last 10 years, thanks to the tireless and heroic work of our military and our counterterrorism professionals, we've made great strides in that effort. We've disrupted terrorist attacks and strengthened our homeland defense. In Afghanistan, we removed the Taliban government, which had given bin Laden and al Qaeda safe haven and support. And around the globe, we worked with our friends and allies to capture or kill scores of al Qaeda terrorists, including several who were a part of the 9/11 plot.

Yet Osama bin Laden avoided capture and escaped across the Afghan border into Pakistan. Meanwhile, al Qaeda continued to operate from along that border and operate through its affiliates across the world.

And so shortly after taking office, I directed Leon Panetta, the director of the CIA, to make the killing or capture of bin Laden the top priority of our war against al Qaeda, even as we continued our broader efforts to disrupt, dismantle, and defeat his network.

Then, last August, after years of painstaking work by our Intelligence Community, I was briefed on a possible lead to bin Laden. It was far from certain, and it took many months to run this thread to ground. I met repeatedly with my national security team as we developed more information about the possibility that we had located bin Laden hiding within a compound deep inside of Pakistan. And finally, last week, I determined that we had enough intelligence to take action, and authorized an operation to get Osama bin Laden and bring him to justice.

Today, at my direction, the United States launched a targeted operation against that compound in Abbottabad, Pakistan. A small team of Americans carried out the operation with extraordinary courage and capability. No Americans were harmed. They took care to avoid civilian casualties. After a firefight, they killed Osama bin Laden and took custody of his body.

For over two decades, bin Laden has been al Qaeda's leader and symbol, and has continued to plot attacks against our country and our friends and allies. The death of bin Laden marks the most significant achievement to date in our nation's effort to defeat al Qaeda.

Yet his death does not mark the end of our effort. There's no doubt that al Qaeda will continue to pursue attacks against us. We must—and we will—remain vigilant at home and abroad.

As we do, we must also reaffirm that the United States is not—and never will be—at war with Islam. I've made clear, just as President Bush did shortly after 9/11, that our war is not against Islam. Bin Laden was not a Muslim leader; he was a mass murderer of Muslims. Indeed, al Qaeda has slaughtered scores of Muslims in many countries, including our own. So his demise should be welcomed by all who believe in peace and human dignity.

Over the years, I've repeatedly made clear that we would take action within Pakistan if we knew where bin Laden was. That is what we've done. But it's important to note that our counterterrorism cooperation with Pakistan helped lead us to bin Laden and the compound where he was hiding. Indeed, bin Laden had declared war against Pakistan as well, and ordered attacks against the Pakistani people.

Tonight, I called President Zardari, and my team has also spoken with their Pakistani counterparts. They agree that this is a good and historic day for both of our nations. And going forward, it is essential that Pakistan continue to join us in the fight against al Qaeda and its affiliates.

The American people did not choose this fight. It came to our shores, and started with the senseless slaughter of our citizens. After nearly 10 years of service, struggle, and sacrifice, we know well the costs of war. These efforts weigh on me every time I, as Commander-in-Chief, have to sign a letter to a family that has lost a loved one, or look into the eyes of a service member who's been gravely wounded.

So Americans understand the costs of war. Yet as a country, we will never tolerate our security being threatened, nor stand idly by when our people have been killed. We will be relentless in defense of our citizens and our friends and allies. We will be true to the values that make us who we are. And on nights like this one, we can say to those families who have lost loved ones to al Qaeda's terror: Justice has been done.

Tonight, we give thanks to the countless intelligence and counterterrorism professionals who've worked tirelessly to achieve this outcome. The American people do not see their work, nor know their names. But tonight, they feel the satisfaction of their work and the result of their pursuit of justice.

We give thanks for the men who carried out this operation, for they exemplify the professionalism, patriotism, and unparalleled courage of those who serve our country. And they are part of a generation that has borne the heaviest share of the burden since that September day.

Finally, let me say to the families who lost loved ones on 9/11 that we have never forgotten your loss, nor wavered in our commitment to see that we do whatever it takes to prevent another attack on our shores.

And tonight, let us think back to the sense of unity that prevailed on 9/11. I know that it has, at times, frayed. Yet today's achievement is a testament to the greatness of our country and the determination of the American people.

The cause of securing our country is not complete. But tonight, we are once again reminded that America can do whatever we set our mind to. That is the story of our history, whether it's the pursuit of prosperity for our people, or the struggle for equality for all our citizens; our commitment to stand up for our values abroad, and our sacrifices to make the world a safer place.

Let us remember that we can do these things not just because of wealth or power, but because of who we are: one nation, under God, indivisible, with liberty and justice for all.

Thank you. May God bless you. And may God bless the United States of America.

<u>END 11:44 P.M. EDT</u>

Appendix 3B: "Ensuring al-Qa'ida's Demise" (Remarks by John Brennan on June 29, 2011)

Remarks as Prepared for Delivery
John O. Brennan
Assistant to the President for Homeland Security and Counterterrorism
Paul H. Nitze School of Advanced International Studies
Washington, DC
Wednesday, June 29, 2011

Ensuring al-Qa'ida's Demise

Good afternoon. Thank you, Dean Einhorn, for your very warm welcome and for your decades of service—in government, global institutions and here at SAIS. And it's a special pleasure to be introduced by John McLaughlin, a friend and colleague of many years and one of our nation's great intelligence professionals.

It's a pleasure to be here at the Paul H. Nitze School of Advanced International Studies, an institution that has instilled in generations of public servants the pragmatic approach to problem-solving that is essential for the effective conduct of foreign policy. I especially want to thank the Merrill Center for Strategic Studies for its emphasis on national security and for joining with the Office of the Director of National Intelligence to introduce students to our Intelligence Community and inspiring the next generation of intelligence professionals.

It's wonderful to see so many friends and colleagues who I've had the privilege to work with over many years. You have devoted your lives to protecting our nation from many threats, including the one that brings me here today, and one that has claimed the lives of some of our friends and colleagues—that is the continued terrorist threat from al-Qa'ida.

Today, we are releasing President Obama's National Strategy for Counterterrorism, which formalizes the approach that we've been pursuing and adapting for the past two and half years to prevent terrorist attacks and to ensure al-Qa'ida's demise. I'm pleased that we are joined today by dedicated professionals from across the federal government who helped to shape our strategy and who work tirelessly every day to keep our country safe. Thank you for being here.

An unclassified summary of our strategy is being posted today to the White House website, WhiteHouse.gov. In the time I have with you, I'd like to put our strategy in context, outline its key goals and principals, and describe how we're putting these principles into practice to protect the American people.

I want to begin with the larger strategic environment that shapes our counterterrorism efforts. This starts with the recognition that this counterterrorism strategy is only one part of President Obama's larger National Security Strategy. This is very important. Our counterterrorism policies do not define our entire foreign policy; rather, they are a vital part of—and are designed to reinforce—our broader national security interests.

Since taking office, President Obama has worked to restore a positive vision of American leadership in the world—leadership defined, not by the threats and dangers that we will oppose, but by the security, opportunity and dignity that America advances in partnership with people around the world. This has enhanced our national security in many areas against many threats.

At the same time, many of the President's broader foreign policy and national security initiatives also help to achieve our more focused counterterrorism goals. They do so by addressing the political, economic and social conditions that can sometimes fuel violent extremism and push certain individuals into the arms of al-Qa'ida.

For instance, when our diplomats promote the peaceful resolution of political disputes and grievances, when our trade and economic policies generate growth that lifts people out of poverty, when our development experts support good governance that addresses people's basic needs, when we stand up for universal human rights—all of this can also help undermine violent extremists and terrorists like al-Qa'ida. Peaceful political, economic, and social progress undermines the claim that the only way to achieve change is through violence. It can be a powerful antidote to the disillusionment and sense of powerlessness that can make some individuals more susceptible to violent ideologies.

Our strategy recognizes that our counterterrorism efforts clearly benefit from—and at times depend on—broader foreign policy efforts, even as our CT strategy focuses more narrowly on preventing terrorist attacks against our interests, at home and abroad.

This, obviously, is also the first counterterrorism strategy to reflect the extraordinary political changes that are sweeping the Middle East and North Africa. It's true that these changes may bring new challenges and uncertainty in the short-term, as we are seeing in Yemen. It also is true that terrorist organizations, and nations that support them, will seek to capitalize on the instability that change can sometimes bring. That is why we are working closely with allies and partners to make sure that these malevolent actors do not succeed in hijacking this moment of hope for their own violent ends.

But as President Obama has said, these dramatic changes also mark an historic moment of opportunity. So too for our counterterrorism efforts. For decades, terrorist organizations like al-Qa'ida have preached that the only way to affect change is through violence. Now, that claim has been thoroughly repudiated, and it has been repudiated by ordinary citizens, in Tunisia and Egypt and beyond, who are changing and challenging their governments through peaceful protest, even as they are sometimes met with horrific brutality, as in Libya and Syria. Moreover, these citizens have rejected the medieval ideology of al-Qa'ida that divides people by faith and gender, opting instead to work together—Muslims and Christians, men and women, secular and religious.

It is the most profound change in the modern history of the Arab world, and al-Qa'ida and its ilk have been left on the sidelines, watching history pass them by. Meanwhile, President Obama has placed the United States on the right side of history, pledging our support for the political and economic reforms and universal human rights that people in the region are demanding. This, too, has profound implications for our counterterrorism efforts.

Against this backdrop, our strategy is very precise about the threat we face and the goals we seek. Paul Nitze once observed that "one of the most dangerous forms of human error is forgetting what one is trying to achieve." President Obama is adamant that we never forget who we're fighting or what we're trying to achieve.

Let me start by saying that our strategy is not designed to combat directly every single terrorist organization in every corner of the world, many of which have neither the intent nor the capability to ever attack the United States or our citizens.

Our strategy of course recognizes that there are numerous nations and groups that support terrorism in order to oppose United States interests. Iran and Syria remain leading state sponsors of terrorism. Hezbollah and HAMAS are terrorist organizations that threaten Israel and our interests in the Middle East. We will therefore continue to use the full range of our foreign policy tools to prevent these regimes and terrorist organizations from endangering our national security.

For example, President Obama has made it clear that the United States is determined to prevent Iran from acquiring nuclear weapons. And we will continue working closely with allies and partners, including sharing and acting upon intelligence, to prevent the flow of weapons and funds to Hezbollah and HAMAS and to prevent attacks against our allies, citizens or interests.

But the principal focus of this counterterrorism strategy—and the focus of our CT efforts since President Obama took office—is the network that poses the most direct and significant threat to the United States, and that is al-Qa'ida, its affiliates and its adherents. We use these terms deliberately.

It is al-Qa'ida, the core group founded by Usama bin Laden, that has murdered our citizens, from the bombings of our embassies in Kenya and Tanzania to the attack on the United StatesS. Cole to the attacks of September 11th, which also killed citizens of more than 90 other countries.

It is al-Qa'ida's affiliates—groups that are part of its network or share its goals—that have also attempted to attack our homeland. It was al-Qa'ida in the Arabian Peninsula (AQAP), based in Yemen, that attempted to bring down that airliner over Detroit and which put explosives on cargo planes bound for the United States. It was the Pakistani Taliban that sent Faisal Shahzad on his failed attempt to blow up an SUV in Times Square.

And it is al-Qa'ida's adherents—individuals, sometimes with little or no direct physical contact with al-Qa'ida, who have succumbed to its hateful ideology and who have engaged in, or facilitated, terrorist activities here in the United States. These misguided individuals are spurred on by the likes of al-Qaida's Adam Gadahn and Anwar al-Awlaki in Yemen, who speak English and preach violence in slick videos over the Internet. And we have seen the tragic results, with the murder of a military recruiter in Arkansas two years ago and the attack on our servicemen and women at Fort Hood.

This is the first counterterrorism strategy that focuses on the ability of al-Qa'ida and its network to inspire people in the United States to attack us from within. Indeed, this is the first counterterrorism strategy that designates the homeland as a primary area of emphasis in our counterterrorism efforts.

Our strategy is also shaped by a deeper understanding of al-Qa'ida's goals, strategy, and tactics. I'm not talking about al-Qa'ida's grandiose vision of global domination through a violent Islamic caliphate. That vision is absurd, and we are not going to organize our counterterrorism policies against a feckless delusion that is never going to happen. We are not going to elevate these thugs and their murderous aspirations into something larger than they are.

Rather, President Obama is determined that our foreign and national security policies not play into al-Qa'ida's strategy or its warped ideology. Al-Qa'ida seeks to terrorize us into retreating from the world stage. But President Obama has made it a priority to renew American leadership in the world, strengthening our alliances and deepening partnerships. Al-Qa'ida seeks to portray America as an enemy of the world's Muslims. But President Obama has made it clear that the United States is not, and never will be, at war with Islam.

Al-Qa'ida seeks to bleed us financially by drawing us into long, costly wars that also inflame anti-American sentiment. Under President Obama, we are working to end the wars in Iraq and Afghanistan responsibly, even as we keep unrelenting pressure on al-Qa'ida. Going forward, we will be mindful that if our nation is threatened, our best offense won't always be deploying large armies abroad but delivering targeted, surgical pressure to the groups that threaten us.

Al-Qa'ida seeks to portray itself as a religious movement defending the rights of Muslims, but the United States will continue to expose al-Qa'ida as nothing more than murderers. They purport to be Islamic, but they are neither religious leaders nor scholars; indeed, there is nothing Islamic or holy about slaughtering innocent men, women, and children. They claim to protect Muslims, but the vast majority of al-Qa'ida's victims are, in fact, innocent Muslim men, women, and children. It is no wonder that the overwhelmingly majority of the world's Muslims have rejected al-Qa'ida and why its ranks of supporters continue to decline.

Just as our strategy is precise about who our enemy is, it is clear about our posture and our goal. This is a war—a broad, sustained, integrated and relentless campaign that harnesses every element of American power. And we seek nothing less than the utter destruction of this evil that calls itself al-Qa'ida.

To achieve this goal, we need to dismantle the core of al-Qa'ida—its leadership in the tribal regions of Pakistan—and prevent its ability to reestablish a safe haven in the Pakistan–Afghanistan region. In other words, we aim to render the heart of al-Qa'ida incapable of launching attacks against our homeland, our citizens, or our allies, as well as preventing the group from inspiring its affiliates and adherents to do so.

At the same time, ultimately defeating al-Qa'ida also means addressing the serious threat posed by its affiliates and adherents operating outside South Asia. This does not require a "global" war, but it does require a focus on specific regions, including what we might call the periphery—places like Yemen, Somalia, Iraq, and the Maghreb. This is another important distinction that characterizes this strategy. As the al-Qa'ida core has weakened under our unyielding pressure, it has looked increasingly to these other groups and individuals to take up its cause, including its goal of striking the United States.

To destroy al-Qa'ida, we are pursuing specific and focused counterterrorism objectives. For example:

- We are protecting our homeland by constantly reducing our vulnerabilities and adapting and updating our defenses.

- We are taking the fight to wherever the cancer of al-Qa'ida manifests itself, degrading its capabilities and disrupting its operations.

- We are degrading the ability of al-Qa'ida's senior leadership to inspire, communicate with, and direct the operations of its adherents around the world.

- We are denying al-Qa'ida any safe haven—the physical sanctuary that it needs to train, plot and launch attacks against us.

- We are aggressively confronting al-Qa'ida's ideology, which attempts to exploit local—and often legitimate—grievances in an attempt to justify violence.

- We are depriving al-Qa'ida of its enabling means, including the illicit financing, logistical support, and online communications that sustain its network.

- And we are working to prevent al-Qa'ida from acquiring or developing WMD, which is why President Obama is leading the global effort to secure the world's vulnerable materials in four years.

In many respects, these specific counterterrorism goals are not new. In fact, they track closely with the goals of the previous administration. Yet this illustrates another important characteristic of our strategy. It neither represents a wholesale overhaul—nor a wholesale retention—of previous policies.

President Obama's approach to counterterrorism is pragmatic, not ideological. It's based on what works. It builds upon policies and practices that have been instituted and refined over the past decade, in partnership with Congress—a partnership we will continue. And it reflects an evolution in our understanding of the threat, in the capabilities of our government, the capacity of our partners, and the tools and technologies at our disposal.

What is new—and what I believe distinguishes this strategy—is the principles that are guiding our efforts to destroy al-Qa'ida.

First, we are using every lawful tool and authority available. No single agency or department has sole responsibility for this fight because no single department or agency possesses all the capabilities needed for this fight. This is—and must be—a whole-of-government effort, and it's why the Obama Administration has strengthened the tools we need.

We've strengthened intelligence, expanding human intelligence and linguistic skills, and we're constantly working to improve our capabilities and learn from our experiences. For example, following the attack at Fort Hood and the failed attack over Detroit, we've improved the analytic process, created new groups to track threat information, and enhanced cooperation among our intelligence agencies, including better information sharing so that all threats are acted upon quickly.

We've strengthened our military capabilities. We increased the size of our Special Forces, sped up the deployment of unique assets so that al-Qa'ida enjoys no safe haven, and ensured that our military and intelligence professionals are working more closely than ever before.

We've strengthened homeland security with a multi-layered defense, bolstering security at our borders, ports and airports; improving partnerships with state and local governments and allies and partners, including sharing more information; increasing the capacity of our first responders; and preparing for bioterrorism. In taking these steps, we are finally fulfilling key recommendations of the 9/11 Commission.

Learning the lessons of recent plots and attempted attacks, we've increased aviation security by strengthening watchlist procedures and sharing information in real-time; enhancing screening of cargo; and—for the first time—ensuring 100 percent screening of all passengers traveling in, to, and from the United States, which was another recommendation of the 9/11 Commission. And we are constantly assessing and improving our defenses, as we did in replacing the old color-coded threat system with a more targeted approach that provides detailed information about specific, credible threats and suggested protective measures.

In addition, we are using the full range of law enforcement tools as part of our effort to build an effective and durable legal framework for the war against al-Qa'ida. This includes our single most effective tool for prosecuting, convicting, and sentencing suspected terrorists—and a proven tool for gathering intelligence and preventing attacks—our Article III courts. It includes reformed military commissions, which at times offer unique advantages. And this framework includes the recently renewed PATRIOT Act. In short, we must have a legal framework that provides our extraordinary intelligence, counterterrorism, and law enforcement professionals with all the lawful tools they need to do their job and keep our country safe. We must not tie their hands.

For all these tools to work properly, departments and agencies across the federal government must work cooperatively. Today, our personnel are working more closely together than ever before, as we saw in the operation that killed Usama bin Laden. That success was not due to any one single person or single piece of information. It was the result of many people in many organizations working together over many years. And that is what we will continue to do.

Even as we use every tool in our government, we are guided by a second principle—the need for partnership with institutions and countries around the world, as we recognize that no one nation alone can bring about al-Qa'ida's demise. Over the past decade, we have made enormous progress in building and strengthening an international architecture to confront the threat from al-Qa'ida. This includes greater cooperation with multilateral institutions such as the United Nations, our NATO allies, and regional organizations such as the Association of Southeast Asian Nations and the African Union.

Over the past two and a half years, we have also increased our efforts to build the capacity of partners so they can take the fight to al-Qa'ida in their own countries. That is why a key element of the President's strategy in Afghanistan is growing Afghan security forces. It's why we'll soon begin a transition so that Afghans can take responsibility for their own security. And it's why we must continue our cooperation with Pakistan.

In recent weeks we've been reminded that our relationship with Pakistan is not without tension or frustration. We are now working with our Pakistani partners to overcome differences and continue our efforts against our common enemies. It is essential that we do so. As frustrating as this relationship can sometimes be, Pakistan has been critical to many of our most significant successes against al-Qa'ida. Tens of thousands of Pakistanis—military and civilian—have given their lives in the fight against militancy. And despite recent tensions, I am confident that Pakistan will remain one of our most important counterterrorism partners.

These kinds of security partnerships are absolutely vital. The critical intelligence that allowed us to discover the explosives that AQAP was shipping to the United States in those cargo planes was provided by our Saudi Arabian partners. Al-Qa'ida in Iraq has suffered major losses at the hands of Iraqi security forces, trained by the United States. Despite the ongoing instability, our counterterrorism cooperation with Yemen continues, and I would argue that the recent territorial gains made by militants linked to AQAP only makes our CT partnership with Yemen more important.

Around the world, we will deepen our security cooperation with partners wherever al-Qa'ida attempts to take root, be it Somalia, the Sahel or Southeast Asia. For while al-Qa'ida seeks to depict this fight as one between the world's Muslims and the United States, it is actually the opposite—the international community, including Muslim-majority nations and Muslim communities, united against al-Qa'ida.

This leads to the third principle of our strategy—rather than pursuing a one-size fits-all approach, we recognize that different threats in different places demand different tools. So even as we use all the resources at our disposal against al-Qa'ida, we will apply the right tools in the right way and in the right place, with laser focus.

In some places, such as the tribal regions between Afghanistan and Pakistan, we will deliver precise and overwhelming force against al-Qa'ida. Whenever possible, our efforts around the world will be in close coordination with our partners. And, when necessary, as the President has said repeatedly, if we have information about the whereabouts of al-Qa'ida, we will do what is required to protect the United States—as we did with bin Laden.

In some places, as I've described, our efforts will focus on training foreign security services. In others, as with our Saudi Arabian and Gulf state partners, our focus will include shutting down al-Qa'ida's financial pipelines. With longtime allies and partners, as in Europe, we'll thwart attacks through close intelligence cooperation. Here in the United States—where the rule of law is paramount—it's our federal, state, and local law enforcement and homeland security professionals who rightly take the lead. Around the world, including here at home, we will continue to show that the United States offers a vision of progress and justice, while al-Qa'ida offers nothing but death and destruction.

Related to our counterterrorism strategy, I would also note that keeping our nation secure also depends on strong partnerships between government and communities here at home, including Muslim and Arab Americans, some of whom join us today. These Americans have worked to protect their communities from al-Qa'ida's violent ideology and they have helped to prevent terrorist attacks in our country. Later this summer, the Obama Administration will unveil its approach for partnering with communities to prevent violent extremism in the United States. And a key tenet of this approach is that when it comes to protecting our country, Muslim Americans are not part of the problem, they're part of the solution.

This relates to our fourth principle—building a culture of resilience here at home. We are doing everything in our power to prevent another terrorist attack on our soil. At the same time, a responsible, effective counterterrorism strategy recognizes that no nation, no matter how powerful—including a free and open society of 300 million Americans—can prevent every single threat from every single individual who wishes to do us harm. It's not enough to simply be prepared for attacks, we have to be resilient and recover quickly should an attack occur.

So, as a resilient nation, we are constantly improving our ability to withstand any attack—especially our critical infrastructure, including cyber—thereby denying al-Qa'ida the economic damage and disruption it seeks. As a resilient government, we're strengthening the partnerships that help states and localities recover quickly. And as a resilient people, we must remember that every one of us can help deprive al-Qa'ida of the success it seeks. Al-Qa'ida wants to terrorize us, so we must not give in to fear. They want to change us, so we must stay true to who we are.

Which brings me to our final principle, in fact, the one that guides all the others—in all our actions, we will uphold the core values that define us as Americans. I have spent more than thirty years working on behalf of our nation's security. I understand the truly breathtaking capabilities of our intelligence and counterterrorism communities. But I also know that the most powerful weapons of all—which we must never forsake—are the values and ideals that America represents to the world.

When we fail to abide by our values, we play right into the hands of al-Qa'ida, which falsely tries to portray us as a people of hypocrisy and

289

decadence. Conversely, when we uphold these values it sends a message to the people around the world that it is America—not al-Qa'ida—that represents opportunity, dignity, and justice. In other words, living our values helps keep us safe.

So, as Americans, we stand for human rights. That is why, in his first days in office, President Obama made it clear that the United States of America does not torture, and it's why he banned the use of enhanced interrogation techniques, which did not work. As Americans, we will uphold the rule of law at home, including the privacy, civil rights, and civil liberties of all Americans. And it's because of our commitment to the rule of law and to our national security that we will never waver in our conviction that the United States will be more secure the day that the prison at Guantanamo Bay is ultimately closed.

Living our values—and communicating to the world what America represents—also directly undermines al-Qa'ida's twisted ideology. When we remember that diversity of faith and background is not a weakness in America but a strength, and when we show that Muslim Americans are part of our American family, we expose al-Qa'ida's lie that cultures must clash. When we remember that Islam is part of America, we show that America could never possibly be at war with Islam.

These are our principles, and this is the strategy that has enabled us to put al-Qa'ida under more pressure than at any time since 9/11. With allies and partners, we have thwarted attacks around the world. We have disrupted plots here at home, including the plan of Najibullah Zazi, trained by al-Qa'ida to bomb the New York subway.

We have affected al-Qa'ida's ability to attract new recruits. We've made it harder for them to hide and transfer money, and pushed al-Qa'ida's finances to its weakest point in years. Along with our partners, in Pakistan and Yemen, we've shown al-Qa'ida that it will enjoy no safe haven, and we have made it harder than ever for them to move, to communicate, to train, and to plot.

Al-Qa'ida's leadership ranks have been decimated, with more key leaders eliminated in rapid succession than at any time since 9/11. For example, al-Qa'ida's third-ranking leader, Sheik Saeed al-Masri—killed. Ilyas Kashmiri, one of al-Qa'ida's most dangerous commanders—reportedly killed. Operatives of AQAP in Yemen, including Ammar al-Wa'ili, Abu Ali al-Harithi, and Ali Saleh Farhan—all killed. Baitullah Mahsud, the leader of the Pakistani Taliban—killed. Harun Fazul, the leader of al-Qa'ida in East Africa and the mastermind of the bombings of our embassies in Africa—killed by Somali security forces.

All told, over the past two and half years, virtually every major al-Qa'ida affiliate has lost its key leader or operational commander, and more than half of al-Qa'ida's top leadership has been eliminated. Yes, al-Qa'ida is adaptive and resilient and has sought to replace these leaders, but it has been forced to do so with less experienced individuals. That's another reason why we and our partners have stepped up our efforts. Because if we hit al-Qa'ida hard enough and often enough, there will come a time when they simply can no longer replenish their ranks with the skilled leaders they need to sustain their operations. And that is the direction in which we're headed today.

Now, with the death of Usama bin Laden, we have struck our biggest blow against al-Qa'ida yet. We have taken out al-Qa'ida's founder, an operational commander who continued to direct his followers to attack the United States and, perhaps most significantly, al-Qa'ida's symbolic figure who has inspired so many others to violence. In his place, the organization is left with Ayman al-Zawahiri, an aging doctor who lacks bin Laden's charisma and perhaps the loyalty and respect of many in al-Qa'ida. Indeed, the fact that it took so many weeks for al-Qa'ida to settle on Zawahiri as its new leader suggests possible divisions and disarray at the highest levels.

Taken together, the progress I've described allows us—for the first time—to envision the demise of al-Qa'ida's core leadership in the coming years. It will take time, but make no mistake, al-Qa'ida is in its decline. This is by no means meant to suggest that the serious threat from al-Qa'ida has passed; not at all. Zawahiri may attempt to demonstrate his leadership, and al-Qa'ida may try to show its relevance, through new attacks. Lone individuals may seek to avenge bin Laden's death. More innocent people may tragically lose their lives.

Nor would the destruction of its leadership mean the destruction of the al-Qa'ida network. AQAP remains the most operationally active affiliate in the network and poses a direct threat to the United States. From the territory it controls in Somalia, Al-Shabaab continues to call for strikes against the

United States. As a result, we cannot and we will not let down our guard. We will continue to pummel al-Qa'ida and its ilk, and we will remain vigilant at home.

Still, as we approach the 10th anniversary of the 9/11 attacks, as Americans seek to understand where we stand a decade later, we need look no further than that compound where bin Laden spent his final days. There he was, holed-up for years, behind high prison-like walls, isolated from the world. But even he understood the sorry state of his organization and its ideology.

Information seized from that compound reveals bin Laden's concerns about al-Qa'ida's long-term viability. He called for more large-scale attacks against America, but encountered resistance from his followers and he went for years without seeing any spectacular attacks. He saw his senior leaders being taken down, one by one, and worried about the ability to replace them effectively.

Perhaps most importantly, bin Laden clearly sensed that al-Qa'ida is losing the larger battle for hearts and minds. He knew that al-Qa'ida's murder of so many innocent civilians, most of them Muslims, had deeply and perhaps permanently tarnished al-Qa'ida's image in the world. He knew that he had failed to portray America as being at war with Islam. In fact, he worried that our recent focus on al-Qa'ida as our enemy had prevented more Muslims from rallying to his cause, so much so that he even considered changing al-Qa'ida's name. We are left with that final image seen around the world—an old terrorist, alone, hunched over in a blanket, flipping through old videos of a man and a movement that history is leaving behind.

This fight is not over. But guided by the strategy we're releasing today, we will never waver in our efforts to protect the American people. We will continue to be clear and precise about our enemy. We will continue to use every tool at our disposal, and apply them wisely. We will continue to forge strong partnerships around the world and build a culture of resilience here at home. And as Americans, we will continue to uphold the ideals and core values that inspire the world, define us as people and help keep us safe.

President Obama said it best last week—we have put al-Qa'ida on a path to defeat, and we will not relent until the job is done. Thank you all very much.

Appendix 3C: National Strategy for Counterterrorism (June 2011)

THE WHITE HOUSE

WASHINGTON

June 28, 2011

As we approach the 10th anniversary of al-Qa'ida's terrorist attacks against the United States on September 11, 2001, it is a time to mark the progress we have made in our war against al-Qa'ida and to rededicate ourselves to meeting the challenges that remain. In the decade since those attacks, we have significantly strengthened our defenses and built a steadfast international coalition. In the past two and a half years, we have eliminated more key al-Qa'ida leaders in rapid succession than at any time since September 11, 2001, including Usama bin Laden, the only leader that al-Qa'ida had ever known. As a result, we now have the opportunity to seize a turning point in our effort to disrupt, dismantle, and ultimately defeat al-Qa'ida.

Despite our successes, we continue to face a significant terrorist threat from al-Qa'ida, its affiliates, and its adherents. Our terrorist adversaries have shown themselves to be agile and adaptive; defeating them requires that we develop and pursue a strategy that is even more agile and adaptive. To defeat al-Qa'ida, we must define with precision and clarity who we are fighting, setting concrete and realistic goals tailored to the specific challenges we face in different regions of the world. As we apply every element of American power against al-Qa'ida, success requires a strategy that is consistent with our core values as a nation and as a people. I am pleased to say that the Counterterrorism Strategy that follows meets these requirements. Indeed, this document reflects the strategy and the policies that we have pursued since the day I took office.

Any such strategy, however, is only as effective as the men and women charged with carrying it out. In this respect, the United States is blessed with thousands of extraordinary military, intelligence, law enforcement, homeland security, and other counterterrorism professionals who keep us safe from terrorist attacks and help carry the fight to al-Qa'ida. Our progress in recent years is a testament to their courage, dedication, and professionalism. Indeed, whatever success awaits us in the months and years ahead will certainly be due to their skill and bravery. On behalf of the American people, I want to congratulate and thank these outstanding professionals for their role in keeping all Americans safe. At the same time, I also call on them to maintain their vigilance, because much work remains to be done.

As President, I have often said that I have no greater responsibility than protecting the American people. Though there are many potential threats to our national security, it is the terrorist threat from al-Qa'ida that has loomed largest in the decade since September 11, 2001. And yet today, we can say with growing confidence – and with certainty about the outcome – that we have put al-Qa'ida on the path to defeat. With an unrelenting focus on the task at hand, and mindful of the challenges still ahead, we will not rest until that job is done.

Introduction

As the President affirmed in his 2010 National Security Strategy, he bears no greater responsibility than ensuring the safety and security of the American people. This National Strategy for Counterterrorism sets out our approach to one of the President's top national security priorities: disrupting, dismantling, and eventually defeating al-Qa'ida and its affiliates and adherents to ensure the security of our citizens and interests.

In response to the attacks of September 2001, the United States embarked on a national effort against al-Qa'ida, the transnational terrorist organization responsible for planning and conducting the attacks. As we approach the 10th anniversary of that day, we can look forward with confidence in our accomplishments and pride in the resiliency of our nation. We have prevented another catastrophic attack on our shores; our citizens have not let the specter of terrorism disrupt their daily lives and activities; our Federal government has worked to become more integrated, efficient, and effective in its counterterrorism (CT) efforts; and we have placed our CT campaign in a context that does not dominate the lives of the American people nor overshadow our approach to the broad range of our interests.

Yet the paramount terrorist threat we have faced—al-Qa'ida and its affiliates and adherents—has also continued to evolve, often in response to the successes of the United States and its partners around the world. Our efforts in Afghanistan and Pakistan have destroyed much of al-Qa'ida's leadership and weakened the organization substantially. Meanwhile, in recent years the source of the threat to the United States and its allies has shifted in part toward the periphery—to groups affiliated with but separate from the core of the group in Pakistan and Afghanistan. This also includes deliberate efforts by al-Qa'ida to inspire individuals within the United States to conduct attacks on their own.

Therefore, this National Strategy for Counterterrorism maintains our focus on pressuring al-Qa'ida's core while emphasizing the need to build foreign partnerships and capacity and to strengthen our resilience. At the same time, our strategy augments our focus on confronting the al-Qa'ida-linked threats that continue to emerge from beyond its core safehaven in South Asia.

Since the beginning of 2011, the transformative change sweeping North Africa and the Middle East—along with the death of Usama bin Laden—has further changed the nature of the terrorist threat, particularly as the relevance of al-Qa'ida and its ideology has been further diminished. Usama Bin Laden's persistent calls for violent regime change in the Arab World and perpetual violence against the United States and our allies as the method to empower Muslim populations stands in stark contrast to the nonviolent movements for change in the Middle East and North Africa. In just a few short months, those movements achieved far more political change than al-Qa'ida's years of violence, which has claimed thousands upon thousands of victims—most of them Muslim. Our support for the aspirations of people throughout the Middle East, North Africa, and around the world to live in peace and prosperity under representative governments stands in marked contrast to al-Qa'ida's dark and bankrupt worldview.

To put it simply: We are bringing targeted force to bear on al-Qa'ida at a time when its ideology is also under extreme pressure. Nevertheless, we remain keenly vigilant to the threat al-Qa'ida, its affiliates, and adherents pose to the United States. As expressed in our National Security Strategy, we face the world as it is, but we will also pursue a strategy for the world we seek. This Strategy articulates how we will achieve a future in which al-Qa'ida and its affiliates and adherents are defeated—and their ideology ultimately meets the same fate as its founder and leader.

Overview of the National Strategy for Counterterrorism

This National Strategy for Counterterrorism articulates our government's approach to countering terrorism and identifies the range of tools critical to this Strategy's success. This Strategy builds on groundwork laid by previous strategies and many aspects of the United States Government's enduring approach to countering terrorism. At the same time, it outlines an approach that is more focused and specific than were previous strategies.

The United States deliberately uses the word "war" to describe our relentless campaign against al-Qa'ida. However, this Administration has made it clear that we are not at war with the tactic of terrorism or the religion of Islam. We are at war with a specific organization—al-Qa'ida.

US CT efforts require a multidepartmental and multinational effort that goes beyond traditional intelligence, military, and law enforcement functions. We are engaged in a broad, sustained, and integrated campaign that harnesses every tool of American power—military, civilian, and the power of our values—together with the concerted efforts of allies, partners, and multilateral institutions. These efforts must also be complemented by broader capabilities, such as diplomacy, development, strategic communications, and the power of the private sector. In addition, there will continue to be many opportunities for the Executive Branch to work with Congress, consistent with our laws and our values, to further empower our counterterrorism professionals with the tools and resources necessary to maximize the effectiveness of our efforts.

Structure of the Strategy. This Strategy sets out our overarching goals and the steps necessary to achieve them. It also includes specific areas of focus tailored to the regions, domains, and groups that are most important to achieving the President's goal of disrupting, dismantling, and defeating al-Qa'ida and its affiliates and adherents while protecting the American people.

The *Overarching Goals* articulate the desired end states that we aim to create, understanding that success requires integrated, enduring, and adaptive efforts. Success also requires strategic patience: Although some of these end states may not be realized for many years, they will remain the focus of what the United States aims to achieve.

The *Areas of Focus* are the specific regions and al-Qa'ida-affiliated groups that the Strategy prioritizes.

The Threat We Face

The preeminent security threat to the United States continues to be from *al-Qa'ida and its affiliates[i] and adherents*.

A decade after the September 11, 2001 terrorist attacks, the United States remains at war with al-Qa'ida. Although the United States did not seek this conflict, we remain committed, in conjunction with our partners worldwide, to disrupt, dismantle, and eventually defeat al-Qa'ida and its affiliates and adherents to ensure the security of our citizens and interests.

The death of Usama bin Laden marked the most important strategic milestone in our effort to defeat al-Qa'ida. It removed al-Qa'ida's founder and leader and most influential advocate for attacking the United States and its interests abroad. But, as the President has made clear, Usama bin Laden's demise does not mark the end of our effort. Nor does it mark the end of al-Qa'ida, which will remain focused on striking the United States and our interests abroad.

Since 2001 the United States has worked with its partners around the globe to put relentless pressure on al-Qa'ida—disrupting terrorist plots, measurably reducing the financial support available to the group, and inflicting significant leadership losses. Despite our many successes, al-Qa'ida continues to pose a direct and significant threat to the United States.

In addition to plotting and carrying out specific attacks, al-Qa'ida seeks to inspire a broader conflict against the United States and many of our allies and partners. To rally individuals and groups to its cause, al-Qa'ida preys on local grievances and propagates a self-serving historical and political account. It draws on a distorted interpretation of Islam to justify the murder of Muslim and non-Muslim innocents. Countering this ideology—which has been rejected repeatedly and unequivocally by people of all faiths around the world—is an essential element of our strategy.

Although its brutal tactics and mass murder of Muslims have undermined its appeal, al-Qa'ida has had some success in rallying individuals and other militant groups to its cause. Where its ideology does resonate, the United States faces an evolving threat from groups and individuals that accept al-Qa'ida's agenda, whether through formal alliance, loose affiliation, or mere inspiration. Affiliated movements have taken root far beyond al-Qa'ida's core leadership in Afghanistan and Pakistan, including in the Middle East, East Africa, the Maghreb and Sahel regions of northwest Africa, Central Asia, and Southeast Asia. Although each group is unique, all aspire to advance al-Qa'ida's regional and global agenda—by destabilizing the countries in which they train and operate, attacking US and other Western interests in the region, and in some cases plotting to strike the US Homeland.

Adherence to al-Qa'ida's ideology may not require allegiance to al-Qa'ida, the organization. Individuals who sympathize with or actively support al-Qa'ida may be inspired to violence and can pose an ongoing threat, even if they have little or no formal contact with al-Qa'ida. Global communications and connectivity place al-Qa'ida's calls for violence and instructions for carrying it out within easy reach of millions. Precisely because its leadership is under such pressure in Afghanistan and Pakistan, al-Qa'ida has increasingly sought to inspire others to commit attacks in its name. Those who in the past have attempted attacks in the United States have come from a wide range of backgrounds and origins, including US citizens and individuals with varying degrees of overseas connections and affinities.

Beyond al-Qa'ida, other foreign terrorist organizations threaten US national security interests. These groups seek to undermine the security and stability of allied and partner governments, foment regional conflicts, traffic in narcotics, or otherwise pursue agendas that are inimical to US interests. Whether these are groups that operate globally, as Hizballah or HAMAS do, or are terrorist organizations located and focused domestically, we are committed to working vigorously and aggressively to counter their efforts and activities even as we avoid conflating them and al-Qa'ida into a single enemy.

Principles That Guide our Counterterrorism Efforts

Although the terrorist organizations that threaten us are far from monolithic, our CT efforts are guided by core principles: Adhering to US Core Values; Building Security Partnerships; Applying CT Tools and Capabilities Appropriately; and Building a Culture of Resilience.

We are committed to upholding our most cherished values as a nation not just because doing so is right but also because doing so enhances our security. Adherence to those core values—respecting human rights, fostering good governance, respecting privacy and civil liberties, committing to security and transparency, and upholding the rule of law—enables us to build broad international coalitions to act against the common threat posed by our adversaries while further delegitimizing, isolating, and weakening their efforts. The United States is dedicated to upholding the rule of law by maintaining an effective, durable legal framework for CT operations and bringing terrorists to justice. United States efforts with partners are central to achieving our CT goals, and we are committed to building security partnerships even as we recognize and work to improve shortfalls in our cooperation with partner nations.

Our CT efforts must also address both near- and long-term considerations—taking timely action to protect the American people while ensuring that our efforts are in the long-term security interests of our country. Our approach to political change in the Middle East and North Africa illustrates that promoting representative and accountable governance is a core tenet of US foreign policy and directly contributes to our CT goals.

At the same time, we recognize that no nation, no matter how powerful, can prevent every threat from coming to fruition. That is why we are focused on building a culture of resilience able to prevent, respond to, or recover fully from any potential act of terror directed at the United States.

Adhering to US Core Values

The United States was founded upon a belief in a core set of values that is written into our founding documents and woven into the very fabric of our society. Where terrorists offer injustice, disorder, and destruction the United States must stand for freedom, fairness, equality, dignity, hope, and opportunity. The power and appeal of our values enables the United States to build a broad coalition to act collectively against the common threat posed by terrorists, further delegitimizing, isolating, and weakening our adversaries.

- **Respect for Human Rights.** Our respect for universal rights stands in stark contrast with the actions of al-Qa'ida, its affiliates and adherents, and other terrorist organizations. Contrasting a positive United States agenda that supports the rights of free speech, assembly, and democracy with the death and destruction offered by our terrorist adversaries helps undermine and undercut their appeal, isolating them from the very population they rely on for support. Our respect for universal rights must include living them through our own actions. Cruel and inhumane interrogation methods are not only inconsistent with US values, they undermine the rule of law and are ineffective means of gaining the intelligence required to counter the threats we face. We will maximize our ability to collect intelligence from individuals in detention by relying on our most effective tool—the skill, expertise, and professionalism of our personnel.

- **Encouraging Responsive Governance.** Promoting representative, responsive governance is a core tenet of US foreign policy and directly contributes to our CT goals. Governments that place the will of their people first and encourage peaceful change directly contradict the al-Qa'ida ideology. Governments that are responsive to the needs of their citizens diminish the discontent of their people and the associated drivers and grievances that al-Qa'ida actively attempts to exploit. Effective governance reduces the traction and space for al-Qa'ida, reducing its resonance and contributing to what it fears most—irrelevance.

- **Respect for Privacy Rights, Civil Liberties, and Civil Rights.** Respect for privacy rights, civil liberties, and civil rights is a critical component of our Strategy. Indeed, preservation of those rights and liberties is essential to maintain the support of the American people for our CT efforts. By ensuring that CT policies and tools are narrowly tailored and applied to achieve specific, concrete security gains, the United States will optimize its security and protect the liberties of its citizens.

- **Balancing Security and Transparency.** Democratic institutions function best in an environment of transparency and open discussion of national issues. Wherever and whenever possible, the United States will make information available to the American people about the threats we face and the steps being taken to mitigate those threats. A well-informed American public is a source of our strength. Information enables the public to make informed judgments about its own security, act responsibly and with resilience in the face of adversity or attack, and contribute its vigilance to the country's collective security. Yet at times, some information must be protected from disclosure—to protect personnel and our sources and methods of gathering information and to preserve our ability to counter the attack plans of terrorists.

- **Upholding the Rule of Law.** Our commitment to the rule of law is fundamental to supporting the development of an international, regional, and local order that is capable of identifying and disrupting terrorist attacks, bringing terrorists to justice for their acts, and creating an environment in every country around the world that is inhospitable to terrorists and terrorist organizations.

—Maintaining an Effective, Durable Legal Framework for CT Operations. In the immediate aftermath of the September 11, 2001 attacks, the United States Government was confronted with countering the terrorist threat in an environment of legal uncertainty in which long-established legal rules were applied to circumstances not seen before in this country. Since then we have refined and applied a legal framework that ensures all CT activities and operations are placed on a solid legal footing. Moving forward, we must ensure that this legal framework remains both effective and durable. To remain effective, this framework must provide the necessary tools to defeat United States adversaries and maintain the safety of the American people. To remain durable this framework must withstand legal challenge, survive scrutiny, and earn the support of Congress and the American people as well as our partners and allies. It must also maintain sufficient flexibility to adjust to the changing threat and environment.

—Bringing Terrorists to Justice. The successful prosecution of terrorists will continue to play a critical role in US CT efforts, enabling the United States to disrupt and deter terrorist activity; gather intelligence from those lawfully held in US custody; dismantle organizations by incarcerating key members and operatives; and gain a measure of justice by prosecuting those who have plotted or participated in attacks. We will work with our foreign partners to build their willingness and capacity to bring to justice suspected terrorists who operate within their borders. When other countries are unwilling or unable to take action against terrorists within their borders who threaten the United States, they should be taken into US custody and tried in US civilian courts or by military commission.

Building Security Partnerships

The United States alone cannot eliminate every terrorist or terrorist organization that threatens our safety, security, or interests. Therefore, we must join with key partners and allies to share the burdens of common security.

- **Accepting Varying Degrees of Partnership.** The United States and its partners are engaged in the full range of cooperative CT activities—from intelligence sharing to joint training and operations and from countering radicalization to pursuing community resilience programs. The United States partners best with nations that share our common

301

values, have similar democratic institutions, and bring a long history of collaboration in pursuit of our shared security. With these partners the habits of cooperation established in other security-related settings have transferred themselves relatively smoothly and efficiently to CT.

In some cases partnerships are in place with countries with whom the United States has very little in common except for the desire to defeat al-Qa'ida and its affiliates and adherents. These partners may not share US values or even our broader vision of regional and global security. Yet it is in our interest to build habits and patterns of CT cooperation with such partners, working to push them in a direction that advances CT objectives while demonstrating through our example the value of upholding human rights and responsible governance. Furthermore, these partners will ultimately be more stable and successful if they move toward these principles.

- **Leveraging Multilateral Institutions.** To counter violent extremists who work in scores of countries around the globe, the United States is drawing on the resources and strengthening the activities of multilateral institutions at the international, regional, and subregional levels. Working with and through these institutions can have multiple benefits: It increases the engagement of our partners, reduces the financial burden on the United States, and enhances the legitimacy of our CT efforts by advancing our objectives without a unilateral, US label. The United States is committed to strengthening the global CT architecture in a manner that complements and reinforces the CT work of existing multilateral bodies. In doing so, we seek to avoid duplicating and diluting our own or our partners' efforts, recognizing that many of our partners have capacity limitations and cannot participate adequately across too broad a range of multilateral fora.

Applying CT Tools and Capabilities Appropriately

As the threat from al-Qa'ida and its affiliates and adherents continues to evolve, the United States must continually evaluate the tools and capabilities we use to ensure that our efforts are appropriate and consistent with US laws, values, and long-term strategic objectives.

- **Pursuing a "Whole-of-Government" Effort:** To succeed at both the tactical and strategic levels, we must foster a rapid, coordinated, and effective CT effort that reflects the full capabilities and resources of our entire government. That is why this Strategy integrates the capabilities and authorities of each department and agency, ensuring that the right tools are applied at the right time to the right situation in a manner that is consistent with US laws.

- **Balancing Near- and Long-Term CT Considerations.** We need to pursue the ultimate defeat of al-Qa'ida and its affiliates without acting in a way that undermines our ability to discredit its ideology. The exercise of American power against terrorist threats must be done in a thoughtful, reasoned, and proportionate way that both enhances US security and delegitimizes the actions of those who use terrorism. The United States must always carefully weigh the costs and risks of its actions against the costs and risks of inaction, recognizing that certain tactical successes can have unintended consequences that sometimes contribute to costs at the strategic level.

Building a Culture of Resilience

To pursue our CT objectives, we must also create a culture of preparedness and resilience[ii] that will allow the United States to prevent or—if necessary—respond to and recover successfully from any potential act of terror directed at our nation.

- **Building Essential Components of Resilience.** Al-Qa'ida believes that it can cause the United States to change course in its foreign and national security policies by inflicting economic and psychological damage through terrorist attacks. Denying success to al-Qa'ida therefore means, in part, demonstrating that the United States has and will continue to construct effective defenses to protect our vital assets, whether they are critical infrastructure, iconic national landmarks, or—most importantly—our population. Presenting the United States as a "hardened" target is unlikely to cause al-Qa'ida and its affiliates and adherents to abandon terrorism, but it can deter them from attacking particular targets or persuade them that their efforts are unlikely to succeed. The United States also contributes to its collective resilience

303

by demonstrating to al-Qa'ida that we have the individual, community, and economic strength to absorb, rebuild, and recover from any catastrophic event, whether manmade or naturally occurring.

Our Overarching Goals

With our core principles as the foundation of our efforts, the United States aims to achieve eight overarching CT goals. Taken together, these desired end states articulate a framework for the success of the US global counterterrorism mission.

- **Protect the American People, Homeland, and American Interests.** The most solemn responsibility of the President and the United States Government is to protect the American people, both at home and abroad. This includes eliminating threats to their physical safety, countering threats to global peace and security, and promoting and protecting US interests around the globe.

- **Disrupt, Degrade, Dismantle, and Defeat al-Qa'ida and Its Affiliates and Adherents.** The American people and interests will not be secure from attacks until this threat is eliminated—its primary individuals and groups rendered powerless, and its message relegated to irrelevance.

- **Prevent Terrorist Development, Acquisition, and Use of Weapons of Mass Destruction.** The danger of nuclear terrorism is the greatest threat to global security. Terrorist organizations, including al-Qa'ida, have engaged in efforts to develop and acquire weapons of mass destruction (WMD)—and if successful, they are likely to use them. Therefore, the United States will work with partners around the world to deter WMD theft, smuggling, and terrorist use; target and disrupt terrorist networks that engage in WMD-related activities; secure nuclear, biological, and chemical materials; prevent illicit trafficking of WMD-related materiel; provide multilateral nonproliferation organizations with the resources, capabilities, and authorities they need to be effective; and deepen international cooperation and strengthen institutions and partnerships that prevent WMD and nuclear materials from falling into the hands of terrorists. Success will require us to work with the international community in each of these areas while establishing security

304

measures commensurate with the threat, reinforcing countersmuggling measures, and ensuring that all of these efforts are sustained over time.

- **Eliminate Safehavens.** Al-Qa'ida and its affiliates and adherents rely on the physical sanctuary of ungoverned or poorly governed territories, where the absence of state control permits terrorists to travel, train, and engage in plotting. In close coordination with foreign partners, the United States will continue to contest and diminish al-Qa'ida's operating space through mutually reinforcing efforts designed to prevent al-Qa'ida from taking advantage of these ungoverned spaces. We will also build the will and capacity of states whose weaknesses al-Qa'ida exploits. Persistent insecurity and chaos in some regions can undermine efforts to increase political engagement and build capacity and provide assistance, thereby exacerbating chaos and insecurity. Our challenge is to break this cycle of state failure to constrict the space available to terrorist networks.

- **Build Enduring Counterterrorism Partnerships and Capabilities.** Foreign partners are essential to the success of our CT efforts; these states are often themselves the target of—and on the front lines in countering—terrorist threats. The United States will continue to rely on and leverage the capabilities of its foreign partners even as it looks to contribute to their capacity and bolster their will. To achieve our objectives, partners must demonstrate the willingness and ability to operate independently, augmenting and complementing US CT efforts with their unique insights and capabilities in their countries and regions. Building strong enduring partnerships based on shared understandings of the threat and common objectives is essential to every one of our overarching CT objectives. Assisting partners to improve and expand governance in select instances is also critical, including strengthening the rule of law so that suspected terrorists can be brought to justice within a respected and transparent system. Success will depend on our ability to work with partners bilaterally, through efforts to achieve greater regional integration, and through multilateral and international institutions.

- **Degrade Links between al-Qa'ida and its Affiliates and Adherents.** Al-Qa'ida senior leaders in Pakistan continue to leverage local and regional affiliates and adherents worldwide through formal and informal alliances to advance their global agenda. Al-Qa'ida exploits local grievances to bolster recruitment, expand its operational reach, destabilize local governments, and reinforce safehavens from which it and potentially other terrorist groups can operate and attack the United States. Together with our partners, we will degrade the capabilities of al-Qa'ida's local and regional affiliates and adherents, monitor their communications with al-Qa'ida leaders, drive fissures between these groups and their bases of support, and isolate al-Qa'ida from local and regional affiliates and adherents who can augment its capabilities and further its agenda.

- **Counter al-Qa'ida Ideology and Its Resonance and Diminish the Specific Drivers of Violence that al-Qa'ida Exploits.** This Strategy prioritizes US and partner efforts to undercut al-Qa'ida's fabricated legitimization of violence and its efforts to spread its ideology. As we have seen in the Middle East and North Africa, al-Qa'ida's calls for perpetual violence to address longstanding grievances have met a devastating rebuke in the face of nonviolent mass movements that seek solutions through expanded individual rights. Along with the majority of people across all religious and cultural traditions, we aim for a world in which al-Qa'ida is openly and widely rejected by all audiences as irrelevant to their aspirations and concerns, a world where al-Qa'ida's ideology does not shape perceptions of world and local events, inspire violence, or serve as a recruiting tool for the group or its adherents. Although achieving this objective is likely to require a concerted long-term effort, we must retain a focus on addressing the near-term challenge of preventing those individuals already on the brink from embracing al-Qa'ida ideology and resorting to violence. We will work closely with local and global partners, inside and outside governments, to discredit al-Qa'ida ideology and reduce its resonance. We will put forward a positive vision of engagement with foreign publics and support for universal rights that demonstrates that the United States aims to build while al-Qa'ida would only destroy. We will apply focused foreign and development assistance abroad. At the same time, we will continue to assist, engage, and connect communities to increase their collective resilience abroad and at home. These efforts strengthen bulwarks against radicalization, recruitment, and mobilization to violence in the name of al-Qa'ida and will focus in particular on those drivers that we know al-Qa'ida exploits.

- **Deprive Terrorists of their Enabling Means.** Al-Qaʻida and its affiliates and adherents continue to derive significant financial support from
donors in the Arabian Gulf region and elsewhere through kidnapping
for ransom and from exploitation of or control over lucrative elements
of the local economy. Terrorist facilitation extends beyond the financial
arena to those who enable travel of recruits and operatives; acquisition
and movement of materiel; and electronic and nonelectronic communication. The United States will collaborate with partner nations around
the world to increase our collective capacity to identify terrorist operatives and prevent their travel and movement of supplies across national
borders and within states. We will continue to expand and enhance
efforts aimed at blocking the flow of financial resources to and among
terrorist groups and to disrupt terrorist facilitation and support activities, imposing sanctions or pursuing prosecutions to enforce violations
and dissuade others. We will also continue our focus on countering kidnapping for ransom, which is an increasingly important funding source
for al-Qaʻida and its affiliates and adherents. Through our diplomatic
outreach, we will continue to encourage countries—especially those
in Europe—to adopt a policy against making concessions to kidnap-
pers while using tailored messages unilaterally and with our partners
to delegitimize the taking of hostages. Mass media and the Internet in
particular have emerged as enablers for terrorist planning, facilitation,
and communication, and we will continue to counter terrorists' ability
to exploit them.

Our Areas of Focus

To prioritize and tailor our efforts to accomplish the Overarching Goals
outlined above, the Strategy articulates more detailed, specific, and localized
Areas of Focus. CT objectives that are best approached from a local
perspective—such as our efforts to diminish specific drivers and grievances
that al-Qaʻida exploits in its efforts to radicalize, recruit, and mobilize
individuals to violence—are best addressed in their regional and group-
specific context.

The Homeland

For the past decade, the preponderance of the United States' CT effort has been aimed at preventing the recurrence of an attack on the Homeland directed by al-Qa'ida. That includes disrupting plots as well as working to constrain al-Qa'ida's ability to plan and train for attacks by shrinking the size and security of its safehavens. Offensive efforts to protect the Homeland have been complemented by equally robust defensive efforts to prevent terrorists from entering the United States or from operating freely inside US borders. To support the defensive side of this equation, we have made massive investments in our aviation, maritime, and border-security capabilities and information sharing to make the United States a hardened and increasingly difficult target for terrorists to penetrate.

These efforts must continue. We know al-Qa'ida and its affiliates continue to try to identify operatives overseas and develop new methods of attack that can evade US defensive measures. At the same time, plots directed and planned from overseas are not the only sort of terrorist threat we face. Individuals inspired by but not directly connected to al-Qa'ida have engaged in terrorism in the US Homeland. Others are likely to try to follow their example, and so we must remain vigilant.

We recognize that the operating environment in the Homeland is quite different from any other country or region. First, the United States exercises sovereign control and can apply the full strength of the US legal system, drawing on the capabilities of US law enforcement and homeland security communities to detect, disrupt, and defeat terrorist threats. Second, in the Homeland, the capabilities and resources of state, local, and tribal entities serve as a powerful force multiplier for the Federal government's CT efforts.

Integrating and harmonizing the efforts of Federal, state, local and tribal entities remains a challenge. As the threat continues to evolve, our efforts to protect against those threats must evolve as well.

The United States will rely extensively on a broad range of tools and capabilities that are essential to our ability to detect, disrupt, and defeat plots to attack the Homeland even though not all of these tools and capabilities have been developed exclusively for CT purposes. Such tools include capabilities related to border protection and security; aviation security and screening; aerospace control; maritime/port security; cargo security; cyber security; nuclear, radiological, biological, and chemical materials and the ability to detect their illicit use; biometrics; critical infrastructure protection; force protection; all hazards preparedness; community engagement; and information sharing among law enforcement organizations at all levels.

We are working to bring to bear many of these capabilities to build resilience within our communities here at home against al-Qa'ida inspired radicalization, recruitment, and mobilization to violence. Although increasing our engagement and partnership with communities can help protect them from the influence of al- Qa'ida and its affiliates and adherents, we must ensure that we remain engaged in the full range of community concerns and interests. Just as the terrorist threat we face in the United States is multifaceted and cannot be boiled down to a single group or community, so must our efforts to counter it not be reduced to a one-size-fits-all approach. Supporting community leaders and influential local stakeholders as they develop solutions tailored to their own particular circumstances is a critical part of our whole-of-government approach that contributes to our counterterrorism goals. As we refine our efforts in support of communities, state and local governments, and across the Federal government, we will continue to institutionalize successful practices and provide advice and guidance where appropriate, with the goal of preventing al-Qa'ida inspired radicalization.

Although this Strategy focuses predominantly on the al-Qa'ida linked and inspired threats, we also need to maintain careful scrutiny of a range of foreign and domestic groups and individuals assessed as posing potential terrorist threats, including those who operate and undertake activities in the United States in furtherance of their overseas agendas. We must be vigilant against all overseas-based threats to the Homeland, just as we must be vigilant against US based terrorist activity—be it focused domestically or on plotting to attack overseas targets.

To ensure that we are constantly addressing any deficiencies or weaknesses in our CT system, the President ordered comprehensive reviews and corrective actions in the immediate aftermath of attempted attacks. Following the tragic attack at Fort Hood, the failed attempt to bomb a Detroit-bound airliner, and the attempted bombing of Times Square, we have taken numerous steps to address information sharing shortfalls within the government, strengthen analysis and the integration of intelligence, and enhance aviation security, including by implementing a new, real-time, threat-based screening policy for all international flights to the United States. Such reviews and attendant corrective actions need to be a constant feature of our CT effort.

South Asia: Al-Qa'ida and its Affiliates and Adherents

Following the September 11, 2001 attacks, it was clear that the United States needed to deny al-Qa'ida a safehaven from which it could launch attacks against the United States or our allies. Currently we are focused on eliminating the al-Qa'ida safehaven in Pakistan while also degrading the Taliban and building up Afghan Security Forces—so that Afghanistan can never again be a safehaven for al-Qa'ida.

From its base of operations in Pakistan's Federally Administered Tribal Areas (FATA), al-Qa'ida continues to pose a persistent and evolving threat to the US Homeland and interests as well as to Pakistan, Afghanistan, India, Europe, and other targets of opportunity. Sustained pressure against al-Qa'ida in Pakistan—in particular since 2008—has forced the group to undergo the most significant turnover in its command structure since 2001 and put al Qa'ida on a path to defeat. Despite these losses, al-Qa'ida is adapting. It is using its safehaven to continue attack planning as well as to produce propaganda; communicate with and convey guidance to affiliates and operational cells in the region and abroad; request logistical and financial support; and provide training and indoctrination to new operatives including some from the United States and other Western countries.

Our CT efforts in Pakistan have far-reaching implications for our global CT efforts. Al-Qa'ida continues to capitalize on its safehaven to maintain communications with its affiliates and adherents and to call on them to use violence in pursuit of its ideological goals. Therefore, the operational dismantlement of Pakistan-based al-Qa'ida will not eliminate the threat to the United States, as we are likely to face a lingering threat from operatives already trained as well as from the group's affiliates and adherents in South Asia and in other parts of the world. Disrupted terrorist attacks in 2009 and 2010—including al-Qa'ida in the Arabian Peninsula's role in the failed December 25, 2009 aviation bombing and the Tehrik-e-Taliban Pakistan's involvement in the May 1, 2010 failed attack in Times Square—suggest that the determination of an expanded and more diverse network of terrorist groups to focus beyond their local environments may persist even with the ultimate defeat of al-Qa'ida in the Afghanistan-Pakistan theater. Other Areas of Focus in the Strategy will address our approach to these al-Qa'ida affiliates and adherents.

In Pakistan our efforts will continue to focus on a range of activities that are pursued in conjunction with the Government of Pakistan to increase the pace and scope of success against key al-Qa'ida and affiliated targets. It is unlikely that any single event—even the death of Usama bin Laden, the only leader al-Qa'ida has ever known—will bring about its operational dismantlement. Therefore, a sustained level of intensified pressure against the group is necessary. As such, US CT activities are focused on working with our partners to ensure the rapid degradation of al-Qa'ida's leadership structure, command and control, organizational capabilities, support networks, and infrastructure at a pace faster than the group is able to recover as well as on further shrinking its safehaven and limiting access to fallback locations elsewhere in Pakistan.

We will defeat al-Qa'ida only through a sustained partnership with Pakistan. The underlying conditions that allow the group to maintain its safe haven and regenerate—including its ability to capitalize on relationships with militant allies—can only be addressed through a sustained local presence opposed to al-Qa'ida. Pakistan has shown resolve in this fight in the face of increasing brutality by al-Qa'ida and its Pakistan-based allies, but greater Pakistani-US strategic cooperation across a broader range of political, military, and economic pursuits will be necessary to achieve the defeat of al-Qa'ida in Pakistan and Afghanistan.

In Afghanistan the US military and NATO's International Security Assistance Force (ISAF) are committed to preventing al-Qa'ida's return and disrupting any terrorist networks located there that have the ability to plan and launch transnational terrorist attacks. US and ISAF efforts to weaken the Taliban, bolster the Afghan Government, and strengthen the capacity of Afghan military and civilian institutions to secure the populace and effectively govern the country also contribute to the protection of our Homeland and to our overall CT objectives in South Asia.

Even if we achieve the ultimate defeat of al-Qa'ida in the Afghanistan-Pakistan theater, an expanded and diverse network of terrorist groups determined to focus beyond their local environments is likely to persist. In South Asia, LeT—the organization responsible for the rampage in Mumbai in 2008 that killed over 100 people, including six Americans—constitutes a formidable terrorist threat to Indian, US, and other Western interests in South Asia and potentially elsewhere. US CT efforts against LT will continue to focus on ensuring that the group lacks the capability to conduct or support operations detrimental to US interests or regional stability, including escalating tensions between Pakistan and India. Much of our effort against LT will continue to center on coordinating with, enabling, and improving the will and capabilities of partner nations—including in South Asia, Europe, and the Arabian Gulf— to counter the group and its terrorist activities.

Arabian Peninsula: Al-Qa'ida and Al-Qa'ida in the Arabian Peninsula (AQAP)

The United States faces two major CT challenges in the Arabian Peninsula— the direct threat posed by al-Qa'ida in the Arabian Peninsula (AQAP), and the large quantity of financial support from individuals and charities that flow from that region to al-Qa'ida and its affiliates and adherents around the world.

In confronting both challenges, we will look chiefly to our partners in the region—Saudi Arabia, United Arab Emirates, Kuwait, Bahrain, Oman, Yemen, and others—to take the lead, with US support and assistance. Our CT efforts in the Arabian Peninsula are part of our overall strategy for the region that includes other objectives such as promoting responsive governance and respect for the rights of citizens, which will reduce al-Qa'ida's resonance and relevancy.

AQAP. The United States faces a sustained threat from Yemen-based AQAP, which has shown the intent and capability to plan attacks against the US Homeland and US partners. Yemen is struggling to contain AQAP amidst an unprecedented confluence of security, political, and economic challenges. Yemen's instability has direct implications for the United States. Even as we work to support Yemen's stability and the aspirations of the Yemeni people, the defeat of AQAP will remain our CT priority in the region, and we will continue to leverage and strengthen our partnerships to achieve this end.

Our CT efforts in Yemen are embedded in a broader effort to stabilize the country and prevent state failure; such a scenario would have significant adverse implications for the United States and the region. The United States is working with regional and international partners to advance a number of political and economic development initiatives that address the underlying conditions that allow Yemen to serve as a safehaven for AQAP. These broader efforts complement those CT initiatives that are focused on building the capacity of Yemeni security services so they are able eventually to disrupt, dismantle, and defeat AQAP with only limited US involvement.

Terrorist Financing. The Arabian Peninsula remains the most important source of financial support for al-Qa'ida and its affiliates and adherents around the world. This is despite the fact that important progress has been made by some of our Gulf partners, especially Saudi Arabia and the United Arab Emirates (UAE), in disrupting terrorist financial support networks. Other countries in the region have not made the same political commitment to prioritize action against al-Qa'ida terrorist financing activity and, as a consequence, remain relatively permissive operating environments for al-Qa'ida financiers and facilitators. The United States will continue to emphasize disrupting the access of terrorists—especially al-Qa'ida, its affiliates, and its adherents—to sources of financial support. We will continue to push for enhanced unilateral action by these governments and closer cooperation with the United States while retaining our ability to take unilateral action as well.

East Africa: Al-Qa'ida in East Africa and Al-Shabaab

In East Africa we pursue a strategy focused on dismantling al-Qa'ida elements while building the capacity of countries and local administrations to serve as countervailing forces to the supporters of al-Qa'ida and the purveyors of instability that enable the transnational terrorist threat to persist

Somalia's chaotic and unsettled political situation has challenged the security environment in East Africa for a generation, undermining regional stability and creating a humanitarian relief challenge that will likely extend well into the future. Partly owing to this persistent instability and disorder, the United States faces terrorist enemies in East Africa that threaten our people, our interests, and our allies.

Al-Qaʻida elements continue to be the primary CT focus of the United States in light of clear indications of their ongoing intent to conduct attacks. Their presence within al-Shabaab is increasingly leading that group to pose a regional threat with growing transregional ties to other al-Qaʻida affiliates and ambitions on the part of some to participate more actively in al-Qaʻida-inspired violence. Influenced by its al-Qaʻida elements, al-Shabaab has used terrorist tactics in its insurgency in Somalia, and could—motivated to advance its insurgency or to further its al-Qaʻida-agenda or both—strike outside Somalia in East Africa, as it did in Uganda, as well as outside the region.

Europe

Europe remains a target of al-Qaʻida and its affiliates and adherents and is a potential gateway for terrorists to attack the US Homeland. Repeated and attempted attacks—such as those in Madrid in 2004, London in 2005 and 2006, and Scotland and Germany in 2007—highlight al-Qaʻida and its affiliates and adherents' continued focus on striking in Europe. Although many individuals involved in plotting within and against European nations have been arrested in recent years, al-Qaʻida and its affiliates and adherents will continue to maintain and build infrastructure in Europe that could potentially support future terrorist attack planning, logistical support, and fundraising efforts. Europe also faces a threat from individuals radicalized by al-Qaʻida ideology to carry out violence despite their lack of formal affiliation with or operational direction from al-Qaʻida or its affiliates.

The foundation of our CT efforts in Europe remains our network of strong and enduring partnerships. Because of the strong will and capacity of most of our European allies to address the threat within their own borders, our role is likely to continue to be focused on providing advisory and support assistance. In instances where capacity-building is required, however, we will work closely with the host country to enhance its CT effectiveness. In addition, the United States will continue to partner with the European Parliament and European Union to maintain and advance CT efforts that provide mutual security and protection to citizens of all nations while also upholding individual rights. In regions of concern beyond Europe, the United States and select European allies will continue strengthening CT partnerships based on a shared understanding of the threat and active collaboration that draws on comparative advantages to contain and mitigate it. These joint endeavors focus chiefly on building the will and capacity of key countries in South Asia, Africa, and the Arabian Peninsula.

Iraq: Al-Qa'ida in Iraq (AQI)

Iraq's security and political situation is improving after years of instability that enabled groups such as al-Qa'ida in Iraq (AQI) to spread chaos and sectarian conflict. AQI continues to be the main focus of US CT efforts in Iraq, as it poses a threat not only to stability but to our military forces. In addition, AQI continues to plot attacks against US interests in the region and beyond.

Iraqi-led CT operations have resulted in the dismantling of AQI's previous senior leadership, but new leaders have assumed control and the group continues to conduct high-profile attacks. Our CT goals are to build Iraqi CT capacity to defeat AQI and to contribute to lasting peace and security in Iraq. Iraqi security forces continue to be plagued by corruption and a judicial and prison system that appears inadequate to manage terrorist detainees, and our CT efforts therefore will need to address these shortfalls. We will continue to watch for AQI attempts to reinvigorate its efforts and draw on a still-significant network of associates that spans the region and includes associates in the United States.

Maghreb and Sahel: Al-Qa'ida in the Lands of the Islamic Maghreb (AQIM)

Al-Qa'ida in the Lands of the Islamic Maghreb (AQIM) has its roots in Algeria but in recent years has shifted its center of gravity southward, where it enjoys a degree of safehaven in northern Mali and exploits the limited CT capabilities of the frontline countries in the Sahel. From this base it has trained fighters from other allied organizations—such as Nigerian-based Boko Haram—and undoubtedly seeks to exploit instability in North Africa to expand its range and access to weapons and recruits. AQIM's high-profile kidnappings of Westerners, generally for ransom or in exchange for prisoners, endanger Western tourists in the region and supply the group with an influx of cash to underwrite its terrorist activities and potentially those of other al-Qa'ida affiliates and adherents. The group has attacked United States and Western citizens and interests, having killed an American in

Nouakchott, Mauritania in 2009 and targeted other Americans and facilities in the region.

The United States' CT efforts against AQIM must draw on and be closely integrated with the broader United States regional strategy, especially since the long-term eradication of AQIM will not be addressed by traditional CT tools alone. Long-term United States capacity building initiatives support many of the frontline and secondary states likely to confront AQIM. But United States citizens and interests in the region are threatened by AQIM today, and we must therefore pursue near-term efforts and at times more targeted approaches that directly counter AQIM and its enabling elements. We must work actively to contain, disrupt, degrade, and dismantle AQIM as logical steps on the path to defeating the group. As appropriate, the United States will use its CT tools, weighing the costs and benefits of its approach in the context of regional dynamics and perceptions and the actions and capabilities of its partners in the region—local governments and European allies. We also will seek to bolster efforts for regional cooperation against AQIM, especially between Algeria and the Sahelian countries of Mauritania, Mali, and Niger as an essential element in a strategy focused on disrupting a highly adaptive and mobile group that exploits shortfalls in regional security and governance.

Southeast Asia: Al-Qa'ida and its Affiliates and Adherents

CT efforts in Southeast Asia have improved markedly in recent years as key countries in the region have enjoyed significant CT successes and put effective pressure on the region's most lethal terrorist organizations. Despite these successes, the region remains potentially fertile ground for local terrorist organizations that share al-Qa'ida's ideology and aspirations. US efforts will aim to ensure that the threat to our Homeland from groups in the region remains low and key partner countries have the capacity to continue to mitigate the al-Qa'ida threat.

As in other regions, our CT strategy is embedded within an overall strategy of enhanced US economic and political engagement with Southeast Asia that fosters peace, prosperity and democracy in the region. This Strategy takes as a critical point of departure the fact that the countries and people of Southeast Asia bear the responsibility for addressing the challenges posed by terrorists in the region. We stand ready to assist in continuing to build the capacity of governments in the region that consistently demonstrate their commitment against al-Qa'ida and its affiliates and adherents in the region. We have developed a robust network of bilateral CT relationships with key countries across the region, including Indonesia, the Philippines, Singapore, Thailand, and Australia. Each of these countries as well as other critical regional players have a role to play in ensuring that the threat from terrorism does not undergo a resurgence in the years ahead and that al-Qa'ida's senior leadership is compelled to look at regions other than Southeast Asia for resources, support, and a potential safehaven.

Central Asia: Al-Qa'ida and Its Affiliates and Adherents

The United States does not face a direct terrorist threat from Central Asia but has an interest in maintaining the security of the US logistics infrastructure supporting operations in Afghanistan, key strategic facilities, and in preventing the emergence of an al-Qa'ida safe haven in Central Asia. We remain vigilant to warning signs in the region and continue to support local efforts to ensure that the threat against United States and allied interests from terrorist groups in Central Asia remains low.

Information and Ideas: Al-Qa'ida Ideology, Messaging, and Resonance

The 21st-century venue for sharing information and ideas is global, and al-Qa'ida, its affiliates and its adherents attempt to leverage the worldwide reach of media and communications systems to their advantage. Be it in traditional media or cyberspace, a successful US strategy in these domains will focus on undermining and inhibiting al-Qa'ida's ideology while also diminishing those specific factors that make it appealing as a catalyst and justification for violence. We must also put forward a positive vision of engagement with Muslim communities around the world so that we are contrasting our vision of the future we are trying to build with al-Qa'ida's focus on what it aims to destroy.

In the global information environment, al-Qa'ida adherents who promote or attempt to commit violence domestically are influenced by al-Qa'ida ideology and messaging that originates overseas, and those who attempt terror overseas often cite domestic US events and policies. At the same time, people—including those targeted by al-Qa'ida with its propaganda—live in a local context and are affected by local issues, media, and concerns.

317

In the arena of information and ideas, we must focus globally and locally and draw on direct and indirect communications and methods. We will continue to make it clear that the United States is not—and never will be—at war with Islam. We will focus on disrupting al-Qa'ida's ability to project its message across a range of media, challenge the legitimacy and accuracy of the assertions and behavior it advances, and promote a greater understanding of United States policies and actions and an alternative to al-Qa'ida's vision. We also will seek to amplify positive and influential messages that undermine the legitimacy of al-Qa'ida and its actions and contest its worldview. In some cases we may convey our ideas and messages through person-to-person engagement, other times through the power of social media, and in every case through the message of our deeds.

Other Terrorist Concerns Requiring Focus and Attention

Although al-Qa'ida is our strategic as well as tactical CT priority, other designated terrorist organizations pose a significant threat to United States strategic interests. Hizballah, HAMAS, and the Revolutionary Armed Forces of Colombia (FARC) remain opposed to aspects of US foreign policy and pose significant threats to US strategic interests as regional destabilizers and as threats to our citizens, facilities, and allies worldwide. Even when their terrorist efforts are not directed at the United States, a successful terrorist operation by one of these groups in and around the key regional fault lines in which they operate increases the likelihood of regional conflict. We remain committed to understanding the intention and capabilities of these groups, as well as working with our partners to disrupt terrorist operations and related activities that threaten regional and international security and threaten our national security objectives. In addition to the threats posed by al-Qa'ida and its affiliates and adherents, US citizens and interests are at times threatened by other violent groups within the Homeland and across the globe. We will remain vigilant to these threats and regularly advise the American people of local risks.

Iran and Syria remain active sponsors of terrorism, and we remain committed to opposing the support these state sponsors provide to groups pursuing terrorist attacks to undermine regional stability.

Conclusion

Our National CT Strategy is one of continuity and of change. As a society we have continued to go about our lives as we have always done, demonstrating the confidence, resolve and resilience that comes with knowing that the final outcome of our war with al-Qa'ida is certain. In the decade since the September 11 attacks, we as a government have become much more effective in executing our CT mission—with a critical measure of this success reflected in the broad array of countries and capabilities that are now arrayed in the fight against al-Qa'ida. Indeed, nobody is more aware of our increased effectiveness than al-Qa'ida and its affiliates and adherents, as their plans are disrupted, their capabilities degraded, and their organizations dismantled. In the weeks since bin Laden's death, it has become clear that the group is struggling to find its footing, that it faces real leadership and organizational challenges, and that its ability to adapt and evolve is being tested now more than ever.

Although we continue to pursue those components of our CT strategy that have proven so successful in recent years in degrading al-Qa'ida, we must at the same time be prepared to adjust our strategy to confront the evolving threat prompted in part by that very success. It is clear that al-Qa'ida the organization has been degraded and has, out of weakness, called on individuals who know the group only through its ideology to carry out violence in its name. In this Strategy we have redoubled our efforts to undercut the resonance of the al-Qa'ida message while addressing those specific drivers of violence that al-Qa'ida exploits to recruit and motivate new generations of terrorists. And even as the core of al-Qa'ida in Pakistan and Afghanistan continues to be dismantled through our systematic CT actions, we have expanded our focus in this Strategy to articulate the specific approaches we must take to counter al-Qa'ida affiliates and adherents on the periphery, be they established affiliated groups in Yemen or Somalia or individual adherents in the Homeland who may be mobilized to violence in al-Qa'ida's name. Although our efforts and those of our partners have yielded undeniable CT successes and kept us safe from attack here in the Homeland, we must nonetheless remain clear eyed to the threat that remains. As some threats have been diminished, others have emerged, and—correspondingly—as some aspects of our approach remain constant, so have others evolved. This Strategy stands to testify to our friends, our partners, and to our terrorist enemies: Here is our plan of action to achieve the defeat of al-Qaʻida and its affiliates and adherents. It is this outcome we seek, and indeed it is the only one we will accept.

Appendix 3C Notes:

i. *Affiliates* is not a legal term of art. Although it includes Associated Forces, it additionally includes groups and individuals against whom the United States is not authorized to use force based on the authorities granted by the Authorization for the Use of Military Force, Pub. L. 107-40, 115 Stat. 224 (2001). The use of *Affiliates* in this strategy is intended to reflect a broader category of entities against whom the United States must bring various elements of national power, as appropriate and consistent with the law, to counter the threat they pose. *Associated Forces* is a legal term of art that refers to cobelligerents of al-Qaʻida or the Taliban against whom the President is authorized to use force (including the authority to detain) based on the Authorization for the Use of Military Force, Pub. L. 107-40, 115 Stat. 224 (2001).

ii. Our principle of creating a culture of resilience is reflected in more detail in Presidential Policy Directive-8, released in May 2011. This PPD is aimed at strengthening the security and resilience of the United States through systematic preparation for the threats that pose the greatest risk to the security of the Nation, including acts of terrorism, cyber attacks, pandemics, and catastrophic natural disasters.

Appendix 3D: Empowering Local Partners to Prevent Violent Extremism in the United States (August 2011)

THE WHITE HOUSE

WASHINGTON

Sadly, the threat of violent extremism in America is nothing new. Throughout our history, misguided groups – including international and domestic terrorist organizations, neo-Nazis and anti-Semitic hate groups – have engaged in horrific violence to kill our citizens and threaten our way of life. Most recently, al-Qa'ida and its affiliates have attempted to recruit and radicalize people to terrorism here in the United States, as we have seen in several plots and attacks, including the deadly attack two years ago on our service members at Fort Hood.

As a government, we are working to prevent all types of extremism that leads to violence, regardless of who inspires it. At the same time, countering al-Qa'ida's violent ideology is one part of our comprehensive strategy to defeat al-Qa'ida. Over the past 2 1/2 years, more key al-Qa'ida leaders – including Usama bin Laden – have been eliminated in rapid succession than at any time since the September 11 attacks. We have strengthened homeland security and improved information sharing. Thanks to coordinated intelligence and law enforcement, numerous terrorist plots have been thwarted, saving many American lives.

Protecting American communities from al-Qa'ida's hateful ideology is not the work of government alone. Communities – especially Muslim American communities whose children, families and neighbors are being targeted for recruitment by al-Qa'ida – are often best positioned to take the lead because they know their communities best. Indeed, Muslim American communities have categorically condemned terrorism, worked with law enforcement to help prevent terrorist attacks, and forged creative programs to protect their sons and daughters from al-Qa'ida's murderous ideology.

The strategy that follows outlines how the Federal Government will support and help empower American communities and their local partners in their grassroots efforts to prevent violent extremism. This strategy commits the Federal Government to improving support to communities, including sharing more information about the threat of radicalization; strengthening cooperation with local law enforcement, who work with these communities every day; and helping communities to better understand and protect themselves against violent extremist propaganda, especially online.

Most of all, this strategy reaffirms the fundamental American principles that guide our efforts. As we approach the 10th anniversary of the September 11 attacks, we remember that al-Qa'ida tried to spark a conflict between faiths and divide us as Americans. But they failed. As this strategy makes clear, we will not waver in defense of our country or our communities. We will defeat al-Qa'ida and its affiliates. We will uphold the civil rights and civil liberties of every American. And we will go forward together, as Americans, knowing that our rich diversity of backgrounds and faiths makes us stronger and is a key to our national security.

321

Empowering Local Partners to Prevent Violent Extremism in the United States

> *"Several recent incidences of violent extremists in the United States who are committed to fighting here and abroad have underscored the threat to the United States and our interests posed by individuals radicalized at home. Our best defenses against this threat are well informed and equipped families, local communities, and institutions. The Federal Government will invest in intelligence to understand this threat and expand community engagement and development programs to empower local communities. And the Federal Government, drawing on the expertise and resources from all relevant agencies, will clearly communicate our policies and intentions, listening to local concerns, tailoring policies to address regional concerns, and making clear that our diversity is part of our strength—not a source of division or insecurity."*

—National Security Strategy, May 2010

A. THE CHALLENGE

The seal of the United States of America is inscribed with the Latin dictum *E Pluribus Unum*—out of many, one. It is our great strength that the American social fabric continues to weave together waves of immigrants to the United States and people from all backgrounds and walks of life as part of an indivisible community. We are a pluralistic Nation and a society that does not just accept diversity; we embrace it, and we are stronger as a result. We surmount the many challenges that we face by remaining committed to the American ideals of freedom, equality, and democracy, which transcend differences of religion, ethnicity, and place of birth. Since America's founding, our country and our ideals have been assailed by forces of hate and division, yet we remain strong, unified, and resilient.

Throughout history, violent extremists—individuals who support or commit ideologically-motivated violence to further political goals—have promoted messages of divisiveness and justified the killing of innocents. The United States Constitution recognizes freedom of expression, even for individuals who espouse unpopular or even hateful views. But when individuals or groups choose to further their grievances or ideologies through violence, by engaging in violence themselves or by recruiting and encouraging others to do so, it becomes the collective responsibility of the US Government and the American people to take a stand. In recent history, our country has faced plots by neo-Nazis and other anti-Semitic hate groups, racial supremacists, and international and domestic terrorist groups; and since the September 11 attacks, we have faced an expanded range of plots and attacks in the United States inspired or directed by al-Qa'ida and its affiliates and adherents as well as other violent extremists. Supporters of these groups and their associated ideologies come from different socioeconomic backgrounds, ethnic and religious communities, and areas of the country, making it difficult to predict where violent extremist narratives will resonate. And as history has shown, the prevalence of particular violent extremist ideologies changes over time, and new threats will undoubtedly arise in the future.

We rely on our local, state, and Federal law enforcement to deter individuals from using violence and to protect communities from harm. But we also must ensure that the right tools are applied at the right time to the right situation. Countering radicalization to violence is frequently best achieved by engaging and empowering individuals and groups at the local level to build resilience against violent extremism. Law enforcement plays an essential role in keeping us safe, but so too does engagement and partnership with communities.

While we can and must prioritize our efforts, our approach should be enduring and flexible enough to address a variety of current and possible future threats. Individuals from a broad array of communities and walks of life in the United States have been radicalized to support or commit acts of ideologically- inspired violence. Any solution that focuses on a single, current form of violent extremism, without regard to other threats, will fail to secure our country and communities. Our threat environment is constantly evolving, which is why we must consistently revisit our priorities and ensure our domestic approach can address multiple types of violent extremism.

Today, as detailed in the *National Security Strategy* and the *National Strategy for Counterterrorism*, al-Qa'ida and its affiliates and adherents represent the preeminent terrorist threat to our country. We know that these groups are actively seeking to recruit or inspire Americans to carry out attacks against the United States, particularly as they are facing greater pressure in their safe-havens abroad. The past several years have seen increased numbers of American citizens or residents inspired by al-Qa'ida's ideology and involved in terrorism. Some have traveled overseas to train or fight, while others have been involved in supporting, financing, or plotting attacks in the homeland. The number of individuals remains limited, but the fact that al-Qa'ida and its affiliates and adherents are openly and specifically inciting Americans to support or commit acts of violence—through videos, magazines, and online forums—poses an ongoing and real threat.

This type of violent extremism is a complicated challenge for the United States, not only because of the threat of attacks, but also because of its potential to divide us. Groups and individuals supporting al-Qa'ida's vision are attempting to lure Americans to terrorism in order to create support networks and facilitate attack planning, but this also has potential to create a backlash against Muslim Americans. Such a backlash would feed al-Qa'ida's propaganda that our country is anti-Muslim and at war against Islam, handing our enemies a strategic victory by turning our communities against one another; eroding our shared sense of identity as Americans; feeding terrorist recruitment abroad; and threatening our fundamental values of religious freedom and pluralism. Violent extremists prey on the disenchantment and alienation that discrimination creates, and they have a vested interest in anti-Muslim sentiment. It is for this reason that our security—preventing radicalization that leads to violence—is inextricably linked to our values: the protection of civil rights and civil liberties and the promotion of an inclusive society.

B. A COMMUNITY-BASED APPROACH

The United States relies on a broad range of tools and capabilities that are essential to prevent violent extremism in the United States, emphasizing, in particular, the strength of communities as central to our approach. The best defenses against violent extremist ideologies are well-informed and equipped families, local communities, and local institutions. Their awareness of the threat and willingness to work with one another and government is part of our long history of community-based initiatives and partnerships dealing with a range of public safety challenges. Communities are best placed to recognize and confront the threat because violent extremists are targeting their children, families, and neighbors. Rather than blame particular communities, it is essential that we find ways to help them protect themselves. To do so, we must continue to ensure that all Americans understand that they are an essential part of our civic life and partners in our efforts to combat violent extremist ideologies and organizations that seek to weaken our society.

We are fortunate that our experience with community-based problem solving, local partnerships, and community-oriented policing provides a basis for addressing violent extremism as part of a broader mandate of community safety. We therefore are building our efforts to counter radicalization that leads to violence in the United States from existing structures, while creating capacity to fill gaps as we implement programs and initiatives. Rather than creating a new architecture of institutions and funding, we are utilizing successful models, increasing their scope and scale where appropriate.

While communities must often lead this effort, the Federal Government has a significant responsibility. Our research and consultations with local stakeholders, communities, and foreign partners have under- scored that the Federal Government's most effective role in strengthening community partnerships and preventing violent extremism is as a facilitator, convener, and source of information. The Federal Government will often be ill-suited to intervene in the niches of society where radicalization to violence takes place, but it can foster partnerships to support communities through its connections to local government, law enforcement, Mayor's offices, the private sector, local service providers, academia, and many others who can help prevent violent extremism. Federal departments and agencies have begun expanding support to local stakeholders and practitioners who are on the ground and positioned to develop grassroots partnerships with the communities they serve.

C. GOAL AND AREAS OF PRIORITY ACTION

Our central goal in this effort is to prevent violent extremists and their supporters from inspiring, radicalizing, financing, or recruiting individuals or groups in the United States to commit acts of violence. The US Government will work tirelessly to counter support for violent extremism and to ensure that, as new violent groups and ideologies emerge, they fail to gain a foothold in our country. Achieving this aim requires that we all work together—government, communities, the private sector, the general public, and others—to develop effective programs and initiatives.

Leveraging Existing Models

The United States has rich experience in supporting locally-based initiatives that connect communities and government to address community challenges through collaboration and the development of stakeholder networks. While recognizing that different challenges require the involvement of different stakeholders, we view community-based problem solving as an effective model of organizing communities and government to counter violent extremism in the homeland. The following provides three examples of this model in practice.

Example One: Comprehensive Gang Model

The Department of Justice's *Comprehensive Gang Model* is a flexible framework that communities can use to reduce or prevent gang activity, involving strategies of community mobilization, social intervention, opportunities for educational and vocational advancements, and organizational change. Local community organizations and government offices responsible for addressing gangs—police, schools, probation officers, youth agencies, grassroots organizations, government, and others—help identify causes, recommend appropriate responses, and select activities for local implementation, supported by integrated Federal, state, and local resources to incorporate state-of-the-art practices in gang prevention, intervention, and suppression. This multi-dimensional, community-led response to gangs—driven by local stakeholders and supported by the Federal Government—has reduced serious gang-related crimes in affected locations across the country.

Example Two: Building Communities of Trust Initiative

The Departments of Justice and Homeland Security established the *Building Communities of Trust (BCOT) Initiative* to improve trust among police, fusion centers, and the communities they serve in order to address the challenges of crime and terrorism prevention. In support of BCOT, a National Planning Team comprised of representatives from Federal, state, and local governments; community organizations; and privacy and civil liberties groups convened and, in select locations, conducted roundtables to explore how to build and maintain relationships of trust. Lessons learned from these roundtables have resulted in official guidance highlighting the importance of meaningful information sharing, responding to community concerns, and distinguishing between innocent cultural behaviors and conduct that may legitimately reflect criminal activity or terrorism precursors.

Example Three: Safe Schools/Healthy Students Initiative

Responding to a series of lethal school shootings in the late 1990s, which culminated with the tragedy at Columbine High School, the Departments of Education, Justice, and Health and Human Services launched the *Safe Schools/Healthy Students (SS/HS) Initiative* to create broader, more comprehensive local programs to prevent violence and substance abuse among our Nation's youth, schools, and communities. In order to receive an SS/HS grant, school districts must partner with local mental health experts, juvenile justice officials, and law enforcement. Proposals must include programs that address violence and substance abuse prevention; social, emotional, and behavioral development; school and community-based mental health services; and early childhood development. According to an ongoing evaluation, the Initiative has resulted in fewer students experiencing or witnessing violence, increased school safety, and an overall decrease in violence in communities where the program is active.

"As extremists try to inspire acts of violence within our borders, we are responding with the strength of our communities, with the respect for the rule of law, and with the conviction that Muslim Americans are part of our American family."

—*President Barack Obama, State of the Union, January 2011*

To support a community-based approach, the Federal Government is working to strengthen partnerships and networks among local stakeholders. There is no single issue or grievance that pushes individuals toward supporting or committing violence, and the path to violent extremism can vary considerably. As a result, it is essential that we empower local partners, who can more readily identify problems as they emerge and customize responses so that they are appropriate and effective for particular individuals, groups, and locations. To that end, we have prioritized three broad areas of action where we believe the Federal Government can provide value to supporting partnerships at the local level and countering violent extremism. Our work will evolve over time as we enhance partnerships and further our understanding of what tools and methods are most effective.

1. Enhancing Federal Engagement with and Support to Local Communities that May be Targeted by Violent Extremists

Communication and meaningful engagement with the American public is an essential part of the Federal Government's work. Our open system of governance requires that we respond to inquiries; educate and share information on our programs, policies, and initiatives; and provide a platform for communities to air grievances and contribute their views on policy and government. We do this consistently in a variety of ways: we convene forums, develop brochures, respond to correspondence, post information on websites, and we make available for comment proposed regulations in the Federal Register. We also reach out to communities directly to answer questions and provide information and guidance, offering opportunities for communities to provide valuable suggestions about how government can be more effective and responsive in addressing their concerns. As such, engagement with local communities provides an opportunity for us to reexamine and improve how we perform our functions. For these reasons, we view effective community engagement as an essential part of good governance and an important end in itself.

The vast majority of our engagement work relates to issues outside the national security arena, such as jobs, education, health, and civil rights. We must ensure that in our efforts to support community- based partnerships to counter violent extremism, we remain engaged in the full range of community concerns and interests, and do not narrowly build relationships around national security issues alone. Where appropriate, we are relying on preexisting Federal Government engagement efforts to discuss violent extremism, ensuring that these forums continue to focus on a wide variety of issues. There are instances when the government needs to build new relationships to address security issues, but these must be predicated upon multifaceted engagement. Indeed, we refuse to limit our engagement to what we are against, because we need to support active engagement in civic and democratic life and help forge partnerships that advance what we are for, including opportunity and equal treatment for all.

Engagement is essential for supporting community-based efforts to prevent violent extremism because it allows government and communities to share information, concerns, and potential solutions. Our aims in engaging with communities to discuss violent extremism are to (1) share sound, meaningful, and timely information about the threat of radicalization to violence with a wide range of community groups and organizations, particularly those involved in public safety issues; (2) respond to community concerns about government policies and actions; and (3) better understand how we can effectively support community-based solutions.

In addition to engaging communities on a wide range of issues, the Federal Government is using its convening power to help build a network of individuals, groups, civil society organizations, and private sector actors to support community-based efforts to counter violent extremism. Myriad groups with tools and capabilities to counter radicalization to violence often operate in separate spheres of activity and therefore do not know one another. The Federal Government, with its connections to diverse networks across the country, has a unique ability to draw together the constellation of previously unconnected efforts and programs to form a more cohesive enterprise against violent extremism.

2. Building Government and Law Enforcement Expertise for Preventing Violent Extremism

Although we have learned a great deal about radicalization that leads to violence, we can never assume that the dynamics will remain the same. We must be vigilant in identifying, predicting, and preempting new developments. This necessitates ongoing research and analysis, as well as exchanges with individuals, communities, and government officials who work on the front lines to counter the threats we all face. In addition, we will continue to hold meetings with foreign partners to share experiences and best practices, recognizing that while not all lessons are transferable to the American context, this sharing can help us improve our approach and avoid common pitfalls.

Government and law enforcement at the local level have well-established relationships with communities, developed through years of consistent engagement, and therefore can effectively build partnerships and take action on the ground. To help facilitate local partnerships to prevent violent extremism, the Federal Government is building a robust training program with rigorous curriculum standards to ensure that the training that communities; local, state, and tribal governments; prison officials; and law enforcement receive is based on intelligence, research, and accurate information about how people are radicalized to accept violence, and what has worked to prevent violent extremism. Misinformation about the threat and dynamics of radicalization to violence can harm our security by sending local stakeholders in the wrong direction and unnecessarily creating tensions with potential community partners. We also are working to support and expand community oriented policing efforts by our state, local, and tribal partners, and to assist them in enhancing cultural proficiency and other foundations for effective community engagement.

3. Countering Violent Extremist Propaganda While Promoting Our Ideals

Radicalization that leads to violent extremism includes the diffusion of ideologies and narratives that feed on grievances, assign blame, and legitimize the use of violence against those deemed responsible. We must actively and aggressively counter the range of ideologies violent extremists employ to radicalize and recruit individuals by challenging justifications for violence and by actively promoting the unifying and inclusive vision of our American ideals.

Toward this end, we will continue to closely monitor the important role the internet and social network- ing sites play in advancing violent extremist narratives. We protect our communities from a variety of online threats, such as sexual predators, by educating them about safety on the internet, and we are using a similar approach to thwart violent extremists. We will work to empower families and communities to counter online violent extremist propaganda, which is increasingly in English and targeted at American audiences.

For example, in the case of our current priority, we must counter al-Qa'ida's propaganda that the United States is somehow at war with Islam. There is no single profile of an al-Qa'ida-inspired terrorist, but extensive investigations and research show that they all believe: (1) the United States is out to destroy Islam; and (2) this justifies violence against Americans. Al-Qa'ida and its supporters spread messages of hate, twist facts, and distort religious principles to weave together a false narrative that Muslims must attack Americans everywhere because the United States is waging a global war against Islam. While al-Qa'ida claims to be the vanguard of Islam, the overwhelming majority of its victims are Muslim.

We will challenge this propaganda through our words and deeds, defined by the very ideals of who we are as Americans. As the President has stated repeatedly, the United States is not, and never will be, at war with Islam. Islam is part of America, a country that cherishes the active participation of all its citizens, regardless of background and belief. We live what al-Qa'ida violently rejects—religious freedom and pluralism. We have emphasized a paradigm of engagement with Muslim communities around the world, based on mutual respect and interest manifest in our new partnerships and programming to promote entrepreneurship, health, science and technology, educational exchanges, and opportunities for women.

But we must remember that just as our words and deeds can either fuel or counter violent ideologies abroad, so too can they here at home. Actions and statements that cast suspicion toward entire communities, promote hatred and division, and send messages to certain Americans that they are somehow less American because of their faith or how they look, reinforce violent extremist propaganda and feed the sense of disenchantment and disenfranchisement that may spur violent extremist radicalization. The Federal Government will work to communicate clearly about al-Qa'ida's destructive and bankrupt ideology, while dispelling myths and misperceptions that blame communities for the actions of a small number of violent extremists.

D. GUIDING PRINCIPLES

How we define and discuss the challenge of radicalization to violence matters. Violent extremism, while of paramount importance given the potential for harm, is only one among a number of threats our Nation is facing. Communities face an array of challenges to their safety, including gang violence, school shootings, drugs, hate crimes, and many others. Just as we respond to community safety issues through partnerships and networks of government officials, Mayor's offices, law enforcement, community organizations, and private sector actors, so must we address radicalization to violence and terrorist recruitment through similar relationships and by leveraging some of the same tools and solutions. In doing so, we are guided by the following principles:

We must continually enhance our understanding of the threat posed by violent extremism and the ways in which individuals or groups seek to radicalize Americans, adapting our approach as needed. As al-Qa'ida and its affiliates and adherents increasingly aim to inspire people within the United States to commit acts of terrorism, we must closely monitor and understand their tactics, both online and offline, remaining nimble in our response, increasing our understanding of the factors that lead individuals to turn to violence, and calibrating our efforts.

We must do everything in our power to protect the American people from violent extremism while protecting the civil rights and civil liberties of every American. Protecting our fundamental rights and liberties is an important end in itself, and also helps counter violent extremism by ensuring nonviolent means for addressing policy concerns; safeguarding equal and fair treatment; and making it more difficult for violent extremists to divide our communities.

As the President said at the National Archives in May 2009, "We uphold our fundamental principles and values not just because we choose to, but because we swear to. Not because they feel good, but because they help keep us safe. They keep us true to who we are …So as Americans, we reject the false choice between our security and our ideals. We can and we must and we will protect both."

We must build partnerships and provide support to communities based on mutual trust, respect, and understanding. We must have honest dialogue between communities and government that is transparent and promotes community-based problem solving.

We must use a wide range of good governance programs—including those that promote immigrant integration and civic engagement, protect civil rights, and provide social services—that may help prevent radicalization that leads to violence. This necessitates a whole-of-government approach, based on the expertise of our traditional national security departments and agencies, as well as other parts of the government, including those with experience in addressing community safety issues.

We must support local capabilities and programs to address problems of national concern. While the demographics of communities and the priorities of local government, communities, and law enforcement vary, our efforts to prevent radicalization to violence and terrorist recruitment must harness the knowledge, expertise, and relationships of local actors, both in and out of government.

Government officials and the American public should not stigmatize or blame communities because of the actions of a handful of individuals. We must instead support communities as partners, recognizing that a particular ethnic, religious, or national background does not necessarily equate to special knowledge or expertise in addressing violent extremism. Where communities have been active in condemning terrorism and confronting violent extremism, we must recognize their efforts; help them build upon their work; and connect them with other communities and stakeholders in order to share best practices.

Strong religious beliefs should never be confused with violent extremism. Freedom of religion is a fundamental American right and one of our most strongly held values. Since our founding, people of diverse and strongly held religious faiths have thrived in America.

Though we will not tolerate illegal activities, opposition to government policy is neither illegal nor unpatriotic and does not make someone a violent extremist. It is a basic tenet of our democracy that citizens of good conscience can respectfully disagree with one another and resolve their differences through peaceful means. Our Nation is built upon the principles of debate, dialogue, and cooperation.

Appendix 4A: The Honorable James R. Clapper, Director of National Intelligence

Statement for the Record by The Honorable James R. Clapper
Director of National Intelligence
Joint Hearing to Mark the 10th Anniversary of 9/11
13 September 2011

Chairman Feinstein, Chairman Rogers, Vice Chairman Chambliss, Ranking Member Ruppersberger and Members of both committees, thank you for convening this Hearing today and for the essential oversight you provide to the Intelligence Community on behalf of all Americans.

The committees meet today in this extraordinary session on a subject of profound importance. This Nation, the Intelligence Community, CIA, and indeed I, are all singularly fortunate that a man of Dave Petraeus' capability, stature, leadership, and patriotism is not only willing, but wants to continue to serve. I am pleased and proud to appear with him today in this crucial Hearing, and honored to be his teammate.

This past week has seen many reflections on those terrible events ten years ago, reflections that have centered on the impact of the attacks and on the state of the terrorist threat today. But no reflections have been more important than those that have centered on the loss of those who perished, and on the sacrifices that have been made by the families and loved ones they left behind.

We all remember where we were on that bright morning that turned so dark. And we have worked with resolve since that day to honor those losses and those sacrifices, and to fight against the scourge that caused-and still seeks to cause-such horrible destruction.

We have seen further sacrifices by those who carry out that fight- in the field and at home, in uniform and in the civilian services. We have lost intelligence officers—courageous men and women- and placed burdens on our families, bringing great sorrow and grief to some.

We have done this with the certainty that there is no other course- that the safety and the security of Americans depends in great measure on the work that we do.

In the last ten years the Intelligence Community has made significant contributions to the effort to combat terrorism and violent extremism. The attacks of 9/11 were the work of al- Qa'ida. That organization is not what it was a decade ago. The relentless pressure we have placed on al-Qa'ida has forced it to change, weakened its central character and capabilities, and caused it to seek other modes of operation.

We have vigorously attacked its leadership, striving to keep it off balance and to cut down those who would direct its activities. We have worked to deny al-Qa'ida any sense of security, to complicate and disrupt its flow of resources, and to undermine its ability to plan and train with well-considered and central direction.

Most notably of course, we have sent Usama bin Ladin to the fate he so clearly deserved. These accomplishments are substantial and real, and they stand as testimony to the dedication and the skill of many intelligence officers and operating elements, and to the extraordinary capabilities they bring to bear in this struggle. The Nation is in many respects safer because of their work- and because of the many actions that have been taken as well by the broad range of federal, state, local, and tribal elements concerned with our security. We have seen ten years of dedicated and relentless effort by all in this fight, and the men and women of the Intelligence Community have worked hard to stand alongside our partners and help to ensure their success.

We have reason, then, to take pride, but it would be an error to conclude that we have reason to gloat, reason to soften our focus, or reason to reduce our concerns or relax our efforts.

The hard fact is that we remain threatened- that terrorists still wish to do us harm, to destroy our institutions, to kill Americans without conscience or concern, and they have the capability to do so.

The nature of the terrorist threat has evolved. Core al-Qa'ida is indeed weaker and less able to recruit, train, and deploy operatives. But it remains the ideological leader of the global extremist movement and it continues to influence terrorists and would-be terrorists through public statements. Its leadership continues to seek openings to push their destructive narrative, and it retains an ability to plot attacks. The group's intent to strike us at home remains strong.

Beyond the threat posed by core al-Qa'ida, we have seen the rising importance of its regional affiliates, groups that support al-Qa'ida's strategy of creating a self-sustaining global extremist movement. These affiliates have increased the scope of their operations, seeking to strike US and Western targets both inside and outside their respective regions.

Perhaps the best known and currently most dangerous of the affiliates is Al-Qa'ida in the Arabian Peninsula (AQAP), based in Yemen. AQAP's two attempted attacks against the US homeland- the unsuccessful airliner attack in December 2009, and its follow-on effort to down two US-bound cargo planes in October 2010-were sobering indications of a determined enemy capable of adjusting tactics to achieve its goals. We have substantial concerns about this group's capability to conduct additional attacks targeting the US homeland and US interests overseas, as well as its continuing propaganda efforts designed to inspire like-minded Western extremists to conduct attacks in their home countries.

There are other important al-Qa'ida affiliates in the Maghreb and in additional regions. These groups, which have varying levels of capability, pose a threat to US interests and remain committed to al-Qa'ida's illegitimate ideology.

We are also concerned about the potential threat posed by homegrown violent extremists who are inspired by al-Qa'ida's global agenda. Increasingly sophisticated English-language propaganda that provides extremists with guidance to carry out attacks on the US homeland remains easily available via the Internet. The Internet has been used, for example, to provide instructions on the use of weapons and the construction of explosives, along with targeting ideas.

English-language web forums also foster a sense of community and further indoctrinate new recruits, predicates that can lead to increased levels of violent activity.

Homegrown extremists may be motivated to carry out violence on the basis of a variety of personal rationales. Such individuals, who may independently plan attacks with no guidance from associates in the US or overseas, are difficult to detect and disrupt, and could carry out attacks with little or no warning.

Homegrown violent extremists are examples of the difficulty and the complexity of defending against terrorist attacks generally, and of the asymmetric measure of success.

Whether initiated by an individual acting alone, or by an international group, a single terrorist success may offset many failures, while our defense against terrorists must seek to prevent or disrupt all attacks.

We confront other sources of terrorism besides al-Qa'ida and its partners, including state- sponsored organizations. I have not touched on those groups in this statement, but I would note that they certainly remain a focus of our interest.

In seeking to counter terrorism, the success of the Intelligence Community has been- and will continue to be- rooted in three critical factors.

The most important factor is the dedication, the skill, and the sharply focused attention of the Community's workforce. No counterterrorism strategy or structure can prevail without the professional achievement of these men and women and their devotion to the intelligence mission, grounded in their oaths to support and defend the Constitution. In the past ten years, we have developed an exceptional workforce that is equipped with singular capabilities. As we look to the years ahead, it will be imperative to preserve and enhance the expertise, the remarkable talents, and the high levels of competence and integrity that are routinely found in the Intelligence Community.

The other two critical factors that determine the success of the Community in countering terrorism are the integration of intelligence activities and the expansion of responsible information sharing, which is enabled by our focus on integration.

The Community has made substantial progress integrating its efforts since 9/11. The mission itself and the lessons learned from 9/11, as well as subsequent events such as the attempted AQAP attacks, underscore the importance of continuing to drive toward greater integration. We have learned a great deal and have taken numerous steps to significantly improve our counterterrorism posture, including the sharing of considerably more counterterrorism information:

- We have instituted policies and mechanisms that permit wider, responsible sharing of the most important information. At the National Counterterrorism Center (NCTC), we have created a central and shared repository for all known and suspected terrorists that catalogues interagency information and serves as the basis for sharing relevant information for the screening of airline passengers, visa applicants, immigrants, and other uses. We are pushing for even greater information integration at NCTC through the establishment of a Counterterrorism Data Layer that ingests terrorism intelligence to better position the Community to identify threats.

- Like the rest of the Community, the Central Intelligence Agency has placed principal emphasis on the prevention of another attack on the homeland and the defeat of terrorists abroad. CIA has a highly integrated partnership of analysts and operators who team routinely with US military forces, other agencies, and foreign partners to pursue and preempt terrorists abroad.

- The Federal Bureau of Investigation has transformed from its virtually exclusive concern with law enforcement to become an intelligence-driven organization that effectively cooperates with Intelligence Community partners and state and local officials to identify and prevent terrorist threats to the homeland. This transformation has notably included the expansion of the FBI-led interagency Joint Terrorism Task Forces, which are now based in 106 cities nationwide. The magnitude of the FBI's transformation is profound.

- The National Security Agency has continued to devote significant resources against high priority threats. As terrorists' operational security practices become increasingly sophisticated, NSA is adapting to address terrorists' use of the latest technologies, while taking great care to protect the civil liberties and privacy of Americans.

- The Department of Homeland Security has established an intelligence component and strengthened its ties to state, local and tribal (SLT) authorities to ensure that they can effectively identify vulnerabilities and respond to threats. In partnership with NCTC and FBI, DHS leads an Interagency Threat Assessment and Coordination Group. This Group is staffed by former and current SLT officials who review intelligence reporting and identify opportunities to further disseminate information to our SLT partners and private sector officials. DHS has also played a leading role in interaction with the National Fusion Center Network covering 50 states and 22 major urban areas.

- The Defense Intelligence Agency has established the Joint Task Force-Combating Terrorism to better support the force protection requirements of the Department of Defense and Combatant Commands, and to provide all-source, national-level terrorism intelligence analysis, warning, and enterprise integration to enable the Department's counterterrorism operations, planning, and policy.

- The National Geospatial-Intelligence Agency has worked to embed and integrate geospatial intelligence analysts and capabilities with its counterterrorism mission partners in the field and in the national community. This has allowed more direct and responsive support to the counterterrorism mission.

- The Department of Defense has partnered with select IC agencies to embed their representative at the Joint Intelligence Operations Centers to improve the support national intelligence agencies provide to combatant commanders.

All other IC components are contributing to this comprehensive mission as well, according to their unique capabilities. The Treasury Department's intelligence professionals, for example, work closely with Community partners to identify terrorist financing sources and often disrupt them through official designations.

I want to particularly note the role of NCTC, which serves as the principal analytic center for the integration of all counterterrorism intelligence, except intelligence that pertains exclusively to domestic terrorists and domestic counterterrorism. In addition, NCTC fulfills an Intelligence Community leadership role with its Director serving on my behalf as the National Intelligence Manager for Counterterrorism. In this role, NCTC identifies opportunities to advance community integration and brings Intelligence Community elements together daily to exchange information and integrate actions as needed.

We have also taken steps to ensure that we promote counterterrorism integration from the most senior levels. I chair regular sessions with the Secretary of Homeland Security and the senior leaders of the FBI, CIA, NSA, DIA, and NCTC to review critical information sharing and integration needs and drive faster responses to them.

There is no better example of the importance- and the power-of intelligence integration than the operation against Usama bin Ladin. As President Obama stated at the time, the success of that mission "marks the most significant achievement to date in our Nation's effort to defeat al-Qa'ida." The success of the operation was the direct result of the determined collection and exhaustive analysis of all available information by Intelligence Community partners across a number of agencies.

That kind of integration has increasingly become routine. As important as the bin Ladin operation was, the high level of integration it illustrated can be seen in intelligence activities every day, and is most clearly evident in the field. In Afghanistan and in many other corners of the globe, intelligence officers from different agencies routinely support each other as second nature in common efforts to achieve their missions and support those they serve. Broadening and deepening the integration of intelligence activities is particularly important to enable and promote the expansion of responsible information sharing, which remains a critical element in our effort to improve intelligence performance.

The Intelligence Community today is producing and sharing more and better streams of intelligence. We are connecting people to people, people to data, and data to data through enhanced collaboration, automation and connectivity. By overcoming policy, technical, and cultural obstacles to sharing, the Intelligence Community is working to ensure that information can be discovered, accessed, evaluated, and integrated faster and more comprehensively than ever before, while remaining consistent with the protection of civil liberties and privacy. It is clear that the progress we have made on information sharing over the last several years has been extensive, profound, and responsive to the 9/11 Commission recommendations, the Intelligence Reform and Terrorism Prevention Act of 2004, and Presidential Executive Orders. There are many examples of this improvement, ranging from the better sharing on counterterrorism matters I have noted to the creation of secure communities of interest that facilitate sharing of highly compartmented intelligence data among analysts working on a particular subject. We have also put in place mechanisms to promote easier and greater collaboration among the Community's analysts, aiming to produce more richly informed intelligence judgments and to enhance our ability to provide intelligence warning. Moreover, we have developed new and updated information sharing agreements with international partners that have enhanced our ability to track and disrupt terrorist threats and transnational criminal activities, and to bolster protection of our borders.

It is also clear, though, that more must be done. As we work towards greater sharing, we are especially mindful of the need to ensure that sharing takes place in a manner that protects against the unauthorized disclosure of information. That need was underscored by the WikiLeaks disclosures, but the importance of our mission demands that we find the best possible solutions to the inherent tension that exists between the need to share information and the need to protect its sources from disclosure. As we seek those solutions, the volume and complexity of the information that we manage and the missions and partners that we support require a broad strategy, with goals and objectives synchronized across the Intelligence Community and the Federal Government.

We are committed to that effort and to such a strategy. An essential element of our approach is improving our capabilities to safeguard our networks and classified information.

Stronger access controls will greatly increase our ability to share intelligence responsibly, and will allow us to increase the amount of intelligence that can be discovered by analysts to further improve intelligence performance.

The principal responsibility of the Director of National Intelligence since establishment of that office has been to spur such improvements and to oversee the development of the most effective Intelligence Community possible. In carrying out that responsibility, my predecessors and I have focused our efforts on three principal concerns underlying intelligence reform. First, we have worked to improve management and cohesion of the Intelligence Community. To that end, we have:

- Provided direction in the National Intelligence Strategy, with new emphasis on supporting homeland security missions, including the sharing of intelligence with law enforcement and homeland security officials at the state and local levels;

- Developed and implemented a planning, programming, budgeting and evaluation system to shape the National Intelligence Program to ensure focus on our critical missions while balancing costs and benefits;

- Led the updating and implementation of Executive Order 12333 to strengthen the ability of the DNI to lead the Intelligence Community as a unified enterprise, and to close seams between the sharing of intelligence collected domestically and intelligence collected overseas; and

- Led security clearance reform efforts, in partnership with the Department of Defense, which have updated investigative standards and reduced timelines for investigations, enabling quicker placement of individuals into key positions and supporting our efforts to keep taking the attack to al-Qa'ida.

Second, we have worked to facilitate and improve the secure sharing of intelligence and information across the Community and with a broader range of recipients. I have already noted improvements, but as a general summary we have:

- Led IC efforts to develop and implement policies that have improved the discovery and availability of intelligence;

- Established strategies for improved information sharing across the Intelligence Community and with federal, state, and local partners; and

- Led efforts to ensure the broadest possible access to, and integration of, information relating to counterterrorism, with appropriate regard for civil liberties and privacy.

Third, we have worked to improve the integration and effectiveness of intelligence. We

- Led efforts, in cooperation with these Committees and the Congress, to modernize the Foreign Intelligence Surveillance Act (FISA) to enable collection against emerging information technologies while protecting the privacy of US citizens and legal residents;

- Integrated the Drug Enforcement Agency into the Intelligence Community, enhancing the integration of intelligence and countemarcotics efforts;

- Established National Intelligence Managers to more comprehensively focus the Community's efforts against the hardest intelligence problems;

- Worked to expand intelligence production for the most senior policymakers to include broader homeland security information and analysis from DHS and the FBI; and

- Developed the Comprehensive National Cyber Initiative to enhance the Intelligence Community's capability to understand, detect, and counter threats to the Nation's information infrastructure, and to contribute to the neutralization of foreign cyber threats while incorporating privacy safeguards.

These and related efforts that we have undertaken have been aimed at increasing the ability of the Intelligence Community to take collective action in a coordinated way, working towards a more integrated enterprise than the Community that existed ten years ago. Today more than ever we are closing the seams between organizations and people, and working as one team to protect the Nation.

The progress that the Intelligence Community has achieved has been made possible by the support of the Congress, and especially by the work and the interest of the intelligence oversight committees. Over the past ten years the Congress, through legislation and oversight, has worked to ensure that the Intelligence Community's elements function effectively and efficiently and have the tools that we need.

The Intelligence Reform and Terrorism Prevention Act, for example, in addition to establishing the Office of the Director of National Intelligence to lead the Community, provided a foundation to improve information sharing and the integration of intelligence activities. The Congress has also taken action to strengthen critical intelligence capabilities in the fight against terrorism, most notably in the USA PATRIOT Act and in amendments to the Foreign Intelligence Surveillance Act.

It is essential that the Community continue its close engagement in this oversight and support relationship as we jointly look to further improve the performance of intelligence. This relationship is critical not only on matters of resources and capabilities, but also on matters of legislation that will be required to keep pace with changes in technology and other developments that affect the dynamics of intelligence.

Certainly in an era when the resources allocated to the Nation's security capabilities will be reduced, it will be critical to ensure that Congress has the best possible information on the demands placed on intelligence and the resources needed to meet those demands. We have a responsibility to provide the context and insight that will be necessary to support the decisions that Congress will make on the scope and the capacity of the Intelligence Community's capabilities.

In providing that context, we have to be clear on the extent of the work that we in the Intelligence Community must do. Our highest priority is to provide the best possible intelligence to protect the people of the United States. As this hearing today demonstrates, the threat from terrorism must be-and is-a principal concern for our resources and our energy.

The Intelligence Community is also called on, though, to provide critical support to protect the Nation- and the Nation's interests- in many other contexts. For example, we live in a world in which the dangers posed by nuclear weapons and nuclear weapons proliferation are clearly evident. We certainly have concerns about the prospect of such weapons, or other WMD, finding their way into the hands of terrorists. But we also have concerns with broader proliferation issues and implications as nations continue to seek these capabilities.

The Intelligence Community must also provide support to help meet the increasingly complex demands placed on United States foreign policy,

345

including support for efforts to capitalize on opportunities that lie in the dynamics of the shifting international environment. As we have all seen, US interests are international and the consequences of events abroad are often felt here at home.

I cite these points as examples, not to distract from the focus of today's hearing, but rather to be clear, without being exhaustive, about the breadth and the importance of the work that the Intelligence Community is charged and relied upon to do.

The Intelligence Community's men and women are carrying out that work with distinction and the Community's leaders, along with the Congress, have a responsibility to ensure that they can continue to do so in the future. To build on the progress that has been made since the attacks of 9/11, further improvements must be pursued in two main spheres of effort.

The first sphere is continued improvement in the management of the Intelligence Community, and especially the management of the National Intelligence Program (NIP) that provides the resources for the Community's capabilities. For sound reasons, the Community is constituted as a group of independent and departmental elements. This is an organizational structure that reflects the disparate demands and missions of intelligence support, yet recognizes the common purpose and the shared strengths of intelligence capabilities. Structural control and management responsibility for the resources of this enterprise, though, are similarly dispersed across departments. This disposition poses problems for the most efficient and effective management of intelligence capabilities, particularly as we move to an era of austerity in resources.

There are steps that can be taken to improve this management arrangement and enable the NIP to be managed as a coherent "whole." These steps would promote agility, accountability, efficiency, and most important, operational effectiveness. Achieving this will require considerable groundwork and will require Congressional support.

The second sphere where we will continue to seek improvement is the broad range of activities that fall into the areas of intelligence integration and information sharing. We have begun the important work of providing the necessary safeguards, through auditing and other measures, to protect intelligence in such a way that it can be shared more readily and responsibly. We will continue that work and we have a strategy in place that will maximize and integrate our sharing and protection capabilities, and strengthen the governance framework that is needed to promote further improvements.

We are similarly focused on greater integration of intelligence activities and are working to make further advances in several areas. Our highest priorities are integration measures that will:

- Better enable analysts to support operations and policymakers;

- Further integrate national intelligence assets with our military partners;

- Increase appropriate sharing with foreign partners to defeat al-Qa'ida abroad and enhance our perspectives on other issues; and

- Support closer working relationships with federal, state, local, and tribal partners.

Working to achieve these improvements will make us more efficient and make responsible information sharing a fact of life in the Intelligence Community.

Before closing, I want to emphasize an important point, which is that we in the Intelligence Community recognize that in all of our work we must exemplify America's values.

We must carry out the Intelligence Community's missions in a manner that draws strength from the richness and diversity of American communities, that retains the trust of the American people, and that remains true to the oaths we have taken to support and defend the Constitution.

Those oaths, along with the nature of intelligence work and the trust placed in us by the American people, demand that we have the highest respect for the rule of law and the protection of civil liberties and privacy. While we move forward aggressively to protect the Nation, we are committed to upholding that trust and exemplifying those values.

In summary, then, I can say that the work of the Intelligence Community over the past ten years has contributed greatly to the safety of Americans. Our efforts have taken place alongside those of many others, from first responders through the whole range of local, state, and federal elements concerned with the defense of the homeland. They have also taken place in concert with the courageous and dedicated efforts of the military and diplomatic services, whose members have carried out much of the counterterrorism effort overseas.

We have put in place remarkable capabilities and achieved significant successes. The nature of terrorism, though, and the nature of the ruthless extreme groups and individuals who subscribe to terrorist ideology, make it impossible to guarantee that every planned attack will be thwarted and every plot disrupted.

Nonetheless, we know that the character and the resilience of the United States and its people will prevail despite the efforts of those who wish to instill fear in our daily routines and alter our way of life. This Nation has risen to every challenge in its history and will continue to do so. All of us in the Intelligence Community are dedicated to taking every possible action to protect Americans and to defeat the scourge of terrorism. I can promise you and the American people that we will not relent in that effort.

Thank you for your attention and for the opportunity to appear today. I would be pleased to answer any questions that you and the other Members of the committees may have.

Appendix 4B: David H. Petraeus, Director of CIA

Statement for the Record
CIA Director David H. Petraeus
Joint Hearing to Mark the 10th Anniversary of 9/11
September 13, 2011

Chairman Feinstein, Chairman Rogers, Vice Chairman Chambliss, and Ranking Member Ruppersberger. Thank you for the opportunity to testify before this joint session of our intelligence oversight committees. And, on behalf of my Agency and my predecessor, thank you for the strong bipartisan backing and effective oversight. In significant part because of your support, today's Central Intelligence Agency is better able to protect our country and our citizens from al-Qa'ida and other terrorist groups. Simply put, the Agency is a stronger, more agile institution than it was before 9/11, and your assistance over the last decade has been critical in making us better and our nation more secure. I thank you for that.

And, here let me recognize the enormous contributions of Leon Panetta, my predecessor at the CIA. As you know, he is a principled, passionate leader who oversaw the accomplishment of some great tasks at the helm of the Agency. And Secretary Panetta will be a close and invaluable partner for us at the Department of Defense.

I want to note, as well, that I am committed to continuing along the path on which Director Panetta embarked with the committees' Members. The CIA's relationship with Congress has been strengthened over the past several years, and I will endeavor, as I emphasized during my confirmation process and in meetings with many of you since then, to strengthen it further.

And it's a pleasure to be here with the Director of National Intelligence, my good friend Jim Clapper. Jim is a true intelligence professional and a great public servant. He and I have worked together closely over the years in a variety of different posts, and I look forward to helping him forge an ever more collaborative, more effective Intelligence Community.

I welcome the opportunity today to present the Central Intelligence Agency's view of the terrorist threat a decade after the 9/11 attacks. One week into the job, but with over a decade of work in close coordination with the

349

Agency in the fight against terror, I have, as I expected, found the CIA to be a true national asset, comprised of selfless, committed, highly intelligent Americans who demonstrate impressive knowledge, skill, ingenuity, and initiative. I am proud to lead the Agency and honored to represent its truly outstanding workforce. I should note humbly, given eight days as the CIA director, that the testimony I am presenting represents the analysis of that outstanding, professional workforce. Indeed, it is a pleasure to be able to rely on the analysis of such exceptional officers in testifying on matters of such fundamental importance to our country.

As a bottom line up front: The CIA assesses that, ten years after the 9/11 attacks, the United States continues to face a serious threat from al-Qa'ida and its worldwide network of affiliates and sympathizers. Although heavy losses to al-Qa'ida's senior leadership appear to have created an important window of vulnerability for the core al- Qa'ida organization in Pakistan and Afghanistan, exploiting that window will require a sustained, focused effort. Moreover, as al-Qa'ida's core has been weakened, we must recognize that the initiative has been shifting somewhat to al-Qa'ida's affiliates and sympathizers outside South Asia. Much work remains to be done. Our nation faces a serious threat from these groups, particularly from those based in Yemen, home to Al- Qa'ida in the Arabian Peninsula, and there are other al-Qa'ida affiliates that present significant threats as well.

In the remainder of my statement, I will first describe the pressure on the core al-Qa'ida organization, then discuss the danger that al-Qa'ida and its affiliates still pose, and then outline the keys to further progress against this enemy, including some of the steps we are taking with our partners throughout the US Government and with our friends overseas.

Core al-Qa'ida Under Growing Strain...

For more than a decade, al-Qa'ida's senior leadership and core organization in Pakistan and Afghanistan have been capable of planning and executing dangerous plots targeting the West. Today, as a result of sustained counterterrorism efforts, a substantial number with our partners in Pakistan and Afghanistan, that core part of al- Qa'ida's organization is much weaker and less capable than when it attacked us on 9/11.

Usama Bin Ladin's death in May dealt a stunning blow to al-Qa'ida. Bin Ladin was, of course, an iconic figure, the group's only leader since its founding. We know now that he was deeply involved until the end in directing al-Qa'ida's operations and strategy more deeply involved than many assessed before we were able to exploit the materials found with him.

Bin Ladin's longtime deputy, Ayman al-Zawahiri, succeeded him in June, but much of al-Qa'ida's support base finds Zawahiri less compelling as a leader. We thus assess that he will have more difficulty than did Usama bin Ladin in maintaining the group's cohesion and its collective motivation in the face of continued pressure.

The layer of top lieutenants under Bin Ladin and Zawahiri—the group responsible for day-to-day management of al-Qa'ida and its operations—has sustained significant losses in recent years as well. Those losses have been especially severe among terrorist plotters, paramilitary commanders, trainers, and bombmakers. Just last week, Pakistan announced the capture with US assistance of Younis al-Mauritani, a senior al-Qa'ida operative who was involved in planning attacks against the interests of the United States and many other countries. Last month, al- Qa'ida lost its second-in- command and senior operational coordinator, Atiyah Abd al-Rahman. That followed the death in June of Ilyas Kashmiri, a senior operational commander. And the organization is struggling to find qualified replacements.

These setbacks have shaken al-Qa'ida's sense of security in Pakistan's tribal areas, driving the remaining leaders underground to varying degrees and shifting a good bit of their attention from terrorist plotting to security and survival. In fact, some mid-level leaders and rank-and-file al-Qa'ida members may increasingly seek safehaven across the border in Afghanistan or decide to leave South Asia. Senior leaders will find it riskier to move and may remain in Pakistan's tribal areas, where trusted local facilitators offer limited freedom of movement, but where their security is threatened. The upshot is that it will, of course, be more difficult to attract and accommodate would-be jihadists wanting to travel to the tribal areas of Pakistan.

All of this amounts, again, to a window of vulnerability for core al-Qa'ida—and a window of opportunity for us and our allies. We must maintain the pressure. We must exploit the opportunity.

. . . But Remains a Serious Threat

Even in decline, with its core leadership having sustained significant losses, al-Qa'ida and its affiliates still pose a very real threat that will require our energy, focus, creativity, and dedication for quite a while. Al-Qa'ida's operatives remain committed to attacks against United States citizens at home and overseas, both to demonstrate strength in the wake of Bin Ladin's death and to continue pursuit of one of al-Qa'ida's principal goals—forcing the United States and a number of our allies to retreat from the world stage. Al-Qa'ida's leaders continue to believe this would clear the way for overthrowing governments in the Islamic world and for the destruction of Israel.

Moreover, despite being less able to conduct large-scale attacks, al-Qa'ida and its sympathizers *do* continue to train and deploy operatives in small numbers for overseas plots. Many of these operatives have nationalities and backgrounds that make them well suited for targeting the United States and Europe. Increasingly, in fact, we see signs of al-Qa'ida's efforts to carry out relatively small attacks that would, nonetheless, generate fear and create the need for costly security improvements. Indeed, we should not forget that one of al-Qa'ida's goals is to force the US and our allies to adopt additional, expensive security safeguards that would further burden our economies. Though we have made very real progress in the campaign to disrupt, dismantle, and defeat al-Qa'ida, we are in this for the long haul.

Initiative Shifting to Affiliates

As I mentioned earlier, the extremist initiative is, to some degree, shifting to al-Qa'ida's affiliates outside South Asia. While linked to al-Qa'ida central, these groups have their own command structures, resource bases, and operational agendas, and they largely operate autonomously. Working with our local partners to cooperate against these affiliates will continue to be crucial to the success of our overall efforts to disrupt, dismantle, and defeat al-Qa'ida's global network.

Al-Qa'ida in the Arabian Peninsula, or AQAP, has emerged as *the* most dangerous regional node in the global jihad. Since December 2009, the group has attempted two attacks on the United States: a plot to blow up a US airliner as it approached Detroit in 2009, and an effort to send bombs hidden in computer printers on two cargo aircraft in 2010. AQAP continues to plot strikes against our nation, US interests worldwide, and our allies.

Since May, moreover, AQAP has launched an offensive against the Yemeni Government in parts of southern Yemen, expelling many government forces from that region and increasing AQAP's freedom of movement. Political unrest in Yemen has helped AQAP co-opt local tribes and extend its influence. Despite all of this, counterterrorism cooperation with Yemen has, in fact, improved in the past few months. That is very important, as we clearly have to intensify our collaboration and deny AQAP the safehaven that it seeks to establish.

State failure and the expansion of extremist networks over the past two decades have made southern Somalia one of the world's most significant havens for terrorists. Al- Qa'ida's affiliate there—al-Shabaab—is large and well-funded relative to most extremist groups, and it has attracted and trained hundreds of foreign fighters, including scores of Americans and dozens from other Western countries. Al-Shabaab suicide bombings in Uganda last year demonstrated the group's ability to operate beyond Somalia.

Sustained pressure on the relatively small circle of leaders and foreign fighters driving al-Shabaab's terrorist plotting and outreach to al-Qa'ida could persuade the organization to turn away from global jihad. Indeed, both the top al-Qa'ida operative in East Africa, Harun Fazul, and the al-Shabaab mastermind behind the Uganda bombings were killed this past June. And Fazul's protégé was killed two years earlier, and al-Shabaab fighters recently left Mogadishu under pressure from African Union troops. Nonetheless, we must continue our work to reduce al-Shabaab's capabilities.

Al-Qa'ida in the Lands of the Islamic Maghreb, or AQIM, has targeted Western interests throughout Northern and Western Africa while continuing to battle the security forces of Algeria, Mali, and Mauritania. Indeed, AQIM staged a deadly double-suicide bombing late last month against the Algerian military. We are working with our regional partners and France to counter AQIM, and those efforts have helped to prevent a significant attack by AQIM against Western interests since late 2007.

In Nigeria, the extremist group Boko Haram conducted a suicide car-bombing in late August against the UN building in Abuja, marking Boko Haram's first known lethal operation against Westerners. Our regional counterparts have stepped up their efforts against this target in the last several months. We work closely with our partners on this threat, and we will seek to intensify our support.

Al-Qa'ida in Iraq, or AQI, has sustained significant losses since the surge in 2007, and it is much farther than it was in 2007 from realizing its goal of overthrowing the government in Baghdad or controlling some portion of Iraq. Nonetheless, AQI remains capable of carrying out sensational attacks, as it showed in mid-August, and the Agency believes that AQI will remain capable of inflicting casualties on government forces and civilians at least through the next few years. Its core members share al-Qa'ida's desire to expand the global jihad, and that could lead AQI to attempt attacks outside Iraq.

Finally, the number of al-Qa'ida-affiliated operatives in Southeast Asia has been significantly reduced over the last decade, thanks to aggressive counterterrorism measures by regional governments. Jemaah Islamiyah—the group responsible for the Bali attacks in 2002 and 2005—has, for example, suffered major losses and is largely focused on rebuilding. Additionally, many terrorist leaders in Southeast Asia are now dead—such as Noordin Top, who planned the July 2009 hotel bombings in Jakarta—or in jail, such as Abu Bakar Bashir, the spiritual leader of extremism in Southeast Asia.

Keys to Future Success

The CIA's global campaign against al-Qa'ida and its affiliates requires both offensive and defensive measures, and they will need to be sustained over a long period to be effective. We target terrorist leaders, for example, to deny them the resources and breathing space needed to plot operations against us and our allies. We cooperate with our foreign partners wherever possible; it is often better to help them than to carry out operations ourselves. Nonetheless, we do act unilaterally when we must.

Our officers work hard to identify and intercept operatives before they can execute attacks, as they did by thwarting al-Qa'ida's plot to smuggle liquid explosives onto transatlantic flights in 2006 and the plot to attack the New York subway in 2009. In a similar fashion, we worked closely with friendly services in the Middle East to help stop AQAP's printer bombs before they could detonate.

We owe these successes to improved tradecraft resulting from the fusion of intelligence disciplines, tight integration with other agencies and the military, the sharing of intelligence with foreign partners, and to the Committees' support. We assess that the Agency and its elements are better at each of these actions now than we were before 9/11. But al-Qa'ida and its affiliates *have* proven resilient. Clearly, we must never underestimate our enemies. And, we at CIA must continue to refine our tactics, techniques, and procedures.

Over the past decade, intelligence collectors, analysts, and technical experts have forged closer, more effective relationships, leading to new flows of vital information and, more importantly, new insights into how and where terrorists operate. That integration of analysis and operations, each feeding the other, has been at the heart of our most important successes.

In fact, our relationships with others in the Intelligence Community and with law enforcement agencies are closer and more cooperative than ever. Improvements in the Watchlisting program and other interagency reporting methods allow us, for example, to quickly disseminate actionable intelligence to federal, state, and local agencies at the lowest possible classification level. We continue to work with the DNI and National Counterterrorism Center to enhance this process and to improve the application of Community resources.

The CIA's close collaboration with the military and with our Intelligence Community partners in taking down Usama Bin Ladin reflected the advances our government has made toward achieving a unified counterterrorism effort. That was, indeed, a success born of interagency collaboration and cooperation.

Our counterterrorism cooperation with governments in Europe, the Mideast, South Asia, and elsewhere around the world is also very strong. Working with our allies and partners, we have disrupted dozens of terrorist plots, and we have arrested hundreds of key operatives and facilitators.

All of this must—and will—continue. Indeed, the Intelligence Community has to continue to be a learning organization, and the CIA will do all that it can to contribute to that effort.

Conclusion

In sum, the structures and processes put in place since the 9/11 attacks have made our government more capable and more effective in carrying out our critical counterterrorism mission—and in protecting our fellow citizens. The key in the Central Intelligence Agency has, of course, been its people—the individuals who, at our Headquarters and in our Stations and Bases around the world, have quietly, selflessly, and expertly gone about the hard work of defending Americans from the constant threat of terrorism. *They* have been the key. In so doing, they and their families have made great sacrifices. We can never thank them enough for that. It is my great privilege to serve with them, to be their Director, and, indeed, to be their advocate.

Thank you very much.

Appendix Notes and References

1. United States District Court, Southern District of New York, "Text: United States Grand Jury Indictment against Usama bin Laden." November 6, 1998. *http://www.fas.org/irp/news/1998/11/98110602_ nlt.html.*

2. The White House, "Remarks by the President on Osama bin Laden." May 2, 2011. *http://www.whitehouse.gov/the-press-office/2011/05/02/ remarks-president-osama-bin-laden.*

3. Brennan, John O. Paul H. Nitze School of Advanced International Studies, "Ensuring al-Qa'ida's Demise." June 29, 2011. *http://www. sais-jhu.edu/bin/a/h/2011-06-29-john-brennan-remarks-sais.pdf.*

4. The White House, "National Strategy for Counterterrorism." June 2011. *http://www.whitehouse.gov/sites/default/files/counterterrorism_ strategy.pdf.*

5. The White House, "Empowering Local Partners to Prevent Violent Extremism in the United States." August 2011. *http://www.whitehouse. gov/sites/default/files/empowering_local_partners.pdf.*

6. Clapper, James R. Senate Select Committee on Intelligence and House Permanent Select Committee on Intelligence, "Joint Hearing to Mark the 10th Anniversary of 9/11." September 13, 2011. *http://intelligence. senate.gov/110913/clapper.pdf.*

7. Petraeus, David P. Senate Select Committee on Intelligence and House Permanent Select Committee on Intelligence, "Joint Hearing to Mark the 10th Anniversary of 9/11." September 13, 2011. *http://intelligence. senate.gov/110913/petraeus.pdf.*

Selected Bibliography

Books

Alexander, M. *Kill or Capture: How a Special Operations Task Force Took Down a Notorious Al-Qaeda Terrorist*. New York: St. Martin's Press; 2011.

Alexander, Y, ed. *Counterterrorism Strategies: Successes and Failures of Six Nations*. Dulles, VA: Potomac Books Inc; 2006.

Alexander, Y. *Terrorists in Our Midst: Combating Foreign Affinity Terrorism in America*. Santa Barbara, CA: Praeger; 2010.

Alexander, Y; Brenner EH, and Krause, ST, eds. *Turkey: Terrorism, Civil Rights, and the European Union*. New York: Routledge; 2008.

Alexander, Y, and Donald, JM, eds. *Terrorism, Documents of International and Local Control*. Vol. 35. Dobbs Ferry, New York: Oceana; 2002.

Alexander, Y and Hoenig, M. *The New Iranian Leadership: Ahmadinejad, Terrorism, Nuclear Ambition and the Middle East*. Santa Barbara, CA: Praeger; 2007.

Alexander, Y, and Kraft, M, eds. *Evolution of U.S. Counterterrorism Policy* (three volumes). Santa Barbara, CA: Praeger; 2007.

Alexander, Y, and Richardson, TB, eds. *Terror on the High Seas: From Piracy to Strategic Challenge*. Santa Barbara, CA: Praeger; 2009.

Alexander, Y, and Swetnam, MS. *Usama bin Laden's al-Qaida: Profile of a Terrorist Network* New York: Transnational Publishers; 2001.

Al-Zayyat, M, and Nimis, S. *The Road to Al-Qaeda: The Story of Bin Laden's Right-Hand Man*. London: Pluto Press; 2004.

Amoore, Louise de GM. *Risk and the War on Terror* New York: Routledge; 2008.

Atwan, A-B. *The Secret History of Al Qaeda*. Berkeley, CA: University of California Press; 2008.

Barnett, TPM. *The Pentagon's New Map: War and Peace in the Twenty-First Century*. Berkeley Trade; 2005.

Benjamin, D, and Simon, S. *The Age of Sacred Terror*. New York: Random House; 2002.

Bergen, PL. *The Longest War: America and Al-Qaeda Since 9/11*. New York: The Free Press; 2011.

Berntsen, G, and Pezzullo, R. *The Attack on Bin Laden and Al-Qaeda: A Personal Account by the CIA's Key Field Commander*. New York: Three Rivers Press; 2006.

Bigo, D, and Tsoukala, A, eds. *Terror, Insecurity and Liberty*. New York: Routledge; 2008.

bin Laden, O; bin Laden, N, and Sasson, J. *Growing up bin Laden: Osama's Wife and Son Take Us Inside Their Secret World*. New York: St. Martin's Press; 2009.

Binkley, B. *Al-Qaeda Strikes Again*. Concord, MA: Infinity Publishing; 2008.

Blin, A, and Chalian, G. *History of Terrorism: From Antiquity to Al Qaeda*. Berkeley, CA: University of California Press; 2007.

Bodansky, Y. *Chechen Jihad: Al Qaeda's Training Ground and the Next Wave of Terror*. New York: Harper Paperbacks; 2009.

Boucek, C and Ottaway, M. *Yemen on the Brink*. Washington, DC: Carnegie Endowment for International Peace; 2010.

Brachman, J. *Global Jihadism Theory and Practice (Cass Series on Political Violence)*. New York: Routledge; 2009.

Brantley, C. *Global Terror: An Overview of the Al-Qaeda Organization, Ideology and Leaders, Including Osama Bin Laden, Ayman Al-Zawahiri, Abu Musa*. UK: Lightning Source UK Ltd; 2011.

Brecher, B; Devenney, M, and Winter, A, eds. *Discourses and Practices of Terrorism: Interrogating Terror*. New York: Routledge; 2010.

Burgat, F and Hutchinson, P. *Islamism in the Shadow of Al-Qaeda*. Austin, TX: University of Texas Press; 2008.

Burke, J. *Al-Qaeda: The True Story of Radical Islam*. London, UK: Penguin; 2007.

Burleigh, M. *Sacred Causes: Religion and Politics from the European Dictators to Al Qaeda*. New York: Harper Perennial; 2007.

Caldwell, D. *Vortex of Conflict: U.S. Policy Toward Afghanistan, Pakistan, and Iraq*. Stanford, CA: Stanford Security Studies; 2011.

Cleland, R. *Al Qaeda's New Strategy: Getting Back to Basics*. Victoria, Canada: Trafford Publishing; 2010.

Coolsaet, R and Peeters, E. *Al-Qaeda: the Myth: The Root Causes of International Terrorism and How to Tackle Them*. Ghent, Belgium: Academia Press; 2005.

Couch, CI. *Managing Terrorism and Insurgency: Regeneration, Recruitment and Attrition*. New York: Routledge; 2009.

Crews, RD and Tarzi, A. *The Taliban and the Crisis of Afghanistan.* Cambridge, MA: Harvard University Press; 2009.

Cronin, AK. *Ending Terrorism: Lessons for Policymakers from the Decline and Demise of Terrorist Groups (Adelphi Papers).* New York: Routledge; 2007.

Cruickshank, P. *Al Qaeda (Critical Concepts in Political Science).* London, UK: Routledge Publishing; 2011.

Davis, PK and Jenkins, BM. *Deterrence and Influence in Counterterrorism: A Component in the War on Al Qaeda.* San Diego, CA: RAND Publishing; 2002.

Devetak, R and Hughes, CW, eds. *Globalization and Political Violence: Globalization's Shadow* (Warwick Studies in Globalization). London, England: Routledge; 2008.

Emerson, S. American Jihad: *The Terrorists Living Among Us.* NY: The Free Press; 2002.

Fury, D. *Kill Bin Laden: A Delta Force Commander's Account of the Hunt for the World's Most Wanted Man.* New York: St. Martin's Griffin; 2009.

Gartenstein-Ross, D. *Why al Qaeda Is Winning: The War We're Fighting, and the War We Think We're Fighting.* New York: Wiley Publishing; 2011.

Geltzer, JA. *US Counter-Terrorism Strategy and Al-Qaeda: Signalling and the Terrorist World-View.* London, UK: Routledge; 2011.

Gerges, FA. *The Rise and Fall of Al-Qaeda.* Oxford: Oxford University Press; 2011.

Graff, GM. *The Threat Matrix: The FBI at War in the Age of Global Terror.* New York: Little, Brown and Company; 2011.

Gray, J. *Al Qaeda and What It Means to be Modern.* London: Faber and Faber; 2007.

Gupta, DK. *Understanding Terrorism and Political Violence (Case Series on Political Violence).* New York: Routledge; 2008.

Hamm, MS. *Terrorism as Crime: From Oklahoma City to Al-Qaeda and Beyond.* New York: New York University Press; 2007.

Harmon, CC. *Terrorism Today (Cass Series on Political Violence).* 2nd ed. New York: Routledge; 2007.

Harrison, J. *International Aviation and Terrorism.* New York: Routledge; 2009.

Harvey, FP. *The Homeland Security Dilemma: Imagination, Failure and the Escalating of Perfecting Security.* New York: Routledge; 2008.

Hassan, HA. *Al-Qaeda: The Background of the Pursuit for Global Jihad.* Almqvist & Wiksell International; 2004.

Hellmich, C. *Al-Qaeda: From Global Network to Local Franchise - Rebels.* London: Zed Books; 2011.

Horgan, J. and Tore, Bjorgo, eds. *Leaving Terrorism Behind: Individual and Collective Disengagement.* Milton Park, Abingdon, Oxon: Routledge; 2009.

Horgan, J; and Braddock, K. eds. *Terrorism Studies: A Reader.* New York: Taylor and Francis; 2009.

Horgan, J. *Walking Away from Terrorism (Case Series on Political Violence).* New York: Routledge; 2008.

Hull, EJ. *High-Value Target: Countering Al Qaeda in Yemen.* VA: Potomac Books Inc; 2011.

Hutchinson, P and Burgat, F. *Islamism in the Shadow of al-Qaeda.* Austin, TX: University of Texas Press; 2010.

Ibrahim, A, and Venzke, B. *The Al-Qaeda Threat: An Analytical Guide to Al-Qaeda's Tactics & Targets.* Tempest Pub; 2003.

Ibrahim, R. *The Al Qaeda Reader.* New York: Broadway Books; 2007.

Isby, DC. *Afghanistan: Graveyard of Empires: A New History of the Borderland.* Winnipeg, Canada: Pegasus Publishing; 2010.

Jenkins, B. *Countering Al Qaeda: An Appreciation of the Situation and Suggestions for Strategy.* San Diego, CA: RAND Publishing; 2002.

Jones, SG. *In the Graveyard of Empires: America's War in Afghanistan.* New York: W. W. Norton & Company; 2010.

Kaplan, J. *Terrorist Groups and the New Tribalism: The Fifth Wave of Terrorism (Case Series on Political Violence).* New York: Routledge; 2010.

Keegan, J. *Intelligence in War: Knowledge of the Enemy from Napoleon to Al-Qaeda.* Toronto, Canada: Key Porter Books; 2003.

Keenan, J. *The Dark Sahara: America's War on Terror in Africa.* London: Pluto Press; 2009.

Keppel, G. *Jihad: The Trail of Political Islam.* Boston: Harvard UP; 2002.

Kessler, R. *The Terrorist Watch: Inside the Desperate Race to Stop the Next Attack.* New York: Crown Forum; 2007.

Kupperman, R and Kamen, J. *Final Warning: Averting Disaster in the New Age of Terrorism.* Doubleday; 1989.

Lambert, R. *Countering Al Qaeda in London.* London: C Hurst & Co Publishers; 2011.

Lang, Jr. AF. *War, Torture, and Terrorism*. New York: Routledge; 2008.

Lankford, A. *Human Killing Machines: Systematic Indoctrination in Iran, Nazi Germany, Al Qaeda, and Abu Ghraib*. Lanham, MD: Lexington Books; 2010.

Levin, C. *The Iraq-Al Qaeda Relationship: An Alternative Analysis*. Scotts Valley, CA: Cosimo Reports; 2005.

Lia, B. *Architect of Global Jihad: The Life of Al-Qaeda Strategist Abu Mus'ab Al-Suri*. London: C Hurst & Publishers; 2009.

Lutz, BJ, and Lutz, JM. *Global Terrorism*. New York: Routledge; 2008.

Mackey, C, and Miller, G. *The Interrogators: Task Force 500 and America's Secret War Against Al Qaeda*. New York: Little, Brown and Company; 2005.

Mandaville, P. *Global Political Islam*. New York: Routledge; 2007.

Mardini, R. *The Battle for Yemen: Al-Qaeda and the Struggle for Stability*. Washington, DC: The Jamestown Foundation; 2011.

Marlin, RO. *What Does Al Qaeda Want: Unedited Communiqués*. Berkeley, CA: North Atlantic Books; 2005.

Masters, EM. *Breaking al-Qaeda: Psychological and Operational Techniques*. Scotts Valley, CA: CreateSpace; 2010.

Menelik, G. *Finances and Networks of Al-Qaeda Terrorists*. Munich, Germany: GRIN Verlag; 2009.

Miniter, R. *Mastermind: The Many Faces of the 9/11 Architect, Khalid Shaikh Mohammed*. New York: Sentinel HC; 2011.

Mockaitis, TR. *Osama bin Laden: A Biography*. Westport, CT: Greenwood Publishing Group; 2010.

Moghadam, A. *The Globalization of Martyrdom: Al Qaeda, Salafi Jihad, and the Diffusion of Suicide Attacks*. Baltimore, MD: Johns Hopkins University Press; 2011.

Mohamedou, M. *Understanding Al Qaeda: Changing War and Global Politics*. London: Pluto Press; 2011.

Mueller, J. *Atomic Obsession: Nuclear Alarmism from Hiroshima to Al Qaeda*. Oxford: Oxford University Press; 2009.

Naylor, DH. *Al Qaeda in Iraq*. Hauppauge, NY: Nova Science Publishers; 2009.

Neal, A. *Exceptionalism and the War on Terror: The Politics of Liberty and Security after 9/11*. New York: Routledge; 2008.

Neumann, PR. *Joining Al-Qaeda: Jihadist Recruitment in Europe*. London: Routledge; 2009.

Norman, P. *Understanding Contemporary Terrorism and the Global Response*. New York: UCLP; 2006.

Peters, G. *Seeds of Terror: How Heroin is Bankrolling the Taliban and Al Qaeda*. Oxford: Oneworld Publications; 2011.

Pope, H. *Dining with al-Qaeda: Three Decades Exploring the Many Worlds of the Middle East*. New York: Thomas Dunne Books; 2010.

Post, JM. *The Mind of the Terrorist: The Psychology of Terrorism from the IRA to al-Qaeda*. Basingstoke, UK: Palgrave Macmillan; 2009.

Rashid, A. *Taliban: Militant Islam, Oil and Fundamentalism in Central Asia*. New Haven, CT: Yale University Press; 2010.

Ressa, M. *Seeds of Terror: An Eyewitness Account of Al-Qaeda's Newest Center*. New York: Free Press; 2011.

Riedel, B. *Deadly Embrace: Pakistan, America, and the Future of Global Jihad*. Washington, DC: Brookings Institution; 2011.

Riedel, B. *The Search for Al Qaeda: Its Leadership, Ideology, and Future*. Washington, DC: Brookings Institution; 2010.

Sans, C. *Al-Qaeda in Egypt: A Brief History of Islamic Jihad Within Mubarak's Egypt*. UK: Lightning Source UK Ltd; 2011 .

Scaglia, B. *Beyond Osama: The Al-Qaeda Organization and the Continued Rise of Militant Islam*. Webster's Digital Services; 2011.

Scheuer, M. *Osama Bin Laden*. Oxford: Oxford University Press; 2011.

Schmid, JA, and Price, E, eds. *Handbook of Terrorism Research, Theories and Concepts*. New York: Routledge; 2008.

Shahzad, SS. *Inside Al-Qaeda and the Taliban Beyond 9/11*. London: Pluto Press; 2011.

Shinn, D. *Al Shabaab's Foreign Threat to Somalia*. Orbis. 2011.

Silber, MD. *The Al Qaeda Factor: Plots Against The West*. Philadelphia, PA: University of Pennsylvania; 2011.

Silverman, ME. *Awakening Victory: How Iraqi Tribes and American Troops Reclaimed Al Anbar and defeated Al Qaeda in Iraq*. Havertown, PA: Casemate Publishers; 2011.

Soufan, A. *The Black Banners: Inside the Hunt for Al Qaeda*. New York: W. W. Norton & Company; 2011.

Taylor, P. *Talking to Terrorists: Face to Face with the Enemy: A Personal Journey from the IRA to Al Qaeda*. New York: Harper Press; 2011.

Tucker, J. *War of Nerves: Chemical Warfare from World War I to Al-Qaeda*. New York: Anchor Books; 2007.

Uhl-Bien, M, and Marion, R. *Complexity Theory and Al Qaeda: Examining Complex Leadership.* Management Department Faculty Publications: University of Nebraska— Lincoln; 2003.

van Linschoten, AS, and Kuehn, F. *An Enemy We Created: The Myth of the Taliban/Al-Qaeda Merger in Afghanistan,* 1970-2010. London: C Hurst & Co Publishers; 2011.

Vinci, A. *Armed Groups and the Balance of Power.* New York: Routledge; 2008.

Wilkinson, P. *Homeland Security in the UK.* New York: Routledge; 2007.

Woodward, B. *Bush at War.* New York: Simon and Schuster; 2002.

Woodward, B. *Plan of Attack.* New York: Simon and Schuster; 2004.

Woodward, B. *Obama's Wars.* New York: Simon & Schuster; 2010.

Wright, L. *The Looming Tower: Al Qaeda's Road to 9/11.* London: Penguin; 2007.

Articles

Aldrich, GH. "The Taliban, Al Qaeda, and the Determination of Illegal Combatants." *The American Journal of International Law.* 2002 Oct; 96(4): 891-898.

Beinart, P, and Katherine, T. "The Almanac of Al Qaeda." *Foreign Policy* [Internet]. 2010 May/June [cited 2011 Aug 8]. Available from: *http:// www.foreignpolicy.com/articles/2010/04/26/the_almanac_of_al_ qaeda.*

Bell, JT. "Trying Al Qaeda: Bringing Terrorists to Justice." *Perspectives on Terrorism.* 2010 Oct. 4; (4): 73-81.

Brachman, JM. "Stealing Al Qaeda's Playbook. *Studies in Conflict and Terrorism.*" 2006 June; 29(4): 309-321.

Braniff, B, and Moghadam, A. "Towards Global Jihadism: Al-Qaeda's Strategic, Ideological and Structural Adaptations since 9/11." *Perspectives on Terrorism.* 2011 May; 5(2): 36-49.

Burke, J. "Al Qaeda is a Global Terrorist Organization." *Foreign Policy* [Internet]. 2004 May [cited 2011 Aug 8]. Available from: *http://www. foreignpolicy.com/articles/2004/05/01/think_again_al_qaeda.*

Byman, DL. "Review: Al-Qaeda as an Adversary: Do We Understand Our Enemy?" *World Politics.* 2003 Oct; 56(1): 139-163.

Coll, S. "The Outlaw." *New Yorker* [Internet]; 2011 May [cited 2011 Aug 8]. Available from: *http://www.newyorker.com/ reporting/2011/05/16/110516fa_fact_coll.*

Cragin, RK. "Early History of al-Qa'ida." *The Historical Journal.* 2008 Dec; 51(4): 1047-10067.

Cronin, AK. "How al-Qaida Ends: The Decline and Demise of Terrorist Groups." *International Security.* 2006; 31(1): 7-48.

Cronin, AK. "Behind the Curve: Globalization and International Terrorism." *International Security.* 2002/2003; 27(3): 30-58.

Dickey, C. "Women of Al Qaeda." *Harman Newsweek LLC* [Internet]. 2005 [cited 2011 Aug 8]. Available from: *http://www.thedailybeast.com/newsweek/2010/01/12/divorce-jihadi-style.html.*

Doran, M. "The Pragmatic Fanaticism of al Qaeda: An Anatomy of Extremism in Middle Eastern Politics." *Political Science Quarterly.* 2002; 117(2): 177-190.

Eilstrup-Sangiovanni, M. "Assessing the Dangers of Illicit Networks: Why Al-Qaida May be Less Threatening than Many Think." *International Security.* 2008 Fall; 33(2): 7-44.

Fettweis, C. "Freedom Fighters and Zealots: Al Qaeda in Historical Perspective." *Political Science Quarterly.* 2009; 124(2): 269-296.

Froneberger, T. "Support Networks of Terrorists Within the US." *Journal of Counterterrorism & Homeland Security International.* 2010 Winter; 16(4): 20-24.

Gartenstein-Ross D. "The Strategic Challenge of Somalia's Al-Shabaab." *Middle East Quarterly;* 2009; 16(4): 25-36.

Gomes, JMdC. "A Financial Profile of the Terrorism of Al-Qaeda and its Affiliates." *Perspectives on Terrorism.* 2010 Oct; 4 (4): 3-27.

Gonzalez-Perez, M. "The False Islamization of Female Suicide Bombers." *Gender Issues.* 2011 April; 28(1-2): 50-65.

Gray, DH, and Head, A. "The Importance of the Internet to the Post-Modern Terrorist and its Role as a Form of Safe Haven." *European Journal of Scientific Research.* 2009 Jan; 25(3): 396-404.

Greenwood, C. "International Law and the 'War against Terrorism." *International Affairs* (Royal Institute of International Affairs 1944). 2002 Apr; 78(2): 301-317.

Hegghammer, T. "Global Jihadism after the Iraq War." *Middle East Journal.* 2006 Winter; 32(4): 11-32.

Heifetz, S, and Wolosky, L. "Regulating Terrorism." *Law & Policy in International Business.* 2002; 34(1): 1-5.

Hellmich, C. "Al-Qaeda: Terrorists, Hypocrites, Fundamentalists? The View from Within." *Third World Quarterly.* 2005; 26(1): 39-54.

Heymann, PB, "Dealing with Terrorism: An Overview." *International Security.* 2001/2002; 26(3): 24-38.

Hobbs, JJ. "The Geographical Dimensions of Al-Qa'ida Rhetoric." *Geographical Review.* 2005 July; 95(3): 301-327.

Hoffman, B. "Terrorism in the West: Al Qaeda's Role in "Homegrown" Terror"." *Brown Journal of World Affairs* [Internet]. 2007 April [cited 2011 Aug 8]; 13(2). Available from: *http://www.bjwa.org/article.php?id =7g2aY29l77OM6LeiDWkwN3o0xvDb53Ysn3fc7sCh.*

Hoffman, FG. "Al Qaeda's Demise - Or Evolution." *Proceedings Magazine,* U.S Naval Institute. 2008 Sept; 134(9): 19-22.

Ibrahim, M. "Somalia and Global Terrorism: A Growing Connection?" *Journal of Contemporary African Studies.* 2010; 28(3): 283-295.

IC Publications Ltd. *Evading the net: Al Qaeda triumvirate of terror.* 2010. Available from: *http://findarticles.com/p/articles/mi_m2742/is_417/ ai_n56516356/?tag=mantle_skin;content.*

Jones, C. "Al-Qaeda's Innovative Improvisers: Learning in a Diffuse Transnational Network." *Review Literature and Arts of the Americas.* 2006; 19(4): 555-569.

Klein, A. "The End of Al Qaeda: Rethinking the Legal End of the War on Terror.".*Columbia Law Review.* 2010 June; 110(5): 1865-1910.

Laipson, E. "While America Slept: Understanding Terrorism and Counterterrorism." *Foreign Affairs* [Internet]. 2003 Jan [cited 2011 Aug 8]. Available from: *http://www.foreignaffairs.com/articles/58630/ ellen-laipson/while-america-slept-understanding-terrorism-and-counterterrorism.*

Lebowitz, MJ. "The Value of Claiming Torture: An Analysis of Al Qaeda's Tactical Lawfare: Strategy and Efforts to Fight Back." *Case Western Reserve University Journal of International Law.* 2011; 43: 357-392.

Lewis, WH. "The War on Terrorism: A Retrospective." *Mediterranean Quarterly.* 2002 Fall; 13: 21-37.

McCabe, TR. "The Strategic Failures of al Qaeda." *Parameters.* 2010 April; 40(1): 60-71.

Mendelsohn, B. "Sovereignty Under Attack: The International Society Meets the Al Qaeda Network." *Review of International Studies.* 2005; 31: 45-68.

Mohamed, I. "Somalia and Global Terrorism: A Growing Connection." *Journal of Contemporary African Studies.* 2010; 28(3): 283-295.

Mokhtari, F. "Dealing with Al Qaeda." *American Foreign Policy Interests.* 2010 March-April; 32(2): 75-82.

Naím, M. "Al Qaeda, the NGO." *Foreign Policy* [Internet]. 2002 March [cited 2011 Aug 8]. Available from: *http://www.foreignpolicy.com/ articles/2002/03/01/al_qaeda_the_ngo.*

Orhan, M. "Al-Qaeda: Analysis of the Emergence, Radicalism, and Violence of a Jihadist Action Group in Turkey." *Turkish Studies.* 2010 June; 11(2): 143-161.

Ould Mohamedou, M-M. "The Militarization of Islamism: Al-Qa'ida and Its Transnational Challenge." *The Muslim World.* 2011; 101(2): 307-323.

Passos, N. "Fighting Terror With Error: The Counter-Productive Regulation of Informal Value Transfers." *Crime, Law, and Social Change.* 2006 Nov 11; 45: 315-21.

Pham, PJ. "Foreign Influences and Shifting Horizons: The Ongoing Evolution of al Qaeda in the Islamic Maghreb." *Orbis.* 2011 Feb: 240-254.

Revell, O. "Law Enforcement Views Radical Islam: Protecting America." *The Middle East Quarterly.* 1995 March; 2(1): 3-8.

Riedel, B, and Saab, BY. "Al Qaeda's Third Front: Saudi Arabia." *The Washington Quarterly.* 2008; 31(2): 33-46.

Riedel, B. "Al Qaeda Strikes Back." *Foreign Affairs* [Internet]. 2007 May/ June [cited 2011 Aug 8]. Available from: *http://www.foreignaffairs.com/ articles/62608/bruce-riedel/al-qaeda-strikes-back.*

Ronfeldt, D. "Al Qaeda and its Affiliates: A Global Tribe Waging Segmental War." *Information Strategy and Warfare: A Guide to Theory and Practice.* Routledge. 2007; p. 34-55.

Schanzer, J. "The Al Qaeda Reader." *Middle East Quarterly.* 2009 April; 16(2): 86-95.

Schwartz, S. "The Terrorist War against Islam: Clarifying Academic Confusions." *Academic Questions.* 2011; 24(1): 59-73.

Shavit, U. "Al-Qaeda's Saudi Origins." *Middle East Quarterly.* 2006; 13(4): 3-13.

Steger, MB. "Religion and Ideology in the Global Age: Analyzing al Qaeda's Islamist Globalism." *New Political Science.* 2009 Dec; 31(4): 529-541.

Stenersen, A. "Blood Brothers or a Marriage of Convenience? The Ideological Relationship between al-Qaida and the Taliban." *International Studies Convention.* 2009 Feb 14-18.

Stern, J. "Muslims in America." *Center for the National Interest* [Internet]. 2011 May/June [cited 2011 Aug 8]. Available from: *http://nationalinterest. org/article/muslims-america-5167?page=show.*

Thomas, TL. "Al Qaeda and the Internet: The Danger of "Cyberplanning"." *Foreign Military Studies Office* (Army) Fort Leavenworth; 2003: 112-123.

Tosini, D. "Al-Qaeda's Strategic Gamble: The Sociology of Suicide Bombings in Iraq." *Canadian Journal of Sociology.* 2010; 35(2): 271-308.

Van Evera, S. "Assessing U.S. Strategy in the War on Terror." *Annals of the American Academy of Political and Social Science.* 2006: 10-26.

Wedgwood, R. " Al Qaeda, Terrorism, and Military Commissions." *The American Journal of International Law.* 2002 April; 96(2): 328-337.

Yin, T. "Anything But Bush: The Obama Administration and Guantanamo Bay." *Harvard Journal of Law & Public Policy.* 2011; 34(2): 453-492.

Zagaris, B. "U.S. Enacts Counter-Terrorism Act with Significant New International Provisions." *International Enforcement Law Reporter.* 2001 December; 17: 522-26.

Zagaris, B. "U.S. Forms New Investigative Team to Target Terrorist Financial Networks." *International Enforcement Law Reporter.* 2001 December; 17: 519-20.

Zagaris, B. "Bush Administration Embarks on New Initiative to Combat Terrorism Financing Amid Broad Criticisms." *International Enforcement Law Reporter.* 2002 December; 18: 491-92.

Government Documents

A Ticking Time Bomb: Counterterrorism Lessons from the U.S. Government's Failure to Prevent the Fort Hood Attack: Hearing Before the Senate Comm. on Homeland Security and Governmental Affairs, 112th Cong., 1st Sess. (February 15, 2011). Available from: *http://hsgac.senate.gov/public/index.cfm?FuseAction=Hearings.Hearing&Hearing_ID=9516c9b9-cbd4-48ad-85bb-777784445444.*

Afghanistan: What Is an Acceptable End-State, and How Do We Get There?: Hearing Before the Senate Comm. on Foreign Relations, 112th Cong., 1st Sess. (May 3, 2011). Available from: *http://foreign.senate.gov/hearings/hearing/?id=8e8aa88e-5056-a032-5211-717689d40315.*

Al Qaeda and the Global Reach of Terrorism: Hearing Before the US House of Representatives Committee on International Relations,107th Cong., 1st Sess. (2001) 107-150 (testimony of Oliver B. Revell).

Al Qaeda, the Taliban & Other Extremist Groups in Afghanistan and Pakistan: Hearing Before the Senate Comm. on Foreign Relations, 112th Cong., 1st Sess. (May 24, 2011). Available from: *http://foreign.senate. gov/hearings/hearing/?id=805120d6-5056-a032-5247-313a14503d33.*

Anti-Terrorist Financing Guidelines: Voluntary Best Practices for U.S. Based Charities; 2005.

Army and Air Force National Guard and Reserve Component Equipment Posture: Hearing Before the House Comm. on Armed Services, 112th Cong., 1st Sess. (April 1, 2011). Available from: *http://armedservices. house.gov/index.cfm/hearings-display?ContentRecord_id=dd921231-7688-43e0-828a-6cc1f085b764.*

Assessing U.S. Foreign Policy Priorities and Needs Amidst Economic Challenges in South Asia: Hearing Before the Subcomm. on the Middle East and South Asia of the House Comm. on Foreign Affairs, 112th Cong., 1st Sess. (April 5, 2011). Available from: *http://foreignaffairs. house.gov/112/65627.pdf.*

Assessing U.S. Foreign Policy Priorities and Needs Amidst Economic Challenges: Hearing Before the House Comm. on Foreign Affairs, 112th Cong., 1st Sess. (1 March 2011). Available from: *http://foreignaffairs. house.gov/hearing_notice.asp?id=1219.*

Assessing U.S. Foreign Policy Priorities and Needs Amidst Economic Challenges in the Middle East: Hearing Before the Subcomm. on the Middle East and South Asia of the House Comm. on Foreign Affairs, 112th Cong., 1st Sess. (March 10, 2011). Available from: *http:// foreignaffairs.house.gov/hearing_notice.asp?id=1225.*

Assessing U.S. Policy and Its Limits in Pakistan: Hearing Before the Senate Comm. on Foreign Relations, 112th Cong., 1st Sess. (May 5, 2011). Available from: *http://foreign.senate.gov/hearings/ hearing/?id=8ec7ae3c-5056-a032-5292-4ec18865f8a0.*

Bush, G; O'Neill, P, and Powell, C. *President Freezes Terrorists Assets*, Remarks by the President. Available from: *http://georgewbush-whitehouse.archives.gov/news/releases/2001/09/20010924-4.html*

Catastrophic Preparedness: How Ready Is FEMA for the Next Big Disaster?: Hearing Before the Senate Comm. on Homeland Security and Governmental Affairs, 112th Cong., 1st Sess. (March 17, 2011). Available from: *http://hsgac.senate.gov/public/index.cfm?FuseAction=Hearings. Hearing&Hearing_ID=a42880b1-22fc-4890-b82c-dd2a369e2aa2.*

Country Reports on Terrorism: 2006. U.S. Department of State. 2006 Apr. 28. Available from: *http://www.state.gov/s/ct/rls/crt/2006/.*

Cummings, A. *IACP Committee on Terrorism at a COT Conference*: 2008 May; Dublin, Ireland.

Current and Future Worldwide Threats to the National Security of the US: Hearing Before the Senate Comm. on Armed Services, 112th Cong., 1st Sess. (March 10, 2011). Available from: *http://armed-services.senate.gov/e_witnesslist.cfm?id=5038*.

Defense Authorization Request for Fiscal Year 2012 and the Future Years Defense Program: Hearing Before the Senate Comm. on Armed Services, 112th Cong., 1st Sess. (February 17, 2011). Available from: *http://armed-services.senate.gov/e_witnesslist.cfm?id=4974*.

Department of Defense Plans and Programs Relating to Counterterrorism, Counternarcotics, and Building Partnership Capacity: Hearing Before the Subcomm. on Emerging Threats and Capabilities in Continuation of the Subcommittee's Open Hearing of Tuesday, April 12, 2011 of the Senate Comm. on Armed Services, 112th Cong., 1st Sess. (May 5, 2011). Available from: *http://armed-services.senate.gov/e_witnesslist.cfm?id=5164*.

Department of Defense Plans and Programs Relating to Counterterrorism, Counternarcotics, and Building Partnership Capacity: Hearing Before the Subcomm. on Emerging Threats and Capabilities of the Senate Comm. on Armed Services, 112th Cong., 1st Sess. (April 12, 2011). Available from: *http://armed-services.senate.gov/e_witnesslist.cfm?id=5136*.

The Diplomat's Shield: Diplomatic Security and Its Implications for U.S. Diplomacy: Hearing Before the Subcommittee on Oversight of Government Management, the Federal Workforce, and the District of Columbia of the Senate Comm. on Homeland Security and Governmental Affairs, 112th Cong., 1st Sess. (June 29, 2011). Available from: *http://hsgac.senate.gov/public/index.cfm?FuseAction=Hearings.Hearing&Hearing_ID=f60764dd-83a9-42cb-85bf-1e0ce3b2e6ef*.

Domestic Security Enhancement Act of 2003. 2003 Jan 9. 108th Congress.

The Emergency Supplemental Appropriations Act for Defense, the Global War on Terror, and Tsunami Relief: 2005; P.L. 109-13.

Evaluating Goals And Progress in Afghanistan and Pakistan: Hearing Before the Senate Comm. on Foreign Relations, 112th Cong., 1st Sess. (June 23, 2011). Available from: *http://foreign.senate.gov/hearings/hearing/?id=fc954f47-5056-a032-527c-2d086e505d32*.

Examining the Spending, Priorities and the Missions of the Bureau of Reclamation and the U.S. Geological Survey's Water Resources Program: Hearing Before the Subcomm. on Water and Power Oversight of the House Comm. on Natural Resources, 112th Cong., 1st Sess. (March 2, 2011). Available from: *http://naturalresources.house.gov/Calendar/EventSingle.aspx?EventID=225146*.

Financial Action Task Force. Detecting and Preventing the Cross-Border Transportation of Cash by Terrorists and Other Criminals: International Best Practices. 2005 Feb. 12. Available from: *http://www.fatf-gafi.org/dataoecd/50/63/34424128.pdf*.

Flowe Jr, Ben H, and Gold, R. *President Bush Waives Glenn Amendment Sanctions Against India and Pakistan and Imposes Additional Sanctions Against Terrorists*: Export Licensing Client Memo. 2001 Sept. 24.

Future of Al-Qaeda: Hearing Before the Subcomm. on Terrorism, Nonproliferation, and Trade of the House Comm. on Foreign Affairs, 112th Cong., 1st Sess. (May 24, 2011). Available from: *http://foreignaffairs.house.gov/hearing_notice.asp?id=1299*.

H.A.S.C. No. 112-24, Developments in Afghanistan: Hearing Before the House Comm. on Armed Services, 112th Cong., 1st Sess. (March 16, 2011). Available from: *http://armedservices.house.gov/index.cfm/2011/3/developments-in-afghanistan*.

The Global Nuclear Revival and U.S. Nonproliferation Policy: Hearing Before the House Comm. on Foreign Affairs, 112th Cong., 1st Sess. (March 17, 2011). Available from: *http://foreignaffairs.house.gov/hearing_notice.asp?id=1231*.

Health and Status of the Defense Industrial Base and Its Science and Technology-Related Elements: Hearing Before the Subcomm. on Emerging Threats and Capabilities of the Senate Comm. on Armed Services, 112th Cong., 1st Sess. (May 3, 2011). Available from: *http://armed-services.senate.gov/e_witnesslist.cfm?id=5163*.

Homeland Security Progress Has Been Made to Address the Vulnerabilities Exposed by 9/11, But Continued Federal Action Is Needed to Further Mitigate Security Risks: 2007 Jan. Report No.: GAO-07-375. Sponsored by the US Government Accountability Office. Available from: *http://www.gao.gov/new.items/d07375.pdf*.

ICE Worksite Enforcement—Up To the Job?: Hearing Before the Subcomm. on Immigration Policy and Enforcement of the House Comm. on the Judiciary, 112th Cong., 1st Sess. (January 26, 2011). Available from: *http://judiciary.house.gov/hearings/hear_01262011.html*.

Iraq: The Challenging Transition to a Civilian Mission: Hearing Before the Senate Comm. on Foreign Relations, 112th Cong., 1st Sess. (February 1, 2011). Available from: *http://foreign.senate.gov/hearings/ hearing/?id=a421f9a1-5056-a032-52ae-3e2b956077c2*.

Juergensmeyer, M. *Global Rebellion: Religious Challenges to the Secular State, from Christian Militias to Al Qaeda*. Berkeley, CA: University of California Press; 2009 June 1. Sponsored by the U.S. Department of the Treasury. Available from: *http://www.treasury.gov/resource-center/ terrorist-illicit-finance/Documents/guidelines_charities.pdf*.

Justice For America: Using Military Commissions To Try The 9/11 Conspirators: Hearing Before the Subcomm. on Crime, Terrorism, and Homeland Security of the House Comm. on The Judiciary, 112th Cong., 1st Sess. (April 5, 2011). Available from: *http://judiciary.house. gov/hearings/printers/112th/112-29_65601.PDF*.

Katzman, K. *Al Qaeda: Profile and Threat Assessment*: CRS Report for Congress; 2005

Libya: Defining U.S. National Security Interests: Hearing Before the House Comm. on Foreign Affairs, 112th Cong., 1st Sess. (March 31, 2011). Available from: *http://foreignaffairs.house.gov/112/65492.pdf*.

Mayfield v. US. District of Oregon. 2007 Sept 26. Civil No. 04-1427-AA.

Mefford, A. *The State of the Terrorist Threat Facing the US*: Hearing Before the Subcommittee on Technology and Homeland Security Subcommittee. 108th Cong., 1st Sess. (2003). Available from: *http:// www.fbi.gov/news/testimony/the-state-of-the-terrorist-threat-facing- the-united-states*.

Morris, MF. *Al-Qaeda as Insurgency*. USAWC Strategy Research Project. March 2005

Mueller, RS. *Hearing Before the Select Committee on Intelligence of the US Senate*. 108th Cong., 1st Sess. (Feb. 24, 2004). Available from: *http:// www2.fbi.gov/congress/congress04/mueller022404.htm*.

National Commission on Terrorist Attacks upon the US Cong. 2004; *Testimony of John S. Pistole*, Executive Assistant Director, Counterterrorism/ Counterintelligence, FBI.

National Commission on Terrorist Attacks. *The 9/11 Commission Report: Final Report of the National Commission on Terrorist Attacks Upon the US*. Boston: W. W. Norton & Company; 2004.

National Security and Foreign Policy Priorities in the Fiscal Year 2012 International Affairs Budget: Hearing Before the Senate Comm. on Foreign Relations, 112th Cong., 1st Sess. (March 2, 2011). Available from: *http://foreign.senate.gov/hearings/hearing/?id=e83cf72d-5056-a032-5281-5af178b5557a.*

North Korea's Sea of Fire: Bullying, Brinkmanship and Blackmail: Hearing Before the House Comm. on Foreign Affairs, 112th Cong., 1st Sess. (March 10, 2011). Available from: *http://foreignaffairs.house.gov/hearing_notice.asp?id=1224.*

Obama, BH. *Remarks on the Death of Al Qaida Terrorist Organization Leader Usama bin Laden*: Daily Compilation of Presidential Documents; 2011.

Open Hearing: *Worldwide Threat*: Hearing Before the Select Committee on Intelligence, 112th Cong., 1st Sess. (February 16, 2011). Available from: *http://intelligence.senate.gov/hearings.cfm?hearingId=e655f9e2809e5 476862f735da1668813.*

Overview of U.S. Relations with Europe and Eurasia: Hearing Before the Subcomm. on Europe and Eurasia of the House Comm. on Foreign Affairs, 112th Cong., 1st Sess. (March 10, 2011). Available from: *http://foreignaffairs.house.gov/hearing_notice.asp?id=1223.*

Patterns of Global Terrorism 2002: U.S. Department of State. 2002 Apr. 30. Available from: *http://www.state.gov/s/ct/rls/crt/2002/html/index.htm.*

Patterns of Global Terrorism 2003: U.S. Department of State. 2004 Apr. 29. Available from: *http://www.state.gov/s/ct/rls/pgtrpt/2003/31644.htm.*

Permanent Provisions of the PATRIOT Act: Hearing Before the Subcomm. on Crime, Terrorism, and Homeland Security of the House Comm. on the Judiciary, 112th Cong., 1st Sess. (March 30, 2011). Available from: *http://judiciary.house.gov/hearings/hear_03302011.html.*

Preserving Progress: Transitioning Authority and Implementing the Strategic Framework in Iraq, Part 1: Hearing Before the Subcomm. on the Middle East and South Asia of the House Comm. on Foreign Affairs, 112th Cong., 1st Sess. (June 1, 2011). Available from: *http://foreignaffairs.house.gov/hearing_notice.asp?id=1302.*

Priorities for U.S. Assistance in the Western Hemisphere: Hearing Before the Subcomm. on the Western Hemisphere of the House Comm. on Foreign Affairs, 112th Cong., 1st Sess. (April 13, 2011). Available from: *http://foreignaffairs.house.gov/hearing_notice.asp?id=1263.*

Protecting Cyberspace: Assessing The White House Proposal: Hearing Before the Senate Comm. on Homeland Security and Governmental Affairs, 112th Cong., 1st Sess. (May 23, 2011). Available from: *http://hsgac.senate.gov/public/index.cfm?FuseAction=Hearings. Hearing&Hearing_ID=96ef8175-e114-4fe0-ab31-b42d45d599ac.*

Providing for consideration of the bill (H.R. 3773) to amend the Foreign Intelligence Surveillance Act of 1978 to establish a procedure for authorizing certain acquisitions of foreign intelligence, and for other purposes. H.R. Res. 3773, 110th Cong. (enacted).

Providing for consideration of the bill (H.R. 6304) to amend the Foreign Intelligence Surveillance Act of 1978 to establish a procedure for authorizing certain acquisitions of foreign intelligence, and for other purposes. H.R. Res. 6304, 110th Cong. (enacted).

Reauthorization of the PATRIOT Act: Hearing Before the Subcomm. on Crime, Terrorism, and Homeland Security of the House Comm. on the Judiciary, 112th Cong., 1st Sess. (March 9, 2011). Available from: *http://judiciary.house.gov/hearings/hear_03092011_2.html.*

Recent Developments in Egypt and Lebanon: Implications for U.S. Policy and Allies in the Broader Middle East: Hearing Before the House Comm. on Foreign Affairs, 112th Cong., 1st Sess. (February 9-10, 2011). Available from: *http://foreignaffairs.house.gov/hearing_notice.asp?id=1207* and *http://foreignaffairs.house.gov/hearing_notice.asp?id=1208.*

Safe for America Act: Hearing Before the Subcomm. on Immigration Policy and Enforcement of the House Comm. on the Judiciary, 112th Cong., 1st Sess. (April 5, 2011). Available from: *http://judiciary.house.gov/hearings/printers/112th/112-27_65602.PDF.*

Secretary of the Treasury O'Neill and Secretary of State Powell on Executive Order: 2001 Sept. 24. Available at: *http://avalon.law.yale.edu/sept11/president_026.asp.*

Secure Visas Act: Hearing Before the Subcomm. on Immigration Policy and Enforcement of the House Comm. on the Judiciary, 112th Cong., 1st Sess. (May 11, 2011). Available from: *http://judiciary.house.gov/hearings/hear_05112011.html.*

Securing the Border: Building on the Progress Made: Hearing Before the Senate Comm. on Homeland Security and Governmental Affairs, 112th Cong., 1st Sess. (March 30, 2011). Available from: *http://hsgac.senate.gov/public/index.cfm?FuseAction=Hearings.Hearing&Hearing_ID=497314c6-9e5b-4448-9783-2a1ddc924df8.*

Securing the Border: Progress at the Federal Level: Hearing Before the Senate Comm. on Homeland Security and Governmental Affairs, 112th Cong., 1st Sess. (May 4, 2011). Available from: *http://hsgac.senate.gov/public/index.cfm?FuseAction=Hearings.Hearing&Hearing_ID=6267a10e-5cc4-4087-b801-b8afb30f7ea3.*

Securing the Border: Progress at the Local Level: Hearing Before the Senate Comm. on Homeland Security and Governmental Affairs, 112th Cong., 1st Sess. (April 7, 2011). Available from: *http://hsgac.senate.gov/public/index.cfm?FuseAction=Hearings.Hearing&Hearing_ID=941a2dc2-43ff-4aba-b1da-d3c3ed1d7a76.*

See Something, Say Something, Do Something: Next Steps for Securing Rail and Transit: Hearing Before the Senate Comm. on Homeland Security and Governmental Affairs, 112th Cong., 1st Sess. (June 22, 2011). Available from: *http://hsgac.senate.gov/public/index.cfm?FuseAction=Hearings.Hearing&Hearing_ID=5cb4a10a-bfd0-4925-a254-de8589cb4745.*

Shifting Sands: Political Transitions in the Middle East, Part 1: Hearing Before the Subcomm. on the Middle East and South Asia of the House Comm. on Foreign Affairs, 112th Cong., 1st Sess. (April 13, 2011). Available from: *http://foreignaffairs.house.gov/hearing_notice.asp?id=1262.*

Situation in Afghanistan: Hearing Before the Senate Comm. on Armed Services, 112th Cong., 1st Sess. (March 15, 2011). Available from: *http://armed-services.senate.gov/e_witnesslist.cfm?id=5058.*

Steps Needed for a Successful 2014 Transition in Afghanistan: Hearing Before the Senate Comm. on Foreign Relations, 112th Cong., 1st Sess. (May 10, 2011). Available from: *http://foreign.senate.gov/hearings/hearing/?id=50dda323-5056-a032-522f-1577e3361280.*

Strategic Implications of Pakistan and the Region: Hearing Before the Senate Comm. on Foreign Relations, 112th Cong., 1st Sess. (May 17, 2011). Available from: *http://foreign.senate.gov/hearings/hearing/?id=5105c3eb-5056-a032-5263-30425149ff2c.*

Strengthening Enforcement and Border Security: The 9/11 Commission Staff Report on Terrorist Travel: Hearing Before US. Cong. Senate Judiciary Committee, Subcommittee on Immigration, Border Security, and Citizenship, and Subcommittee on Terrorism, Technology, and Homeland Security. 109th Cong., 1st Sess. S. Rept. 109-71. Available from: *http://frwebgate.access.gpo.gov/cgi-bin/getdoc.cgi?dbname=109_senate_hearings&docid=f:22470.pdf.*

Sudan at the Crossroads: Hearing Before the House Comm. on Foreign Affairs, 112th Cong., 1st Sess. (January 18, 2011). Available from: *http:// republicans.foreignaffairs.house.gov/hearing_notice.asp?id=1204.*

Ten Years after 9/11: A Report from the 9/11 Commission Chairmen: Hearing Before the Senate Comm. on Homeland Security and Governmental Affairs, 112th Cong., 1st Sess. (March 30, 2011). Available from: *http://hsgac.senate.gov/public/index.cfm?FuseAction=Hearings. Hearing&Hearing_ID=759efc68-191f-4dfd-b362-c3197c6cb624.*

Ten Years after 9/11: Improving Emergency Communications: Hearing Before the Senate Comm. on Homeland Security and Governmental Affairs, 112th Cong., 1st Sess. (July 27, 2011). Available from: *http://hsgac.senate.gov/public/index.cfm?FuseAction=Hearings. Hearing&Hearing_ID=609036b2-6858-452b-9e7b-3dcdfa0cadc3.*

Ten Years after 9/11: Is Intelligence Reform Working? Part I: Hearing Before the Senate Comm. on Homeland Security and Governmental Affairs, 112th Cong., 1st Sess. (May 12, 2011). Available from: *http://hsgac.senate. gov/public/index.cfm?FuseAction=Hearings.Hearing&Hearing_ ID=2a16d2d9-22b9-4858-984e-a50d92a0a0ab.*

Ten Years after 9/11: Is Intelligence Reform Working? Part II: Hearing Before the Senate Comm. on Homeland Security and Governmental Affairs, 112th Cong., 1st Sess. (May 19, 2011). Available from: *http://hsgac.senate.gov/public/index.cfm?FuseAction=Hearings. Hearing&Hearing_ID=4d3c8208-2bc3-47ed-b8b5-e742028a4bdf.*

Ten Years after 9/11: Preventing Terrorist Travel: Hearing Before the Senate Comm. on Homeland Security and Governmental Affairs, 112th Cong., 1st Sess. (July 13, 2011). Available from: *http://hsgac.senate.gov/public/ index.cfm?FuseAction=Hearings.Hearing&Hearing_ID=af5eac3a-fe02-493e-89ea-64fab7c88259.*

Terrorist Financing: Better Strategic Planning Needed to Coordinate U.S. Efforts to Deliver Counter-Terrorism Financing Training and Technical Assistance Abroad. 2005. Sponsored by the U.S. Government Accountability Office. Available from: *http://www.gao.gov/new.items/ d0619.pdf.*

The United Nations: Urgent Problems That Need Congressional Action: Hearing Before the House Comm. on Foreign Affairs, 112th Cong., 1st Sess. (January 25, 2011). Available from: *http://foreignaffairs.house. gov/hearing_notice.asp?id=1203.*

Understanding the Power of Social Media as a Communications Tool in the Aftermath of Disasters: Hearing Before the Ad Hoc Subcomm. on Disaster Recovery and Intergovernmental Affairs Of the Senate Comm. on Homeland Security and Governmental Affairs, 112th Cong., 1st Sess. (May 5, 2011). Available from: *http://hsgac.senate.gov/public/index.cfm?FuseAction=Hearings.Hearing&Hearing_ID=e928effc-4bfd-4024-9017-130bb45b4ed4*.

U.S. of America v. John Phillip Walker Lindh: US District Court for the Eastern District of Virginia, Alexandria Division. 2002 Feb.

US Policy Towards Iraq: Hearing Before the Senate Comm. on Armed Services, 112th Cong., 1st Sess. (February 3, 2011). Available from: *http://armed-services.senate.gov/e_witnesslist.cfm?id=4967*.

US Policy in Yemen: Hearing Before the Subcomm. on Near Eastern, South and Central Asian Affairs of the Senate Comm. on Foreign Relations, 112th Cong., 1st Sess. (July 19, 2011). Available from: *http://foreign.senate.gov/hearings/hearing/?id=6dfc834d-5056-a032-5221-41d3cf94e791*.

USA PATRIOT Act: Dispelling the Myths: Hearing Before the Subcomm. on Crime, Terrorism, and Homeland Security of the House Comm. on the Judiciary, 112th Cong., 1st Sess. (May 11, 2011). Available from: *http://judiciary.house.gov/hearings/hear_05112011_02.html*.

USA PATRIOT bill H.R. 3162, 107 Cong. (2001) (enacted).

USA PATRIOT Improvement and Reauthorization Act of 2005: H.R. Res. 3199, 109th Cong. (enacted).

What Should the Department of Defense's Role in Cyber Be?: Hearing Before the Subcomm. on Emerging Threats and Capabilities of the House Comm. on Armed Services, 112th Cong., 1st Sess. (February 11, 2011). Available from: *http://armedservices.house.gov/index.cfm/hearings-display?ContentRecord_id=90d8a16a-23b7-4b9c-a732-cb10ab20e579*.

Databases/Websites

American Enterprise Institute for Public Policy Research. War on Terror. Available from: *http://www.aei.org/ra/100075*.

Brookings Institution. Foreign Policy. Available from: *http://www.brookings.edu/foreign-policy.aspx*.

Carnegie Middle East Center. Available from: *http://carnegie-mec.org/?lang=en*.

Center for a New American Security. Terrorism, Irregular Warfare and Crime. Available from: *http://www.cnas.org/node/3647.*

Center for Strategic & International Studies. Homeland Security and Counterterrorism Program. Available from: *http://csis.org/program/ homeland-security-program.*

Chicago Project on Security and Terrorism. Available from: *http://cpost. uchicago.edu/research.php.*

Congressional Research Service [CRS] Reports. Homeland Security. Available from: *http://www.fas.org/sgp/crs/homesec/index.html.*

Congressional Research Service [CRS] Reports. Terrorism. Available from: *http://www.fas.org/sgp/crs/terror/index.html.*

Council on Foreign Relations. Terrorism. Available from: *http://www.cfr. org/issue/terrorism/ri135.*

Foundation for Defense of Democracies. Center for Law & Counterterrorism. Available from: *http://www.defenddemocracy.org/index.php?option= com_content&view=article&id=1341&Itemid=334.*

Foundation for Defense of Democracies. Center for Terrorism Research. Available from: *http://www.defenddemocracy.org/index. php?option=com_content&view=article&id=515778&Itemid=343.*

Foundation for Defense of Democracies. Terrorist Media. Available from: *http://www.defenddemocracy.org/index.php?option=com_content&vi ew=article&id=1343&Itemid=337.*

Foundation for Defense of Democracies. Iran/Hezbollah Project. Available from: *http://www.defenddemocracy.org/index.php?option=com_conte nt&view=article&id=1349&Itemid=369.*

Hudson Institute. Homeland Security. Available from: *http://www. hudson.org/index.cfm?fuseaction=research_publications_ list&resType=Homeland.*

Hudson Institute. International Security and Terrorism. Available from: *http:// www.hudson.org/index.cfm?fuseaction=research_publications_ list&resType=IntSec.*

International Institute for Counter-Terrorism. Available from: *http://www.ict. org.il/.*

Leiken, RS. "Al Qaeda's New Soldiers". *The New Republic.* 2004 Apr 26. Available from: *http://www.cftni.org/publications/FairGame.pdf.*

Leiken, R. "Bearers of Global Jihad?: Immigration and National Security after 9/11". The Nixon Center. 2004 Mar. Available from: *http://www. mafhoum.com/press7/193S23.pdf.*

Levitt, M. "Navigating the U.S. Government's Terrorist Lists." The Washington Institute for Near East Policy. *Policy Watch*. 2001 Nov 30. Available from: *http://www.washingtoninstitute.org*.

Lieven, A. "How The Afghan Counterinsurgency Threatens Pakistan." *The Nation*.2011 Jan. Available at: *http://www.thenation.com/article/157160/how-afghan-counterinsurgency-threatens-pakistan*.

Middle East Institute. Publications. Available from: *http://www.mei.edu/Publications.aspx*.

National Consortium for the Study of Terrorism and Responses to Terrorism. Available from: *http://www.start.umd.edu/start/data_collections/*.

National Counterterrorism Center. Available from: *http://www.nctc.gov/*.

National Counterterrorism Center. Worldwide Incidents Tracking System. Available from: *https://wits.nctc.gov/FederalDiscoverWITS/index.do?Rcv=Perpetrator&N=0*.

National Security Network. Terrorism & National Security. Available from: *http://www.nsnetwork.org/issues/terrorism*.

New America Foundation. Counterterrorism Strategy Initiative. Available from: *http://counterterrorism.newamerica.net/*.

RAND Corporation. Terrorism and Homeland Security. Available from: *http://www.rand.org/topics/terrorism-and-homeland-security.html*.

Rogan, H. "Jihadism Online - A study of how al-Qaida and radical Islamist groups use the Internet for terrorist purposes". *FFI Rapport* [Internet]. 2006 [cited 2011 Aug 8]. Available from: *http://rapporter.ffi.no/rapporter/2006/00915.pdf*.

Rowswell, B. "Ogdensburg Revisited: Adapting Canada-US Security Cooperation to the New International Era." Center for Strategic and International Studies. 2004. Available from: *http://csis.org/files/media/csis/pubs/pp0405rowswell%5B1%5D.pdf*.

The Al-Qaida and Taliban Sanctions Committee - 1267. United Nations Security Council. Available from: *http://www.un.org/sc/committees/1267/consolist.shtml*.

The Al-Qaida and Taliban Sanctions Committee. United Nations. Available from: *www.un.org/docs/sc/committees/1267/1267ListEng.htm*.

The Heritage Foundation. Terrorism. Available from: *http://www.heritage.org/Issues/Terrorism*.

The Jamestown Foundation. Global Terrorism Analysis. Available from: *http://www.jamestown.org/programs/gta/*.

The Long War Journal. Available from: *http://www.longwarjournal.org/*.

The Washington Institute for Near East Policy. Available from: *http://www.washingtoninstitute.org/template101.php*.

US Department of State Bureau of Diplomatic Security (OSAC). Available from: *https://www.osac.gov/Pages/Home.aspx*.

Selected Bibliography

Index

D

I

About the Authors

Yonah Alexander

Director, Inter-University Center for Terrorism Studies
Director, International Center for Terrorism Studies
Potomac Institute for Policy Studies
and
Co-Director, Inter-University Center for Legal Studies
The International Law Institute

Professor Yonah Alexander is a Senior Fellow, Member of the Board of Regents, and Director of the International Center for Terrorism Studies of the Potomac Institute for Policy Studies, Arlington, VA, US. Concurrently, he is Director of the Inter-University Center for Terrorism Studies and Co-Director of the Inter-University Center for Legal Studies, a consortia of universities and think tanks throughout the world. Professor Alexander previously directed the Terrorism Studies Program at George Washington University, Washington, DC, US, and the Institute for Studies in International Terrorism at the State University of New York (US).

He was awarded a PhD from Columbia University (NY), MA by the University of Chicago (IL), and received his baccalaureate degree from Roosevelt University of Chicago (IL). With over 35 years experience devoted to the field of terrorism studies, Professor Alexander has held academic appointments at The George Washington University, American University, the Columbus School of Law at Catholic University of America, Tel Aviv University, The City University of New York, and The State University of New York, and has lectured at numerous institutions and universities throughout the world, and is a member of the International Institute of Strategic Studies, London, UK.

Dr. Alexander is Founder and Editor-in-Chief of the international academic journals *Terrorism; Minorities and Group Rights*; and *Political Communication and Persuasion*. Since 2010, he has served as Editor-in-Chief of the *Partnership for Peace Review*, a journal published under the auspices of NATO. He has published over 100 books including *Terrorists in Our Midst: Combating Foreign Affinity Terrorism in America*; *Terrorism on the High Seas: From Piracy to Strategic Challenge*; *Evolution of U.S.*

Counterterrorism Policy (three volumes); *Turkey: Terrorism, Civil Rights, and the European Union*; *The New Iranian Leadership: Terrorism, Nuclear Ambition, and the Middle East Conflict*; and *Counterterrorism Strategies: Success and Failures of Six Nations.* Translated into more than two dozen languages, Professor Alexander's personal papers and collection on terrorism are housed at the Hoover Institution Library and Archives at Stanford University, Palo Alto, CA (US).

Michael S. Swetnam

CEO and Chairman
Potomac Institute for Policy Studies

Michael Swetnam was one of the principal founders of the Potomac Institute for Policy Studies in 1994. Since its inception, he has served as Chairman of the Board and currently serves as the Institute's Chief Executive Officer. His authored and edited publications include: *Cyber Terrorism and Information Warfare (vols 1-4)*; *Usama bin Laden's al-Qaida: Profile of a Terrorist Network*, (with Yonah Alexander); ETA: Profile of a Terrorist Group (with Yonah Alexander and Herbert M. Levine); and *Best Available Science: Its Evolution, Taxonomy, and Application*, co-authored with A. Alan Moghissi, Betty R. Love and Sorin R. Straja.

Mr. Swetnam is currently a member of the Technical Advisory Group to the United States Senate Select Committee on Intelligence. In this capacity, he provides expert advice to the US Senate on research and development (R&D) investment strategy for the US Intelligence Community (IC). He has also served on the Defense Science Board (DSB) Task Force on Counterterrorism, and the Task Force on Intelligence Support to the War on Terrorism.

From 1990 to 1992, Mr. Swetnam served as a Special Consultant to President Bush's Foreign Intelligence Advisory Board (PFIAB) and provided expertise on Intelligence Community issues inclusive of budget, community architecture, and major programs. He was also involved in authoring the Board's assessment of Intelligence Community support to Operations Desert Storm and Shield.

Prior to forming the Potomac Institute for Policy Studies, Mr. Swetnam worked in private industry as a Vice President of Engineering at the Pacific-Sierra Research Corporation, Director of Information Processing Systems at GTE, and Manager of Strategic Planning for GTE Government Systems.

Previously, he worked for the Director of Central Intelligence as a Program Monitor on the Intelligence Community Staff (1986-1990), was responsible for the development and presentation to Congress of the budget of the National Security Agency, and helped develop, monitor and present the DOE Intelligence Budget to Congress. Mr. Swetnam was assigned as the IC Staff Representative to inter-governmental groups responsible for developing the INF and START treaties, and assisted in presenting these treaties for Congressional ratification. His collateral duties included serving as the host to the DCI's Nuclear Intelligence Panel, and Co-Chairman of the Science and Technology Requirements' Analysis Working Group.

Mr. Swetnam served in the US Navy for 24 years as an active duty and reserve officer, Special Duty Cryptology. He has served in several public and community positions and serves on the Board of Directors of Space and Defense Systems Inc., Dragon Hawk Entertainment Inc., and the Governing Board of The Potomac Institute of New Zealand

The Hon. Charles E. Allen

Principal, Chertoff Group

At the Chertoff Group, the Hon. Charles E. Allen brings to bear his extensive experience in intelligence program management, analysis and production; intelligence collection management; system acquisition and warning intelligence. He has held a number of senior governmental positions, including: Under Secretary for Intelligence and Analysis, US Department of Homeland Security (2007–2009); Assistant Secretary for Information Analysis and Chief of Intelligence, U.S. Department of Homeland Security (2005 – 2007); and Assistant Director of Central Intelligence for Collection, Central Intelligence Agency (CIA; 1998-2005).

At the Department of Homeland Security, Mr. Allen developed intelligence architecture, integrated intelligence activities, and ensured continuous alignment with the department's evolving priorities. He was also responsible for the development of accelerated and expanded departmental processes for sharing intelligence with state and local security and law enforcement agencies.

Mr. Allen became the principal adviser to the Director of Central Intelligence (DCI) on collection management, where he revolutionized the way the various national intelligence agencies coordinate and target their activities. As well, he chaired the National Intelligence Collection Board, which united all intelligence agencies under common collection strategies. He served as the CIA's National Intelligence Officer for Warning, Director of the National Warning Staff, National Intelligence Officer for Counterterrorism, Deputy Chief for Intelligence of the Agency's Counterterrorism Center, and directed the DCI Hostage Location Task Force, which focused on locating American hostages held by Hezballah in Lebanon.

Mr. Allen is a graduate of the University of North Carolina, a distinguished graduate of the Air War College, and completed graduate studies at Auburn University.